GENERAL PLANT AND ANIMAL BIOLOGY
BIOLOGY BOOK I

SECONDARY SCIENCE SERIES

The books in this series adopt the latest approach to science teaching for secondary schools and the new middle schools. The students are encouraged to discover as much as possible for themselves rather than simply to verify what they are told to be true. Scientific knowledge is acquired through a largely experimental approach, related always to everyday life and experience.

Most of the experiments are simple and require the minimum of equipment. To help readers who do not have access to full laboratory facilities, the conclusions to be drawn from investigations are incorporated later in the text. At the end of most chapters there is a *Test yourself* section to reinforce knowledge and understanding of important points.

SI units have been used throughout the series.

These volumes, **General Plant and Animal Biology**, Biology Book I, and **Human Biology and Hygiene**, Biology Book II, are designed to follow on from the first volume, **Foundation Science,** which provided a two-year course in basic science. They are intended to take pupils up to the standard required by the CSE Biology Examination. The majority of topics required by the various GCE Boards, particularly with regard to the newer syllabuses, have also been covered.

The parallel volumes are **Chemistry**;
General Science Book I: **Matter and Energy**;
General Science Book II: **Man and His Environment**;
Physics (in two parts).

The **Chemistry** and **General Science** volumes are already available; the **Physics** volumes will appear later.

SECONDARY SCIENCE SERIES

GENERAL PLANT AND ANIMAL BIOLOGY

Biology Book I

E. J. Ewington and D. F. Moore

Illustrated by David and Maureen Embry

London and Boston
Routledge & Kegan Paul

*First published 1971
by Routledge & Kegan Paul Ltd
Broadway House, 68–74 Carter Lane, London EC4V 5EL
and 9 Park Street, Boston, Mass. 02108, U.S.A.*

*Printed in Great Britain by
Butler & Tanner Ltd, Frome and London
Reprinted 1972, 1973*

© *E. J. Ewington and D. F. Moore 1971*

*No part of this book may be reproduced in
any form without permission from the
publisher, except for the quotation of
brief passages in criticism*

ISBN 0 7100 7028 4

SECONDARY SCIENCE SERIES

SERIES EDITORS

L. J. Campbell, B.Sc.
R. J. Carlton, B.Sc.

CONTRIBUTORS TO THE SERIES

L. J. Campbell, B.Sc.
   Assistant Education Officer, Isle of Wight
   Formerly Head of Science Department, Hinchley Wood C.S. School.
   Formerly Chairman, Science Panel, South East Regional Examinations Board for the CSE.

R. J. Carlton, B.Sc.
   Head of Science Department, Ashford North Modern Boys' School.
   Correspondent, Science Panel and Physics sub-Panel, South East Regional Examinations Board for the CSE 1962 to 1966.
   Chief Moderator in Physics, South East Regional Examinations Board for the CSE.
   Member of Kent Teachers Panel for Metrication.

E. J. Ewington, B.Sc.
   Headmaster, Howard of Effingham School.
   Formerly Senior Master, Hinchley Wood C.S. School.

D. F. Moore, B.Sc., M.I.Biol.
   Senior Lecturer, Hockerill College of Education.
   Formerly member of Biology sub-Panel, South East Regional Examinations Board for the CSE.

N. E. Savage
   Senior Physics Master, Technical High School for Girls, Canterbury.
   Member, Science Panel and Physics and Integrated Science sub-Panels, South East Regional Examinations Board for the CSE.

R. H. Stone, M.Sc., A.R.I.C.
   Senior Chemistry Master, The Judd School, Tonbridge.

D. W. H. Tripp, B.Sc., A.R.C.S., Teacher's Diploma (Lond.)
   Senior Chemistry Master, Brighton, Hove and Sussex Grammar School. Member of the Radiochemistry Committee, Association for Science Education.

R. S. Wood
   Science Master, Faversham C.S. School.
   Chairman of the Science Panel, South East Regional Examinations Board for the CSE.
   Chairman of the Physics sub-Panel, South East Regional Examinations Board for the CSE.

Contents

Introduction   ix

TOPIC A: THE NATURE OF LIFE

1 Features of Living Organisms   2

2 Cells: The Units of Life   12

TOPIC B: THE VARIETY OF LIVING ORGANISMS

3 Naming and Grouping   24

4 Simple Animals   36

5 More Animals without Backbones   54

6 More about Insects   65

7 Animals with Backbones   87

8 The Plant World: Plants without Flowers   106

9 The Flowering Plant   129

TOPIC C: THE WORKING OF THE PLANT

10 Food-making by Plants: Photosynthesis   152

11 Plants and Water   164

12 Reproduction in the Flowering Plant   184

13 Surviving the Winter   211

14 Plants and their Senses   228

TOPIC D: LIVING TOGETHER—THE COMMUNITY

15 The Economy of Nature   244

16 Soil   257

17 Communal Life   273

    Analytical Contents List   295

    Analytical Contents List for Book II   299

    Index   303

Introduction

This volume, *General Plant and Animal Biology*, Biology Book I, together with its companion volume, *Human Biology and Hygiene*, Biology Book II, presents a course of biology suitable for pupils in the age range 13–16. Those who have worked through the introductory book in this series, *Foundation Science*, will find these volumes a natural extension of that work.

The authors have, throughout, kept in mind the requirements of the various Examining Boards, particularly those of the Certificate of Secondary Education. The two volumes provide adequate preparation for CSE papers in biology. Moreover, in the choice of topics and depth of treatment, the authors have anticipated the needs of candidates for biology at the Ordinary level of the General Certificate of Education.

Whilst some topics are necessarily dealt with in a descriptive manner, the general approach is experimental. The investigations are an integral part of the text and, through them, the students are led to discover facts for themselves rather than to verify what they have been told. The apparatus used is of the simple, unsophisticated type which is likely to be available in most schools, and in quantities which make group and individual practical work possible. However, schools that are unable to carry out the investigations, or do not wish to, will find that the conclusions to be drawn from them are incorporated later in the text. Where an investigation involves any element of danger, a clear warning appears in the margin.

Much biological knowledge can be taught through accurate line drawings and, for this reason, the text is very fully illustrated. In many cases the drawings are sufficiently simple for the pupils to copy, if required.

As in the other books in this series, SI units have been used throughout.

The vocabulary has been kept as simple as possible, commensurate with accuracy of description. Where technical terms are desirable, their first mention has been printed in bold type for easy back reference.

At the end of each chapter a 'test your understanding' section provides a simple yet searching inquiry into the knowledge gained by the pupil. Completion of these tests will also provide a useful summary of the important factual content.

The early chapters of this volume, *General Plant and Animal Biology*, introduce the pupil to the fundamental characteristics of living organisms and to the principles of classification. The major animal and plant groups are then described, mainly from an evolutionary standpoint. In the section entitled 'The Working of the Plant', the pupil is presented with those fundamental aspects of plant anatomy and physiology which can best be approached in a practical way using simple apparatus. In the final section of the book the interdependence of plants and animals, and the importance of the environment, are emphasized. In the hope that pupils will be given an opportunity to carry their studies out of doors, a fuller treatment of ecological field work is given than in most books aimed at this age group.

E. J. E.
D. F. M.

TOPIC A: THE NATURE OF LIFE

Chapter 1

Features of Living Organisms

1.1. Living and non-living things

This book is all about **Biology**, that is, the study of living things. We will begin by considering how living things may be distinguished from non-living things. In many cases there is little difficulty in placing something in the correct group. For instance, we all know that oak trees, buttercups, spiders and horses are living things, whilst lead, glass, granite and polythene are non-living. However, it is not always so easy to decide whether something is living or not. As an example, let us consider **viruses**. These are the cause of many diseases in animals and plants, including, in man, the diseases poliomyelitis, the common cold, German measles, mumps and chickenpox. Viruses are so small that, until the electron microscope was invented, it was not possible to see them at all. To give you some idea of their size, let us imagine that we magnify a virus and a man by the same amount. If the man was magnified so that he was 56 km (35 miles) tall, a polio virus, magnified by the same amount, would still be little larger than a pinhead. The electron microscope has shown us that viruses are simple in shape, being familiar geometric shapes of rods and spheres (see Figure 1.1).

A great deal has been learnt about small organisms such as bacteria by culturing them in glass dishes in the laboratory. If fed with the right materials the bacteria grow and multiply, and are obviously living things. Viruses, however, do not exist outside the

Figure 1.1 Examples of virus shape

VIRUS causing mosaic disease of tobacco plants

VIRUS causing measles

VIRUS infecting bacteria

body of a living organism, that is, they are unable to lead a separate existence. Are they living or non-living? In appearance they resemble crystals more than living creatures, but their chemical composition links them with the living world. Scientists are coming to realize that the distinction between the living and the non-living world is not a rigid one. Everything, whether living or non-living, is composed of **molecules**, and exactly when a group of molecules becomes a living organism is not easy to say.

CHARACTERISTICS OF LIVING ORGANISMS

Although there may be some doubt about viruses, we have said that it is usually quite obvious whether a thing is living or not. This is because living organisms possess certain features not shown by non-living matter. Perhaps, when considering these features, it will help us to think of a mouse and a runner bean plant as examples of living things, and a crystal and a motorcar as examples of non-living things.

1.2. Movement

If you turn over a stone or an old log you will soon see whether it hides any living creatures, because they will rapidly move away when disturbed. Do all living things move? Certainly our mouse, like the majority of animals, is constantly moving around. What about the runner bean? Actually this does move, but in a much less obvious way. The tip of the climbing stem moves round and round, seeking a support around which to grow. Can non-living things move? Of course they can; the car is an obvious example. What is the difference between the movement of the mouse and that of the car? The car needs a driver to move, whereas the mouse is able *to move under its own power.*

1.3. Respiration

You will have learnt, elsewhere, that **energy** is required if work is to be done. A motorcar requires energy in order to move, and this is obtained from the explosive combustion of the fuel, namely, petrol. This release of energy from petrol requires oxygen from the air, for it is a process of oxidation. The petrol is not completely converted into energy, for water and waste gases are also produced. The 'fuel' used by living things is, of course, their food, which contains energy-rich substances such as sugars and fats. The breakdown of these substances also involves oxidation, and water and carbon dioxide gas are produced as waste. The process whereby energy is released from food is called **respiration**. It may be summarized as follows:

sugar + oxygen → energy + carbon dioxide + water

We know that respiration is taking place in the mouse, because the animal **breathes**. Its chest expands and contracts, causing air to flow in and out of its lungs. This air brings in the essential oxygen and removes the waste carbon dioxide. Respiration in the runner bean plant is less obvious. However, plants do consume oxygen and release carbon dioxide in respiration.

1.4. Growth

If you have kept mice or planted bean seeds, you will know that these organisms grow. What is meant by growth? Does it occur in any non-living things? Perhaps we can best answer these questions by performing a simple investigation.

Investigation 1a. Observing the growth of a crystal and of a bean seed

Into a 400 cm^3 beaker pour about 300 cm^3 of water. Place the beaker on a tripod and gauze, and heat gently with a bunsen burner. Add crystals of potash alum (potassium aluminium sulphate) to the water, and stir with a glass rod. Continue adding crystals until no more will dissolve; any further crystals will then settle at the bottom of the beaker. The solution is now saturated. Filter the hot liquid, and allow the filtrate to cool overnight. Meanwhile, place three runner or broad bean seeds in a beaker of water. Leave them overnight to swell.

On the following day, decant the saturated alum solution into a clean beaker. From the residual crystals, select one that is of good shape and suspend it in the alum solution, as shown in Figure 1.2a. Remove the bean seeds from the water and place each in a jar, as shown in Figure 1.2b. Alternatively, all three seeds may be placed in one jar.

Leave both sets of apparatus where they will not be disturbed, and top up the liquids in the containers as necessary. Observe the crystal and the beans over a period of three or four weeks. Then try to answer these questions:

1. What similarity exists between the 'growth' of the crystal and that of the bean?
2. In what way does the growth of the bean differ from that of the crystal?
3. Which type of growth, that of the crystal or that of the bean, would you say was more complex?

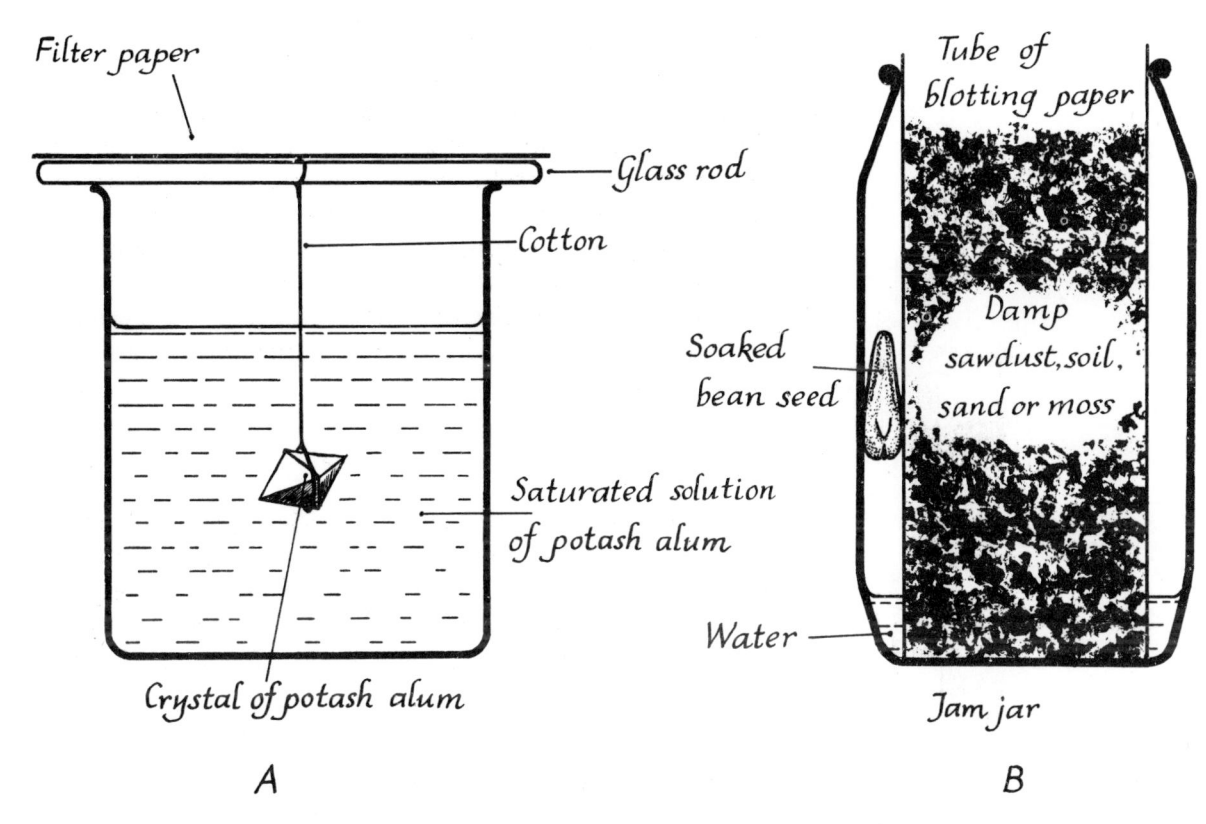

Figure 1.2 Investigating growth

1.5. Nutrition

All living things must obtain a constant supply of food. The food must provide:

a. 'Fuel', or *substances rich in energy*, which can be released by respiration.

b. *Materials for growth*, that is, for increase in size and for the development of new structures or the replacement of damaged ones.

c. *Health substances*, essential for the prevention of disease.

The act of obtaining food is called **feeding**, and the whole process whereby food is used, or utilized, is termed **nutrition**. We shall learn later in this chapter that animals differ from most plants in their method of nutrition.

Bearing in mind the three purposes of food, can we say that a motorcar feeds on petrol or that a crystal feeds on alum?

1.6. Excretion

We have learnt that the process of respiration results in the production of a waste gas, namely carbon dioxide. Many other waste substances are produced by living organisms; as some of these products are poisonous, they must be eliminated. The process whereby an organism gets rid of waste products is called **excretion**. In complex animals such as the mouse, many excretory products are eliminated in the urine. Simpler animals, such as the earthworm and snail, do not produce urine, but they do have their own excretory mechanisms. In plants, excretory substances may be deposited in certain parts of the plant. Thus the heartwood of trees contains waste products such as tannins and resins. It is strange that the beautiful tints of autumn leaves are largely due to deposits of excretory substances.

1.7. Irritability

If it is to survive, it is essential that a living organism should be **sensitive** to what is happening around it. Furthermore, it must be able to **respond** to any changes in its surroundings, and the response must be 'sensible'; in other words, it must be one which will ensure the survival of the organism. We can illustrate this by performing a simple investigation.

Investigation 1b. Irritability in woodlice

Figure 1.3 shows the construction of a simple choice chamber, which can be used with such animals as insects or other small arthropods. In such a chamber we are able to provide an insect with a 'choice' between two environments. Perspex petri dishes are used, and it is best to have four bases, or four lids. The halves are glued together with 'Araldite' or a glue made by dissolving a few pieces of Perspex in a little chloroform. Place water in one half of the chamber and calcium chloride in the other. Cover with a sheet of zinc gauze. Place about six woodlice on the gauze and cover with the double lid. Observe the behaviour of the animals. In which half do they congregate? What effect has calcium chloride on the amount of water vapour in the air? Do the woodlice move towards damp or dry conditions? Why should they react in this way? To what must woodlice be sensitive, if they are to survive?

The capacity to sense changes in the environment and to respond to them is called **irritability**. It is less obvious that plants are irritable, for their responses tend to be slow, growth movements. Thus, for instance, the tip of the runner bean stem is sensitive to touch. When it comes into contact with a surface it grows to entwine it, thus gaining support. In this way it is able to reach up into the light without having a strong stem of its own.

Can a motorcar be said to be irritable? Is it sensitive to changes

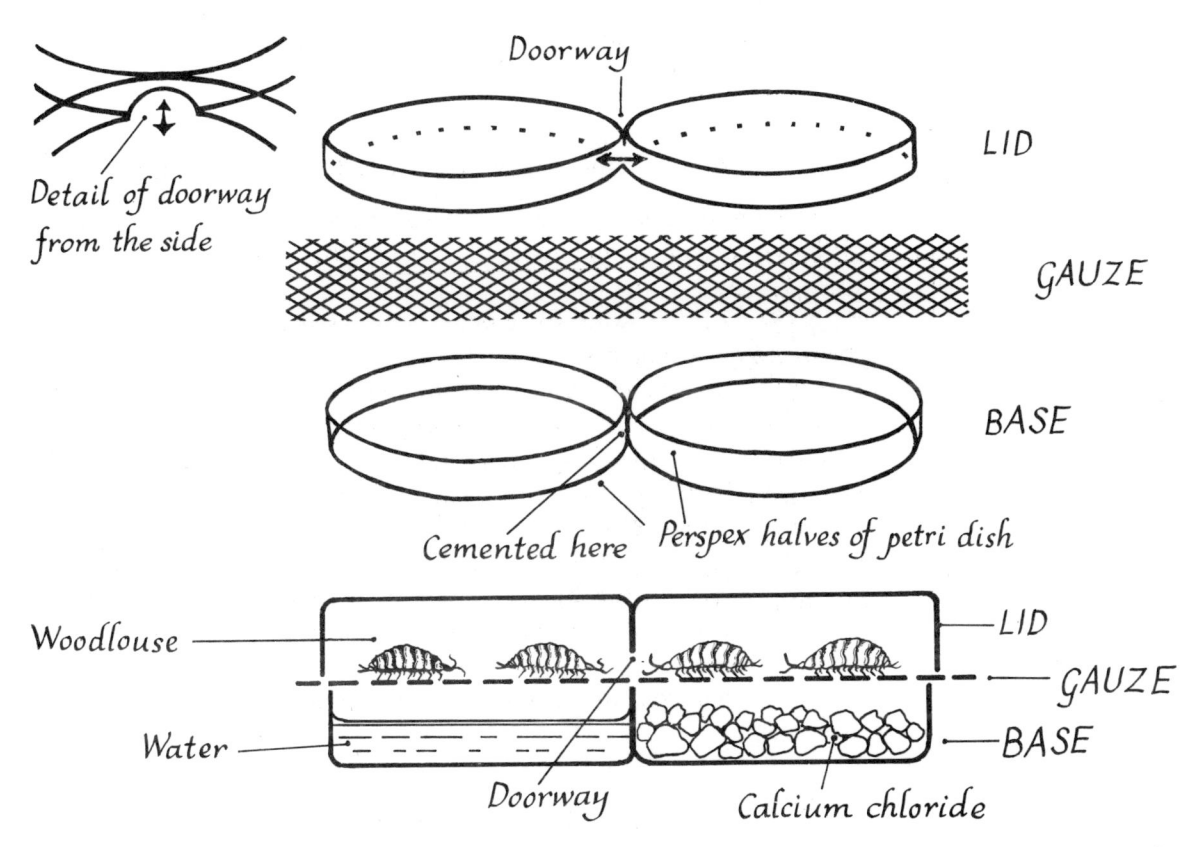

Figure 1.3 Construction of a simple choice chamber

in its surroundings? Does it react as a living thing would, in a manner likely to improve its chances of survival?

1.8. Reproduction

Every living organism has a certain life-span, which may be as short as a few minutes, as in some bacteria, or as long as hundreds of years, as in some trees. If the race is to survive, it follows that new individuals must constantly be produced. The process whereby an organism gives rise to new individuals which are like itself is called **reproduction**. In some plants and animals only one parent is required to produce offspring. This is known as **asexual** reproduction, or reproduction not involving sexes. More commonly, **sexual** reproduction occurs. Here there are two parents, a male and a female, each producing sex cells, or **gametes**. **Fertilization** involves the fusion of a male gamete (for example, sperm) with a female gamete (for example, egg). The product of this fusion is a **zygote**, which develops firstly into an **embryo** and ultimately into an **adult**, itself capable of taking part in sexual reproduction.

Non-living things are unable to reproduce themselves. Thus, at the end of its 'life-span', the motorcar is suitable only for the scrap heap, and has left no offspring.

1.9. Summary of the characteristics of living organisms

The seven characteristics of living organisms are as follows:

a. *Movement*, or locomotion, whereby the position of the whole body, or part of the body, is changed.

b. *Respiration*, whereby energy is released from sugar or other high-energy substances.

c. *Growth*, whereby the organism increases in size or weight, or changes in form, or replaces damaged parts.

d. *Nutrition*, whereby the organism obtains and utilizes food materials necessary for growth, respiration and the prevention of disease.

e. *Excretion*, whereby waste products are eliminated.

f. *Irritability*, whereby the organism senses changes in its surroundings and reacts to these changes in such a way as to increase its chances of survival.

g. *Reproduction*, whereby the organism produces more individuals like itself.

1.10. Comparing plants and animals

Although plants and animals are alike in that they are living organisms and therefore carry out the processes listed above, they differ in several ways. Most of these differences arise out of their different methods of nutrition.

Plants are **producer** organisms, for they are able to build up their own food materials from simple, inorganic substances. They absorb carbon dioxide, water and simple salts. From these simple substances all the complex materials of the plant body are built.

In the green parts of plants the carbon dioxide and water are combined, using the energy of sunlight, to form sugar. This process is called **photosynthesis**. It may be expressed as follows:

$$\text{carbon dioxide} + \text{water} + \text{sunlight} \rightarrow \text{sugar} + \text{oxygen}$$
$$\text{(energy)} \qquad \text{(waste product)}$$

Many plants store the sugar, formed in photosynthesis, as **starch**.

Animals, on the other hand, are unable to produce their own food, but must obtain it 'second-hand' from other organisms. Thus they are termed **consumer** organisms. Animals which feed on plants are called **herbivores**, whilst those which feed on other animals are called **carnivores**. Horses, rabbits and greenfly are examples of herbivorous animals, whilst snakes, owls and lions are carnivorous.

Since the food of animals is complex and insoluble, it has to be **digested**, or broken down, before it can be absorbed by the tissues of the body.

These differences in nutrition lead to other differences between plants and animals. Can you think of the reason why animals usually move about, while plants are usually stationary? Why is the body of an animal compact, whilst that of a plant is more branched? Which type of organism will develop the keenest senses and react fastest?

1.11. The balance of nature

We have said that animals such as rabbits feed on plants. As they feed they grow, and eventually they produce offspring which again feed on plants. Thus, to some extent, the numbers of certain plants are kept down by rabbits. What controls the number of rabbits? The answer is, of course, that rabbits form the food of carnivores, such as foxes. Thus one animal controls the number of another. A **food-chain** exists, where each member of the chain feeds on the one 'below' it, and is eaten by the one 'above' it. For instance, we might imagine the following food-chain in fresh water:

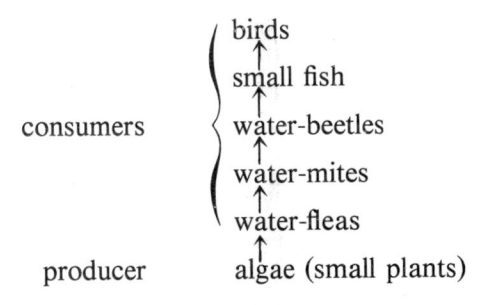

```
                    ┌ birds
                    │   ↑
                    │ small fish
                    │   ↑
    consumers       ┤ water-beetles
                    │   ↑
                    │ water-mites
                    │   ↑
                    └ water-fleas
                          ↑
    producer        algae (small plants)
```

Food-chains are over-simplifications. Thus, in the example given, the mites feed on other animals besides water-fleas, and the beetles on other animals besides mites. In reality, there exists a complex **food-web**, where each animal feeds on a range of other animals, and is itself preyed upon by several predators. At the base of all food-webs are plants. A simple food-web is shown in Figure 1.4.

Because one organism controls the number of another, the living world tends to reach an equilibrium, or **balance**. In this balance, plants and smaller animals are present in greatest numbers. The larger the animal the fewer its number. Thus one mite will need to eat many water-fleas, and one water-beetle will eat many water-mites.

Sometimes the balance of nature is upset, and the numbers of one type of animal rise above the normal. Often the rise is seasonal, as in the case of flies in the summer. The plague of frogs, described in the Bible, was probably such a seasonal rise. In winter, the number of influenza viruses may rise, producing an epidemic. These are examples of an upset in the balance of nature. Often man is

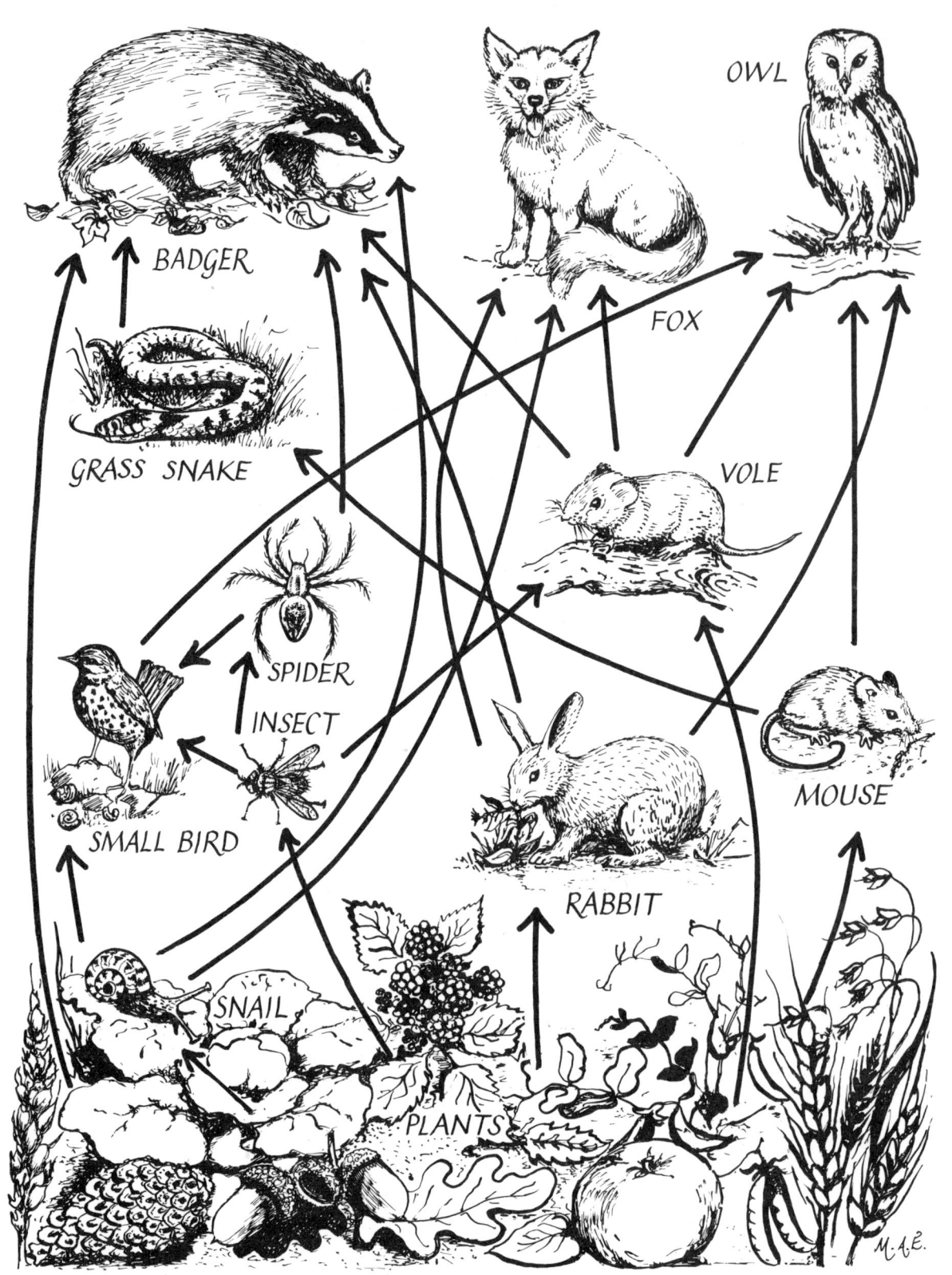

Figure 1.4 A simple food-web

responsible for these, as, for instance, when he introduced rabbits into Australia. Owing to the absence of predators, such as foxes, the rabbits multiplied rapidly, and their numbers were not kept down. The result was that vast areas of land were devastated by the enormous population of rabbits that developed. We should realize, then, that disturbance of the balance of nature may have far-reaching effects.

A more detailed consideration of food-chains, food-webs and the balance of nature will be found in Chapter 15.

Test your understanding

1. What is the important difference between the movement of a mouse and that of a motorcar?
2. What is the purpose of respiration?
3. Write a word equation which summarizes respiration.
4. How does the growth of a bean differ from that of a crystal?
5. Give three reasons why living things require food.
6. What name is given to the process whereby living things eliminate waste matter?
7. What is meant when we say that a living thing is irritable?
8. What is reproduction?
9. Distinguish between asexual and sexual reproduction.
10. Write a simple word equation for photosynthesis, the process whereby green plants make food.
11. Distinguish between herbivores and carnivores.
12. Give two examples of omnivores, animals that feed on both plants and animals.
13. Give your own example of a food-chain.
14. Give your own example of how man has upset the balance of nature.

Chapter 2

Cells: The Units of Life

2.1. Looking at cells: cell structure

In the last chapter we discovered that living things, regardless of type or form, all carry out certain processes which are essential to life. Thus the fly and the elephant, the daisy and the oak tree may be very different in appearance, but, to remain alive, they have the same requirements. These include a source of food and oxygen, together with mechanisms which can take these into the body and make use of them. Waste products must be eliminated or rendered harmless. The organism must be sensitive to what is happening around it and must be able to protect itself. Finally, since all living things have only a certain life-span, reproduction must occur so that the race can be continued.

We must now ask ourselves the question—if living things are so uniform in their requirements, is there any uniformity in their structure? To begin to find an answer to this question we must repeat an investigation that was first performed over 300 years ago.

Investigation 2a. Microscopical examination of cork

For this investigation you will need a bottle cork, a sharp razor-blade (single-edged), a microscope, a glass slide and a cover-slip. The purpose of the investigation is to examine a very thin slice of the cork under the microscope. Unless the slice is thin, light will not pass through it, and the cork will appear very dark.

Holding the cork between the thumb and first two fingers, cut thin slices with the razor-blade (see Figure 2.1). *Keep your thumb well clear of the emerging blade.* The slices need not be whole; indeed, the thinnest areas are often the edges of fragments. Cut a large number of slices so that you have plenty to choose from. Select one which has a thin edge (indicated by its transparency). Place this section on the microscope slide together with a little water. Place a cover-slip over the section, and examine the thin edge under the low power of the microscope. What can you see when you examine the cork? Is it composed of compartments? Are there many of these?

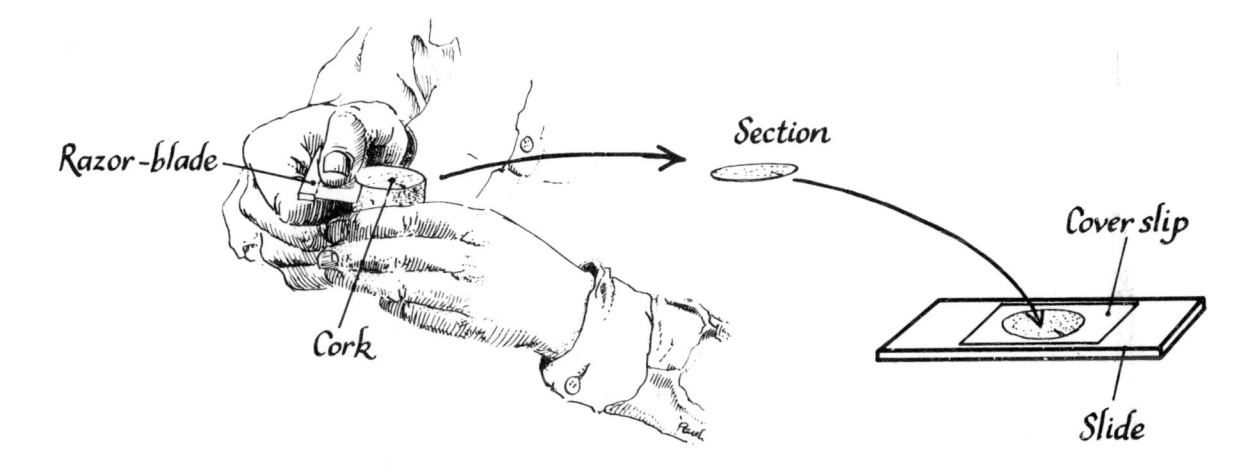

What shape are they? Do they look alike? Draw a few of these compartments so that you will remember their appearance.

Figure 2.1 Preparing cork for examination under the microscope

This investigation was first carried out by an Englishman, **Robert Hooke**, in 1665. He was the inventor of the microscope as we know it today. Using his invention, Hooke examined a variety of things around him, just as you would if you were given a microscope as a present. When he examined a slice of cork, Robert Hooke was struck by its porous nature, and by the walls of the tiny compartments. Since the structure reminded him of a honeycomb, he called the compartments **cells**. Hooke tried to estimate the size of the cells, and also their number. Since there were some 65 cells in 1·5 mm, he deduced that a cubic centimetre would contain over 75 000 000. Hooke now asked himself whether these cells occurred in any other vegetable tissue. His interests were so wide that he was not able to spend as much time on this subject as he might have liked, but he did examine sections from vegetables such as the carrot, and from the pith of burdock, teasels and fern. In all of these materials he found cells such as he had first seen in cork, though their shape and arrangement varied.

Let us now examine, for ourselves, another plant material under the microscope.

Investigation 2b. Microscopical examination of onion epidermis

In this investigation we are going to remove from an onion bulb a piece of tissue called **epidermis**. This is extremely thin, so we shall be able to see its structure without the need for sectioning. The tissue forms the surface layer of the swollen leaf-bases, which form the bulk of the bulb.

Begin by cutting the bulb into quarters (see Figure 2.2a, b). Taking one quarter, cut off the small portion of stem at the base and, with your fingers and thumb, separate the remaining portion into its parts (see Figure 2.2c). Each part is the base of a leaf, swollen with food reserves. Notice the glistening, transparent skin on the inner surface. Peel off a small portion of this skin (see Figure 2.2d) and mount it on a microscope slide with a little water or 70% alcohol (see Figure 2.2e). Examine the tissue under the low power of the microscope. Can you see the cells? What shape are they? Are they like those of cork? Can you think of a way to estimate their length?

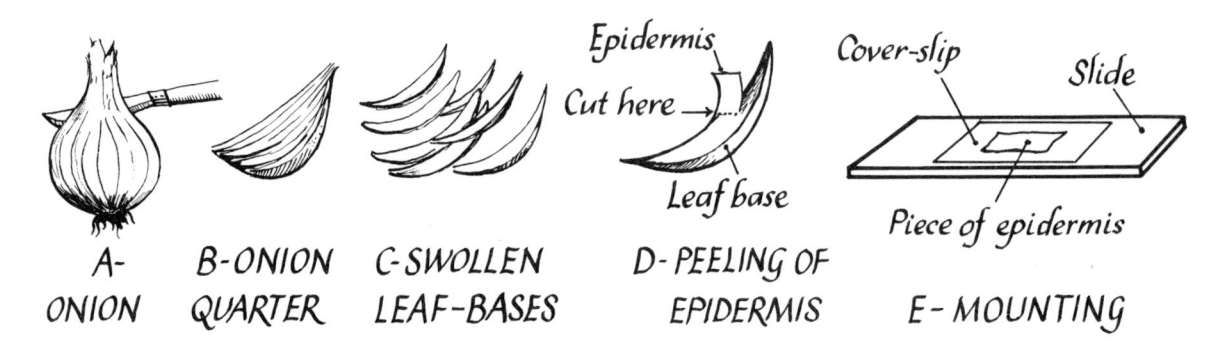

A- ONION B- ONION QUARTER C- SWOLLEN LEAF-BASES D- PEELING OF EPIDERMIS E- MOUNTING

Figure 2.2 Preparing onion epidermis for examination under the microscope

With a teat pipette, place one drop of 'iodine solution' (iodine crystals dissolved in potassium iodide solution or in 70% alcohol) close against one edge of the cover-slip (see Figure 2.3a). Cut a piece of filter paper or blotting paper to the same width as the cover-slip, and hold this paper against the edge of the cover-slip opposite to the drop of iodine (see Figure 2.3b). The paper will draw some of the 'iodine' under the cover-slip and around the specimen, a process called **irrigation**.

Now re-examine the onion cells under low power and then under high power of the microscope, concentrating on the contents of the cells. Are you able to see a dark blob in each cell? This is called the **nucleus**. Is there a granular substance lining the cells? This is the **cytoplasm**. The nucleus and the cytoplasm are composed of living matter, or **protoplasm**. The cell wall is not living, but is produced by the cytoplasm.

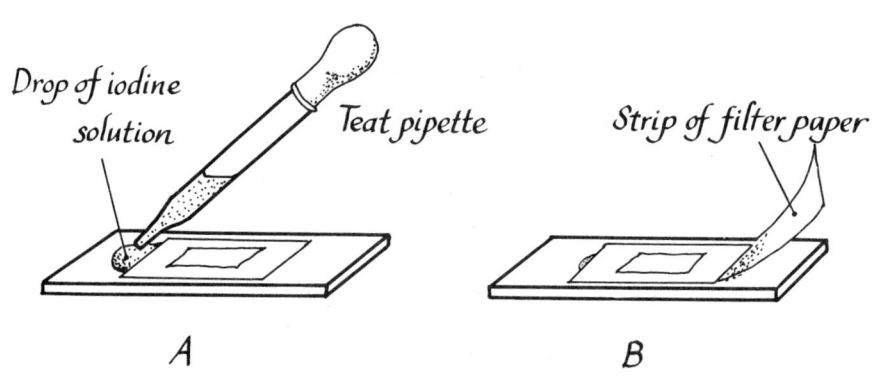

Figure 2.3 Irrigation technique

A   B

14

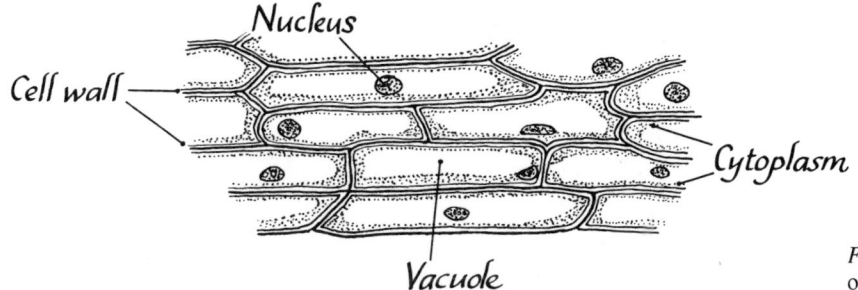

Figure 2.4 Cells from an onion epidermis

Finally, draw a few cells to show their shape and contents (see Figure 2.4). What purpose did the 'iodine' serve in this investigation?

That each cell contains a nucleus was first discovered by **Robert Brown** (1773–1858), following an examination of the cells of orchids. The significance of cytoplasm was not appreciated until the work of the German biologists **Schleiden** and **Schwann**. Before we consider their work, we must turn our attention away from plant tissues and take a look at some animal cells.

Investigation 2c. Looking at some animal cells

It is quite easy to demonstrate that the bodies of animals, like those of plants, are built from cells. In this investigation we shall examine cells from the linings of our own mouths.

Place a drop of water on a clean microscope slide. Sterilize the blade of a blunt scalpel by dipping it in disinfectant (for example, diluted Dettol). With this blade, carefully scrape the inner lining of your cheek. Add the scrapings to the water on the slide and mix them together. The water should now appear slightly creamy. Add a drop of 'iodine', methylene blue or Delafield's haematoxylin. Cover with a cover-slip. Examine under the low power of the microscope, keeping the light fairly well shut down. Can you see the cells? What indications are there that, in the mouth, the cells are joined together to form a sheet? What shape are the cells? What tells us that the cells are extremely thin? Are you able to see the nucleus? What is its shape? How do these cells differ from those of the onion? Draw one or two cells carefully (see Figure 2.5).

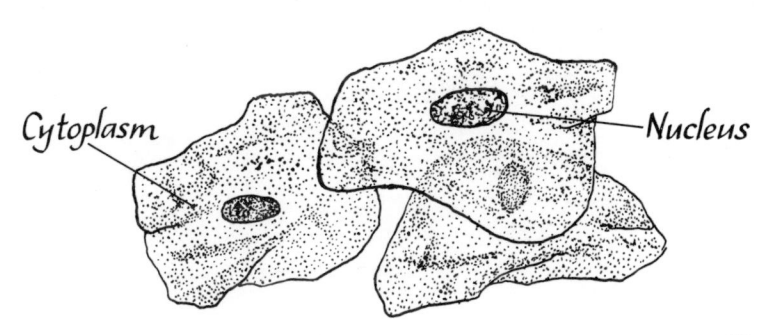

Figure 2.5 Cells from the lining of the cheek

15

2.2. Plant and animal cells

From our investigations we have seen that differences exist between plant and animal cells. One obvious difference concerns the boundary of the cell. In the cork and onion tissues, we saw that each cell was bounded by a distinct **cell wall**. This wall is composed of **cellulose**, though other substances may be added to it. The cells of our cheek lining did not have this wall. If you were to examine many plant and animal tissues, you would find that this distinction is true. *Plant cells have cell walls, whilst those of animals do not.*

The cytoplasm of plant and animal cells differs in its distribution. In plant cells, especially older ones, the cytoplasm does not fill the cell, but forms a lining to the cell wall. The centre of the cell is occupied by a space, or **vacuole**, which is filled with **cell sap**. In animal cells, on the other hand, the cytoplasm largely fills the cell, and any vacuoles present tend to be small.

When we examine cells from the green part of a plant, we discover another important difference between plant and animal cells.

Investigation 2d. Examination of cells from a moss leaf

The leaves of most green plants are too thick to allow light to pass through, so for an examination of leaf cells sections have to be made. The leaves of mosses, however, are much thinner, and their cells can be observed without the need for sectioning.

Remove one or two moss leaves and mount them in a little water on a microscope slide. Examine them under the low power of the microscope. How do the cells differ from those of the onion epidermis? Why does the leaf appear green?

The green bodies in the cells are concerned with food-making, and are called **chloroplasts**. The presence of chloroplasts largely obscures the cytoplasm and nucleus, but, with careful observation, you may be able to see them. *Animal cells do not contain chloroplasts, but the green parts of plants do.* Some moss cells are shown in Figure 2.6.

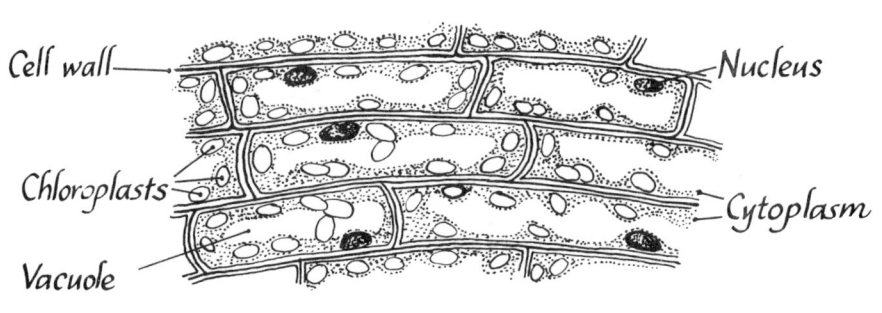

Figure 2.6 Cells of a moss leaf

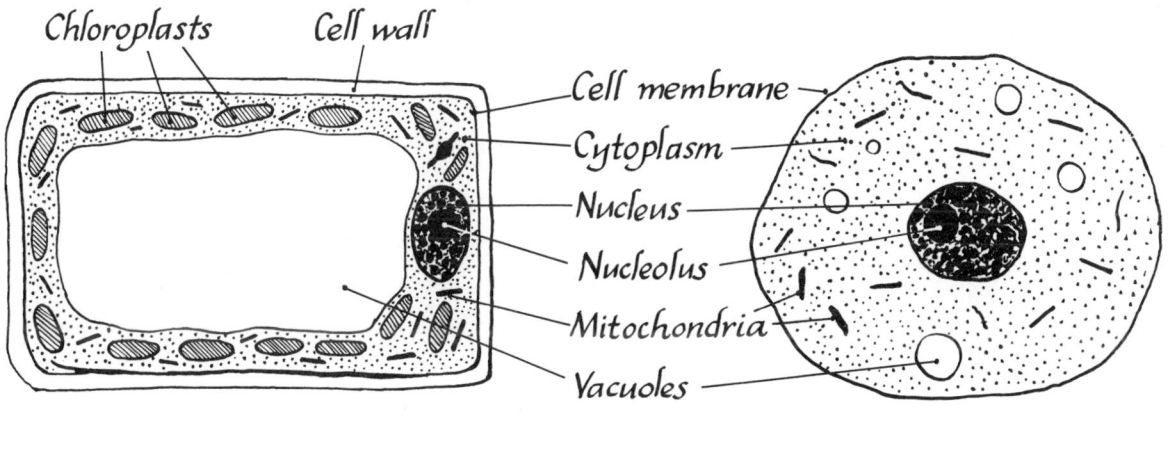

Figure 2.7 Typical plant and animal cells

We may now summarize the essential differences between plant and animal cells. These differences are illustrated in Figure 2.7.

TABLE 2.1. DIFFERENCES BETWEEN PLANT AND ANIMAL CELLS

Plant Cells	Animal Cells
1. Bounded by a cellulose cell wall.	1. No cell wall.
2. Cytoplasm often confined to a lining just inside the cell wall.	2. Cytoplasm tends to fill the cell.
3. Large central vacuole.	3. If present, vacuoles are small and dispersed.
4. Cells of the green parts of plants contain chloroplasts.	4. No chloroplasts.

The biologists Schleiden and Schwann were the first to realize the importance of the nucleus and the cytoplasm. What Robert Hooke saw in his cork tissue were only dead and deformed cell walls. The living contents had long since rotted away, as cork is a dead tissue. Schleiden and Schwann were the first to put forward the theory that the bodies of all plants and animals are built from cells, and from structures formed by cells. This belief, or **cell doctrine**, was one of the major landmarks in the development of modern biology.

2.3. The parts of the cell and their uses

a. *Plasma membrane*. The cytoplasm of all plant and animal cells is bounded by a thin, elastic 'skin' or membrane. This membrane is **semi-permeable**; that is, it permits some substances to pass through it, but holds back others. It exercises, therefore, important control over the contents of the cell.

b. *Cell wall.* The cellulose cell wall of plant cells serves to give mechanical support to the cell.

c. *Cytoplasm.* In some respects, the cell is like a factory, with the cytoplasm being the 'assembly line', for here the main work of the cell takes place. New, complex substances such as proteins are built up from simpler substances, just as on an assembly line complicated mechanisms may be built up from simpler parts. The build-up of new substances is called **synthesis,** or **anabolism**. In the cytoplasm other substances are broken down to simpler substances, a process known as **katabolism**. The general term for the chemical working of the cell, involving build-up and breakdown, is **metabolism**. The metabolic processes are very complicated, and are far from being fully understood.

d. *Mitochondria.* To carry out its metabolic work, the cell needs a supply of energy, just as a factory needs power. This energy is released in the process of respiration, which occurs at special sites in the cell called mitochondria.

e. *Nucleus.* The nucleus has been referred to as the 'Board of Governors' of the cell, for it is the controlling centre. Within it are thread-like bodies, called **chromosomes**, that carry the hereditary units, or **genes**. Each gene can be thought of as a set of instructions for the synthesis of a particular chemical substance. The genes remain in the nucleus, but their instructions are carried to the cytoplasm, where the actual synthesis of new substances takes place. A diagrammatic representation of this process is given in Figure 2.8. It should be realized that every cell in the body contains the same set of genes. In any particular cell, not all of the genes will actually be active in forming new substances. In the same way, a cook does not use all the recipes in her cookery book at the same time.

f. *Chloroplasts.* These occur in the cytoplasm of the cells of the green parts of plants. They contain **chlorophyll**, a green pigment which is able to absorb some of the energy of sunlight. Chloroplasts are the centres of photosynthesis, the process whereby green plants build up their own food materials (carbohydrates) from simple substances (carbon dioxide and water).

2.4. Types of cell

The bodies of some plants and animals are composed of only one cell. Such organisms are termed **unicellular**. It follows that this single cell must perform all the functions necessary for life. In Chapter 4 you will learn how an organism such as the amoeba carries out these functions. Most plants and animals, however, are **multicellular**, having bodies composed of many cells. In these organisms there is no need for every cell to perform all of the functions of life. Division of labour is possible between the cells, and each cell can become adapted or specialized to carry out one, or more, particular functions. This affects the appearance of the cell. Thus, for instance, a cell responsible for movement (muscle cell) will look different from a cell forming part of a bone (bone cell). A few types of plant and animal cell are shown in Figure 2.9.

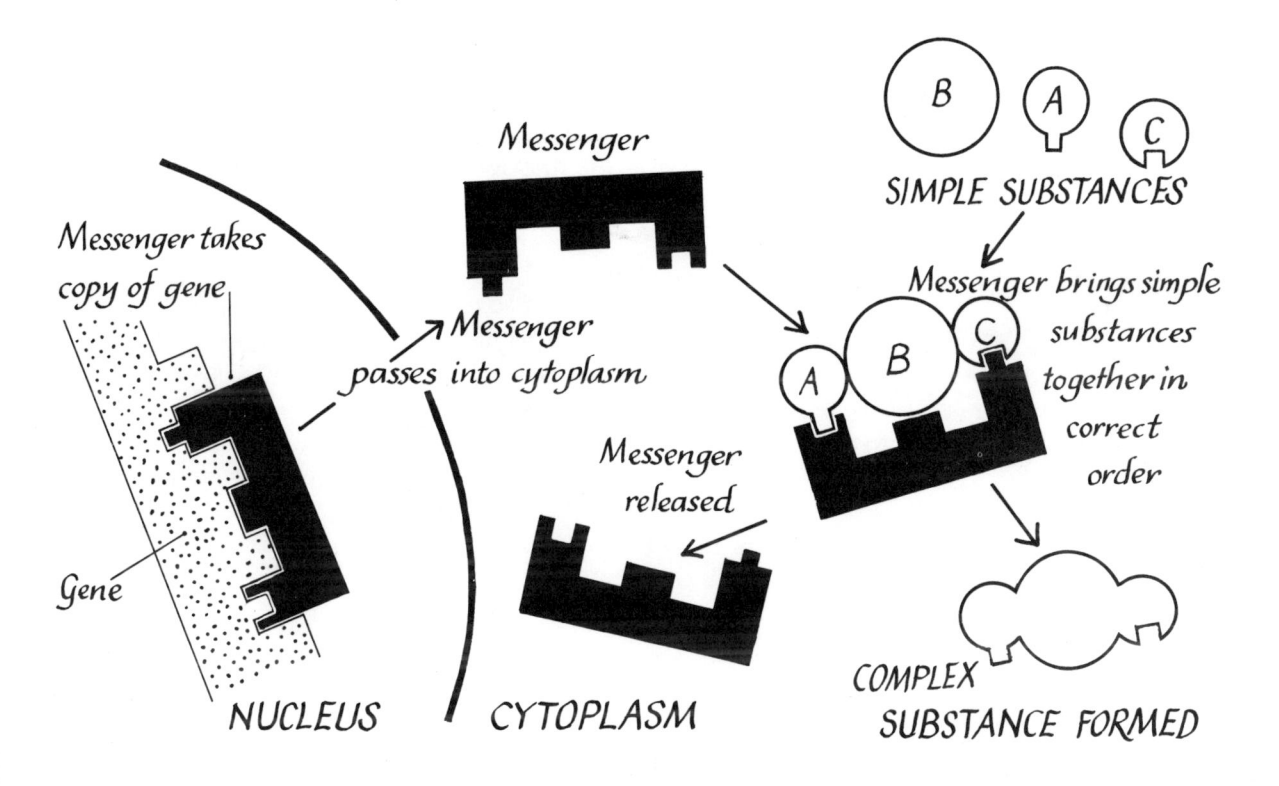

Figure 2.8 Simple representation of the action of a gene in forming a new substance in the cytoplasm

Figure 2.9 Various shapes of plant and animal cells

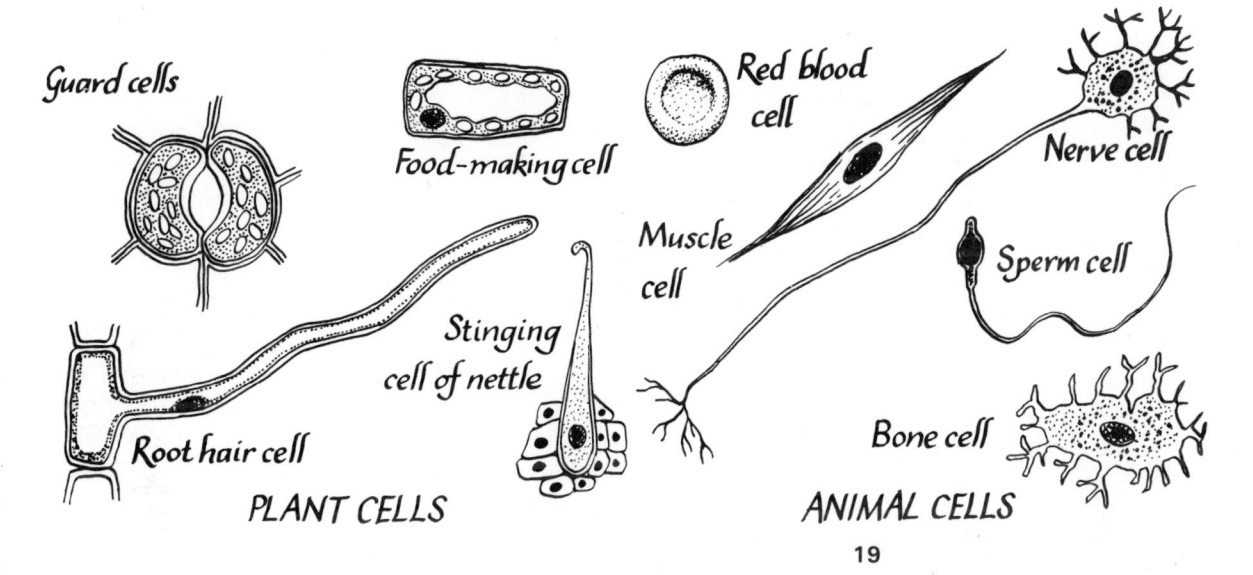

2.5. How cells arise: cell division

The idea that the body is 'a cell state in which every cell is a citizen' was first put forward, in 1858, by the German physician, **Rudolf Virchow**. He was also the first to realize that a new cell can only arise by division of an existing cell. Most organisms begin their lives as a single cell, such as an egg cell; all the cells of the organism are descendants of this original cell.

How, then, does a cell give rise to a new one? You might imagine that the cell would simply split into two halves, haphazardly, but this is very rare in nature. You will recall that the nucleus contains chromosomes which carry the hereditary units, or genes. It is vital that the new cell should possess a full set of these genes, and not just half of them. Because of this, the process of cell division (**mitosis**) is very complex. Before the cytoplasm can split into two halves, the chromosomes must duplicate, or double themselves. During mitosis there is a careful and exact sharing-out of these duplicates (see Figure 2.10).

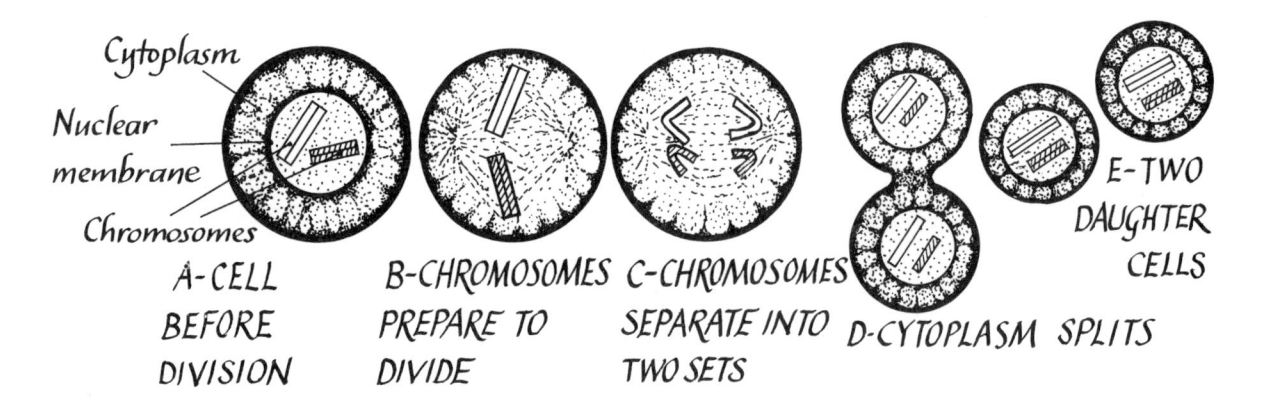

Figure 2.10 Outline of cell division (mitosis)

The time taken for a cell to divide varies a great deal, and depends on the nature of the organism, on which particular tissue is involved, and on factors such as temperature and oxygen supply. A bacterial cell may divide as rapidly as once every twenty minutes, but in higher organisms division is slower.

2.6. The fate of dead cells

Just as an individual has a certain life-span which varies from species to species, so also does a cell have a life-span which varies from cell to cell. Some cells, such as those of our brains, live for the whole span of life of the individual, and when we die the same brain cells die with us. In other cases, the span of life of the cell is much shorter than that of its 'owner'. Thus, a human red blood cell lives only for some 110 days, and a bone cell for some seven years. It follows that dead cells must be replaced, if the organism is to survive. It has been estimated that, of every hundred cells in the human body, one or two die every day. The problem of replacement is, therefore, a vast one, and cell division must continue throughout life. In this sense, then, we never 'stop growing'.

2.7. Cells, tissues, organs and organisms

In society, several men performing the same task often work alongside each other. In the same way, cells performing the same function are grouped together to form a **tissue**. All the cells in a tissue are similar. The skin that we peeled from an onion was a tissue called epidermis. In our bodies we, also, have a surface skin or epidermis, as well as having bone tissue, muscular tissue, skeletal tissue, nervous tissue, etc.

Again, in a factory or office, groups of people with different duties will all be working to the same end, such as the production of an article or the provision of a service. So, also, various tissues work together in an **organ**. The organ performs some major body function. We may take as an example the heart, an organ responsible for the circulation of blood. It is built from several types of tissue, including muscle tissue, nervous tissue, blood tissue, etc.

Finally, we should realize that an individual **organism** is really a collection of organs, each of which contributes, in some way, to the maintenance of its existence.

Test your understanding

Copy and complete the following:

Cells were first observed by ....[1], when he examined a thin slice of cork under his microscope. However, since cork is a dead tissue, only the ....[2] remain. Examination of onion epidermis reveals that living cells contain a lining of ....[3] The organizing centre of the cell is called the ....[4] One of the main differences between plant and animal cells is that plant cells are bounded by a ....[5], composed of ....[6], whilst animal cells are not. In those plant cells that are concerned with food-making, there are green bodies, called ....[7]

The cell doctrine states that all ....[8] and ....[9] are composed of ....[10], and from structures formed by them. Whilst there are some unicellular organisms, most plants and animals are ....[11] It is then possible for cells to become ....[12] for particular purposes.

New cells can only arise by ....[13] of existing ones. During mitosis, there is a careful and exact duplication of the ....[14], to form two similar sets. A group of similar cells, performing a similar function, is called a ....[15]

1. What contribution to our knowledge of cells was made by each of the following: Hooke, Brown, Schleiden and Schwann, Virchow?

2. Make a list of those components which are present in both plant and animal cells.
3. Explain the meaning of the terms 'unicellular' and 'multicellular', and give the advantages of the latter condition.
4. Why is cell division such a complex process?
5. Distinguish between a cell, a tissue, an organ and an organism. Give an example of each.

TOPIC B: THE VARIETY OF LIVING ORGANISMS

Chapter 3

Naming and Grouping

3.1. The meaning of classification

Supposing that you were asked to make a list of all the various animals that you have seen, read about or heard of, how many do you think that you could list? Possibly a hundred or so? Do you realize that there are over one and a quarter million different animals known to scientists? As there are, in addition, over a third of a million types of plant, the total number of types of living organism is very large indeed. Obviously, no one scientist could study all of these creatures, nor would he wish to do so. More probably, he will wish to study a few organisms in detail, whilst having a general knowledge of the living world as a whole.

Although there are all of these different creatures, they are not all different from each other in every respect. Many possess common features, such as the possession of a similar shape, skeleton or number of limbs. The living world will be easier to talk about if we group together organisms according to their observed common features. Such a grouping is known as **classification**.

The need for classification is not confined to biology. The good stamp collector classifies his stamps, the librarian his books, and the supermarket its foods.

Investigation 3a. Grouping living creatures

Arrange on a table as many different specimens, living or preserved, as possible. Pictures of creatures may be used, if you wish. Now rearrange the specimens so that they are in groups of your own choosing. Place beside each group a piece of paper listing the features common to all members of the group. When you have finished, compare your classification with that adopted by other members of the class. Discuss the merits of each method. Realize that it is possible to classify the same organisms in different ways. Do not be surprised to find that not all scientists classify living things in the same way.

thods of classification

...ine attempt to classify living creatures was made by ...opher **Aristotle**, around 350 BC. Only some thousand ...nown at this time.
...d the plants thus:

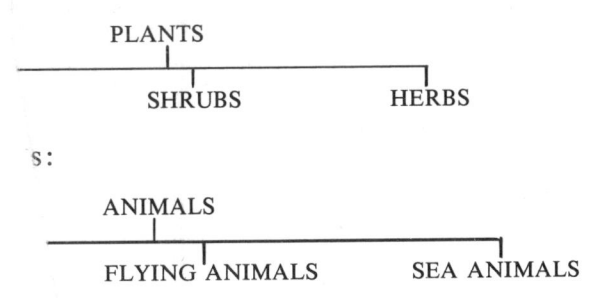

```
              PLANTS
          ┌─────┴─────┐
        SHRUBS      HERBS
```

s:

```
              ANIMALS
          ┌─────┴─────┐
     FLYING ANIMALS  SEA ANIMALS
```

...objections to this system? Why is it unsound ...cuttlefish and swordfish in the same group? ...**John Ray**, we owe the belief that individual ... natural groups called **species**. He suggested ...comprise individuals having similar features, and that 'a species is never born from the seed of another species'. The idea of the species is very important in modern classification. In Ray's time, the seventeenth century, the number of species known did not exceed ten thousand.

3.3. The work of Linnaeus

The modern method of classification is based on the work of the Swedish naturalist **Karl Linnaeus** (1707–78). Linnaeus proposed a natural system based on the idea of the species. In his book entitled *Systema Naturae*, he listed several thousand different species of plant and animal. Linnaeus soon realized that the names given to these species would have to be made more sensible. The common names in use at that time would not be of any use in a scientific classification. These common names varied from country to country, and even from locality to locality. As an example, we may quote the common hedgerow flower, which is known in some localities as 'Cuckoo Pint'. In other localities, the same plant is known as 'Lords and Ladies', 'Jack-in-the-Pulpit' and 'Wake Robin'. Such common names are confusing, also, in that different creatures are sometimes given the same name in different localities. For example, in different parts of the U.S.A., the name 'gopher' is given to a type of burrowing rodent, to a ground squirrel and to a kind of turtle! You can see how confusing this is to scientists.

Linnaeus proposed a **binomial system of nomenclature**, whereby each species was given a double name, in Latin. Why do you think that Latin was chosen? Thus the plant mentioned above as 'Cuckoo

Pint', etc., was named *Arum maculatum*. The first part of the name (*Arum*) is called the **generic name**, and indicates to which genus the plant belongs. A **genus** is a group of species having similar features. The second name (*maculatum*) is the **specific name**, and indicates which species of the genus is being referred to. It frequently describes some prominent feature of the organism (*maculatum* means 'spotted'); *Arum maculatum* is thus the Latin name for the spotted arum lily.

Generic names begin with capital letters, whilst specific names have small ones, unless they are derived from the name of a person (for example, *Williamsii*). Here are some examples of this system of naming:

THE 'DOG' GENUS (*Canis*)

Canis familiaris (dog)
Canis lupus (wolf)
Canis aureus (northern jackal)
Canis dingo (dingo)
Canis latrans (prairie-wolf)
Canis lupaster (Egyptian jackal)
Canis mesomelas (black-backed jackal)

THE 'BUTTERCUP' GENUS (*Ranunculus*)

Ranunculus acris (Meadow Buttercup)
Ranunculus repens (Creeping Buttercup or Crowfoot)
Ranunculus bulbosus (Bulbous Buttercup)
Ranunculus arvensis (Corn Crowfoot)
Ranunculus parviflorus (Small-flowered Buttercup)
Ranunculus auricomus (Goldilocks)
Ranunculus aquatilis (Common Water Crowfoot)

These names are universally accepted, so if an English scientist reads in an American book about *Larus argentatus*, he knows that the animal being referred to is our common 'sea-gull', the Herring Gull. We see, then, that the system first proposed in the eighteenth century by Linnaeus has done much to make classification more accurate.

3.4. What is a species?

No two individuals are exactly alike, whether they be human beings, houseflies or dandelions. Nevertheless, it is possible to think of, say, a 'human type' that all humans resemble to some extent. Similarly, there must be a 'housefly type' and a 'dandelion type'. Groups of individuals, each a slight variation of a common type, form a species. All the individual members of a species resemble each other more than they resemble the members of another species. Thus, for instance, the various breeds of dog, from Pekinese to Great Danes, are all members of the same species, *Canis familiaris*.

Figure 3.1 All breeds of dog and all races of man form single species

Similarly, all humans, whether they be Europeans, Red Indians, Mongolians or Negroes, constitute a single species, *Homo sapiens* (see Figure 3.1).

The members of a species can breed together, producing offspring which are *fertile*; in other words, the offspring are able to breed when they become adult. Individuals belonging to different species do not usually breed together, and if they do the offspring, or **hybrids**, are usually infertile. For example, the horse and the ass belong to different species. If a jackass (male ass) is bred with a horse mare, the offspring is a mule. Only very rarely does a cross between a male and a female mule produce offspring.

Hybridization (the formation of hybrids) is more common in plants than in animals, and many of our garden plants, such as roses and rhododendrons, have been developed in this way. Once developed hybrid plants are propagated by vegetative means (cuttings, etc.).

3.5. Grouping species together

We have seen that Linnaeus grouped similar species into **genera** (singular: genus). All members of a genus have common features. Thus, all members of the cat genus, *Felis*, have five digits on the fore-limb and five on the hind-limb, the toes are clawed and the feet bear walking-pads. Genera having common features are grouped into **families**. Thus the modern 'cats', including cats, pumas, leopards, lions, tigers and jaguars, belong to the same family (the Felidae) as the sabre-toothed tigers that roamed the earth some 40 million years ago, and which have been extinct for 25 000 years (see Figure 3.2).

A group of similar families is called an **order**. Thus cats, dogs, bears, stoats, badgers and seals are members of the order Carnivora, distinguished by their flesh-eating habit and their similar teeth. Orders with common features are grouped into **classes**. The Carnivora is one of the orders in the important class Mammalia, which includes not only such animals as rats, rabbits, moles, bats, pigs, horses, whales, kangaroos and apes, but also man himself. All mammals possess hairy skin, teeth of various types, sweat glands and the ability to feed their young on milk produced in mammary glands.

Classes are grouped into major divisions, called **phyla** (singular: phylum). Mammals are members of the phylum Chordata, which includes all animals with backbones. Other chordates are fishes, amphibians, reptiles and birds. Finally, phyla are grouped into **kingdoms**. Chordates, together with arthropods, molluscs, annelid worms, etc., are members of the Animal Kingdom. (*Note*. In the classification of plants, the term phylum tends to be replaced by the term **division**.)

Figure 3.2 Members of the cat family (Felidae)

Thus the classification of the domestic cat could be summarized as follows:

Kingdom: Animalia
Phylum: Chordata
Class: Mammalia
Order: Carnivora
Family: Felidae
Genus: *Felis*
Species: *Felis domestica*

3.6. The use of keys

As there are so many species of animals and plants, deciding to which species a particular individual belongs is not easy. In order to discover to which phylum the specimen belongs, it is best to use a simple key. In such a key, the classifier is presented with a series of paired features. The features in each pair are opposites, and only one can be possessed by the specimen under examination. Let us see how such a key operates.

Investigation 3b. Using a key to place an animal in the correct phylum

Key

1a. Microscopic .... phylum PROTOZOA
 b. Clearly visible to naked eye .... go on to 2

2a. Body spongy—perforated with holes .... phylum PORIFERA (sponges)
 b. Body not spongy .... go on to 3

3a. Has internal bones .... phylum CHORDATA (backboned animals)
 b. Not bony .... go on to 4

4a. Soft-bodied; no shell .... go on to 5
 b. External shell or hard coarse skin .... go on to 8

5a. Tubular, sac-like body, with tentacles round mouth .... phylum COELENTERATA (polyps and medusae)
 b. Worm-like with front and rear ends .... go on to 6

6a. Body flat and leaf-like .... phylum PLATYHELMINTHES (flatworms)
 b. Body more rounded in section .... go on to 7

7a. Body not divided by rings .... phylum NEMATODA (roundworms)
 b. Body segmented; divided by rings .... phylum ANNELIDA (ringed worms)

8a. Definite shell; skin not spiny .... go on to 9
 b. Skin spiny; body star-shaped; five-rayed .... phylum ECHINODERMATA (starfishes)

9a. Shell segmented and jointed; body bears paired limbs .... phylum ARTHROPODA (insects, crabs, etc.)
 b. Shell not segmented or jointed; body protruding as a muscular foot .... phylum MOLLUSCA (snails, etc.)

Using the key

Examine your specimen carefully and look at the first pair of contrasted features. If your specimen is microscopic it may belong to the phylum **Protozoa**, although there are other possibilities (for example, a larva of a larger animal). If the specimen is clearly visible to the naked eye, you should proceed to features 2a and 2b. If the body is spongy, the animal belongs to the phylum **Porifera**; if not, you should proceed to features 3a and 3b. Continue in this way until you have made a choice which indicates the phylum to which the animal belongs.

The key given is a very simple one, for it does not list many features. However, the key does give some guide as to the probable phylum, and will give valuable practice which will help you to use more complex keys later.

Having identified the phylum to which the animal belongs, it is now necessary to establish its class within that phylum. Two very important phyla are the **Arthropoda**, which contains over three-quarters of a million invertebrate animals, and the **Chordata**, which includes all the animals with backbones. Keys to the classes within these two phyla are given here.

Key to the classes of arthropods

1a. Body long and thin, with no distinct regions; many segments, with one or two pairs of legs per segment . . . . class MYRIAPODA (centipedes and millipedes)
 b. Body shorter and wider, with distinct regions; fewer segments; not more than five pairs of walking legs . . . . go on to 2

2a. Two pairs of antennae; five pairs of walking legs; small limbs along abdomen; mainly marine animals . . . . class CRUSTACEA (crabs, shrimps, etc.)
 b. One pair of antennae, or none; less than five pairs of walking legs; no limbs on abdomen; mainly land animals . . . . go on to 3

3a. Three pairs of walking legs; body has three regions (head, thorax and abdomen) . . . . class INSECTA (flies, beetles, etc.)
 b. Four pairs of legs; body divisible into two regions only . . . . class ARACHNIDA (spiders, scorpions, etc.)

Key to the classes of chordates

1a. Fish-like animals, with fins . . . . go on to 2
 b. Animals with legs, wings or flippers, but no fins . . . . go on to 3

2a. Mouth terminal; scales smooth; gills covered by bony flap (see Figure 7·4) . . . . class OSTEICHTHYES (bony fish)
 b. Mouth ventral; scales rough and tooth-like; five pairs of visible gill openings; small hole (spiracle) behind each eye (see Figure 7·4) . . . . class CHONDRICHTHYES (gristly or cartilaginous fishes)

3a. Skin thin, moist and loose-fitting; no hair or scales .... class AMPHIBIA (frogs, newts, etc.)
 b. Skin thick, tough, hairy or scaly .... go on to 4

4a. Body entirely covered with scales .... class REPTILIA (snakes, lizards, etc.)
 b. Body with wings and feathers .... class AVES (birds)
 c. Body bearing hair .... class MAMMALIA (cats, dogs, rabbits, etc.)

3.7. The value of classification

We have seen that we are able to place plants and animals in groups because the members of a group share certain common features. Thus, for instance, all mammals have hair, two sets of teeth, mammary glands, sweat glands and a constant body temperature. To be told that an animal is a mammal gives a great deal of information about it, even though we may never have seen the animal. It is more important, therefore, for the biologist to know the general features of the group than to know a great deal about one member of the group. Classification helps us to understand the general structure of all animals and plants and to catalogue them in our mind. Classification is not, however, a mere pigeon-holing. We must ask ourselves *why* the members of a group share common features. Biologists believe it is because they are *related*, just as the members of a human family share common features because they are related. We believe that the dog and the wolf, for example, are more closely related to each other than either is related to, say, the cat. In other words, classification suggests that the dog and the wolf have a **common ancestor.**

Classification, therefore, serves to catalogue organisms and to express relationships between them.

Some suggestions for further work

1. Make a collection of plants which all belong to the same group (for example, members of the buttercup genus, *Ranunculus*).
2. Devise a key to enable your collection to be identified.
3. Construct keys, similar to those given for arthropods and chordates, for groups such as molluscs and annelids.

TABLE 3.1. OUTLINE CLASSIFICATION OF ANIMALS

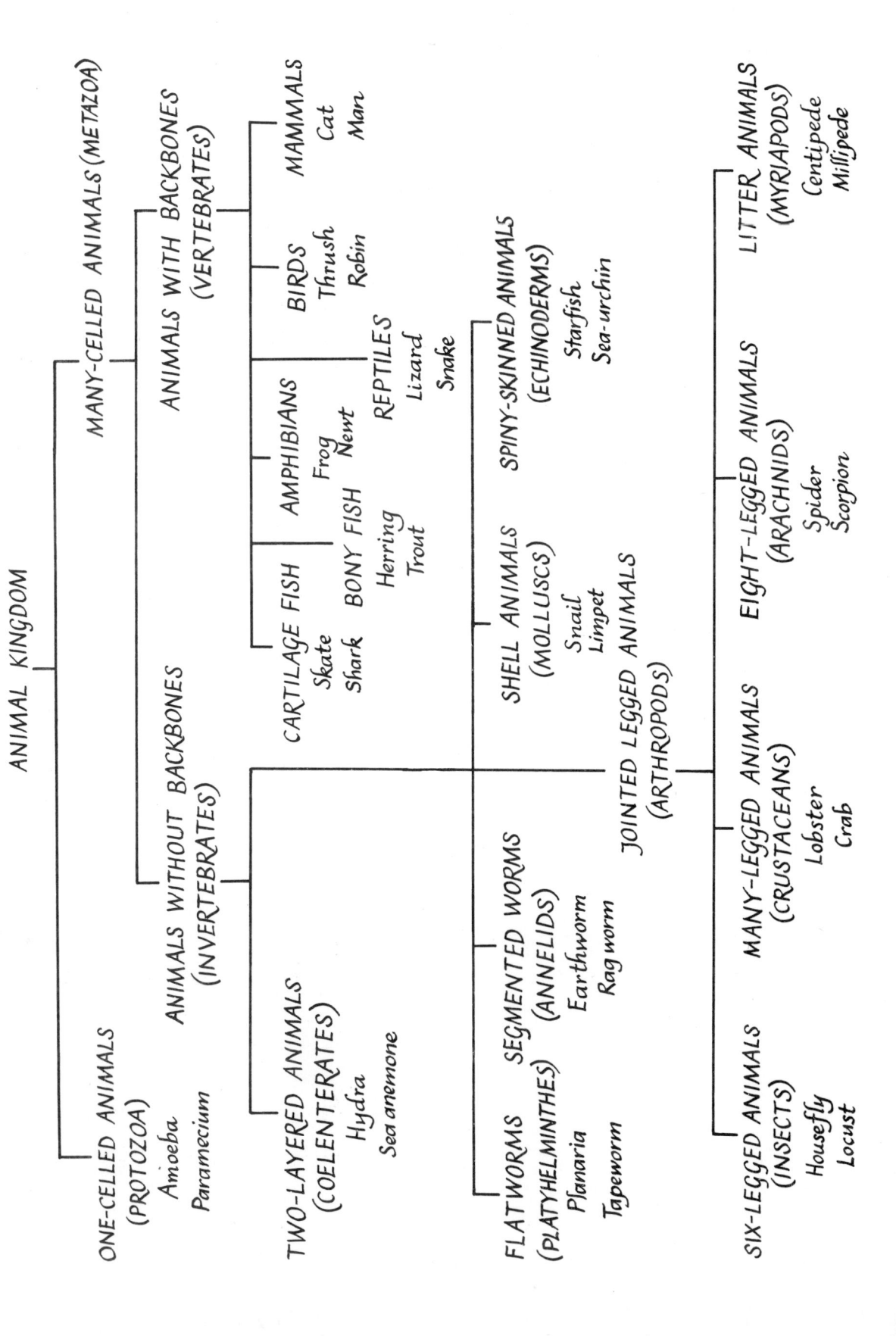

ANIMAL KINGDOM

- MANY-CELLED ANIMALS (METAZOA)
  - ANIMALS WITH BACKBONES (VERTEBRATES)
    - CARTILAGE FISH
      - Skate
      - Shark
    - BONY FISH
      - Herring
      - Trout
    - AMPHIBIANS
      - Frog
      - Newt
    - REPTILES
      - Lizard
      - Snake
    - BIRDS
      - Thrush
      - Robin
    - MAMMALS
      - Cat
      - Man
  - ANIMALS WITHOUT BACKBONES (INVERTEBRATES)
    - ONE-CELLED ANIMALS (PROTOZOA)
      - Amoeba
      - Paramecium
    - TWO-LAYERED ANIMALS (COELENTERATES)
      - Hydra
      - Sea anemone
    - FLATWORMS (PLATYHELMINTHES)
      - Planaria
      - Tapeworm
    - SEGMENTED WORMS (ANNELIDS)
      - Earthworm
      - Ragworm
    - SHELL ANIMALS (MOLLUSCS)
      - Snail
      - Limpet
    - SPINY-SKINNED ANIMALS (ECHINODERMS)
      - Starfish
      - Sea-urchin
    - JOINTED LEGGED ANIMALS (ARTHROPODS)
      - SIX-LEGGED ANIMALS (INSECTS)
        - Housefly
        - Locust
      - MANY-LEGGED ANIMALS (CRUSTACEANS)
        - Lobster
        - Crab
      - EIGHT-LEGGED ANIMALS (ARACHNIDS)
        - Spider
        - Scorpion
      - LITTER ANIMALS (MYRIAPODS)
        - Centipede
        - Millipede

TABLE 3.2. OUTLINE CLASSIFICATION OF PLANTS

THE PLANT KINGDOM

- SIMPLE PLANTS
  - ALGAE
  - FUNGI
  - LICHENS
  - BACTERIA
- MOSSES and LIVERWORTS
  - MOSSES
  - LIVERWORTS
- FERN-LIKE PLANTS
  - TRUE FERNS
  - HORSETAILS
  - CLUB MOSSES
- SEED-BEARING PLANTS
  - NAKED SEED PLANTS (GYMNOSPERMS)
  - FLOWERING PLANTS (ANGIOSPERMS)
    - BROAD LEAF PLANTS (DICOTYLEDONS)
    - NARROW LEAF PLANTS (MONOCOTYLEDONS)

Test your understanding

Copy and complete the following paragraphs:

The total number of types of living organism is approximately ....[1] The placing of plants and animals in groups is called ....[2], and is based on the possession of similar ....[3] The modern method of grouping began with the work of the Swedish naturalist ....[4] He gave each plant and animal a ....[5] name and a ....[6] name, both names being in the ....[7] language. Thus all cats are placed in the genus ....[8], whilst the dog and the ....[9] are members of the genus *Canis*.

Similar genera are grouped into ....[10], whilst a class contains a number of similar ....[11] The major divisions of the animal kingdom are called ....[12], and those of the plant kingdom ....[13] The easiest way to identify unknown creatures is by the use of ....[14] The great value of classifying plants and animals is that it not only catalogues them but also shows how they are ....[15]

1. Why is classification necessary?
2. Why were early methods of classification unsatisfactory?
3. What is (a) a species and (b) a genus?
4. What is meant by the binomial nomenclature?
5. Devise a simple key to enable any six current models of cars to be identified. Set out your key as shown in Section 3.6.
6. Similarly, devise a simple key to enable any six breeds of dog to be identified.
7. Why is biological classification more difficult than, say, classification of stamps or books?

Chapter 4

Simple Animals

4.1. The simplest animals: protozoans

We have seen in Chapter 2 that all living organisms are made up of units or cells, each cell comprising living matter, or protoplasm. Each cell has an organizing centre, the nucleus, which is surrounded by the cytoplasm. The simplest animals, having bodies composed of a single cell, the unicellular animals, are grouped together in the phylum **Protozoa**. This name comes from two Greek words meaning 'first animals', and reminds us that the protozoans alive today probably resemble the first animals to live on the earth. The Protozoa includes many species of animal, which differ considerably in their body form and way of life. As an example of a unicellular animal, we will examine the common freshwater protozoan, the amoeba.

4.2. Amoeba: a common protozoan

If some pond mud or soil water is examined very carefully, it will almost certainly be found to contain tiny white specks, barely visible to the naked eye. These specks are small species of amoeba. To examine the structure of this animal it is best to obtain a culture of the larger species, *Amoeba proteus*, which measures up to 1 mm across.

Investigation 4a. Examination of living amoebae

Amoebae may be cultured in a petri dish containing water to which a few boiled wheat grains have been added. Examine such a culture under the lowest power of the microscope (a binocular microscope is preferable). Recognize the amoebae by their dark-grey, granular appearance and their irregular shape. Using a fine-drawn teat pipette, suck up one or two amoebae and transfer them to a cavity slide, together with a little water. Add a cover-slip and examine them under the low power of the microscope. Keep the light shut well down, and observe the animal moving about. Compare your animal with that shown in Figure 4.1.

Figure 4.1 The structure of *Amoeba proteus*

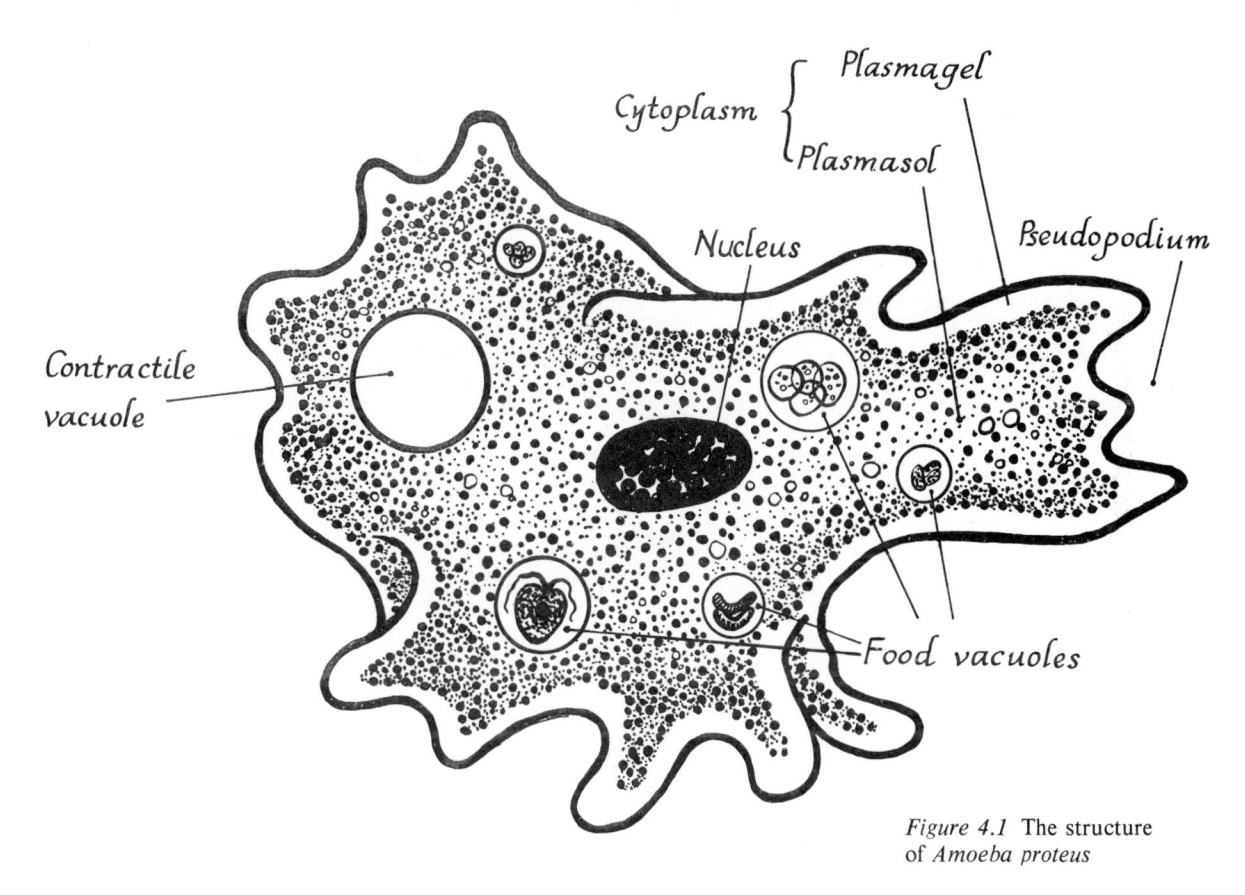

4.3. How an amoeba moves

Within the cell of an amoeba, the cytoplasm is liquid (**plasmasol** or **endoplasm**), whilst at the surface it becomes jelly-like (**plasmagel** or **ectoplasm**). When the animal is observed under the microscope, the granular plasmasol may be seen to stream forward, causing outpushings of the body, called **pseudopodia**. The exact cause of this streaming is not understood. It is believed that, when the plasmasol reaches the advancing tip, it solidifies to form plasmagel. The reverse occurs at the temporary rear end, where plasmagel liquefies to plasmasol (see Figure 4.2).

It is interesting that we have cells in our own blood, the so-called white cells, which are able to move in this strange, amoeboid fashion. It follows that an amoeba is constantly changing shape as it streams along a surface. When the animal is not in contact with a surface it extends pseudopodia in all directions. Look for such a star-shaped amoeba in the culture dish.

4.4. How an amoeba feeds

An amoeba feeds on other microbes (microscopic organisms) which inhabit the water around it. These include diatoms and desmids

Figure 4.2 Locomotion of an amoeba

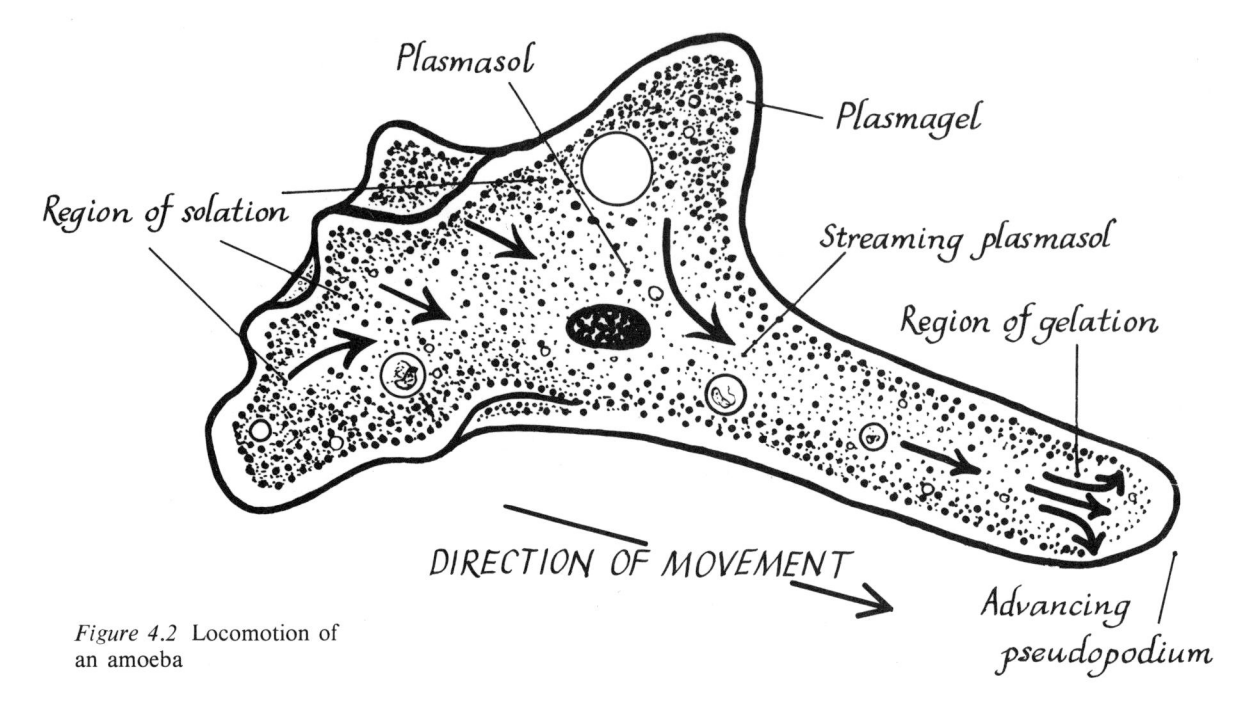

(plants), and ciliates (protozoans). If an amoeba comes into contact with such an organism, it extends pseudopodia around it, until it is completely engulfed. The prey, together with a little water, forms a **food vacuole** within the body of the amoeba. The process of ingestion of food can be followed in Figure 4.3.

The ingested organism lives for a brief period within the food vacuole, moving about in the small volume of water. It dies when the cytoplasm secretes first acid and then enzymes into the vacuole. These juices digest the body of the prey. Useful products are then absorbed into the cytoplasm, after which any undigested matter is simply left behind the advancing amoeba.

Figure 4.3 Amoeba feeding

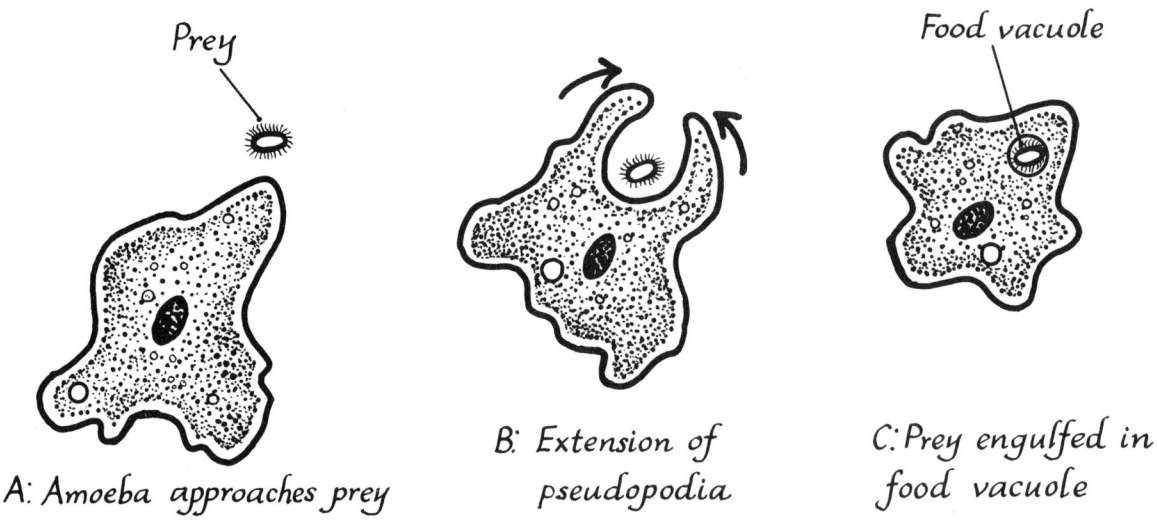

The white cells in our blood are not only able to move like an amoeba but are also able to ingest organisms in the same way. This is of great importance in the body's defence against disease.

4.5. Respiration, excretion and the control of water content

Since an amoeba is so small, it has a very large surface area compared to its volume. In other words, every part of its body is close to the surface through which simple substances diffuse (see Figure 4.4). The diffusion occurs from regions of high concentration to regions of low concentration. Thus oxygen diffuses into the body from the surrounding water, whilst the respiratory waste product, carbon dioxide, diffuses in the reverse direction. The amoeba, therefore, needs no special respiratory structures. Other waste products are also able to leave the body by diffusion.

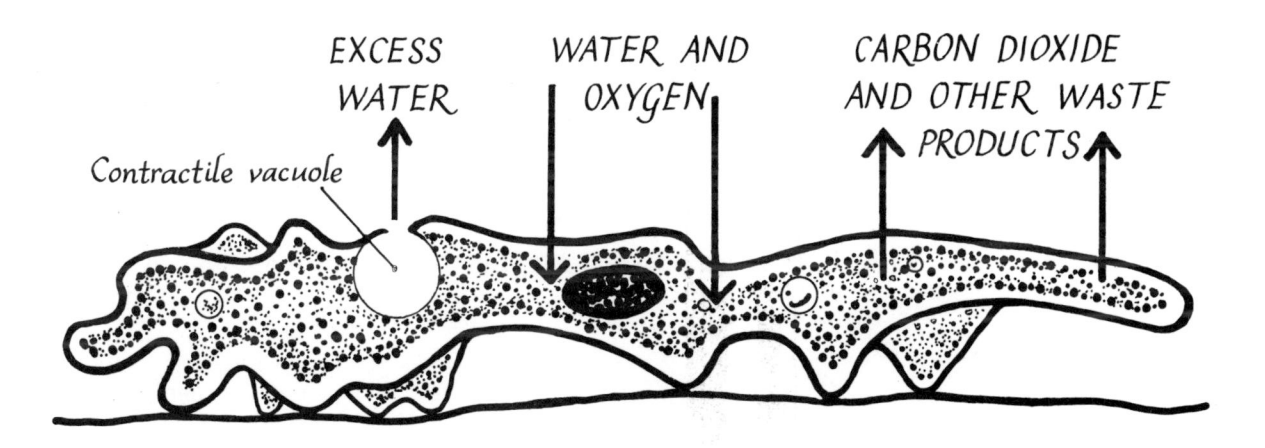

Figure 4.4 Lateral view of an amoeba in contact with a surface, showing the exchange of materials with the surrounding water

The amoeba does, however, possess a special structure for the removal of excess water which enters the body by osmosis (see Chapter 11). This structure is the **contractile vacuole**, visible as a clear space in the plasmasol. It may be seen to increase in size gradually, as water flows into it. Suddenly, it collapses like a burst balloon, ejecting its watery contents. Observe an amoeba, and time the filling and emptying of the contractile vacuole. The time varies from a few minutes to as many as twenty minutes.

4.6. Reproduction

Amoebae reproduce in a very simple manner. The process is asexual, being performed by a single animal. The nucleus divides into two, by mitosis, the daughter nuclei being identical copies of the parent nucleus. As the daughter nuclei move apart, the cytoplasm constricts and splits into two (see Figure 4.5). The new amoebae

A: DIVISION OF NUCLEUS

B: CONSTRICTION OF CYTOPLASM

C: DAUGHTER AMOEBAE

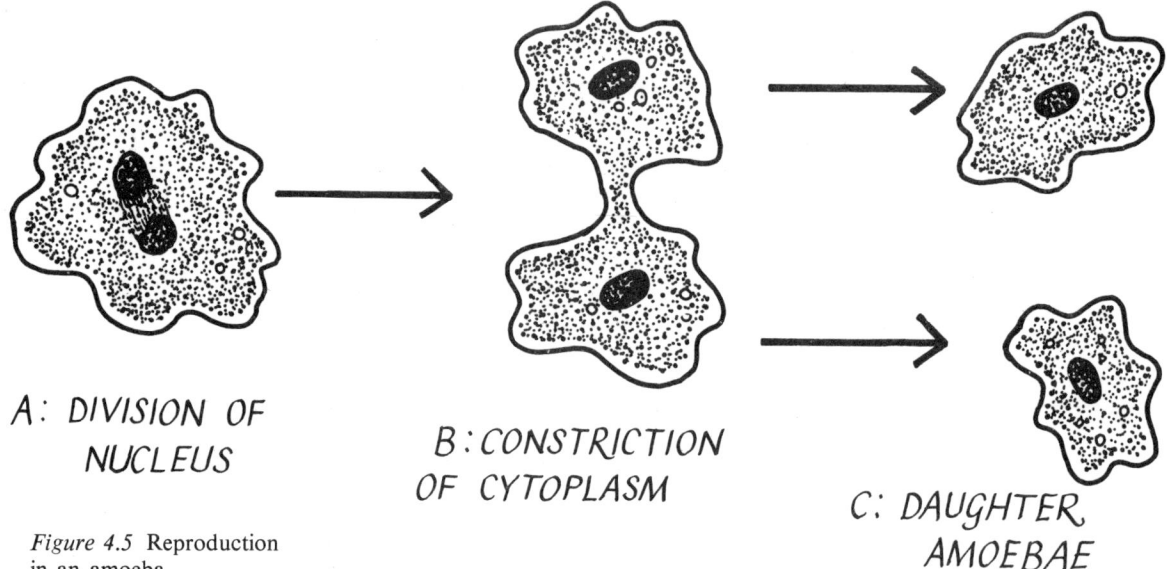

Figure 4.5 Reproduction in an amoeba

feed and grow until they, too, reach the size when they are able to divide. This simple method of reproduction is known as **binary fission**, and is common in unicellular organisms.

4.7. Encystment

Amoebae are able to withstand unfavourable conditions, such as coldness or drought, by enclosing themselves in a protective cyst. Pseudopodia are withdrawn and a tough coat of **chitin** is secreted by the cytoplasm (Figure 4.6). When favourable conditions return, the cyst wall ruptures. Inside, the amoeba has divided repeatedly, so

Figure 4.6 Encystment in an amoeba

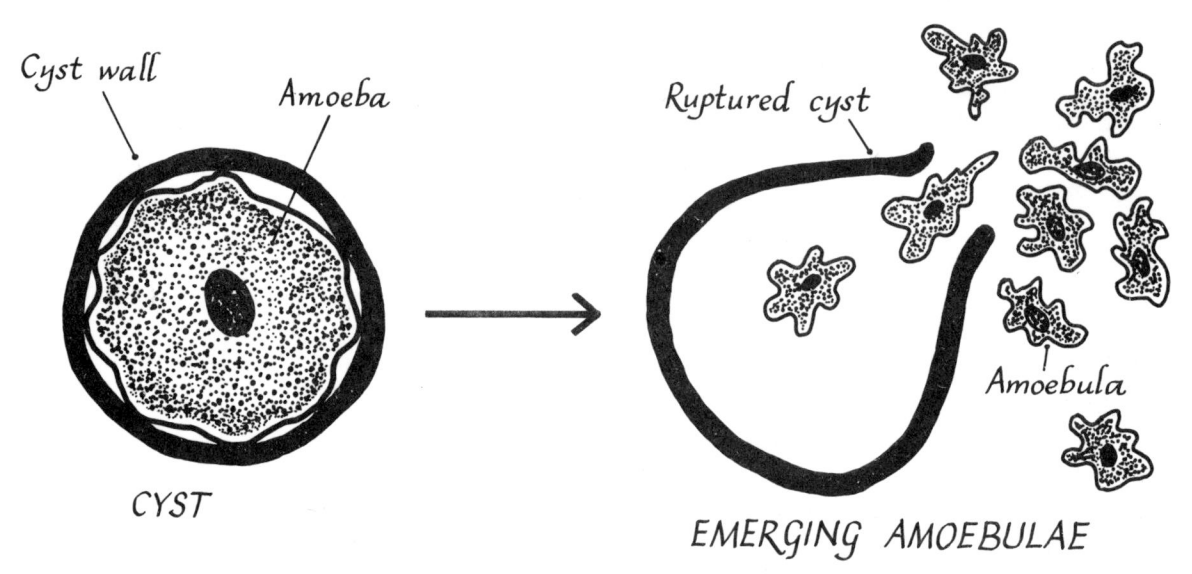

CYST

EMERGING AMOEBULAE

that many small amoebae (**amoebulae**) escape. Thus a new population of amoebae is soon established. Encysted amoebae may also be carried to new habitats in the dust blown from dry ponds.

4.8. Other protozoans

Some 15 000 different species of protozoans are known. Many of them are **parasites**; in other words, they live within the bodies of animals and plants, often causing harm. Commonly, their presence causes disease. One form of amoeba, called Entamoeba, inhabits the intestines of man, sometimes causing the disease dysentery. Other diseases caused by protozoans are malaria and sleeping-sickness, two diseases that still cause millions of deaths each year in tropical countries.

It seems surprising, perhaps, that there are so many forms of unicellular animal (see Figure 4.7). Within a single cell, however, protozoans have developed many complex structures, so that they belie the label 'simple'.

4.9. Multicellular animals: metazoans

The Protozoa is the only group of unicellular animals: all other animals are multicellular. It should be remembered, however, that most multicellular animals begin life as a single cell. This egg cell, after fertilization by a sperm cell, undergoes division, or **cleavage**, to form a ball of cells. As the number of cells increases they become **differentiated**. In other words, they take on different forms as they come to take on different functions in the body. We say that the cells become specialized. In one-celled animals the single cell has to perform all the functions of life (feeding, respiration, etc.), but in multicellular animals division of labour is possible. A cell which is adapted to serve one particular function is more efficient. Thus, the body is like a factory and the cells like the workers, each of whom is skilled at his own particular job and each of whom contributes to the common good.

Differentiation and specialization of cells may be seen in the freshwater polyp, hydra.

4.10. Hydra: a simple multicellular animal

Investigation 4b. Establishing a culture of hydra

In late spring or early summer, collect weeds and dead, submerged leaves from a pond or slow-moving stream. Allow these to stand in a small aquarium of pond water. In a day or two examine for the presence of living hydra, some of which may have become attached to the glass. Hydra are colourless, green or brown animals

Figure 4.7 Various unicellular animals (protozoans)

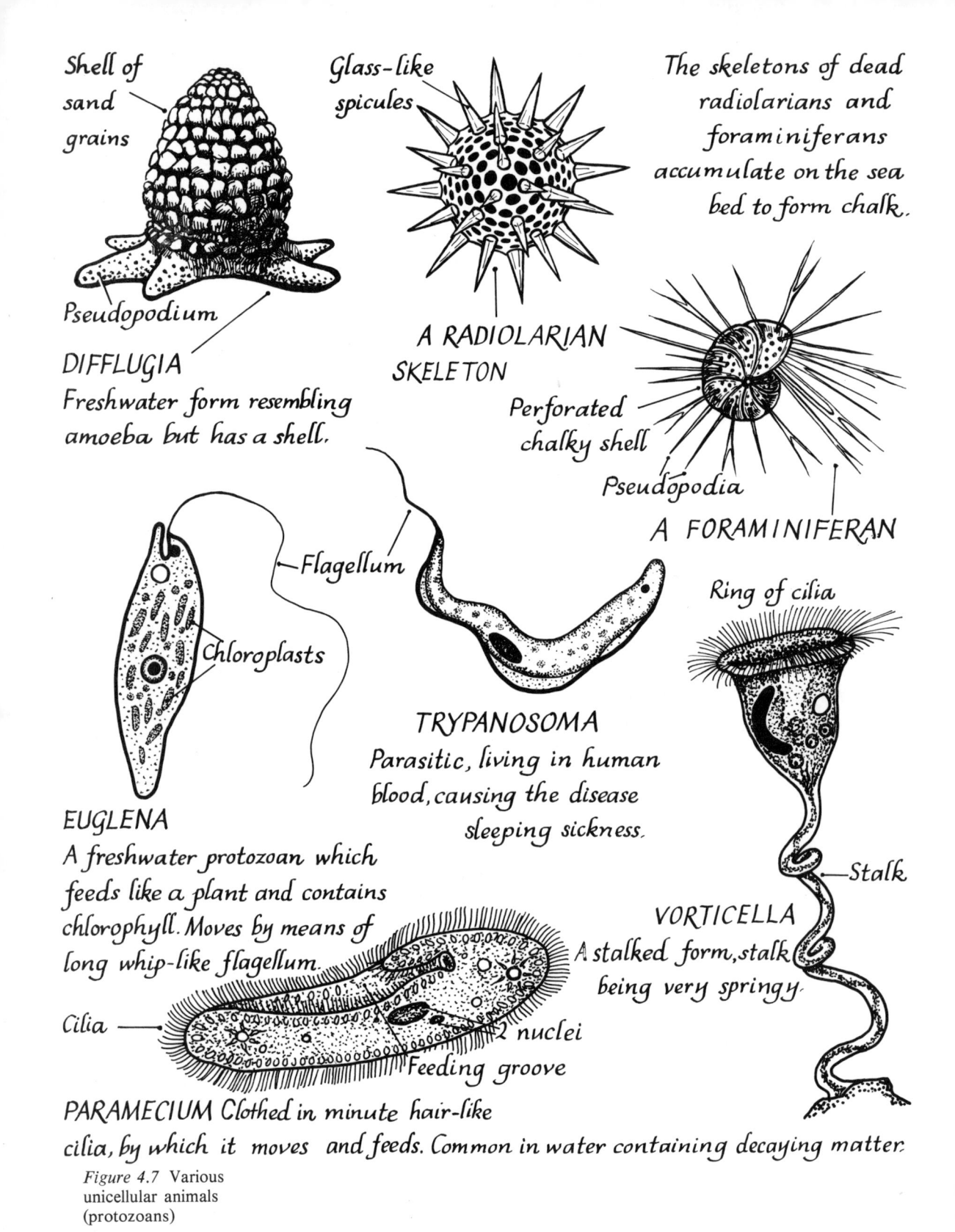

which, when extended, may reach 2 cm in length. The slightest disturbance results in contraction of the body to a short, fat stump. Place the aquarium near a window, but away from direct sunlight, and feed at intervals by adding living water-fleas (*Daphnia*). For examination under the microscope, transfer the hydra to a cavity slide or small watchglass.

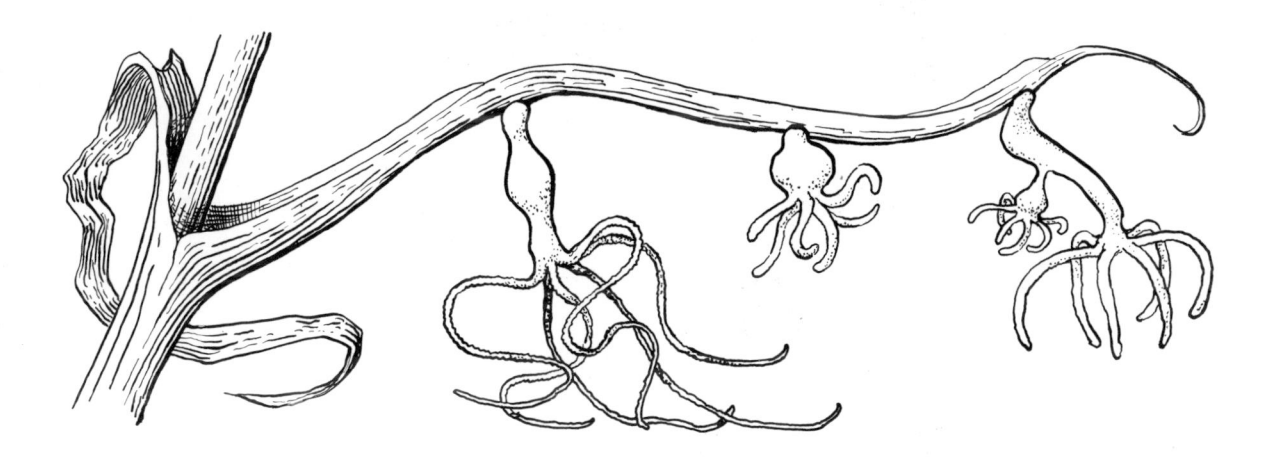

Figure 4.8 Hydra attached to a water weed

4.11. The structure of the body (see Figure 4.9)

The body of the hydra is a hollow cylinder, the interior comprising a digestive cavity, or **enteron**. At one end of the body is an adhesive disc, by which the animal attaches itself to a water-weed, etc. (see Figure 4.8). At the other end the body is extended into six to eight **tentacles**, which surround the single opening, the **mouth**. Both the body and the tentacles are capable of great elongation when the animal is 'fishing' for its prey.

The body wall is composed of two layers of cells separated by a jelly-like substance called **mesogloea**. The outer layer of cells is the **ectoderm** and the inner layer the **endoderm**. The various types of cell present in these layers are illustrated in Figure 4.10.

a. Ectodermal cells

Musculo-epithelial cells. These are the commonest cells in the protective ectoderm. The base of each cell is extended as a pair of muscular processes or **muscle-tails**. These extend longitudinally and, by contracting, cause rapid shortening of the body and tentacles.

Cnidoblast (stinging) cells. These cells are important in the capture of water-fleas or other prey. When the trigger, or cnidocil, is stimulated, the coiled thread contained within the cell is suddenly discharged, piercing the tissues of the prey or entwining some part of its body. The thread is tubular, allowing poison to pass down into

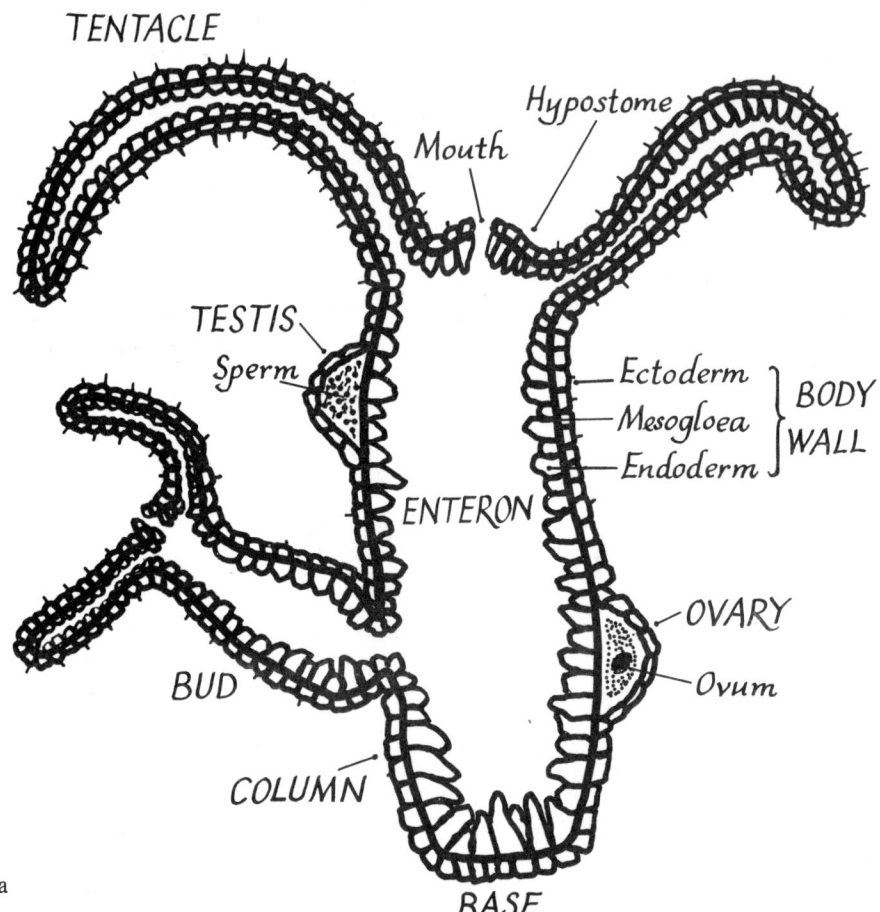

Figure 4.9 Hydra: longitudinal section of a contracted animal

the prey. This poison paralyses the flea so that it cannot escape. The threads may also aid the attachment of the hydra during somersaulting (see Section 4.12).

Sensory cells. Any changes in the water surrounding the hydra cause the sensory cells to be excited, or **stimulated**. The stimulus is then passed on to the nerve-net.

Interstitial (replacement) cells. These cells are capable of developing into any of the other cell types. This is especially necessary in the case of the stinging cells for, once discharged, they cannot be 'reloaded', and must be replaced.

Nerve cells. Nerve cells actually lie in the mesogloea where they are linked to form a network. By means of this **nerve-net**, nervous impulses are able to be passed from the sensory cells to all parts of the body.

Glandular (adhesive) cells. In order to attach the base of the hydra to a water-weed, the glandular cells produce a sticky exudation.

b. Endodermal cells

The cells of the endoderm are mainly concerned with nutrition for they line the digestive cavity, or enteron.

Secretory cells. These pass digestive juices into the enteron. In these juices are enzymes which bring about the digestion of the tissues of the prey.

Flagellate cells. The flagella attached to these cells lash the water in the enteron, so keeping it circulated.

Pseudopodial cells. Like amoebae, these cells are able to extend their cytoplasm as pseudopodia, engulfing particles of partly digested prey.

The endoderm cells, like the musculo-epithelial cells of the ectoderm, possess muscle-tails. Here, however, the tails extend in a circular direction, their contraction causing the body or tentacles to become thinner and longer.

Figure 4.10 Part of the body wall of a hydra, showing the various types of cell

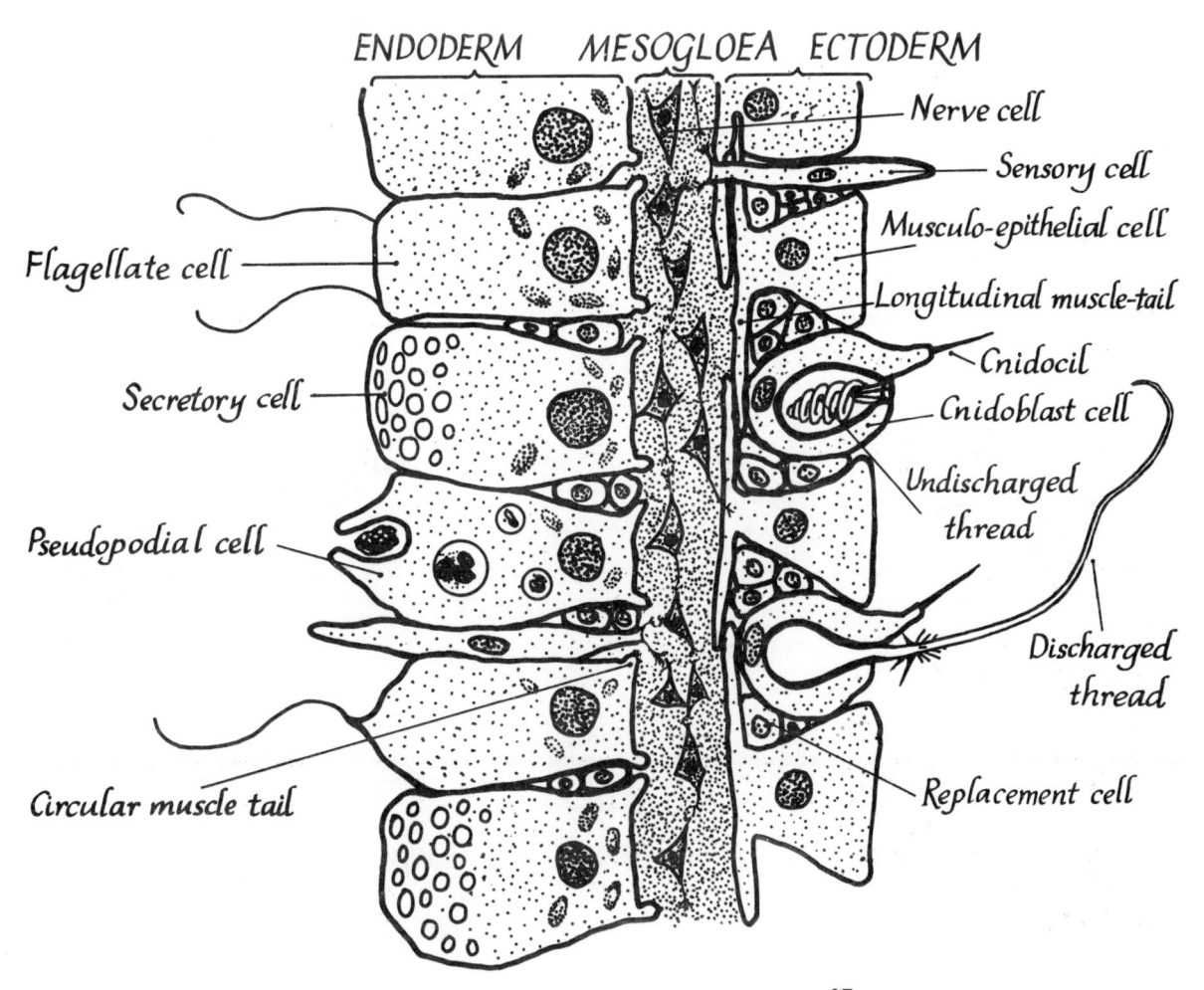

The colour of the green hydra (*Hydra viridis*) is due to the presence in the endoderm cells of abundant microscopic green plants or algae, of the type known as **zoochlorellae**. They live in a state of **symbiosis**, or partnership, with the hydra. Apart from the obvious benefit of gaining shelter, the algae are also able to use the carbon dioxide and nitrogenous waste products of the hydra. Similarly, the hydra benefits from the association for it is able to use the oxygen given off by the algae during photosynthesis. Examples of such symbiotic partnerships are common in the living world.

4.12. Locomotion

Once the animal is suitably placed to extend its tentacles and catch prey, it tends to remain stationary for long periods. It is capable of movement either by **looping** or **somersaulting**. These movements are best understood by studying Figure 4.11. Think about which set of muscle-tails will be contracting at each stage.

4.13. Feeding and digestion

When the hydra is in the 'fishing' position, the tentacles are very long and thin, extending to 20 cm in some species. If a water-flea swims into a tentacle the cnidoblast cells discharge their stinging threads. Some of these pierce, poison and paralyse the prey, whilst others help to hold the prey by becoming entangled in the bristles of its body. The more the flea struggles, the more it comes into contact

Figure 4.11 Locomotion of a hydra

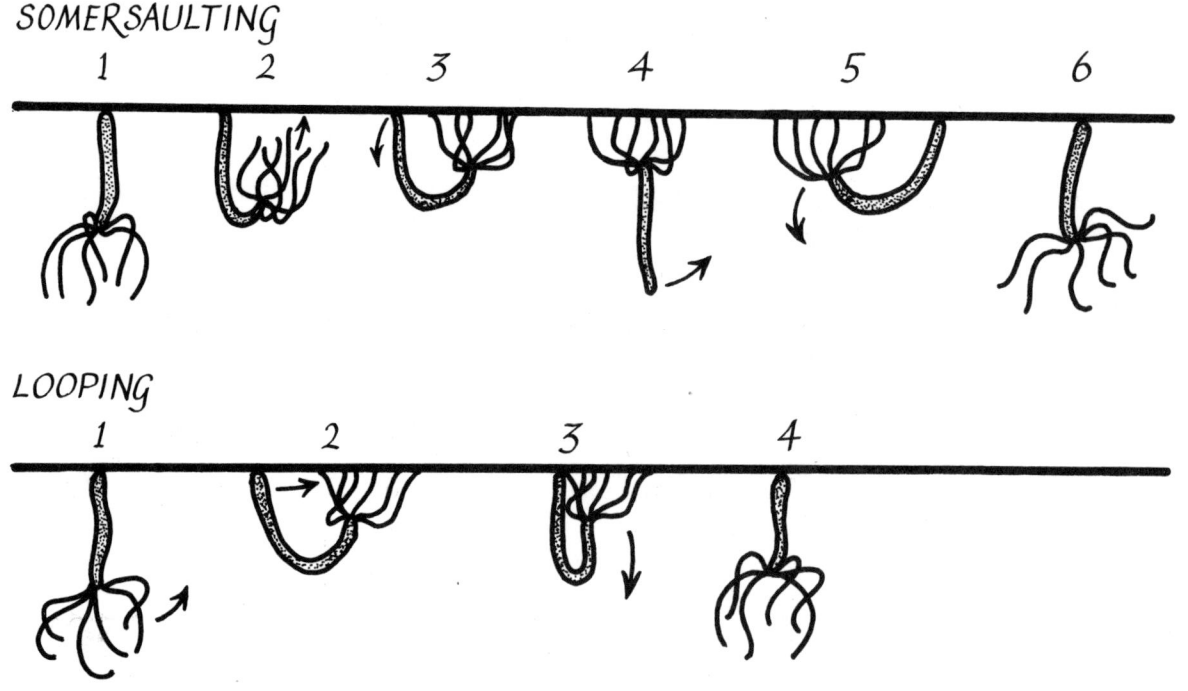

Figure 4.12 Hydra trapping a water-flea

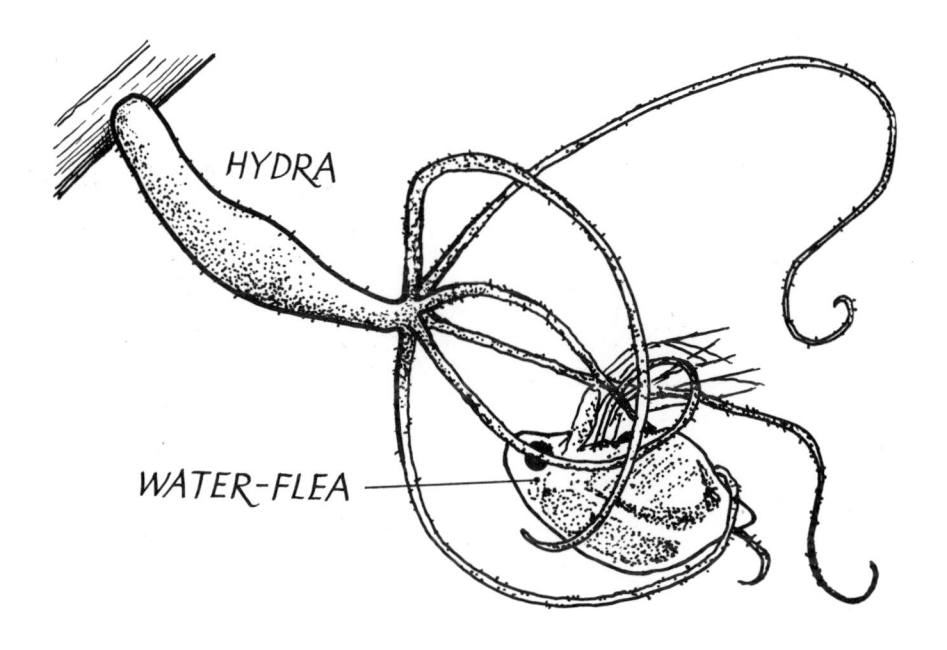

with other tentacles, which, in turn, discharge their threads into it (see Figure 4.12).

The tentacles then contract, drawing the prey towards the mouth, which opens to permit **ingestion** into the enteron. The prey is visible as a distinct bulge in the body of the hydra. Within the enteron, the secretory cells secrete enzymes which reduce most of the prey to soluble form. Small particles of this partly digested food are then engulfed by the pseudopodial cells, in whose vacuoles digestion is completed. The useful products of digestion are then **assimilated** by the surrounding cells. Undigested matter accumulates in the enteron from where it is discharged through the mouth, there being no anus in this animal.

4.14. Respiration and excretion

One of the advantages of the body structure of hydra is that almost all of the cells are bathed in water. As in unicellular animals, therefore, no special respiratory or excretory structures are required, as the animal can rely on simple **diffusion** for the exchange of materials with its surroundings.

4.15. Reproduction and life-history

a. Asexual budding

During the summer months when food is plentiful, the hydra is able to reproduce asexually by a process of budding. At one point on the body wall, interstitial cells multiply, causing a bulge. As this enlarges, tentacles and a mouth develop. The daughter hydra then breaks free, as shown in Figure 4.13.

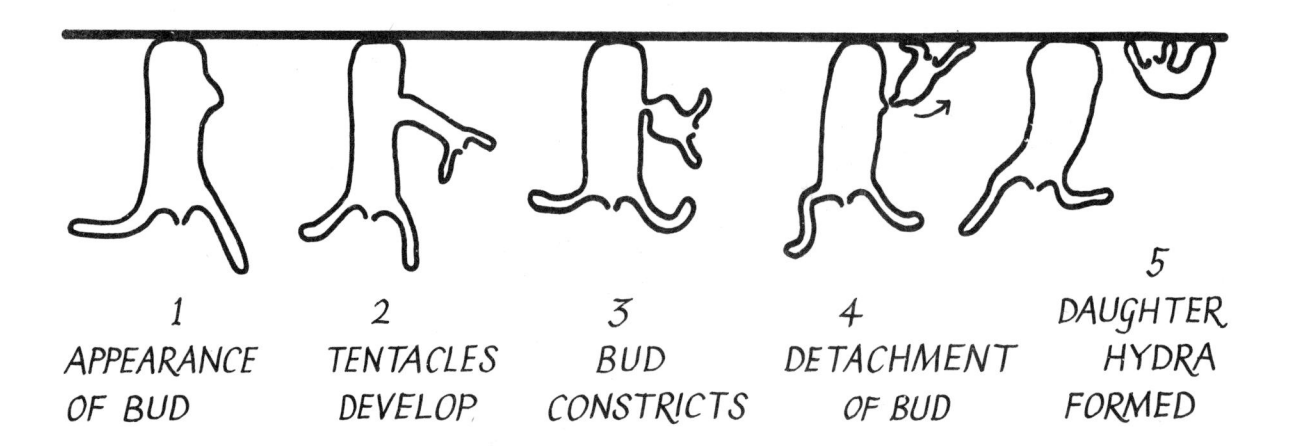

1	2	3	4	5
APPEARANCE OF BUD	TENTACLES DEVELOP	BUD CONSTRICTS	DETACHMENT OF BUD	DAUGHTER HYDRA FORMED

Figure 4.13 Stages in asexual budding of hydra

b. Regeneration

Hydra have considerable ability to replace lost or damaged parts, a process known as regeneration. Should an individual become broken into two, each fragment regenerates the missing half, so that two individuals result. Quite small fragments may produce new hydra in this way.

c. Sexual reproduction

At certain seasons of the year, particularly in the autumn, hydra reproduce sexually. Each animal is **hermaphrodite,** that is, it bears both male and female sex organs (gonads). The male organs, or **testes**, develop at the tentacle end of the body, and appear before the female **ovaries**, which occur nearer the base. Within the testes interstitial cells multiply and become active male gametes, or **spermatozoa**. These are released into the water by the rupture of the testis wall. The sperm are attracted by chemicals given out by the ovary. Each ovary develops in a similar way to the testis, but one cell, the female gamete, or **ovum**, develops at the expense of the other cells (see Figure 4.14).

One sperm penetrates the ovum and fertilizes it. The fertilized ovum, or **zygote**, divides into a ball of cells (blastula) which secretes a protective cyst around itself. Within the cyst the cells form a new ectoderm and endoderm. The encysted hydra, lying at the bottom of the pond, is able to withstand the unfavourable conditions of winter. In spring the cyst wall ruptures and the new hydra emerges, soon developing a mouth and tentacles. It then moves until it reaches a position suitable for feeding.

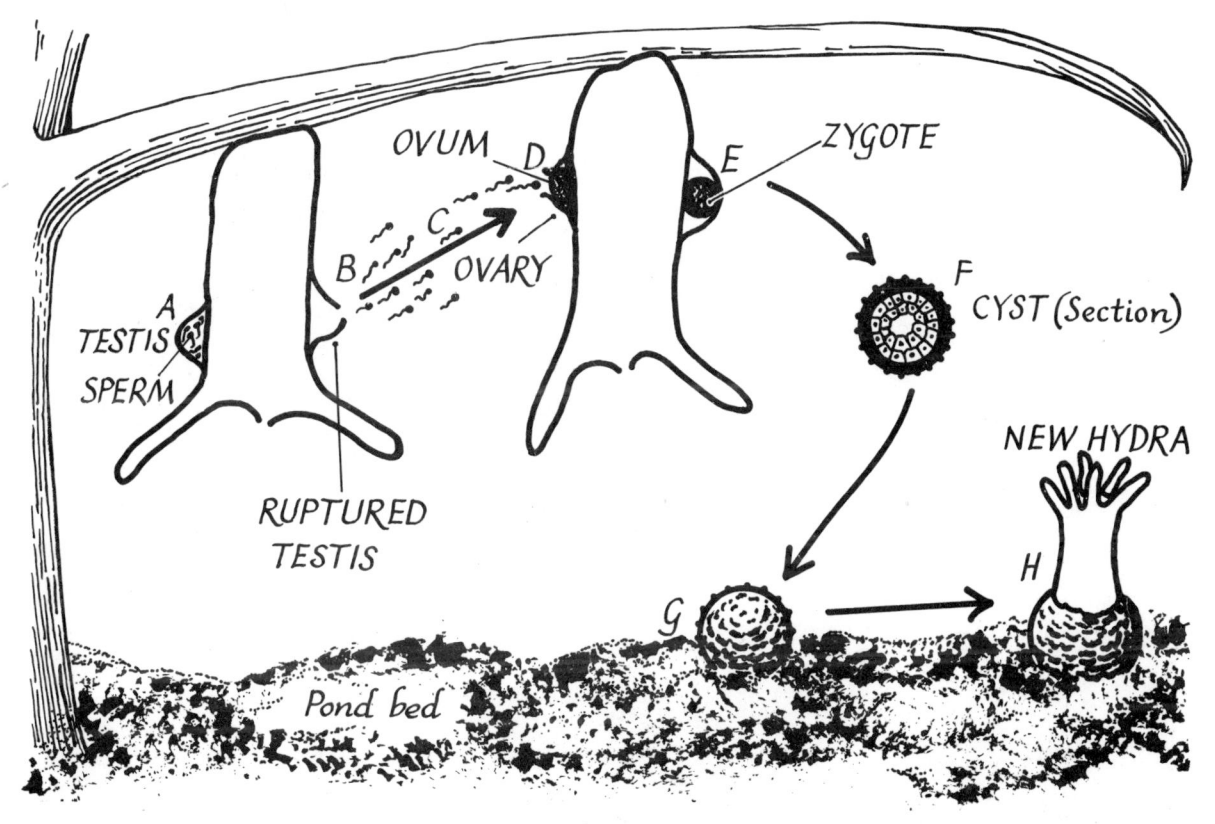

Figure 4.14 Stages in the sexual reproduction of hydra

4.16. Animals related to the hydra

Multicellular animals which, like the hydra, have a body wall composed of two layers of cells are placed in the phylum **Coelenterata** (*coelenteron*: a hollow cavity). Many of these animals (see Figure 4.15) form **colonies**, which resemble plants in their branched nature. **Corals** are an example of such colonial forms, the individual polyps secreting a chalky skeleton around themselves. This skeleton persists after the death of the polyps, and forms the foundation of coral-reefs. Each polyp of the coral colony resembles the familiar sea-anemones of our rock pools.

Some colonial coelenterates form free-swimming **medusae** to disperse their offspring. Medusae are minute bell-shaped organisms forming part of the plankton in the surface waters of the sea. Some medusae have become much larger to form **jelly-fish**. The bulk of their bodies is made up of the jelly-like mesogloea that formed only a thin layer in the hydra. One of the largest and most complex coelenterates is the **Portuguese Man-of-war**, a massive colony, the sting from which can paralyse quite large fish and can be very painful to man.

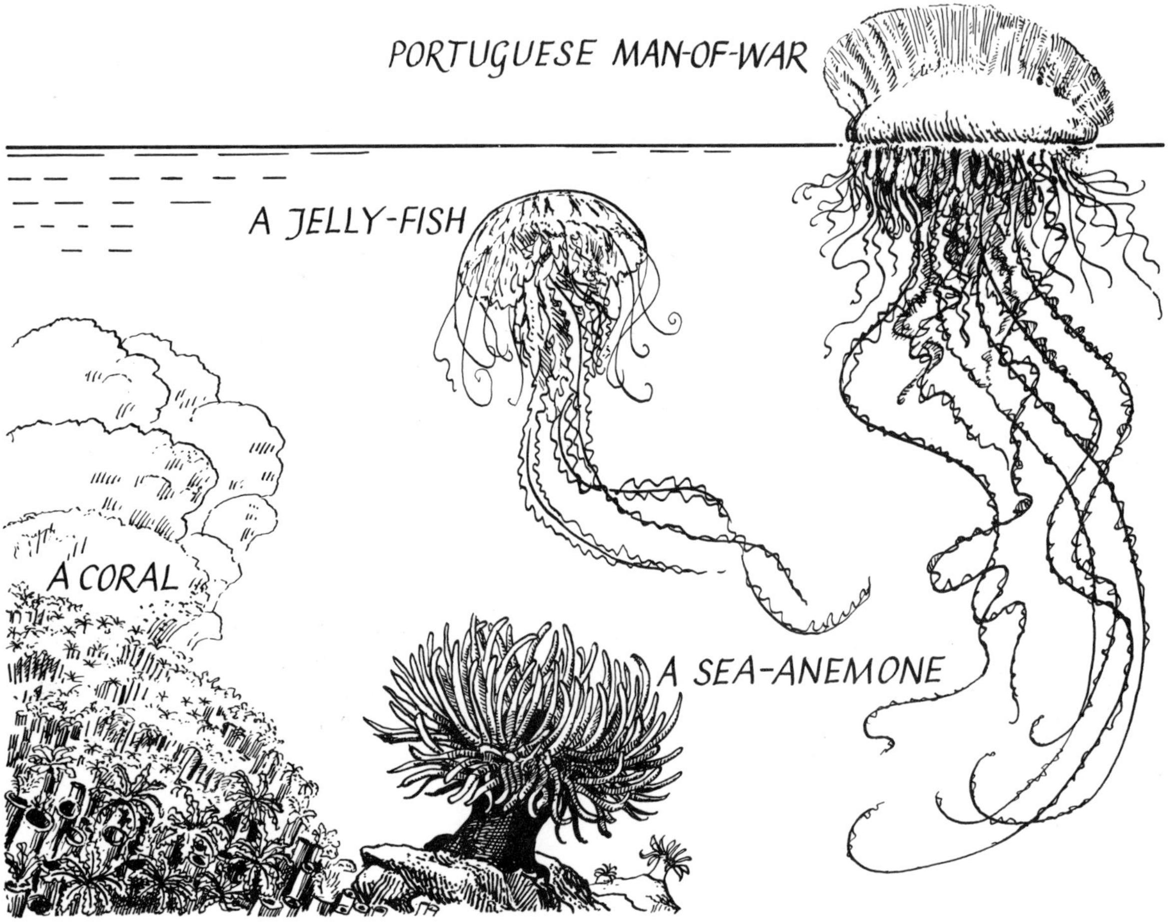

Figure 4.15 Various coelenterates

4.17. Three layers of cells

We have seen that coelenterates are tubular animals with a body wall composed of two layers of cells. Although this condition has the advantage that all cells are near to food and oxygen, it has certain disadvantages. Firstly, growth in these animals tends to involve increase in length, and immobile colonies are common. Secondly, there is insufficient depth of cells to form organs.

In the next group of animals, the phylum **Platyhelminthes**, or flatworms, we find the development of a third layer of cells, called the **mesoderm**, lying between the ectoderm and endoderm. The mesoderm is always many cells thick, so that the body is more solid. The enteron is restricted and, with part of the mesoderm, forms the **gut**. The new mesodermal layer forms important systems of the body, such as the muscular and excretory systems. In higher animals it also forms the skeletal and blood systems. Thus, the development of this third layer was an important landmark in animal evolution. As an example of a simple three-layered animal we will briefly consider the freshwater flatworm, planaria.

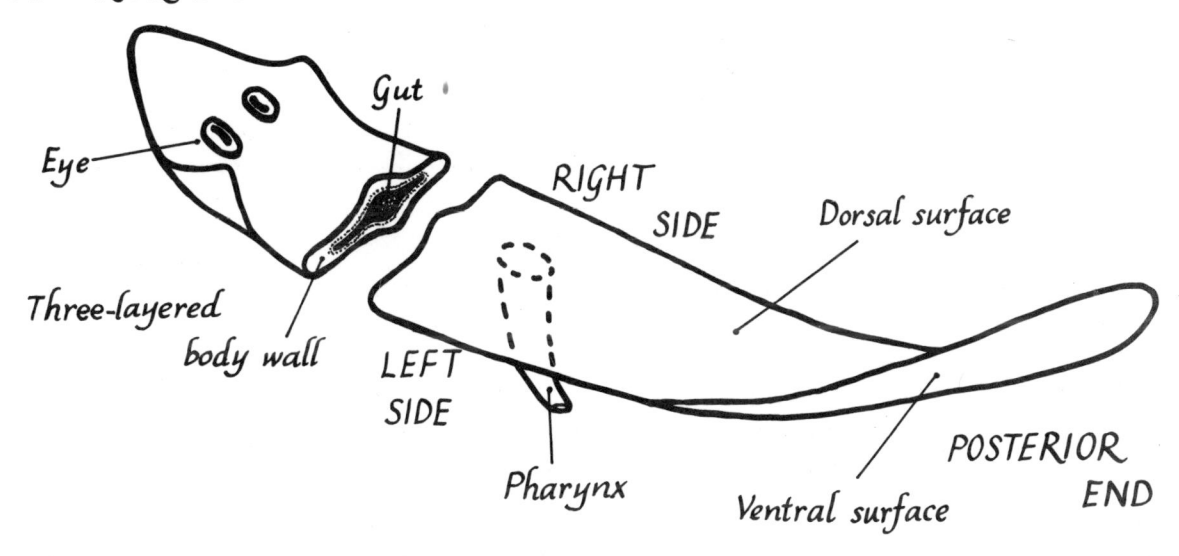

4.18. Planaria: a simple three-layered animal

Planaria is a leaf-like, black creature, about 1 cm long. It inhabits ponds and slow-moving streams, where it will be found under stones and vegetation. Figure 4.16 shows that the body is **bilaterally symmetrical**; in other words, it has distinct anterior and posterior ends, right and left sides, and dorsal and ventral surfaces. The ventral, or lower, surface bears minute **cilia**, the beating of which enables the animal to glide along. Movement can also be effected by waves of muscular contraction passing down the body, but this is not the usual method of locomotion.

Planarians, like the hydra, have remarkable powers of regeneration. Surviving cells are able to produce the types of cell which have been destroyed by injury; complete worms may be produced from very small pieces. If a worm is cut at the head end, and the two halves are kept from growing together again, a two-headed 'monster' results (see Figure 4.17).

Figure 4.16 A planarian, partly shown in section

Figure 4.17 Two-headed planarian, produced by making a cut at the anterior end

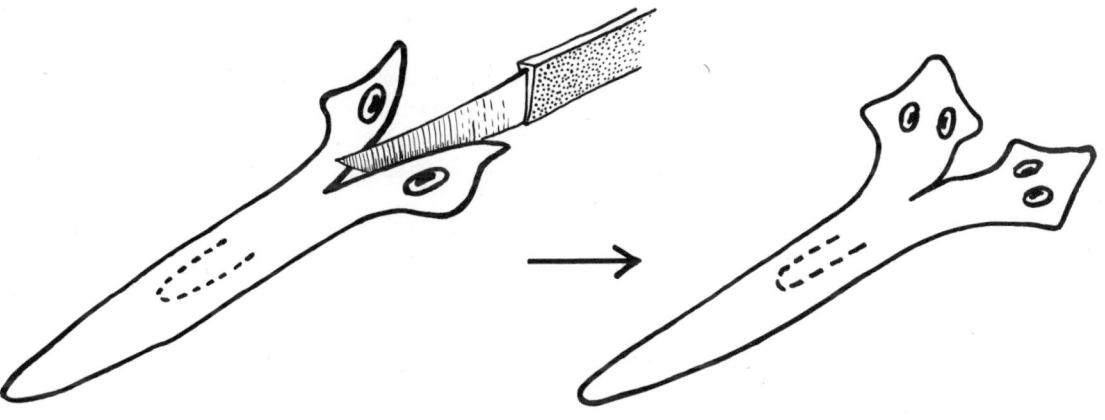

4.19. Other flatworms

Planarians are free-living flatworms, but the majority of animals in this group are parasites. They are particularly suited for life within the gut of vertebrates, for their thin bodies do not block the passage. Familiar parasitic flatworms are **tapeworms** (for example, tapeworm of dog) and **flukes** (for example, liver fluke of sheep).

Test your understanding

Copy and complete the following paragraphs:

a. *Amoeba*

The amoeba is a ....[1] animal; in other words, it is composed of a single cell. It has no definite ....[2] for it is continually pushing out ....[3] These are also used to enclose particles of food which, with a little ....[4], form a food ....[5] The food is then ....[6] by enzymes and the useful materials ....[7]

The amoeba reproduces by splitting into two, a process known as ....[8] The ....[9] divides first, followed by the ....[10] When conditions become ....[11] the amoeba surrounds itself with a ....[12] When the case bursts minute ....[13] emerge.

b. *Hydra and flatworms*

The hydra is an example of a ....[1] animal, since its body is composed of many ....[2] The animal is found in ....[3] where it may be attached to ....[4] Since it has a hollow body almost all of the hydra's cells are bathed in ....[5] This enables the animal to ....[6] and excrete by the simple process of ....[7] The hydra moves by contracting ....[8] attached to some of its cells. The animal can move either by looping or by ....[9], and feeds on such animals as ....[10], which it traps by means of stinging cells on its ....[11] The prey is partly digested in the ....[12], after which particles complete their breakdown within the cells of the ....[13]

Hydra can reproduce both ....[14] and ....[15], the latter usually occurring at the onset of an unfavourable season. Sperm and ova are produced within the same animal, that is, the hydra is ....[16] The sperm are attracted to the ....[17] of another animal, after which ....[18] occurs. The zygote develops into a hollow ball of cells which survives the unfavourable season as a ....[19]

Flatworms are distinguished by the presence of a third layer of cells, called the ....[20] This lies between the ....[21] and the ....[22] One of the interesting features of lowly animals such as hydra and planarians is that they are able to ....[23] lost or damaged parts.

1. Briefly explain how an amoeba (a) moves, (b) feeds and (c) reproduces.
2. Why is a study of protozoans of importance to man?
3. What major difference exists between the structure of the amoeba and hydra?
4. Describe how the hydra traps, ingests and digests a water-flea, mentioning the types of cell involved at each stage.

5. Why do the amoeba and hydra require no special organs of respiration and excretion?
6. Briefly describe how the hydra reproduces (a) asexually and (b) sexually.
7. What is the important difference in body structure between Coelenterates and Platyhelminthes?

Chapter 5

More Animals without Backbones

5.1. The segmented worms: annelids

When we refer to 'worms' we usually mean those animals that belong to the phylum **Annelida**, of which the earthworm is the most familiar example. The word annelid comes from a word meaning 'ringed'; this refers to the presence in the skin of a series of rings extending round the body. Each ring marks the position of an internal partition dividing the body into a number of compartments, or **segments**. Certain body organs are repeated in each segment. We may compare the animal to a train in which each coach corresponds to a segment. One coach is similar to the next, having similar compartments, corridors, windows, doors, etc., but some parts, such as heating pipes, communication cords and electrical wiring, are continuous from coach to coach. If you examine Figure 5.2 you will see how the gut, nerve cord and main blood vessels extend from segment to segment. Returning to our train, we may remind ourselves that some sections have special features for they have special purposes. In this category are the guard's van and the engine. So, also, in a segmented animal certain segments have special parts to play and possess special organs. In earthworms this is especially true of the first twenty segments of the body.

One important advance over the flatworms is that the annelid worms have a cavity, or **coelom**, surrounding the gut. The development of this cavity was another important landmark in animal evolution, for it freed the gut to enable it to work independently of the body wall. In simpler terms, this means that food can be moved along the gut without the necessity for the whole animal to move. Another important development was the **blood system**, whereby substances such as food and oxygen can be transported within the body.

5.2. Various annelids

The earthworm lives underground, but most annelids are aquatic, commonly occurring on the sea-shore (see Figure 5.1). The **ragworm**

Figure 5.1 Various annelid worms

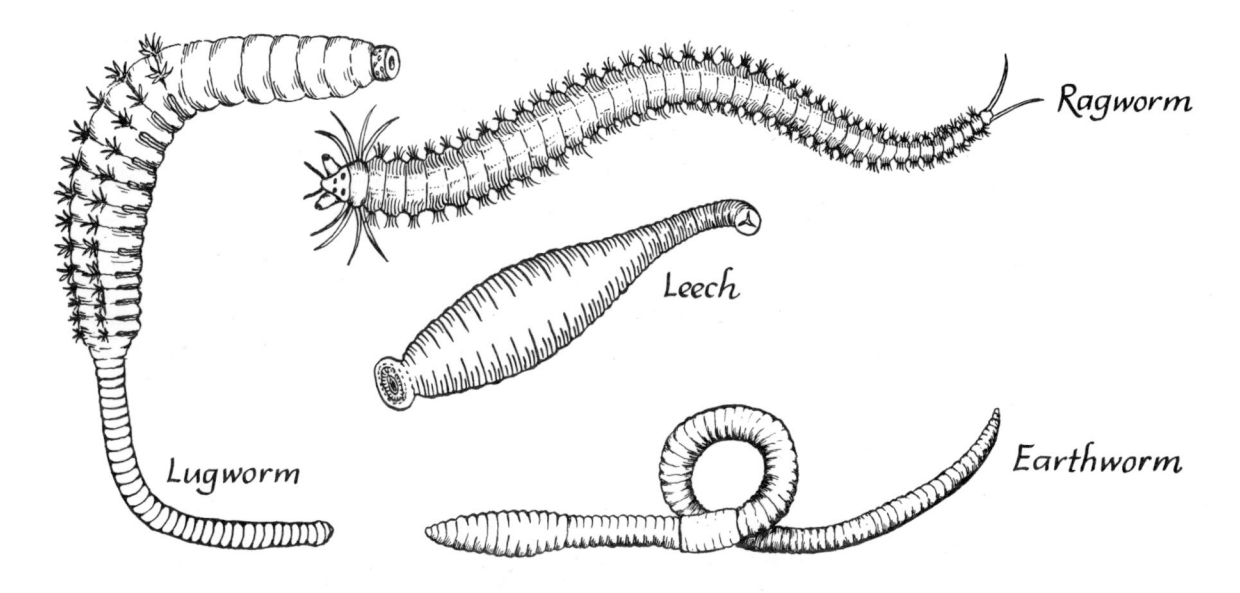

(*Nereis*) is a common sea-shore animal, which has sharp jaws for seizing the small animals on which it preys. Each segment bears a pair of fleshy limbs, carrying bunches of stiff bristles which are used to 'row' the animal along. Many of the annelids of the sea-shore live a burrowing existence in the sand or mud. The **lugworm** (*Arenicola*) is one such burrower, and is widely used as bait by fishermen. Some tube-dwelling annelids have beautiful, feathery gills, giving them a flower-like appearance. Apart from their use in respiration, these gills are sometimes used to sieve minute food particles from the water, a process known as filter-feeding.

Quite different from these creatures are **leeches**, which are parasites. Using special suckers, a leech attaches itself to an animal such as a fish or amphibian. Its sharp jaws pierce the skin, and the leech sucks a meal of blood from its 'host'. Then the parasite detaches itself and swims freely in the water until it comes into contact with a new host. Leeches were once much used in medicine for 'blood-letting', a treatment which was thought to relieve many ills. The number of leeches used was so great that, in some districts, the particular species used became extinct.

Examination of a range of annelid worms will remind us that animals become highly **adapted** to suit them for particular ways of life.

5.3. Earthworms

Earthworms are annelids which have become adapted for life in the soil. They rarely leave their burrows, because their delicate skins are unable to withstand dry conditions. The body bears no external projections for these would be damaged during burrowing.

Thus, there are no tentacles, gills or limbs, and bristles are reduced to only four pairs per segment (see Figure 5.2). The skin is kept moist by **mucous glands** in the skin; the mucus also enables the worm to slide along in its burrow easily. The skin is the sole respiratory surface. Near the head end the skin is swollen into a 'saddle', or **clitellum**. Here there are abundant mucous glands which serve to form the egg cocoon.

Earthworms are of great value to agriculture, a fact which was well established by the famous naturalist **Charles Darwin**. He showed that the common earthworm improves the fertility of soil in four ways:

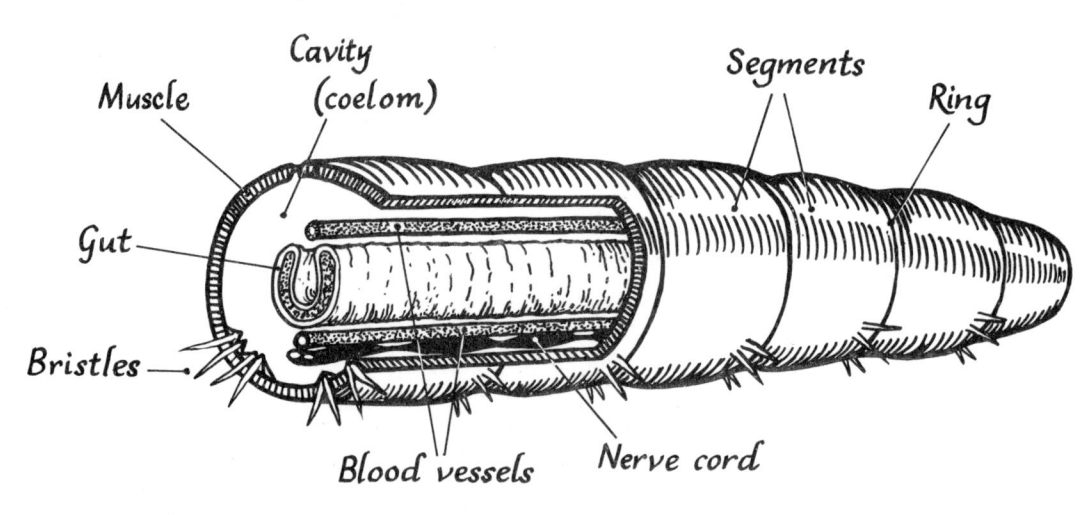

Figure 5.2 The earthworm, cut to show some of its internal structures

a. By *burying* dead and decaying matter which would otherwise accumulate on the surface of the soil. Earthworms feed on this matter, dragging it down into their burrows. Thus the worm does what the good farmer or gardener does when he digs rotted matter into the soil.

b. By *aerating* and *draining* the soil. The burrows of the worms enable air to enter the soil and water to run away. This keeps the soil healthy and prevents it from becoming waterlogged.

c. By *ploughing* the soil. When burrowing, the worms take soil into their food-tubes. From this soil they obtain nourishing food matter, the residual soil passing out of their bodies to be deposited on the surface as **worm-casts**. In this way worms are constantly bringing the deeper soil to the surface, from as deep as half a metre. This activity caused Darwin to refer to earthworms as 'Nature's Ploughmen'. He estimated that in an acre (about 4 000 square metres) there are some 53 000 worms and that in a year these bring to the surface some 10 tons (some 10 000 kilogrammes) of soil. In five years that amount of soil would cover the surface to a depth of one inch ($2\frac{1}{2}$ cm). This may not sound much, but over the years, the effect is considerable. Darwin observed one particular field over a period of thirty years. At the beginning of the period, the field was covered with a layer of stones which were large enough to hinder the progress of a horse. After thirty years of worm activity, a horse could be ridden across the field without its hooves striking a single stone of any size.

d. By *powdering* the soil. If you examine a dried worm-cast you will find that the soil is very finely powdered, due to the grinding activity of the worm's gut. This fine soil is the perfect medium for the germination of small seeds. Again, during its passage through the worm's gut, any acidity in the soil has been neutralized by the addition of chalky matter. Seeds grow best in such soil.

Investigation 5a. Setting up a wormery

A wormery consists of two sheets of glass placed in a wooden frame so that they are about 3 cm apart. These may be purchased, or may be constructed fairly easily. Alternatively, an old aquarium may be used (see Figure 5.3).

Into the wormery place alternate layers of garden soil, sand and leaf mould (or peat). Water each layer lightly as it is added. Sprinkle a layer of leafy matter on to the surface. Add a good

Figure 5.3 A simple wormery

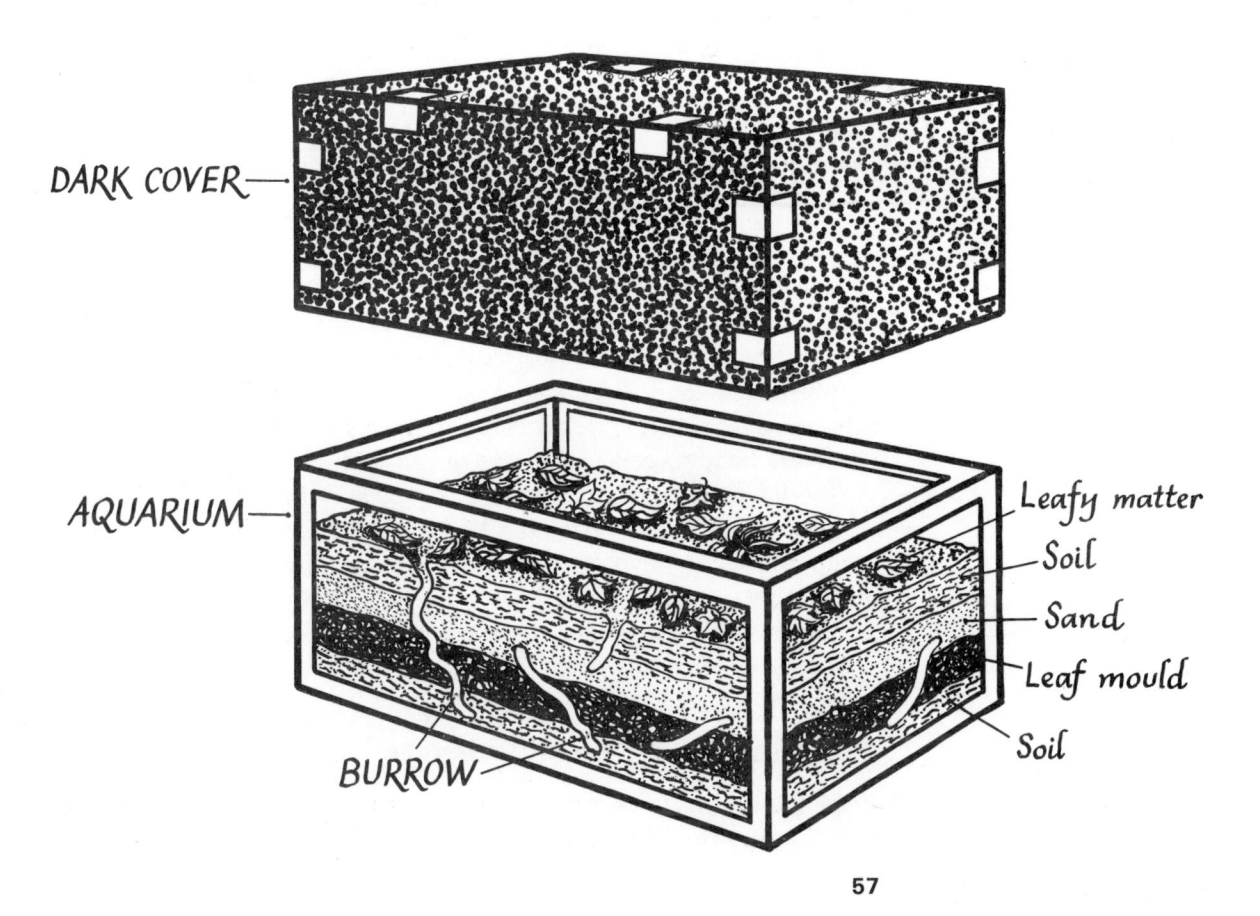

number of garden worms and leave them for a week, keeping the sides of the aquarium covered with dark paper. This will encourage the worms to burrow near the glass. Find out what kinds of food your worms like to eat by adding various items (beetroot, celery, cabbage, etc.) to the surface and by noticing which are eaten by the worms.

5.4. Animals with jointed legs: arthropods

Of all the animal groups without backbones, the Arthropoda is by far the most important. It includes such animals as crabs, lobsters, grasshoppers, bees, spiders and centipedes. Let us consider how these animals resemble each other. An important feature is that the body is encased in a hard shell, or **exoskeleton**, which is composed of chitin. This armoured layer, known also as the **cuticle**, lies on the outside of the normal skin, which is responsible for its formation.

The cuticle (see Figure 5.4) serves many purposes in arthropods. Its presence is a major reason for the great success of the group. It

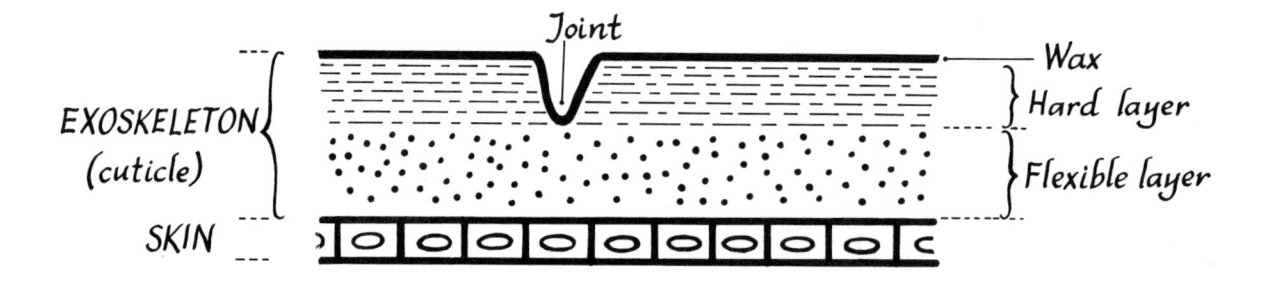

Figure 5.4 Structure of the arthropod cuticle

supports the softer parts of the body and protects them from damage. The body muscles are attached to its inner surface and pull on it. The arthropod body, like that of annelids, is segmented. Between each segment the cuticle is thin and flexible, forming a **joint**. Muscles attach to each side of the joint and, by their contraction, cause the body to bend at this point (see Figure 5.5).

Another important feature of arthropods is that, typically, each segment bears a pair of **jointed limbs**. From these the name of the group is derived (*arthro:* jointed, *pod:* limb). One of the interesting things about these animals is the variety of uses to which the limbs are put in the various species. We will now consider how the basic arthropod pattern has been modified in the various classes.

5.5. Crustaceans: aquatic arthropods

At the beginning of their history, arthropods were water-dwelling animals, and the crustaceans are the modern representatives of this

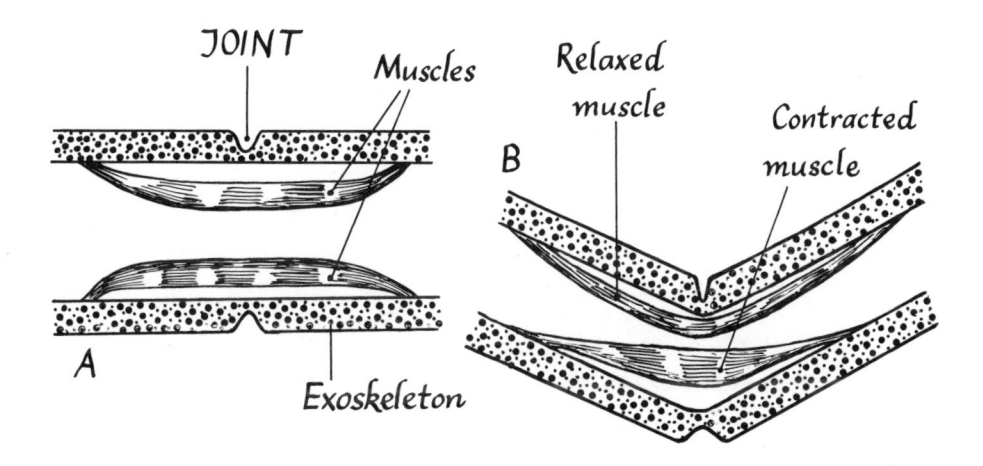

Figure 5.5 Muscles bend the arthropod body at joints

group. Most crustaceans live in the sea, commonly on the sea-shore (for example, crabs, shrimps and prawns). The cuticle is very hard and 'crusty', being hardened by calcium salts from the sea water. Some of the limbs have special **pincers**, which enable them to grip the rocks and seaweed. Larger pincers are used for defence and for catching prey. **Lobsters** and **crabs** are giant crustaceans. Many crustaceans are much smaller, some so minute that they form part of the microscopic **plankton** in the surface layer of the sea. The familiar **water-fleas** are freshwater crustaceans, which are important sources of food for larger animals.

The strangest crustaceans are, without doubt, the **barnacles**. Encased in their hard, chalky shells, and attached to rocks, piers, ships, etc., they were once thought to be related to the limpets and mussels (molluscs). However, a study of their development showed that they

Figure 5.6 Various crustaceans

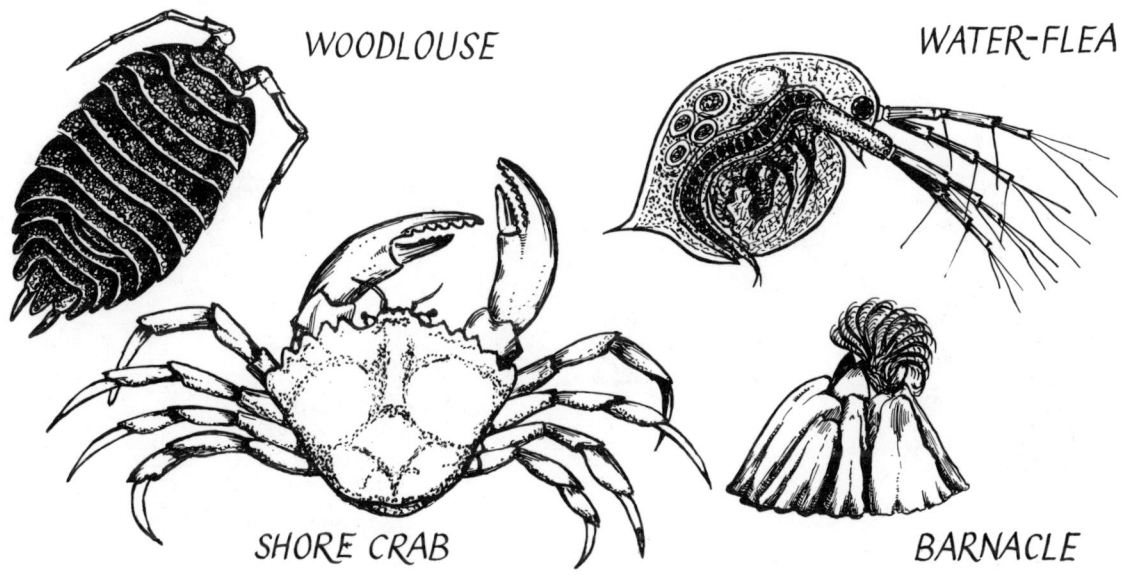

are crustaceans, for the eggs develop into minute larvae resembling those of other crustaceans. The barnacle has a strange way of life, for it spends its whole existence lying on its back inside its shell. When covered by the tide, two small doors in the shell open, and the barnacle extends feathery limbs to sweep small particles of food from the sea water.

Other unusual crustaceans are the **woodlice**. They inhabit damp places under stones and logs, and are the nearest that the crustaceans have come to evolving a land form. Two major problems facing any land animal are the problem of respiration in air and the problem of resisting desiccation (drying up). Woodlice breathe through their limbs, which are specially adapted for this purpose. If exposed to desiccation, some species are able to roll themselves into a ball.

5.6. Insects: highly successful land arthropods

The insects are the group of arthropods that includes such familiar animals as ants, bees, houseflies, beetles, butterflies, moths and grasshoppers (see Figure 5.7). They are an extremely successful group, having the greatest number of species (some three-quarters of a million). The number of actual individuals is enormous. Insects inhabit vast areas of territory and, in some tropical areas, compete successfully with man. The diversity of insects is such that they are able to inhabit almost every known habitat and to feed on a wide range of food materials. Here, again, they compete with man, for many of these foods are also food for man. Thus, insects attack our crops and consume our stored products. They are also responsible for transmitting disease, such as malaria, sleeping-sickness and plague.

Not all insects, however, are harmful. Some, such as bees and butterflies, are important agents in the pollination of flowers. Insect

Figure 5.7 Various insects

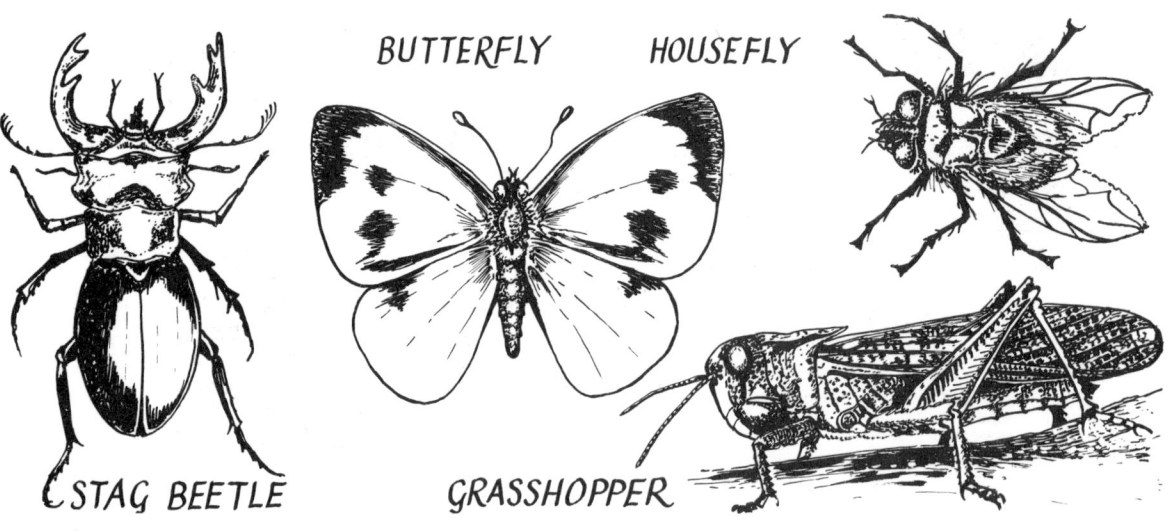

products that are used by man include silk, wax, shellac and cochineal. On balance, however, insects are man's most powerful enemies.

Although there are so many different types of insect, they have certain common features which make recognition fairly easy (see Figure 6.1, page 65). The body is divided into three regions: the head, thorax and abdomen. The **head** bears a pair of sensory **antennae** and a pair of large **compound eyes**, the surfaces of which are divided into many hexagonal lenses. The six **walking-legs** are attached to the **thorax**, which may also bear one or two pairs of **wings**. The wings are composed of a double layer of cuticle, and usually show a distinct pattern of 'veins'. The **abdomen** bears no limbs and is visibly divided into about ten **segments**.

Insects are such an important group of animals that the next chapter will be devoted entirely to them.

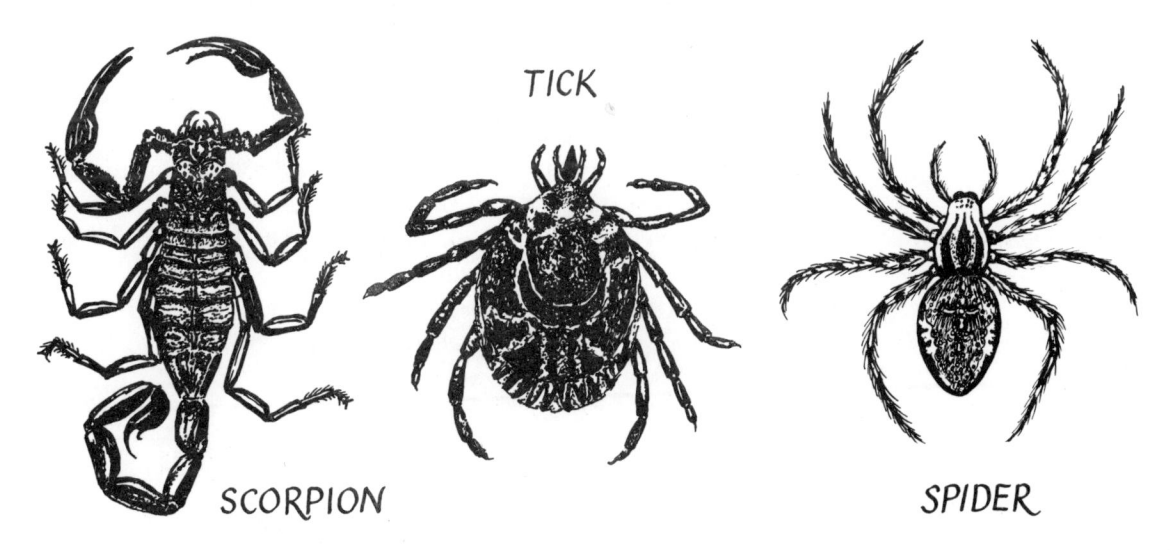

Figure 5.8 Some arachnids

5.7. Arachnids

Of all the animal groups Arachnida is probably the one we like least (see Figure 5.8). The mere mention of spiders and scorpions conjures up horror in many people's minds. This is due, no doubt, to the animals' habit of hiding in dark places, from which they emerge on eight long legs to pounce on their prey. **Spiders** trap their prey in webs, and this adds to our distaste. **Scorpions** feed on other land arthropods which are paralysed by the poisonous sting in the scorpion's tail. The tail is arched over the head when the scorpion strikes at its prey.

Ticks and **mites** are extremely small arachnids, but they cause considerable harm to man and to his livestock and crops. In Asia they transmit serious diseases such as typhus and spotted fever.

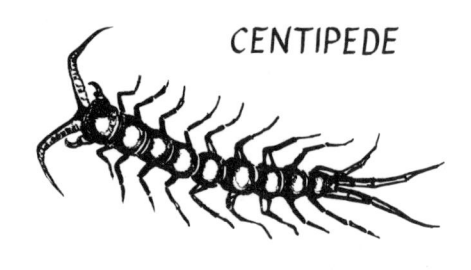

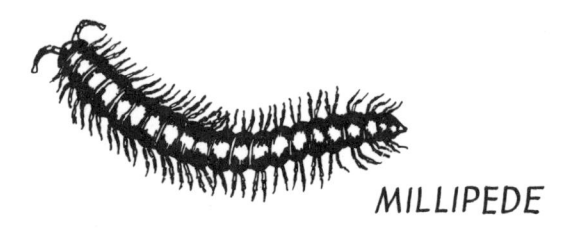

Figure 5.9 Myriapods

5.8. Myriapods: the many-legged arthropods

The fourth, and last, group of arthropods is Myriapoda, a name which means 'many legs' (see Figure 5.9). We are also reminded of this abundance of legs in the names of the two subdivisions: the centipedes ('hundred legs') and millipedes ('thousand legs'). In actual fact, centipedes have varying numbers of legs according to the species, the average being about thirty-six, whilst millipedes have about twice as many. Apart from the possession of many legs, the two groups have little in common.

Centipedes are carnivores and feed on insects, earthworms and slugs. They hunt in the dark, seizing their prey with powerful jaws equipped with poison glands. Their bodies are flattened, oval in section, and each segment bears one pair of limbs only. **Millipedes** (wireworms), on the other hand, are herbivores and feed on soft vegetable matter such as strawberries and potatoes. Their bodies are more rounded in section and the segments are fused in pairs, so that each division of the body bears two pairs of limbs.

Figure 5.10 Various molluscs

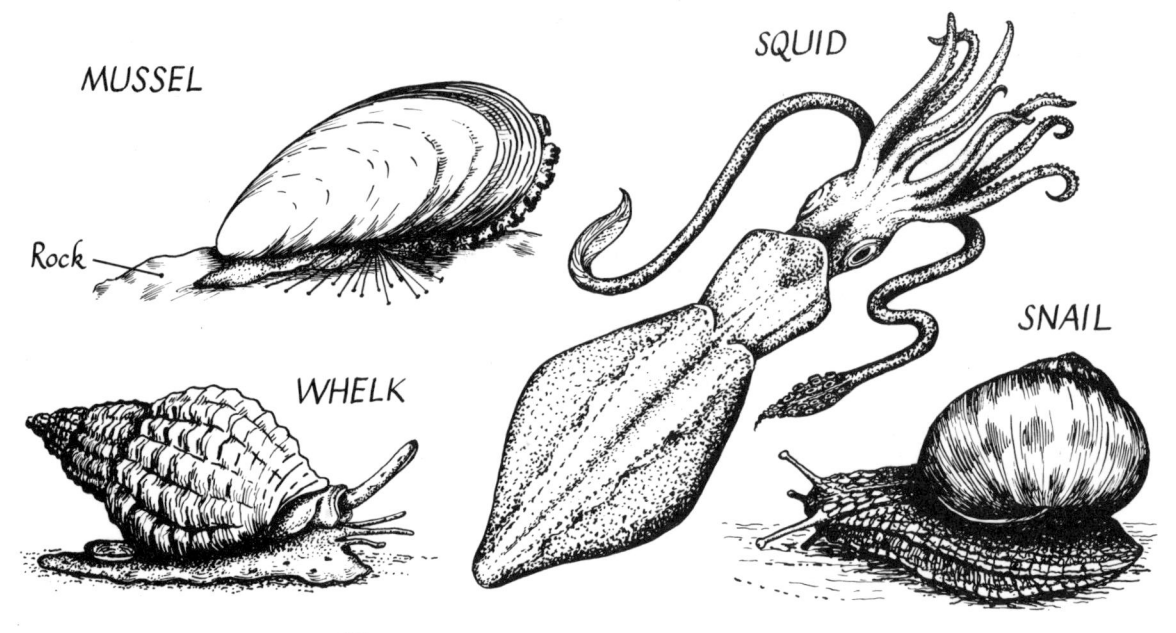

5.9. The soft-bodied animals: molluscs

Second only to the arthropods in number of species and range of body form are the molluscs, a group which includes snails, slugs, winkles, whelks, mussels, oysters, octopuses and squids (see Figure 5.10). At first sight there would not seem to be much resemblance between a snail and an octopus, for their ways of life are so different. The snail is a sluggish, creeping animal, which browses on vegetation, whilst the octopus is an extremely active carnivore, which preys on crustaceans. A closer study, however, does indicate a relationship between the two animals.

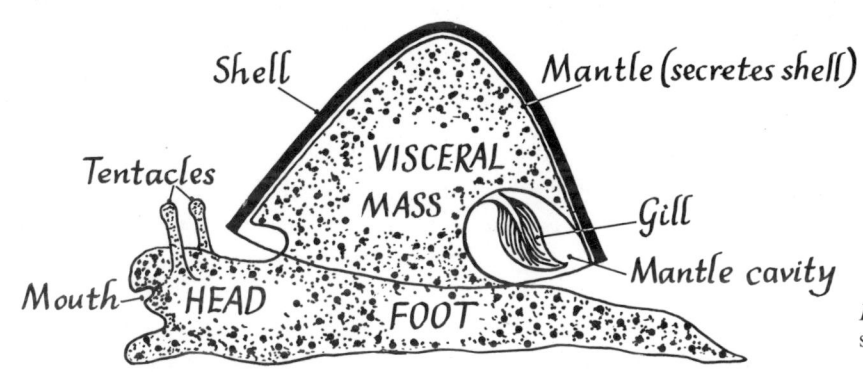

Figure 5.11 Parts of a simple mollusc

The name mollusc means 'soft-bodied', and this is a common feature. The lack of any hard internal parts makes molluscs popular 'sea-foods'. The body is divisible into three parts: the **head**, usually bearing eyes and tentacles; the fleshy **foot**, used for locomotion; and the **visceral mass**, containing vital body organs such as the digestive and reproductive systems. The visceral mass is protected by a hard **shell**, the inner surface of which is often 'mother of pearl'. The shell varies considerably in the various groups of molluscs. It may be single, like a chinese hat (limpet), double, the two halves hinging together (mussel), coiled (snail), embedded in the skin (cuttlefish), or absent altogether (slug). In octopuses and squids the shell is much reduced to enable the animal to be more active, since a shell, like a suit of armour, is a weighty structure to carry around.

It is interesting that, just as the crustaceans have developed some land forms, so also have the molluscs. The land snail has no gills, but has developed a simple lung from the mantle cavity (see Figure 5.11). The head and foot can also be withdrawn into this cavity should the animal be in danger of damage or of drying up.

5.10. The spiny-skinned animals: echinoderms

The last group of animals without backbones, Echinodermata, has little in common with the other groups (see Figure 5.12). The most familiar echinoderm is the **starfish**, of which there are some

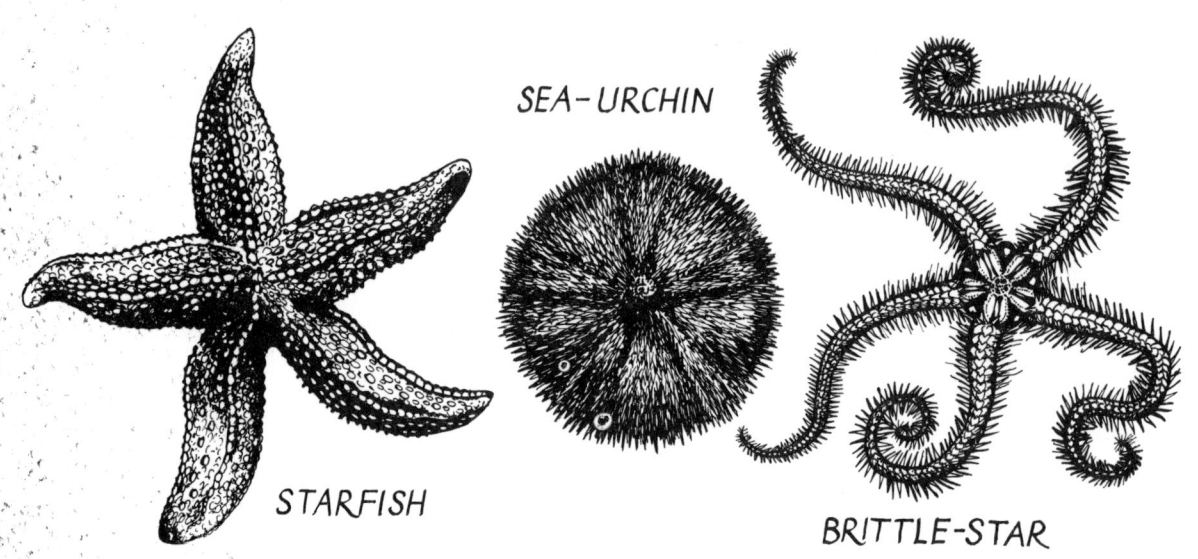

Figure 5.12 Various echinoderms

thousand species. Other echinoderms are the brittle-stars, sea-urchins, sand-dollars and sea-cucumbers. The very names suggest unusual animals. All live in the sea, and the most obvious common feature is that the body is star-like, or **radially symmetrical**, so that it may be cut into similar halves by a radial cut passing through the centre of any 'arm'. The skeleton is chalky and forms plates which may be fused into a shell, as in sea-urchins, or scattered in a leathery skin, as in starfishes. This rough surface is reflected in the word echinoderm, which really means 'hedgehog-skinned'. Movement of echinoderms is by strange tubular feet which move when water is forced into them from a system of canals. It is interesting that these strange animals develop from minute larvae which closely resemble those of primitive chordates. Strange as it may seem, the echinoderms may be our closest relatives in the invertebrate world.

Test your understanding

1. What is meant when we say that the body of an annelid worm is segmented?
2. In what way is a leech an unusual annelid?
3. List three ways in which earthworms enrich the soil.
4. Crabs and spiders are arthropods. Write down the names of three other members of this group.
5. In what important ways does the body of an arthropod differ from that of an annelid?
6. Try to find a connection between crustaceans and some whales.
7. Why do we refer to insects as a very successful group?
8. Suggest three ways in which insects may do harm to man.
9. What are the main differences between centipedes and millipedes?
10. The snail is a mollusc. Write down the names of three other molluscs.
11. What do we mean when we say that echinoderms, such as starfish, are radially symmetrical animals?

Chapter 6

More about Insects

6.1. The insect body

We learnt in the last chapter that the insect body is encased in a hard skeleton, or cuticle, forming a series of armoured plates along the back, underside and sides of the animal. The body has three regions: the head (six segments, fused together), the thorax (three segments) and the abdomen (approximately ten segments) (see Figure 6.1). There are joints between the segments of the thorax, and between those of the abdomen. Insects breathe by a system of air-tubes, or **tracheae**, which open to the outside at holes called **spiracles**. Let us now consider each region of the body in a little more detail.

The head bears a pair of large **compound eyes**, whose surfaces are marked by many tiny facets, or lenses. Each lens marks the position

Figure 6.1 Parts of a typical insect

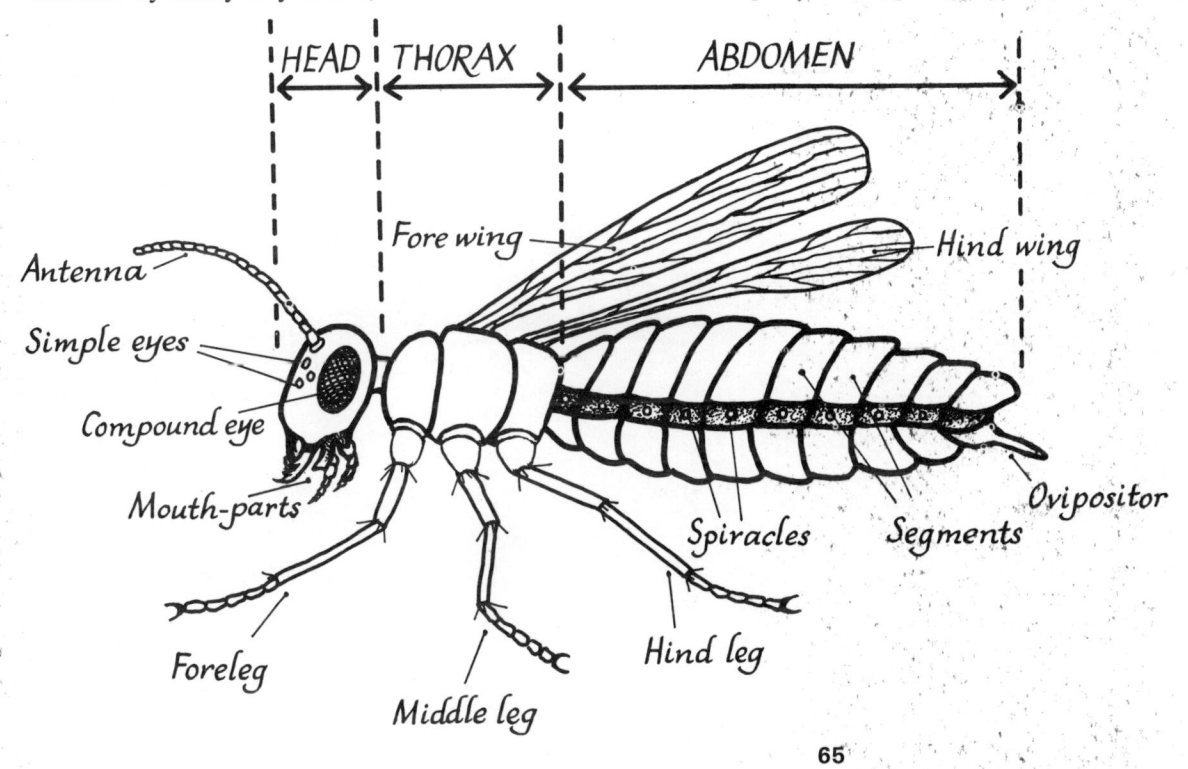

of a minute optical unit, capable of 'seeing' part of the field of view. All the 'pictures', or images, from the hundreds of optical units are put together to build up a full image, rather as a newspaper picture is built up from a series of dots. Also on the head are the **antennae**, or feelers, which are long slender structures bearing sensitive bristles. Antennae are very sensitive to touch and to movements of the air around the insect. Around the mouth of the insect are small leg-like structures called **mouth-parts**. The nature of these parts varies considerably from insect to insect, according to the nature of the diet. Thus the mouth-parts of a locust, which feeds on solid, vegetable matter, will differ from those of, say, a greenfly, which sucks the sap from plants.

The thorax bears the **wings** and the six **walking-legs**. Not all insects have wings, one exception being the 'silverfish', sometimes found scuttling about in our kitchens. Most insects, however, have one or two pairs of wings, which are usually transparent with a distinct pattern of 'veins'. Each walking-leg has several joints, and ends in a pair of claws, sometimes accompanied by an adhesive pad. It should be realized that the bristles protruding from the insect's body, and from its legs, are important sensory devices.

The abdomen houses most of the digestive and reproductive organs, but shows few external features, apart from its clear segmentation. The last segment often bears structures concerned with copulation and egg-laying.

Examine the diagram of the grasshopper (Figure 6.2). Can you see any way in which this animal differs from the typical insect we have described? Try to think of the reasons for any special features. In other words, how is the grasshopper adapted?

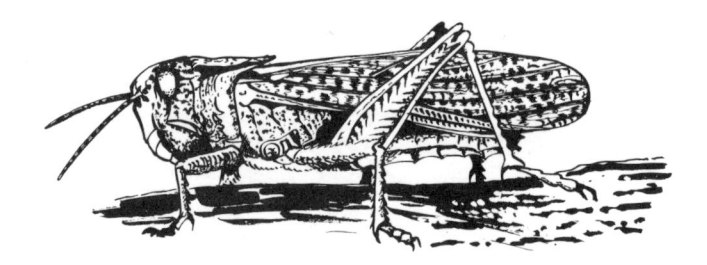

Figure 6.2 The grasshopper

6.2. The butterfly

Over two thousand species of butterfly or moth occur in Britain. As an example we will consider the **large white butterfly** (*Pieris brassicae*), which is a common sight in our gardens in summer (see Figure 6.3).

The wings of all butterflies and moths are covered with minute **scales**, each scale being a flattened bristle. The scales have stalks

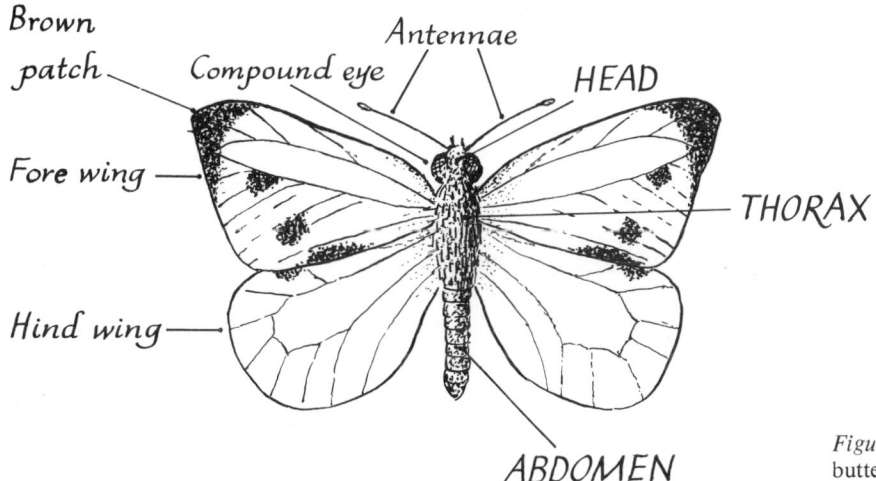

Figure 6.3 The large white butterfly (female)

by which they fit into sockets in the wing, and overlap, rather like tiles on a roof (see Figure 6.4). The scales are easily dislodged if the wings are touched by hand, and appear on the fingers as fine dust. The beautiful coloration and patterns on the wings of butterflies and moths are due to these scales which may be pigmented, or may produce colour by their effect on light in the same way as oil does on water.

Butterflies and moths are placed in an order of insects called the **Lepidoptera** (from Greek *lepis*: a scale, *pteron*: a wing). There is no hard and fast distinction between butterflies and moths, though the antennae of butterflies usually have club-shaped ends, whilst those of moths do not. The adult insects feed mainly on the sweet nectar from flowers, though they may also suck the juice from over-ripe fruits.

The mouth-parts have become adapted to use this food, which is always in liquid form. The **proboscis** consists of two gutter-shaped processes, which are brought together to form a tube up which nectar

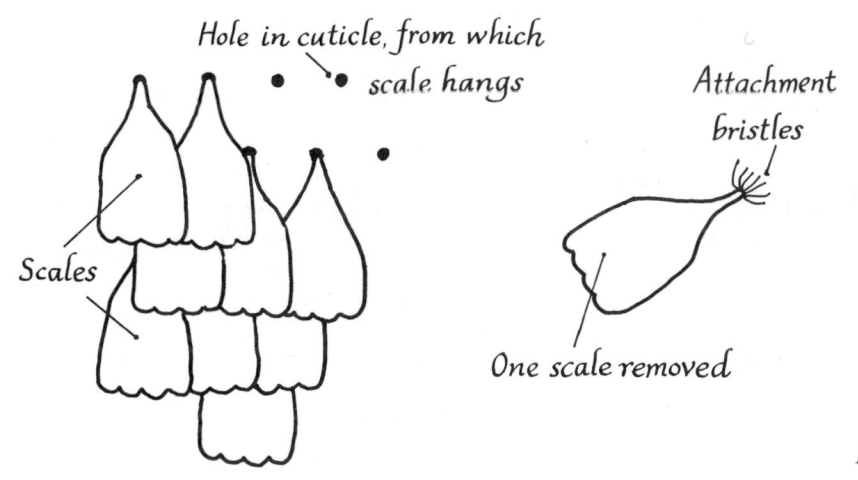

Figure 6.4 Butterfly scales

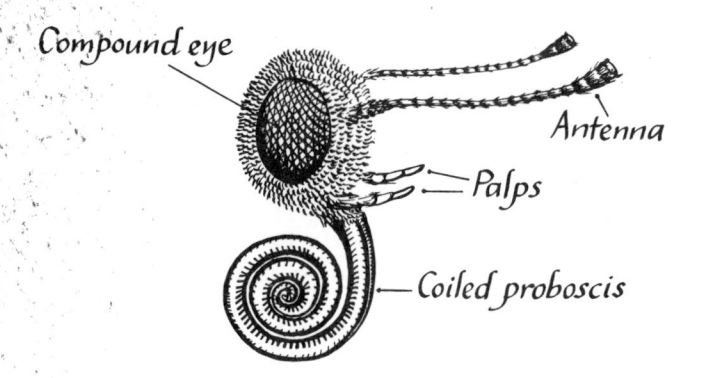

Figure 6.5 Lateral view of the head of a butterfly to show the proboscis

can be sucked. When not in use the proboscis is stowed away under the head, coiled like a watchspring (see Figure 6.5).

Butterflies, and some moths, are useful insects for they bring about the transfer of pollen when they go from flower to flower. This **pollination** is essential if seeds are to develop (see Chapter 12).

6.3. The life-history of the large white butterfly

a. **The eggs.** After mating has occurred between the male and female adults, the female lays batches of 60 to 100 fertilized eggs on the underside of leaves, chiefly of cabbage. Eggs may be laid in April or May, or in August or September. Each egg is attached by a sticky secretion, and its yellowish egg case is beautifully sculptured. After eight to ten days the larva, or caterpillar, emerges, eating first the egg shell and then the leaf.

b. **The larva.** The caterpillar has a head and thirteen segments, equivalent to a thorax and abdomen. The head bears simple eyes and short antennae. The mouth-parts differ from those of the adult butterfly, for they are adapted for biting (see Figure 6.6). Caterpillars

Figure 6.6 The larval stage of the large white butterfly: (a) side view and (b) front view of head

68

are able to produce liquid silk, and this emerges from the **spinneret** to set as a strand of silk. The next three segments of the body represent the thorax and each bears a pair of short, jointed legs. Some of the abdominal segments also bear leg-like structures, known as **prolegs**, or false legs. Unlike the true, thoracic legs, these prolegs are not jointed, but are fleshy, stumpy structures with a circlet of hooks at the end. The last segment of the body bears a pair of fleshy **claspers.**

The yellowish-green larva rapidly consumes the cabbage leaf, using its strong, jaw-like mandibles to cut pieces away. As the larva grows, it moults (ecdyses) its cuticle four times, and after about thirty days reaches its full size. It is now about 40 mm long.

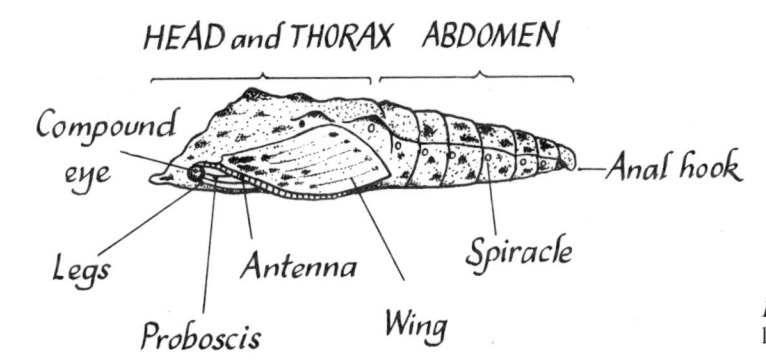

Figure 6.7 The pupa of the large white butterfly

c. **The pupa or chrysalis** (see Figure 6.7). The larva now leaves the food plant and climbs to a more sheltered spot, such as a fence, wall or tree-trunk. Here it spins a pad of silk, and to this it fixes its claspers. It also supports itself by a loose girdle of silk, made by passing two silk threads round the abdomen to each side of the support. Considerable changes now occur in the body, and after a final moult the larval skin is lost and the pupa is revealed. It hangs suspended from the pad of silk, to which it is attached by special anal hooks. The soft cuticle of the pupa soon hardens and becomes dark in colour, so that it blends well with its background. Within the pupal case the larval tissues are broken down and the butterfly body is built. Some of the adult structures become visible through the pupal case.

d. **The adult or imago.** After about two weeks, the cuticle splits and the adult butterfly gradually emerges from the pupa. It cannot fly until the wings have dried and expanded, which takes about two hours. Eggs laid in August or September give rise to pupae which remain in their sheltered situation for the whole winter, the adult butterfly emerging in the spring.

The life-cycle is summarized in Figure 6.8.

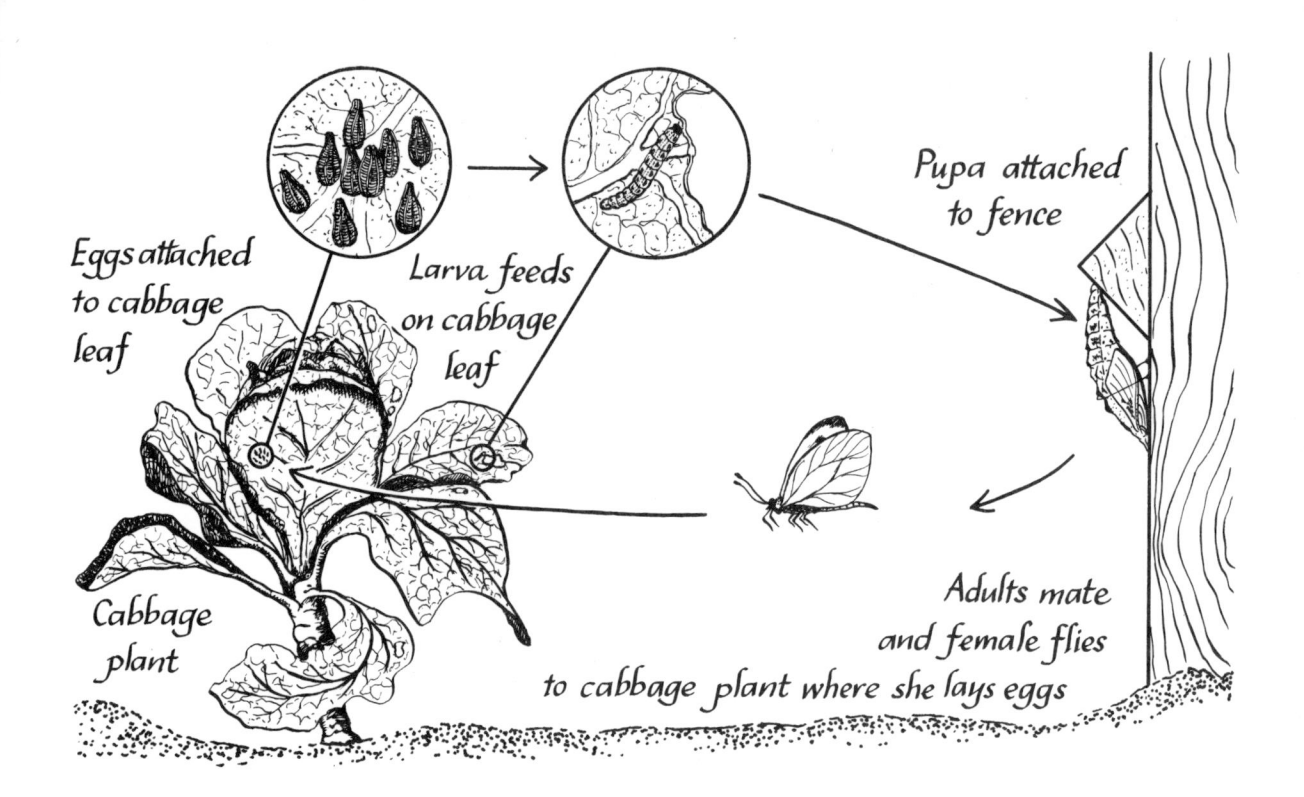

Figure 6.8 Summary of the life-cycle of the large white butterfly

6.4. The meaning of metamorphosis

We have seen that the butterfly exists in two forms, which are quite different in their structure and methods of feeding. The adult flies from flower to flower, seeking the sweet nectar. It does not grow in size, but does mate with the opposite sex. The larva, on the other hand, cannot fly and its sole purpose in life is to eat leaves and grow rapidly. During the pupal stage the larva undergoes transformation into the adult form, this transformation being known as **metamorphosis**. Such changes of form are not confined to insects, for larvae occur in the life-cycles of other animals, such as aquatic crustaceans and molluscs. The frog tadpole is a larva which undergoes metamorphosis into the adult form.

6.5. A social insect: the honey bee

The butterfly is a solitary insect; the adults do not associate together, except during mating. The honey bee (*Apis mellifica*), on the other hand, is a social insect, for the adults live together in communities, or **hives**. The hive contains a large number of bees, sometimes reaching as many as 50 000 in a large hive.

Within the hive there is a division of labour, each bee having its own task to perform in the service of the community. The continuance of the hive is all-important, and every bee is dedicated to its preservation. The hive has been compared to some human societies which have strict regimes, but it is true to say that no human society has such rigorous requirements of its members as does a beehive.

6.6. Castes of bees (see Figure 6.9)

Honey bees are either male or female. The males, or **drones**, may be recognized by their larger size and by the fact that their wings extend beyond their short, stumpy abdomens. Drones do not possess a sting. A hive contains only a few hundred of these male bees, whose sole purpose is to fertilize the queen during her nuptial flight (see Section 6.9). The female bees are of two types, the queen and the worker. There is only one **queen** in the hive. She is larger than the worker and has a conical abdomen which is longer than the wings. Queen bees are able to sting; the sting is unbarbed so that it may be withdrawn easily after use. The queen is responsible for laying all of the eggs that will develop into future inhabitants of the hive, or will establish new hives. Like the drones, the queen is unable to seek food and must be fed by the workers.

The **workers** form the vast majority of the bees in the hive. A worker is smaller than the queen and drone, its wings being about the same length as the abdomen. Workers have a barbed sting, which is not easily withdrawn from the victim's body. Frequently, the sting is torn from the worker's body as it tries to get away, and the resulting injuries often cause death.

The body of the worker is highly adapted for its many duties, especially that of collection of food. The **mouth-parts** are used to take

Figure 6.9 The three castes of honey bee

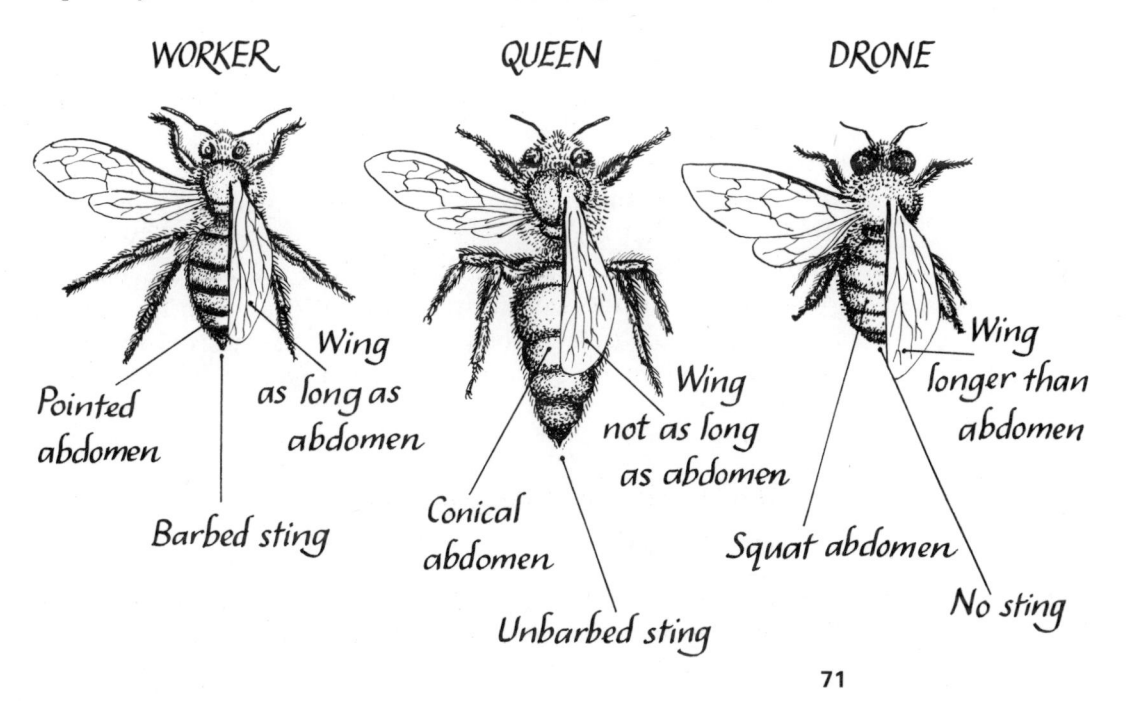

up nectar from flowers (see Figure 6.10). They comprise a central tube (ligula), which has a very fine bore. Small amounts of nectar pass up this tube by capillarity. Larger amounts can be sucked up when all the mouth-parts are closed together, and the ligula in the centre is worked up and down like a piston.

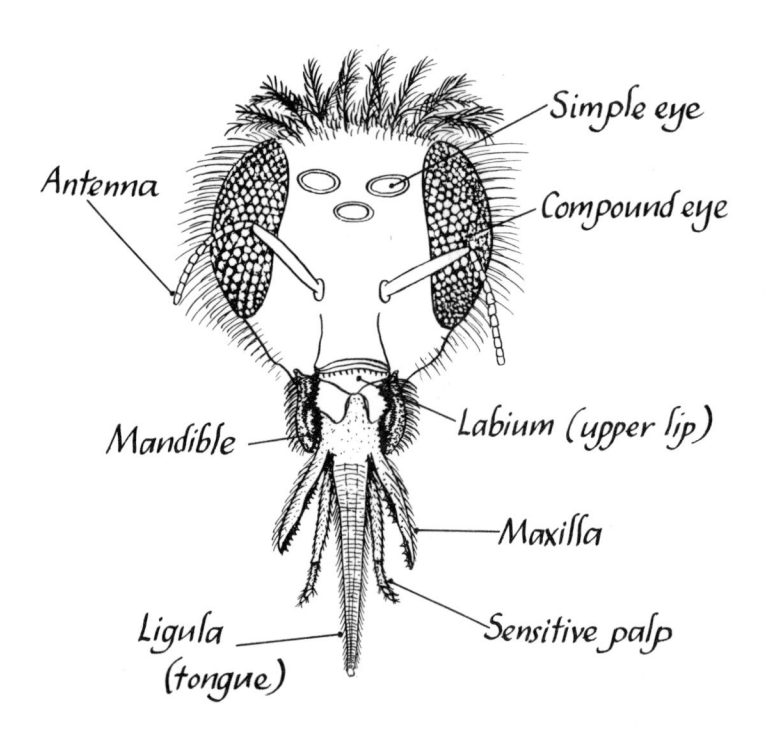

Figure 6.10 The worker honey bee: front view of head showing mouth-parts

The legs of the worker are adapted for the collection of pollen. When the bee visits a flower, seeking nectar, its hairy body becomes covered with this yellowy powder. Using the special brush of hairs on the third leg, the bee sweeps the pollen from its body into a basket-like structure on the third leg of the opposite side (see Figure 6.11). During summer, if you watch carefully, you will often see a bee with its hind legs bulging with their pollen load. When it returns to the hive it ejects the pollen from the baskets, using a special 'prong' on the second pair of legs. Pollen which falls on the head of the bee cannot be collected into baskets, but is swept away by the hairy front legs, which also bear a notch for cleaning the antennae.

6.7. The life-history of the honey bee

a. Comb construction

We may conveniently begin a consideration of the life-history of bees with the **swarm**. A swarm of bees comprises a queen, together with several thousand of her workers. They leave the old hive in May or June. The reasons for this are not fully understood, though overcrowding is probably an important factor. The swarm settles in a tight cluster, say, in a tree or on a fence. Some of the workers act as scouts, leaving the swarm to seek a suitable site for a new hive. Once such a site has been found the mass of bees flies to it, and the work of comb construction begins.

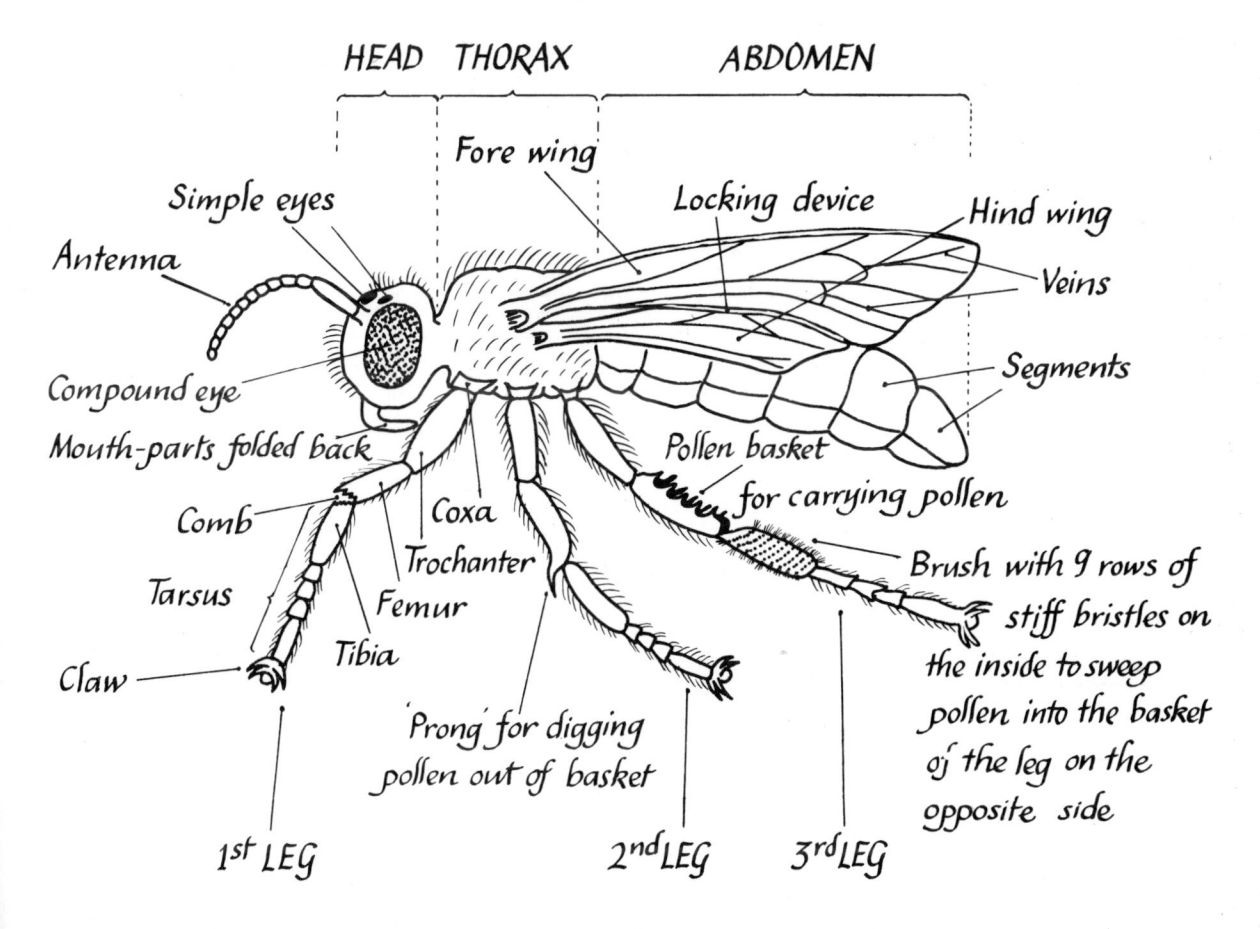

Figure 6.11 Structure of the worker honey bee

A hive comprises a series of vertical **combs** formed from **wax**. Each comb contains many compartments or 'cells'. These cells are the rooms of the hive and are used for a number of purposes. Some are used for storing honey or pollen (**storage cells**), whilst others are used for rearing the young bees (**brood cells**). The structure of part of a comb is shown in Figure 6.12.

Wax is formed in special glands on the underside of the abdomen of the worker. The wax is pushed out between the segments and, after emergence, sets to form a thin scale. This is then 'chewed' by the mandibles to render it more pliable, after which it is placed in position, like a building brick. The comb has a wonderfully symmetrical construction, each cell being hexagonal in shape.

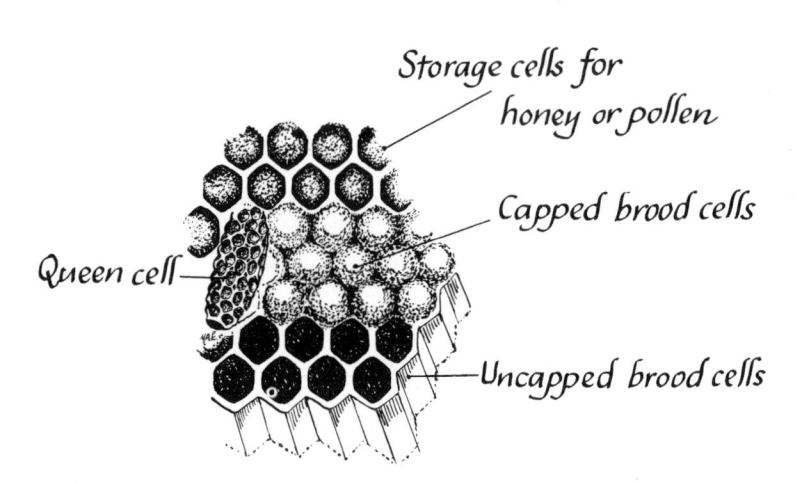

Figure 6.12 Comb structure

b. Egg-laying (see Figure 6.13)

As stated before, only the queen is able to lay eggs. In order to maintain the hive, she must lay a thousand, or more, each day during the breeding period (February to October). The queen places each egg in the bottom of a brood cell, attaching it by a sticky secretion. The egg is a minute, transparent structure, just over 1 mm long, and is, therefore, not easily seen with the naked eye. After three days a minute grub, or larva, emerges.

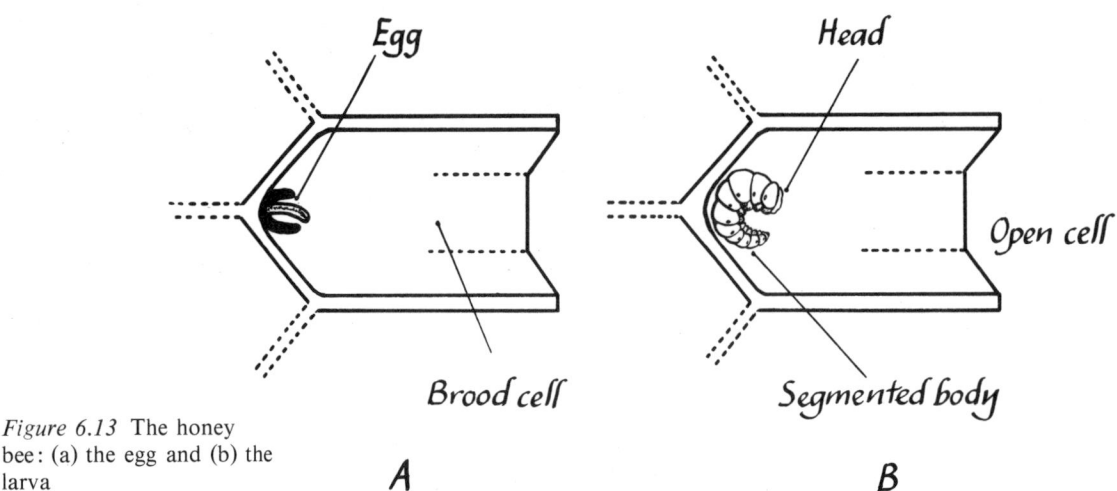

Figure 6.13 The honey bee: (a) the egg and (b) the larva

c. The worker larva

Throughout its development the larva is fed by the workers, at first on a special secretion of their salivary glands, called **royal jelly**. This is very nourishing and the larva grows rapidly. After three days the diet of the worker larva is changed to a mixture of honey and pollen. In two more days the larva is fully grown. Since it is well protected in its brood cell, and does not actively have to seek its own food, the larva is very simple in structure. Its creamy-white body has a head and thirteen segments, as has the butterfly larva, but it has no limbs and has very reduced mouth-parts. During its growth the larva moults several times.

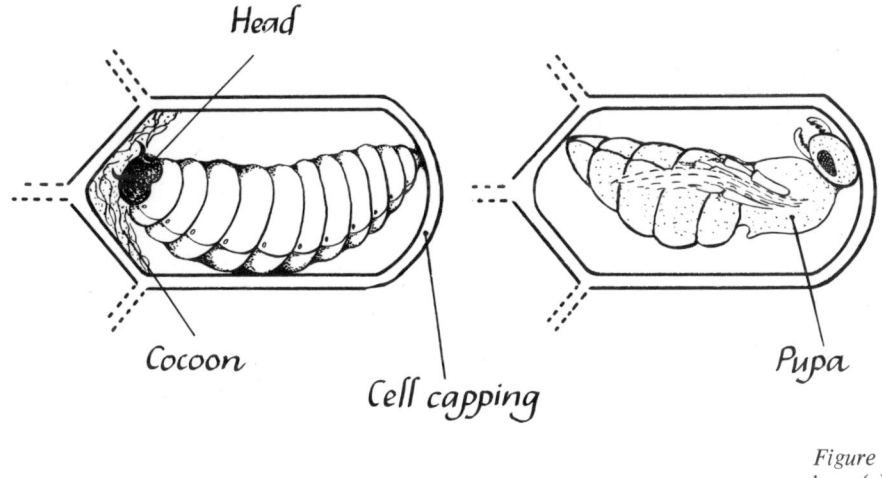

Figure 6.14 The honey bee: (a) the older larva and (b) the pupa

d. The pupa (see Figure 6.14)

On the ninth day after the egg was laid, the cell containing the fully grown larva is 'capped' by the workers. The wax cap is dome-like, and enables brood cells to be easily distinguished from storage cells, which are capped with flat tops. The larva now secretes silk and spins a partial cocoon. On about the fourteenth day it undergoes a final moult and the pupa emerges.

Within the pupal case the larval tissues are broken down and those of the adult constructed. At the end of about eight days, the adult bee emerges, using its strong mandibles to bite through the capping of the cell.

The complete development of the worker bee, from egg-laying to the emergence of the adult, has taken some twenty-one days.

6.8. The duties of the worker

During the active season of February to October the life-span of a worker is as little as six weeks. During this short but highly active life, the worker performs many different tasks. When it emerges from its brood cell some of the internal organs are not fully developed, so for a few days the worker is engaged in cleaning out the used cells. Later in the first week it feeds the older larvae on their diet of pollen and honey, which it obtains from the storage cells. In its second week, the worker is able to secrete its own royal jelly and is therefore able to feed the younger larvae. After about ten days the wax glands become functional, and the worker changes to the task of comb construction, either building new combs or repairing old ones.

Not until it is three weeks old does the worker go to the entrance of the hive to take up guard duty. Here its life may come to an abrupt end, for if the hive is attacked, say by wasps, the worker will be required to repel the attacker by the use of its sting. Guards are also required, on very hot days, to ventilate the hive, driving a current of cool air into it by the action of their wing-beat. During this period the worker will also make short flights, and will become used to locating the position of the hive.

For the second half of its life the worker becomes a forager, spending the daylight hours collecting nectar and pollen for the benefit of the hive. It has been found that a worker who has found a rich source of food performs a special dance on its return to the hive. The other workers follow this dance, and by the pattern of its movements gain information about the exact location of the food source.

6.9. Development of the queen and drone

Drones develop from eggs which are unfertilized. They are reared in cells which are somewhat broader than those of workers, and their development takes a few days longer. Queens are reared only at swarming time, unless the old queen should die or become unable to lay fertilized eggs. The queen cell has a special shape, and lies at right angles to the other cells (see Figure 6.12). The young queen larva is fed on royal jelly for the whole of her development, which is completed in from fifteen to nineteen days.

Five days after emergence the queen takes her first flight. Later, she makes a **nuptial flight**, during which she mates with a drone. She flies from the hive followed by all of the drones. One by one, the drones become exhausted and give up the chase. Finally, one drone reaches the queen and mating occurs, often in the air. The drone then falls to the ground, in a dying condition, whilst the queen returns to the hive. The sperm received from this one drone will be kept alive in the body of the queen, and will be used to fertilize all the eggs that she lays.

No hive can have two queens and, should a new queen emerge whilst the old one is still alive, they will fight until one is stung to death. However, if the old queen has left with the **swarm**, the newly emerged queen will take her place.

When autumn comes, the workers cut the wings from the drones and cast them out of the hive, where they soon perish. This avoids the necessity of feeding the drones during the winter, and thus conserves the food reserve in the hive. The bees rely on the pollen and honey in their storage cells to sustain them during the long winter. In very cold weather they form a tight cluster in the very centre of the hive, huddling together to insulate themselves against the cold.

6.10. A harmful insect: the housefly

Flies belong to the order of insects called the **Diptera** (*di:* two, *pteron:* wing), the members of which possess only one pair of wings. Over five thousand species of fly occur in Great Britain alone. The most common fly in our houses is *Musca domestica*, the housefly. It is important that we should know something of the life and habits of this animal, for it is responsible for the transmission of many diseases. These include cholera, typhoid, dysentery, infantile diarrhoea, leprosy, tuberculosis and poliomyelitis. These diseases are caused by micro-organisms such as bacteria and viruses. We shall see that the natural habits of the fly cause it to transfer these germs from infected persons to healthy ones.

6.11. The life-history of the housefly

a. Egg-laying

Being cold-blooded animals, flies are unable to remain active during the cold conditions of winter. Exactly how they spend this period is not fully known. The adult fly may well remain dormant in protected places within buildings, etc., but it is also possible that it overwinters as a dormant larva or pupa. The fly first becomes active in late spring, when egg-laying begins. The eggs are laid in batches of 100 to 150 in any moist, fermenting, organic matter, such as horse manure. They may also be laid in human faeces. Each egg is a whitish, sausage-shaped object, about 1 mm in length. Hatching occurs within a period of eight hours to three days, according to temperature. Eggs and larva are shown in Figure 6.15.

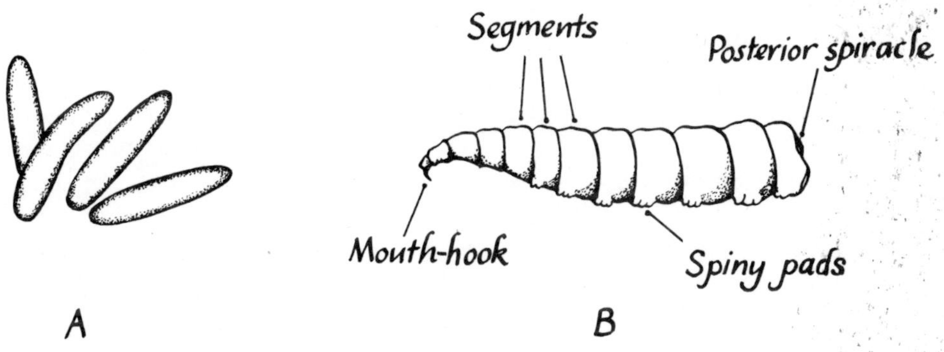

Figure 6.15 The housefly: (a) the eggs and (b) the larva

b. The larva

Each egg hatches into a minute, whitish larva or maggot, about 2 mm in length. Its body tapers considerably, the mouth being at the pointed end. There are twelve segments, the second and last bearing **spiracles**. The larva is limbless, and has none of the normal insect mouth-parts. Instead, the mouth bears a pair of sharp **hooks** which, with the aid of the **spiny pads** on the underside of the body, enable the larva to grip the surface as it wriggles along. The mouth-hooks are also used to tear the surface apart, and any liquid matter is then sucked into the mouth. Although there are no eyes, the larva is sensitive to light, and its burrowing constantly takes it away from the surface. Moulting occurs twice during its growth and, in warm weather, it will be fully grown in only forty-two hours.

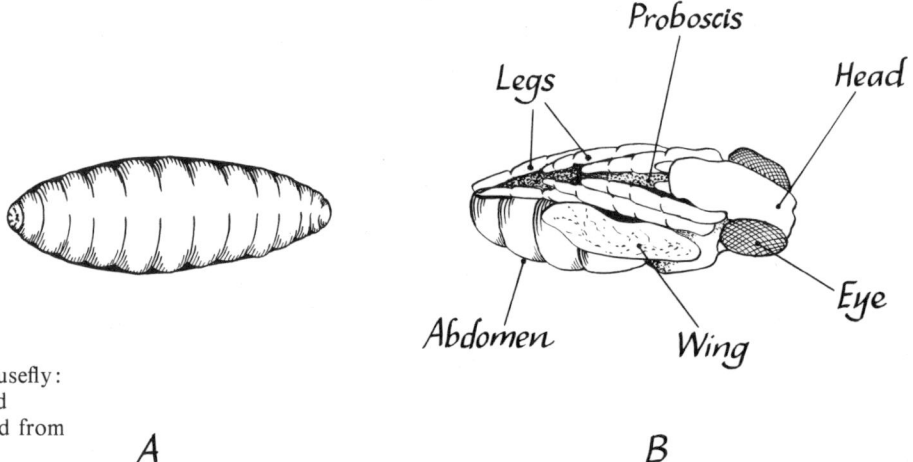

Figure 6.16 The housefly: (a) the puparium and (b) the pupa removed from the puparium

c. The pupa (see Figure 6.16)

Once it is fully grown, the larva moves to a drier and cooler place. Unlike most insect larvae, there is no final moult, but the larval cuticle is retained as a case, or **puparium**, around the pupa. The puparium is barrel-shaped, and dark reddish-brown in colour. Within four days the larval tissues have been broken down and those of the adult constructed. The fly then emerges from the puparium by forcing off one end. A special balloon-like sac on the head of the fly is repeatedly dilated and withdrawn; this puts pressure on the puparium, which eventually bursts open.

d. The adult or imago (see Figure 6.17)

When it first emerges, the body of the fly lacks colour, and is very shrunken. Within an hour it assumes its normal coloration, and the wings expand. In about fourteen days the new fly will itself be able

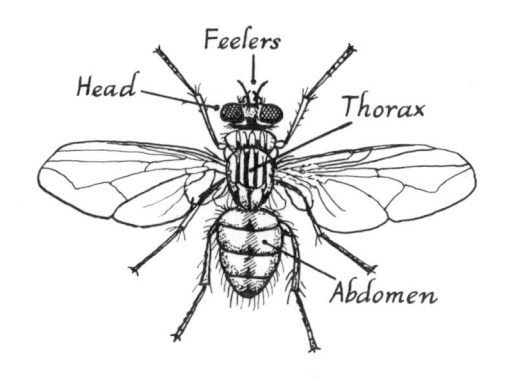

Figure 6.17 (left) The adult housefly

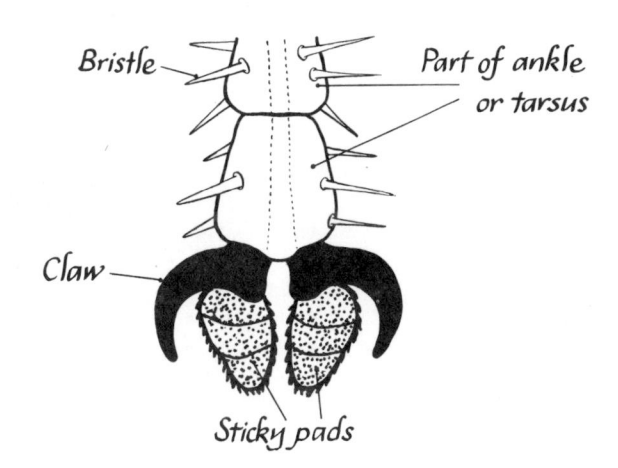

Figure 6.18 (above) The housefly: end of leg, showing claws and sticky pads

to lay eggs. Thus the whole life-cycle may be completed in three weeks, and there may be as many as nine generations in the year. Since each adult may lay several batches of eggs during her life, it is easy to understand why flies become so numerous as the summer season proceeds.

The wings of the fly correspond to the fore-wings of those insects that have two pairs of wings (for example, honey bee). The hind wings are represented by a pair of sensory flaps, called **halteres**, or balancers. During flight, these vibrate in time with the wings, and any disturbance in the line of flight will affect them. It has been shown that the presence of halteres is essential for controlled flight, and if they are cut off the fly will crash to the ground.

The legs of the fly are adapted to enable it to walk on surfaces of different types. Each leg ends in a pair of claws which can grip curtains, wallpaper and other similar soft surfaces. Between these claws are two sticky pads, which enable the fly to walk across very smooth surfaces, such as glass. The legs bear many bristles which are used to brush dust from the body (see Figure 6.18).

The fly has none of the cutting mouth-parts possessed by many insects, for its diet is entirely fluid. The fly feeds on many human foods, especially such foods as meat, milk, cheese, jam and fruit. It also feeds avidly on human excrement. The fly feeds by sucking up the food through a fleshy tube or proboscis, which is jointed halfway down, so that it may be retracted under the head when not in use. At the end of the proboscis are two fleshy lobes between which is the mouth. These lobes can be folded or straightened out, and have a number of grooves on them running towards the mouth. Thus, they act as gutters to deliver food to the mouth. When feeding, the fly dissolves solid food by vomiting saliva on to the surface of the food. The liquid food then runs up the proboscis to the mouth (see Figure 6.19).

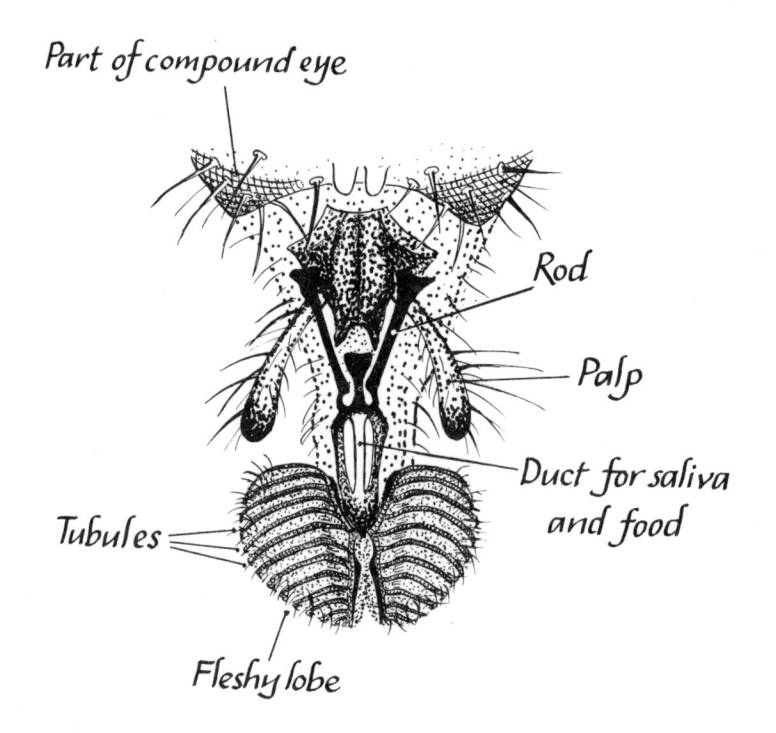

Figure 6.19 The mouth-parts of the adult housefly (front view)

6.12. Flies and disease

The transmission of disease by flies is due to their habit of feeding on excrement and other decaying matter, and on human foods. The faeces of an infected person may contain the germs causing disease, and these germs may be taken up by the fly in one of two ways. Firstly, they may be ingested during feeding, and if they are able to survive within the alimentary canal they may leave the body with the fly faeces or may be deposited as the fly regurgitates its food. Secondly, the germs may be carried on the hairs on the legs and body of the fly. Thus, if a fly then proceeds to land on human food, it may transfer the germs to it, either by bodily contact or through its excreta. It is possible to demonstrate this transference of micro-organisms by the following method.

Investigation 6a. The transference of micro-organisms by flies

Thoroughly sterilize two petri dishes (see Figure 6.20) by heating in an autoclave or pressure cooker (15 lb in^{-2} or 100 kN m^{-2} for fifteen minutes). Pour some sterilized nutrient agar into each dish.

Replace the lids quickly and allow the agar to set. The agar contains food for the growth of bacteria and other micro-organisms. Clip the wings from a housefly and allow it to walk across the agar in dish A, keeping the lid on while this is happening. Dish B is the control, the agar being left unexposed. After removing and killing the fly, leave both dishes in a warm place, or in an incubator at 37°C, for a day or two. Finally, observe the surface of the agar in each dish. Are there any colonies of bacteria in dish A? Do these patches appear in the control? Have any bacteria grown in the control? How do you explain these results?

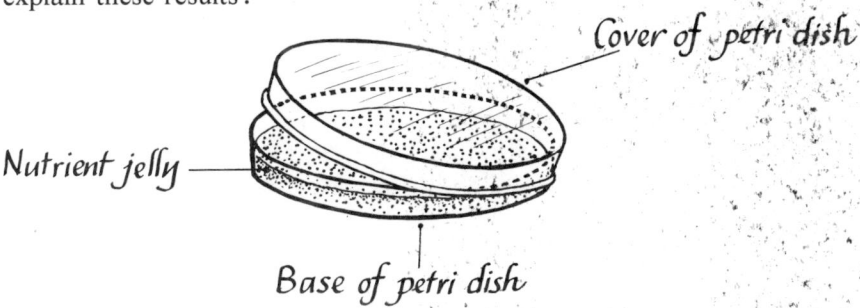

Figure 6.20 Dish used in Investigation 6a

The prevention of spread of disease by flies

This may be considered under three headings: food protection, killing adult flies and prevention of breeding.

Food protection. We have seen that germs may enter our bodies in food that has been contaminated by flies. Obviously, if this contamination can be prevented, the battle against disease may be won. No food should be left exposed to flies. Meat and milk should be covered with gauze, if no refrigerator is available. It is also of prime importance that flies should not be allowed access to human excreta.

Killing adult flies. Flies may be killed by swatting, trapping and by chemicals (insecticides). Swatting is the least desirable method, for the squashed body of the fly is still a source of disease organisms. Flies should never be swatted near food. Flies can be trapped with sticky fly-paper but, again, this is not a desirable method. It is far better to kill them with insecticides. Dead bodies of flies should, of course, be disposed of immediately, preferably by burning.

Prevention of breeding. Flies lay eggs in organic refuse, such as manure, compost, kitchen waste, etc. Manure and compost will, if stacked properly and covered by grass, generate enough heat to kill the fly eggs. Dustbins should have tightly fitting lids and should be sprayed with a fly-repellent. Wherever possible, refuse should be burnt.

Only by constant vigilance in our sanitary habits will we gain the upper hand against this very harmful insect, the housefly.

6.13. The mosquito

Mosquitoes, gnats and midges belong to the same group of insects as the housefly, namely the Diptera. Of the twenty-nine species of mosquito that occur in this country, only three are really common around our homes. These are as follows:

> *Culex pipiens:* the common gnat
> *Theobaldia annulata:* our largest mosquito
> *Anopheles maculipennis*

In tropical countries, mosquitoes of the genus **Anopheles** transmit the dreaded disease **malaria**. Until the Middle Ages malaria occurred in England, when it was known as ague. A study of the life and habits of mosquitoes has enabled man to wage war against malaria, but millions of people still die from the disease each year. The transmission of the disease is due to the practice of the female mosquito of supplementing her normal diet of nectar and fruit juices with meals of blood. The female *Culex* sucks the blood of birds, but the other two mosquitoes listed above will also suck human blood. It used to be thought that the female had to take a meal of blood before egg-laying. However, some mosquitoes have been found to lay a batch of eggs before blood-sucking has begun. Again, other mosquitoes occur in the Arctic where there can be little opportunity of obtaining blood.

6.14. The life-history of the mosquito

a. Egg-laying

Mosquitoes lay their eggs in any still water such as swamps, shallow ponds, rainwater butts, etc. The female *Culex* will lay some 200 eggs at one time, cementing each egg to the next to form a raft, about 5 mm across (see Figure 6.21a). Air trapped between the eggs causes the raft to float. The female *Anopheles*, on the other hand, lays her eggs separately, each egg having a pair of floats (see Figure 6.21b). Inside the egg the larva develops. After two or three days it hatches out by forcing off a cap from one end of the egg case.

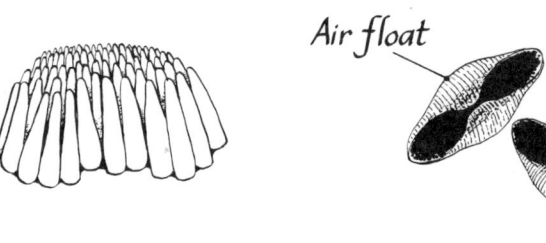

Figure 6.21 The eggs of mosquitoes: (a) *Culex* and (b) *Anopheles*

Figure 6.22 The larvae of mosquitoes: (a) *Culex* and (b) *Anopheles*

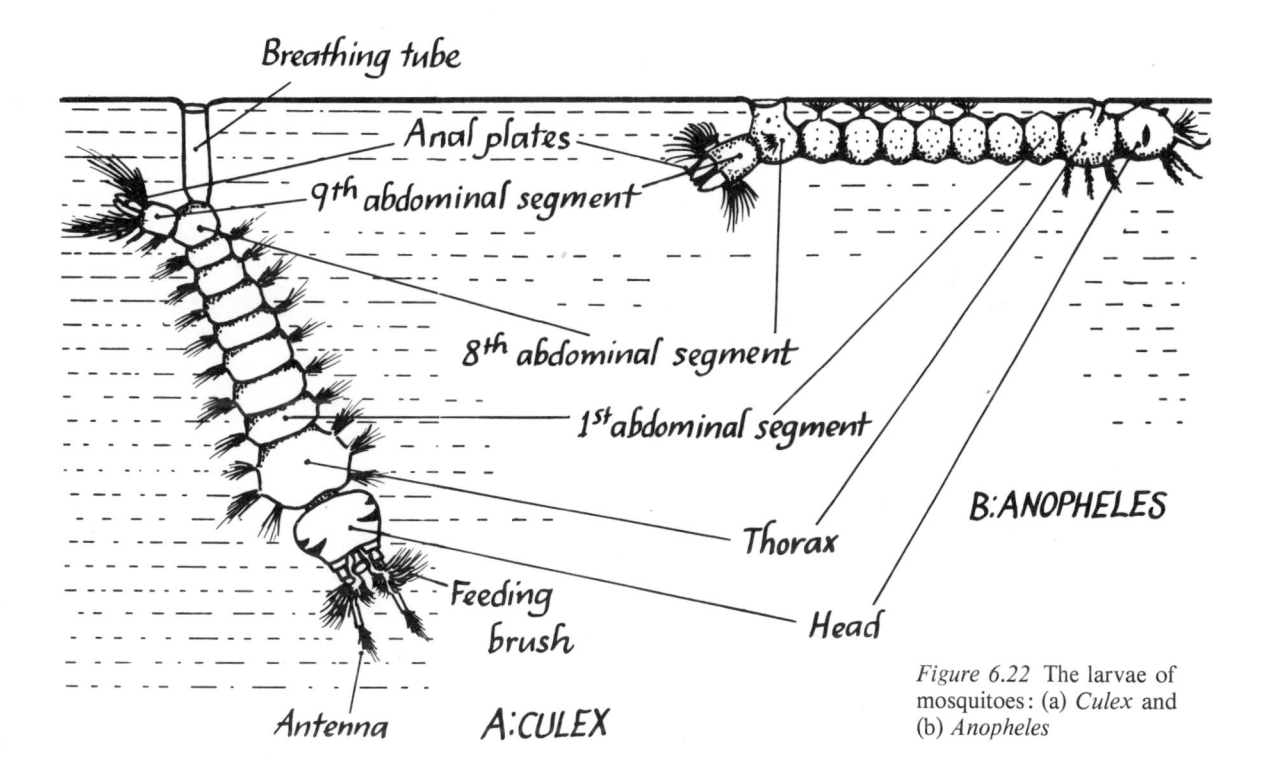

b. The larva

The mosquito larva is highly adapted for life in fresh water. Its structure is shown in Figure 6.22. Although it spends its life in the water, the larva is air-breathing. Attached to the eighth abdominal segment is a tube, containing two spiracles, through which air can enter the body. When the larva breathes it pushes the tube through the surface film of the water and hangs head downwards in the water. The larva feeds whilst it is breathing. The mouth-parts bear many bristles which constantly sweep the water and filter food particles from it. If the larva is disturbed, the entrance to the breathing tube is closed by five small flaps, which are greased to repel water, and the larva sinks from the surface. To reach the surface again, it swims upwards by wriggling its limbless body. Living in fresh water, one of the problems facing the larva is the steady loss of salts from the body by diffusion. It would seem that the anal plates reabsorb some of the lost salts.

The larva of *Anopheles* differs only in that it lies parallel to the surface of the water.

c. The pupa

The larva lives for about two to three weeks, during which time it moults three times. It undergoes a final moult to reveal the comma-shaped pupa (see Figure 6.23). Unlike most insect pupae, this is able to move by flicking its curved abdomen. It does not feed but hangs from the surface film, taking in air through a pair of trumpet-like tubes. If disturbed, the pupa jerks its abdomen, thus propelling itself downwards, after which it floats passively back to the surface. After a few days, the pupal case splits down the back, and the adult mosquito crawls out. For the first five minutes or so, during which the wings expand and harden, the adult uses the split pupal case as a raft. It then flies off.

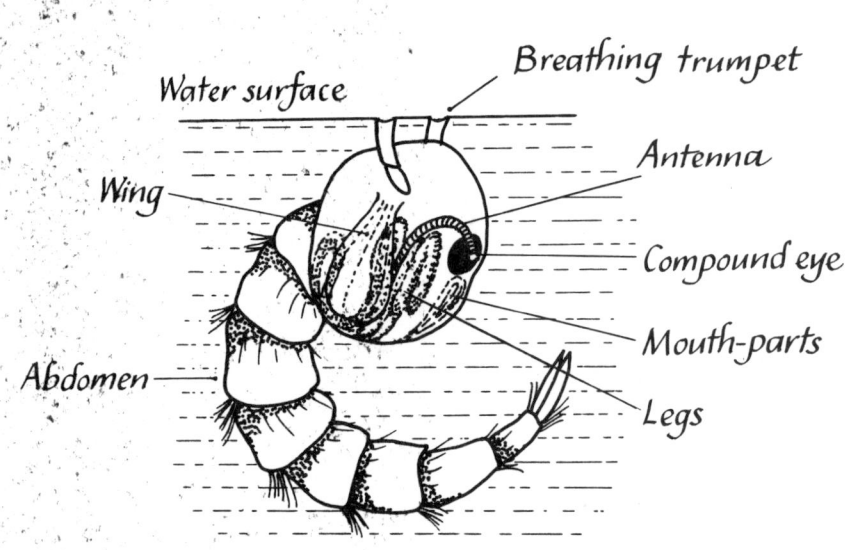

Figure 6.23 The pupa of a mosquito

d. The adult or imago

The structure of the female adult mosquito is shown in Figure 6.24. The body, legs and wings are all very slender. During flight the wings vibrate very rapidly, producing the high-pitched whine that you have, no doubt, heard on a warm summer's night heralding a probable 'bite'. The antennae differ in the two sexes. In the male they are very bushy, whilst in the female they are slender and thread-like. The mouth-parts of the female comprise a deeply grooved lower lip, or **labium**, which houses six needle-like **lancets**. One of these, the **labrum**, or upper lip, forms a tube for the uptake of blood, whilst another carries the salivary duct.

The process of taking a blood meal is as follows: the mosquito settles on the skin, so lightly that it is probably unperceived by the victim; the labium 'feels' across the surface of the skin, its lobes pinpointing a suitable point of entry; the lancets are thrust downwards, piercing the skin, and as this happens the labium is bent back; saliva, which contains a substance which prevents the blood from clotting, is passed down into the wound; blood is sucked up the labrum into the body of the insect. It will be seen from this description that we are not really 'bitten' by a mosquito, but punctured. It is not understood what causes the irritation of mosquito 'bites'.

The mouth-parts of the male mosquito are unable to pierce skin, and he has, therefore, to feed on nectar and fruit juices alone. In the autumn, the male *Culex* and *Anopheles* die but the female overwinters, hibernating on the walls of buildings. Some other mosquitoes pass the winter as larvae.

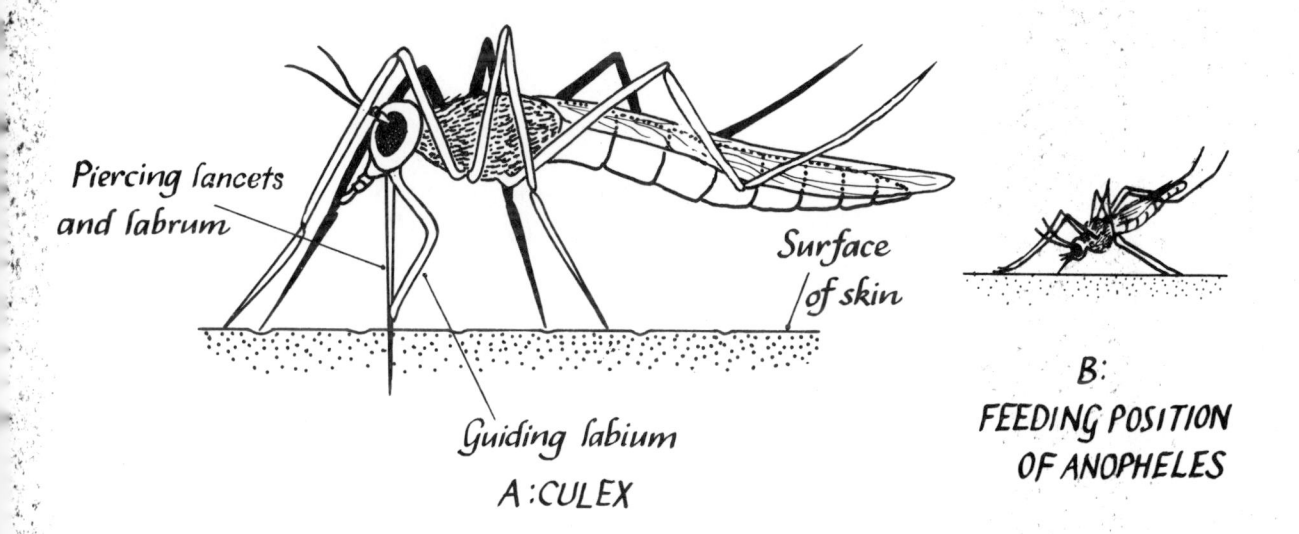

Figure 6.24 Female mosquitoes taking a meal of blood

6.15. Mosquitoes and malaria

Malaria is caused by a microscopic, protozoan animal, belonging to the genus **Plasmodium**. These animals multiply in the blood of humans and other vertebrates, such as birds, monkeys, etc. In humans the multiplication results in malarial fever, and, unless treatment is given, death ensues. If a mosquito takes blood from an infected person, the disease organisms continue their life-cycle within the body of the insect. Should a healthy person then be bitten, the malarial germs are passed into this person's blood with the saliva of the mosquito. More details of the disease, and the means used to control it, will be found in Book II, Chapter 16.

Test your understanding

1. List the three main regions of the insect body and, against each, name the structures attached to that region.
2. How do the wings of butterflies and moths differ from those of other insects?
3. What do butterflies feed on, and how do they obtain this nourishment?
4. Write down five important features of the body of a caterpillar.

5. What changes occur when a caterpillar becomes a butterfly, and what name is given to this transformation?
6. What do we mean when we say that the honey bee is (a) a social insect and (b) an example of division of labour?
7. What are the duties of (a) the queen bee, (b) the worker bee and (c) the drone?
8. Describe the composition of a swarm and how it establishes a new hive.
9. Mention three important ways in which the larva of a honey bee differs from that of a butterfly.
10. Describe what happens on a nuptial flight.
11. Describe how a beehive overwinters.
12. Name three diseases transmitted by houseflies.
13. Explain the various ways in which disease organisms may be transmitted by flies.
14. Describe how a housefly feeds.
15. Suggest five ways by which we can prevent the transmission of disease by flies.
16. What disease is transmitted by mosquitoes, and how is this transmission brought about?
17. Why is it incorrect to say that we have been 'bitten' by a mosquito?

Chapter 7

Animals with Backbones

7.1. The general features of chordate animals

Look at the animals shown in Figure 7.1. These are all members of one phylum of animals, called the **Chordata**. Why are we able to place these animals in the same group? What features have they in common? At first sight they do not appear to be much alike. The lancelet, trout and dogfish all possess fins, but the lizard and man have limbs. The chaffinch differs from the others in that it possesses wings. Again, whilst the lancelet, trout and dogfish breathe by gills, the other animals have lungs. The surfaces of the animals are, apparently, quite different. The lancelet has a smooth, thin skin, with no scales. The trout and the dogfish have a scaly skin, but, on closer examination, it is evident that the scales are of different types. The frog's skin lacks scales, and is very thin and loose-fitting, feeling moist to the touch. The lizard is quite different, for its skin is very dry, and is armoured with bony plates. Feathers protrude from the skin of the chaffinch, whilst the boy's skin has a covering of hair.

It seems, therefore, that whatever common features are shared by these seven animals, they do not show externally. A study of their internal structure is more rewarding. Three important, common features are then apparent:

   a. There is a backbone or **vertebral column**.
   b. The **nerve cord** is dorsal and tubular.
   c. The pharynx or throat has **gill slits**.

These structures are so important that we must consider each in a little more detail.

a. The vertebral column

All chordates have a skeleton which is internal, that is, an **endoskeleton** (see Figures 7.2 and 7.3). This contrasts with the exoskeleton we have seen in such animals as insects and molluscs. The main part of the endoskeleton of chordates is the backbone or vertebral column. In the developing chordate, the vertebral column begins life as a stiff rod, the **notochord**, formed from a gristly

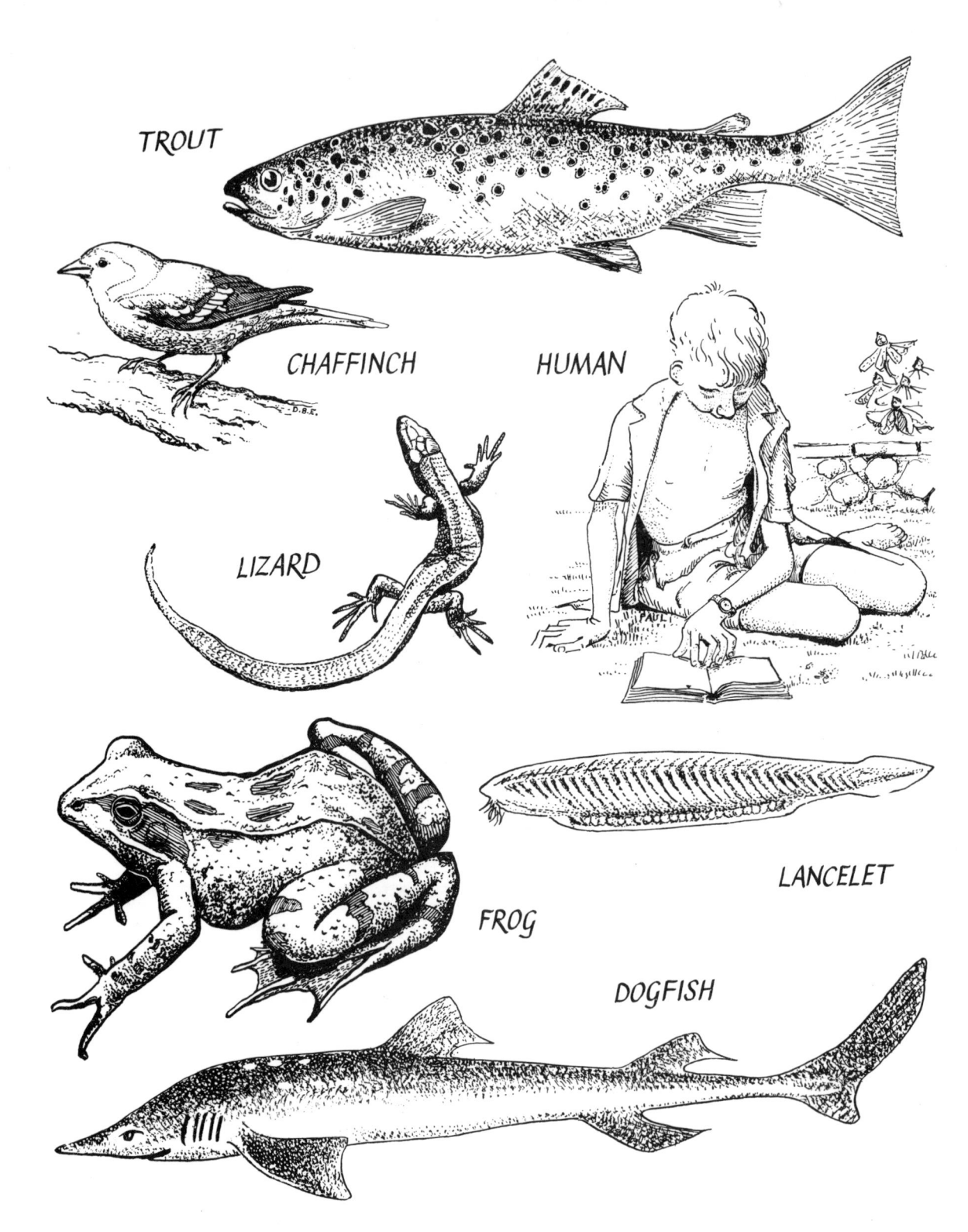

Figure 7.1 Various chordates

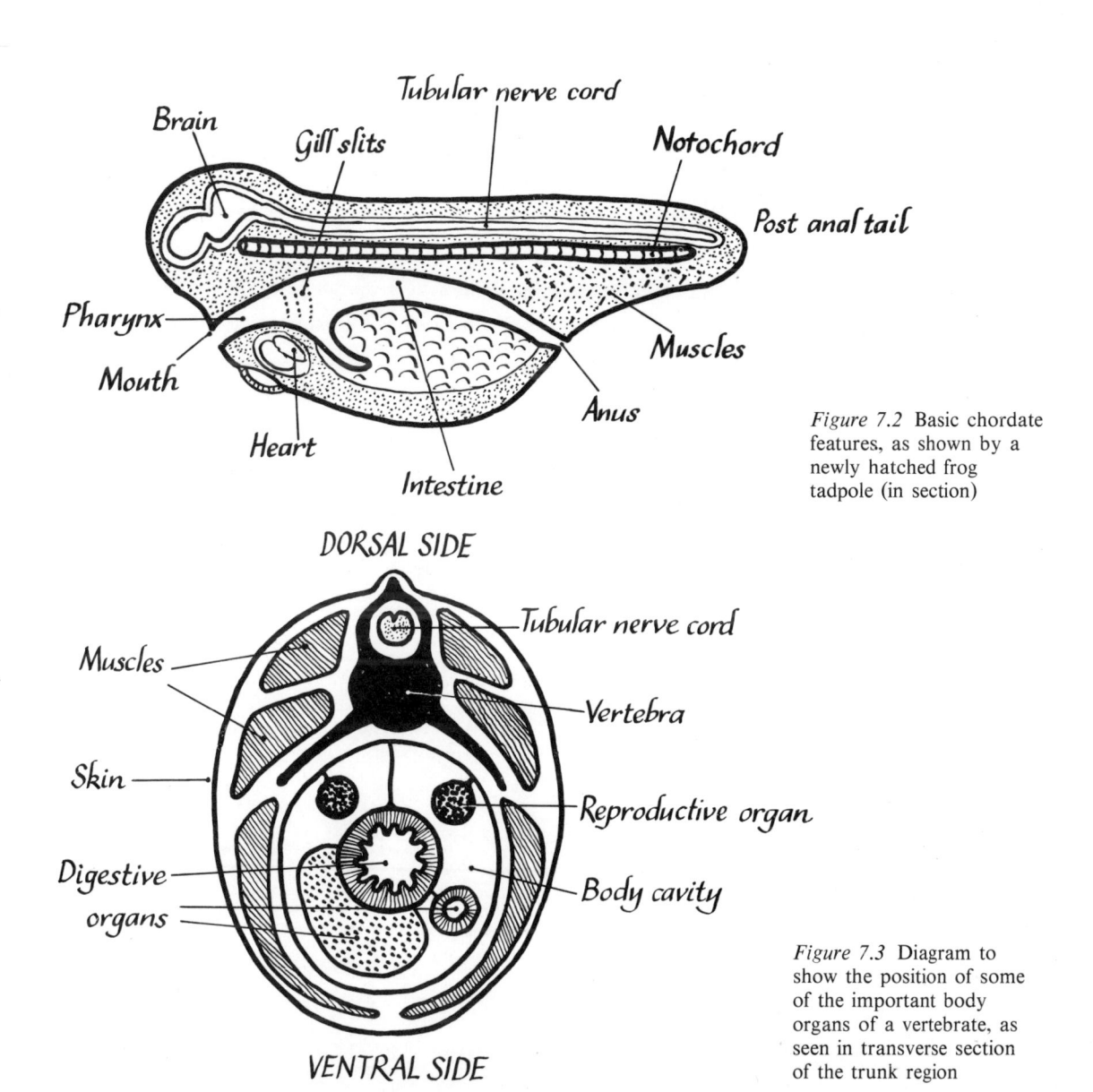

Figure 7.2 Basic chordate features, as shown by a newly hatched frog tadpole (in section)

Figure 7.3 Diagram to show the position of some of the important body organs of a vertebrate, as seen in transverse section of the trunk region

substance. It is flexible, but sturdy, as is a ruler. In the lancelet, the notochord persists into the adult, but this is unusual in chordates. In most members of the group the notochord becomes replaced by a series of bones called **vertebrae**, which come to surround the nerve cord. Most chordates, therefore, are also **vertebrates**.

b. The nerve cord

In chordates, the nerve cord develops above the notochord; in other words, it is dorsal in position. Invertebrate animals have a ventral nerve cord (see Figure 5.2). The chordate nerve cord is tubular, and is expanded in the head to form a **brain**. The brain is

89

protected by the part of the skeleton that we call the skull (cranium), whilst, as we have seen, the nerve cord is protected by the vertebrae. The nerve cord and vertebrae are referred to as the **spine.**

c. The gill slits

If you examine a dogfish, you will see that on the sides of the head and just behind the eyes are a series of slits. It is possible to pass a rod into the mouth and out of the slits, which lie in the wall of the throat, or **pharynx**. The trout has similar slits, but they are covered by a bony flap. Lancelets have a pharynx which is so perforated by gill slits that it resembles a basket. Now you may well be saying to yourself 'but I haven't got gill slits'. This is true, and in this respect you resemble the adult frog, lizard and chaffinch. However, in all these animals, including man, gill slits do develop in the **embryo** (before hatching or birth). In the frog, the gill slits function in the tadpole, but, in the lizard, chaffinch and man they are never functional.

7.2. Fishes

Investigation 7a. Types of fish

For this investigation you will need a dogfish and a whiting or herring. If these are not available, examine Figure 7.4.

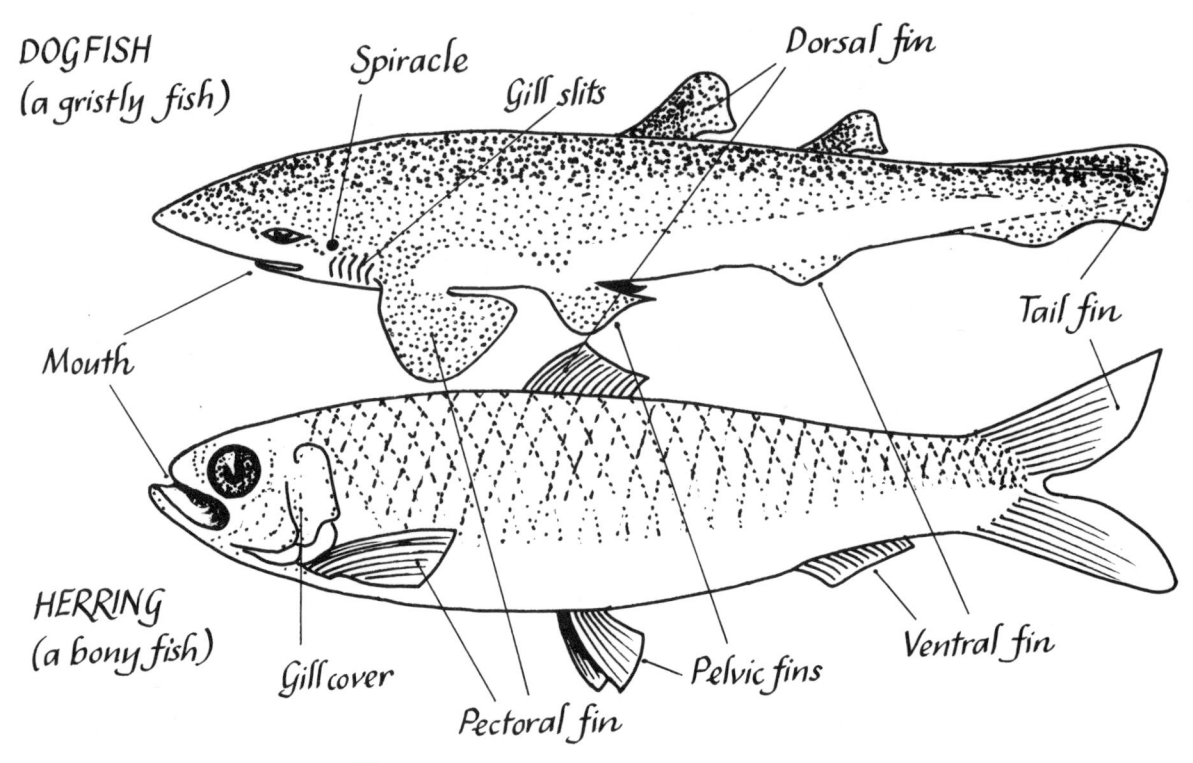

Figure 7.4 Two fish, for comparison

Place the animals side by side and examine them closely. Are they similar in appearance? What are the main differences between them? To help you think of these differences, here is a table for you to copy and complete. The first line is done for you.

TABLE 7.1. COMPARING THE FEATURES OF THE DOGFISH AND WHITING

Feature	Dogfish	Whiting
1. Appearance of gill slits	There are five visible gill slits.	Gill slits are obscured by bony flap.
2. Feel of skin		
3. Position of mouth		
4. Shape of tail fin		
5.		
6.		

For features 5 and 6 insert any other differences that you can see.

I think you will agree that these two fish show considerable differences. Because of this, zoologists place them in separate classes within the phylum Chordata. The dogfish is a member of the class **Chondrichthyes**, the gristly fishes. The skeleton in these fish is formed not of bone, but of **cartilage** or gristle. The best known member of the group is the shark, one of the most feared animals in the sea. The skate is a flattened form of gristly fish. There are no members of the group living in fresh water. The whiting and the herring, on the other hand, are placed in the class **Osteichthyes**, the bony fishes, for here the skeleton is formed of true bone. The group contains freshwater fish such as the roach, perch, carp and pike, whilst the cod, mackerel, halibut and herring are examples of marine forms. Plaice are flattened bony fish, just as skate are flattened gristly fish. There is an interesting difference in the direction of flattening of these two. See if you can find out what it is.

There are more species of bony fish than of any other class of chordates. Each species is adapted to its own particular way of life; that is, for where it lives, how it feeds, breeds and avoids its enemies. When you look at a fish, try to think how it is suited to its way of life. Some bony fish are shown in Figure 7.5.

7.3. Locomotion in fishes

Watch a fish moving in an aquarium. How does it propel itself? Notice the flexible tail flicking from side to side. If you cannot see

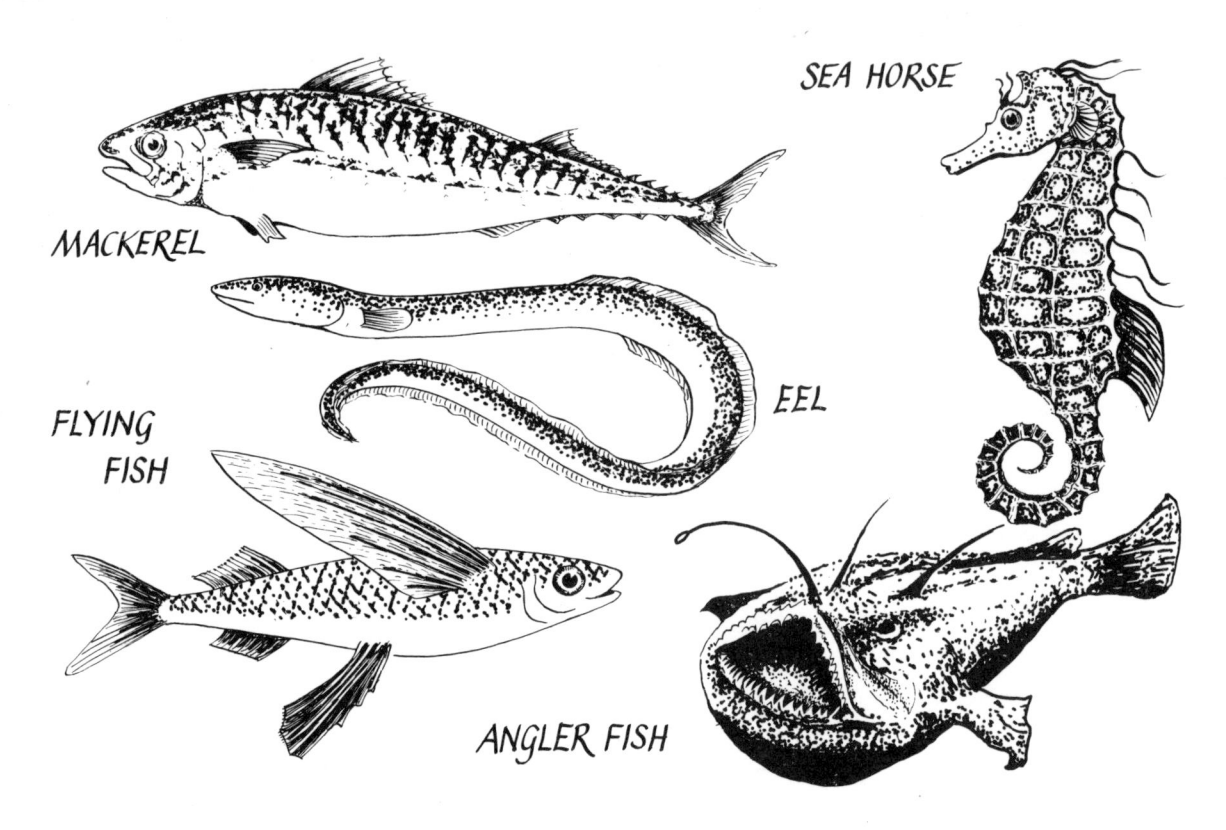

Figure 7.5 Various bony fish

how this lateral movement of the tail can cause the fish to move forward, look at Figure 7.6 and remember that this method of sculling a boat involves moving the oar from side to side.

Notice that, just as the oar ends in a flattened blade, so the tail of the fish ends in a broadly flattened **tail fin**. Think of the purpose of the blade and of the tail fin.

Figure 7.6 Moving an oar from side to side causes the boat to move foward. Movement of the fish tail causes the fish to move in a similar way

What is the purpose of the other fins of the fish? We can best illustrate the answer to this question by performing a simple investigation.

Investigation 7b. Establishing the purpose of the flight of a dart

For this investigation you will need a dartboard and a dart from which the flights can be removed (see Figure 7.7).

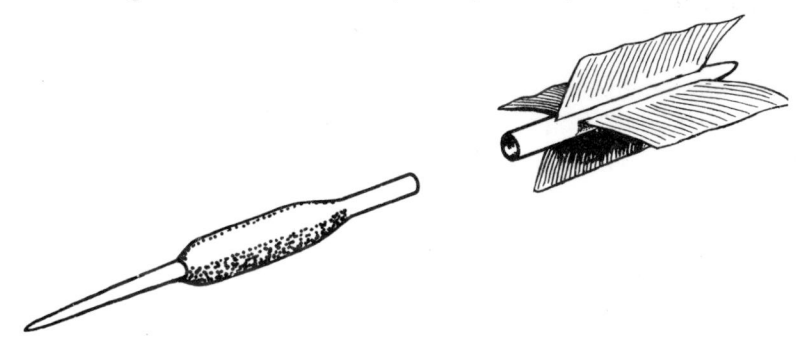

Figure 7.7 Dart with removable flights

Remove the flights and throw the dart at the dartboard. Which end of the dart arrived at the board first? Repeat the test several times. Now replace the flights, and again throw the dart several times. Try throwing the dart, flights first. Come to a conclusion as to the purpose of the flights.

A fish without its fins would be like a dart without its flights. We say that the fins **stabilize** the fish, so that it stays on course, and does not pitch, roll or yaw. **Pitching** is the tendency for the tail to rise and the head to sink, or vice versa. **Rolling** is a corkscrew motion of the body, whilst **yawing** is the tendency for the tail to catch up with the head. Just as a dart has vertical and horizontal flights, so the fish has vertical fins (dorsal and ventral) and horizontal fins (pectoral and pelvic).

7.4. Other adaptations shown by fishes

Fishes have existed for at least 300 million years, and they could not have survived if they were not well adapted for life in the water. We have seen how they are adapted for locomotion. Some of their other adaptations will now be considered.

a. Prevention from sinking

Fishes are denser than water and, therefore, tend to sink. Bony fish prevent this by having a **swim-bladder**, a gas-filled tube inside the trunk. You have, no doubt, seen this bladder as a silvery streak inside herrings, pilchards or sardines. Gristly fish have no swim-bladder. They keep themselves up rather as an aeroplane does. Water striking the wing-like pectoral fins is deflected downwards, just as an aeroplane wing deflects air downwards. Deflection of the water causes an upthrust which raises the head end of the fish. As the tail lashes sideways, the unequal lobes of the tail fin cause an upthrust at this end of the body. It is interesting that the two types of fish have different solutions to the problem of sinking.

b. Streamlining

Just as a dart is shaped so that it flies easily through the air, so a fish is streamlined to enable it to pass easily through the water. The body is smoothly tapered at each end and all projecting parts have their leading edges curved backwards (see Figure 7.4).

c. Camouflage

The coloration of a fish depends on the depth of the water it inhabits. Deep-dwelling forms have dark upper surfaces to blend with the dark sea-bed beneath them. Forms living nearer the surface are dark on the upper side but light on the lower. When viewed from underneath, they are difficult to see against the brightly lit, surface waters, and when viewed from above they blend with the dark appearance of the water. Some fish have a patterned coloration which helps them to blend well with the weeds, rocks or corals around them. Other fish, such as the plaice, are able to change colour to match the sea-bed on which they are lying.

d. Respiration

Fish are able to breathe under water because they have **gills**. Each gill is a comb-like structure, comprising rows of delicate finger-like filaments supported by a bony gill-bar. Water is taken into the mouth of the fish and passed out of the gill slits. The delicate gill filaments are bathed by this current of water and absorb oxygen from it, also passing out waste carbon dioxide into it.

e. Sensitivity

The **eyes** of fishes are placed on the side of the head, giving almost all-round vision. Because the eyes are placed in this way, the fish is not able to judge distance very well. The **ears** are embedded in the head and serve mainly as balance organs. In addition, along the sides of the body and on the head are a series of **lateral-line organs**. These are sensitive to vibration and are so named because, in many fish, their presence is indicated by a distinct line along the side of the body. The organs are useful when the fish is swimming in a shoal, for they pick up vibrations from neighbouring fish. The organ of **smell** is very well developed in fishes, especially in sharks and other fish which hunt their prey.

7.5. Conquest of the land: amphibians

It seems certain that life first arose in the water and, today, the simplest forms of life are still aquatic. We have seen that fishes are highly adapted for life in the water, yet the highest vertebrates, the reptiles, birds and mammals, are land animals. When did this conquest of the land occur? What were the earliest land vertebrates like, and why did they forsake their watery home? These questions have interested zoologists for a long time.

Figure 7.8 The Australian lung-fish

Fossils of strange fishes have been found in rocks which are 280 million years old. They were like other fish in shape, but bore limbs instead of fins. They also possessed a simple lung, indicating that they were probably able to breathe air. A few survivors of this strange group of **lung-fish** still exist in Australia, Africa and South America (see Figure 7.8).

Lung-fish occur in tropical areas where rivers and lakes are liable to dry up. When this happens, lung-fish have a better chance of survival than ordinary fish, for they can live for a while in the dry mud, breathing air. Alternatively, they may be able to use their limbs to move over land for short distances, possibly enabling them to reach water again. We see, therefore, how the first land vertebrates might have arisen from a group of animals intent on getting back into the water!

From these lung-fish arose the first **amphibians**, animals able to live in water or on land. In time, the limbs and lungs improved, and many different forms of amphibians dwelt on the earth during the Carboniferous era. This was the period, some 250 million years ago, when coal was formed. Amphibians dominated the wet swamps, marshes and forests of those ancient times. Some reached $1\frac{1}{2}$ metres in length. As they developed more forms, some became adapted

Spotted salamander

Tree frog

Crested newt

Figure 7.9 Modern amphibians

more to life on land, whilst others returned to the water to escape competition. Eventually, amphibians became almost extinct when they came into competition with the reptiles. Today, few species exist, the main forms being the frogs, toads, newts and salamanders (see Figure 7.9). They are mostly small animals, but the Giant Salamander of Japan is almost 2 metres in length.

The conquest of the land involved changes other than the development of lungs and limbs. A stronger skeleton was required, since land animals do not have water to support them. Strong muscles had to develop, to enable the animal to raise itself from the ground. A skin which was resistant to drying was also essential. Look at Figure 7.10 and notice how the fish form has given way to the compact land form of the amphibian.

You will be reminded of the ancestry of amphibians if you watch the movement of a newt on land. When moving slowly, it raises itself on its legs, but when frightened and moving rapidly it 'swims on land', curving its body like a fish, with the limbs hardly touching the ground (see Figure 7.11).

When we look at amphibians, therefore, we must remember that they are survivors of a very important period in the history of animals. All amphibians are tied to the water, for they are unable to breed on land.

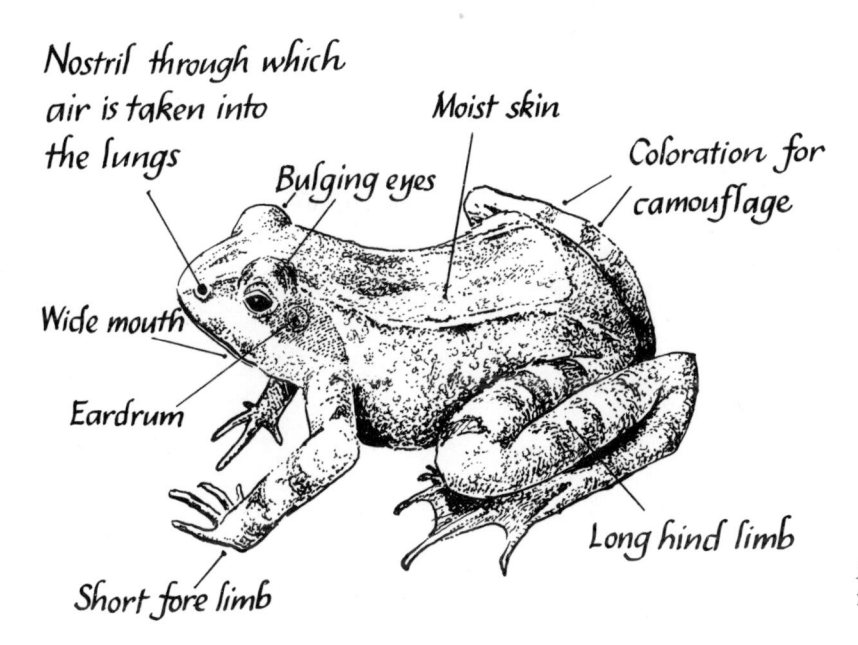

Figure 7.10 Terrestrial features of the frog

7.6. Reptiles

Reptiles differ from amphibians in that they are not only able to live on land, but also to breed there. This is because they lay shelled eggs in which the developing embryo is surrounded by membranes enclosing a pool of water. (In a few reptiles, however, the eggs develop inside the female and the young are born alive.) Unlike amphibians, therefore, reptiles do not have to live near water, and, in fact, many reptiles inhabit very dry situations, such as deserts. Such

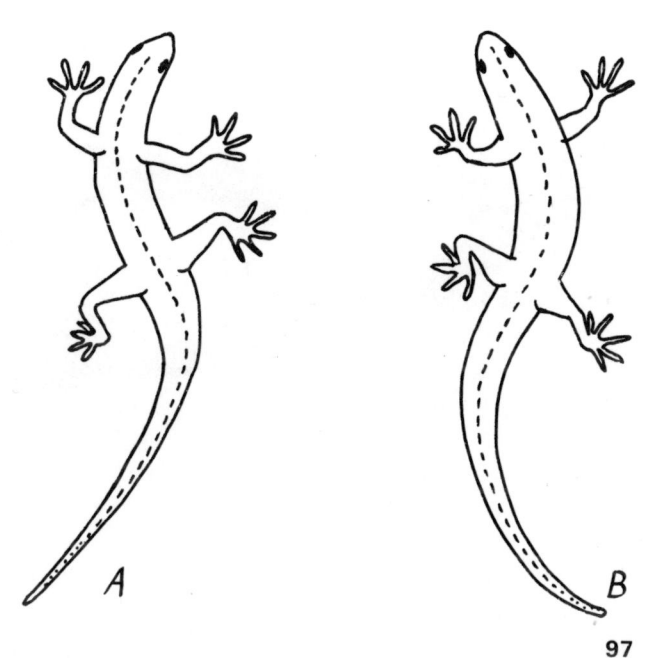

Figure 7.11 A newt 'swimming on land'

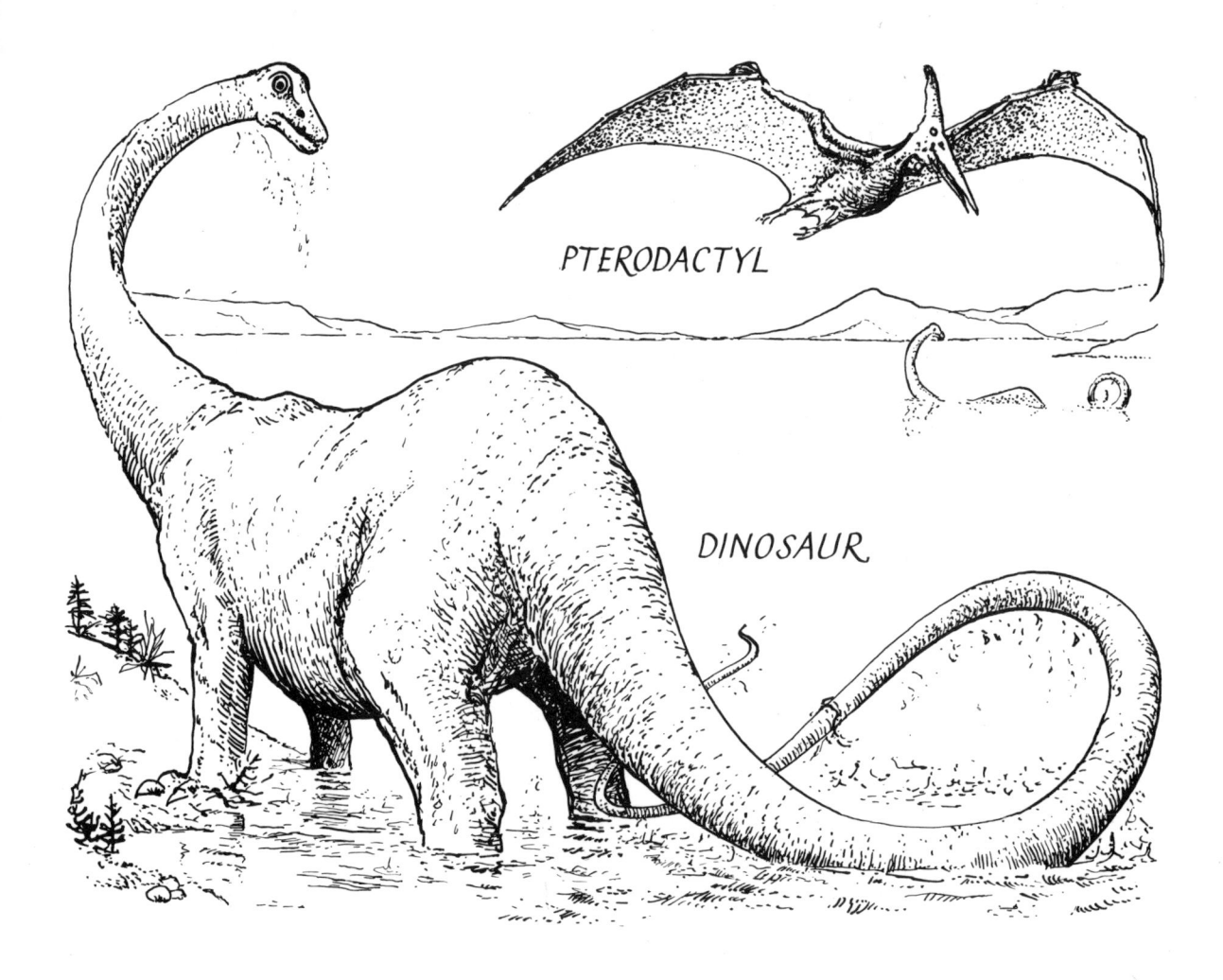

Figure 7.12 Ancient reptiles

reptiles are able to save or conserve water, which is a valuable commodity to them. The skin is dry and covered with scales or bony plates. Most reptiles, like amphibians, are tetrapods, that is, they have four limbs.

Reptiles arose from amphibians, and dominated the earth during the **Age of Reptiles**, between 200 and 140 million years ago. At this time plant food must have been very plentiful, and reptiles increased both in number of forms and in body size. On land, the **Dinosaurs** were the largest animals the world has ever known. One dinosaur, **Diplodocus**, was 25 metres (80 feet) long and weighed some 50 800 kilogrammes (50 tons). This animal probably lived partly immersed in water, since otherwise its enormous weight would have prevented movement. Another great group of reptiles, the **Ichthyosaurs**, returned to the water, again producing very large creatures. The third group, the **Pterodactyls**, took to the air, and were the world's first flying vertebrates. All these animals became extinct at least 70 million years ago, probably because the climate became colder and they were unable to compete with the warm-blooded birds and mammals. Some ancient reptiles are shown in Figure 7.12.

Modern reptiles (see Figure 7.13)

Today, most reptiles inhabit the warmer regions of the earth, but a few species do live in temperate countries such as ours. They live

Figure 7.13 Modern reptiles

successfully alongside birds and mammals. The **tortoises** are a link with the past, for their form reminds us of ancient reptiles. Their short bodies are heavily armoured with bony plates covered with horny shell. The weight of this exoskeleton makes them slow-moving animals. When water can take some of the weight, as in the **turtles**, they can be more active.

In all reptilian groups there has been a tendency for aquatic forms to develop. It should be remembered, however, that although they may live in water, reptiles still breathe air, and must lay their eggs on land. The **crocodiles** and **alligators** are further examples of reptiles that have returned to the water.

The most modern and advanced reptiles are the **lizards** and **snakes**. The many forms of lizard inhabit various situations. Apart from those on land, there are burrowing, tree-dwelling, aerial and aquatic forms. The famous iguana reaches 2 metres in length. An interesting lizard is the chameleon, inhabiting the forests of Africa and India. Its skin is able to change colour rapidly to match its surroundings. The eyes work independently, looking in different directions, and the animal can suddenly eject its long, sticky tongue, to catch insects. Without doubt, this is one of the strangest living creatures.

Snakes are highly advanced reptiles that have developed a unique method of locomotion. There are no limbs; instead the snake 'rows' itself along on its ribs, which have been considerably extended. Snakes kill their prey either by biting with their poisonous fangs, as in the vipers and rattlesnake, or by crushing, as in the boa constrictor and pythons. Some snakes have returned to the water. Only three types of snake occur naturally in the British Isles: the grass snake, the smooth snake and the viper or adder. Only the last of these is poisonous. It is an interesting fact that all snakes are deaf. It is the movement of the snake-charmer, and not the music, that charms the snake!

7.7. Birds

The problems of flight have been solved in four groups of animals, namely insects, pterodactyls, birds and bats. In each case the structures used in flying are different. Basically, in order to fly an animal must be light, have a large surface area compared with its weight, and have powerful muscles. No one can doubt that birds have thoroughly mastered the problems of the air. The skeleton is very light and the wings present a large surface area. Powerful flight muscles attach to the wings and anchor on the breast-bone. These muscles are the breast meat of the chicken. Since the fore-limbs have been converted to wings, birds are **bipedal** creatures.

Figure 7.14 Diversity among birds

Features of birds (see Figure 7.14)

All birds have **feathers**: any animal that has feathers is a bird. Apart from their use in flying, feathers insulate the body against heat loss. Birds are warm-blooded animals; in other words, their bodies have an almost constant temperature, day and night, summer and winter. Being such active animals, the muscles are constantly producing heat, and the feathers help to retain this heat. In very hot weather, birds are not as efficient as mammals at getting rid of excess heat, for they are unable to sweat.

Compared with the size of an adult bird, the eggs are very large. This is because the egg must contain all the materials required for the full development of the bird, a larval stage being impossible. There is abundant yolk and, as in reptiles, the embryo is surrounded firstly by a watery sac, and then by a hard shell. Birds are more advanced than reptiles in their breeding behaviour, for they build nests and give their young **parental care**. Birds have well-developed brains and good eyesight.

Birds are an easy group to recognize, for the body form does not change to any great extent in the various groups. The parts of the body, however, show interesting adaptations to different ways of life. This variation occurs in the wings, plumage, feet and beaks.

EAGLE - flesh eater

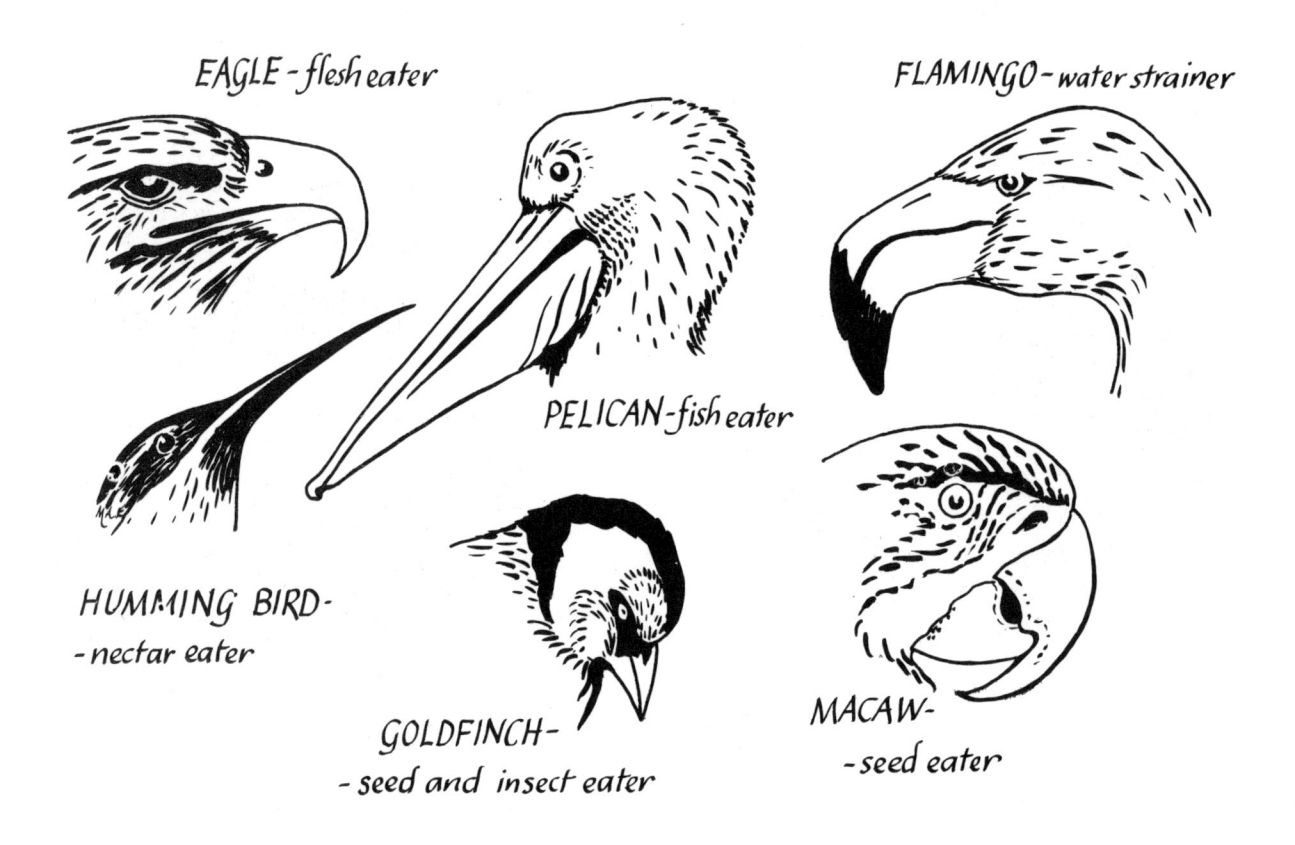

FLAMINGO - water strainer

PELICAN - fish eater

HUMMING BIRD - nectar eater

GOLDFINCH - seed and insect eater

MACAW - seed eater

Figure 7.15 Birds' beaks are adapted to deal with various types of food

As an example, some bird beaks are shown in Figure 7.15. No bird has teeth, and the beak has to be adapted to deal with various types of food.

History

Birds arose from reptiles, over 100 million years ago, but we know very little about how this occurred. Few fossils have been found, possibly because the bird skeleton is easily crushed. It seems likely that a running form of reptile developed first, with powerful back legs. In some way, its scaly front legs became feathered wings and it was able to soar into low trees. A period of gliding from tree to tree was followed by true flapping flights. These changes must have taken millions of years to occur.

Not all birds are able to fly. The emu and the cassowary of Australia, the kiwi of New Zealand, the rhea of South America and the ostrich of Africa are all examples of flightless birds. Naturally, they have been able to develop a greater body size than flying forms, from which they probably developed. They are unable to survive fierce competition with land mammals; hence their confinement to countries such as Australia and New Zealand.

7.8. Mammals

Finally, in our survey of the vertebrates, we come to the group which is the most advanced, the mammals. They have five important features in which they differ from the reptiles and birds:

a. The body bears a covering of **hair**. Apart from the general body fur, this has many specialized forms, such as eyelashes, cat whiskers, hedgehog spines, and horse and zebra tails. Hair is only found in mammals.

b. Like birds, mammals are warm-blooded, but, unlike birds, they possess **sweat glands** to cool themselves when overheated. Being warm-blooded, some mammals are able to live in the colder parts of the earth, including the Arctic and Antarctic.

c. The embryo of the mammal is retained inside the mother's womb, where it is nourished through an organ called the **placenta**. When it is born it is quite advanced in development.

d. After birth, the young are fed on **milk** from special **mammary glands**. The word 'mammal' comes from 'mamma', which refers to the teat from which the young animal sucks milk.

e. Mammals have very good **brains**, and are the most intelligent of all animals.

Unusual mammals

What we have said above regarding the reproduction of mammals applies to the vast majority of the class, but two variations do exist. The **Monotremes**, namely the duck-billed platypus and spiny anteater (*Echidna*) of Australia, do not produce their young alive, but lay eggs. The second strange group are the **Marsupials**, the pouched mammals of Australia and South America. This group includes the kangaroos, wallabies, koala bears and opossums. The young are born at a very early stage in development—in the opossum after only eight days, and in the kangaroo after thirty-nine days of growth. Development is completed in a pouch, which is a deep intucking in the mother's skin, housing the teats.

7.9. Diversity among mammals

Although mammals have the common features that we have listed, they show many differences in body form (see Figure 7.16). If you compare a mouse and an elephant; a lion and a whale; a squirrel and a giraffe; you will realize how diverse mammals have become.

History

Mammals arose from reptiles, but, since the features by which we distinguish them are not recognizable in a fossil, it is hard to say

Figure 7.16 Diversity among mammals

when this occurred. Mammals were present during the great age of dinosaurs as timid, insignificant creatures, probably eating insects and worms. As conditions changed and the reptiles declined, mammals came into their own, and increased in number and variety. Eventually, they replaced the reptiles as the dominant life-form, a position they have held ever since. The story of mammals culminated with the origin of man. His ability to use his hands, his upright posture, keen brain and eyesight, all suggest an ancestry in tree-dwelling forms, which also gave rise to the monkeys and apes.

Test your understanding

1. What is meant by a vertebrate?
2. What are gill slits and which animals possess them as adults?
3. Explain five features by which you can distinguish a bony fish from a gristly fish.
4. Name three examples of bony fish and three examples of gristly fish.
5. What have the plaice and skate in common? How do they differ?
6. Which part of a fish is the main organ of propulsion?
7. What is the purpose of the median (dorsal and ventral) fins?
8. How does a bony fish prevent itself from sinking?
9. Why are the eyes of the fish placed on the side of the head?
10. What is the purpose of the lateral-line organs?
11. Explain how the first land vertebrates may have arisen.
12. What is an amphibian, and what are the main types alive today?
13. Which features of the frog suit it for life on land?
14. What are dinosaurs, and why did they become extinct?
15. Name five modern reptiles that live in the water.
16. In what respects is the chameleon an unusual animal?
17. What are the three basic requirements of any flying animal?
18. Name the four different groups of flying animal.
19. Which animals are warm-blooded, and what does this mean?
20. How are birds more advanced in their reproduction than reptiles?
21. Draw the feet of as many different birds as you can, so as to show adaptations to different ways of life. Under each sketch, state the nature of the adaptation.
22. Why are mammals so called?
23. Make a list of five important features of mammals.
24. In what respects are the duck-billed platypus and kangaroo unusual mammals?
25. What features possessed by man point to a tree-dwelling ancestor?

Chapter 8

The Plant World: Plants without Flowers

8.1. From the past

Ever since plant life first appeared on the earth, perhaps 3 000 million years ago, it has been *evolving* from small, simple forms to the large, complex plants of today. During this process of **evolution**, plants have not just become larger and more complicated, they have become specially adapted to the particular conditions under which they live.

As the climatic and other conditions have changed on the earth during the last 3 000 million years, so has the plant life. On many occasions successful forms of vegetation were cut off in their prime as conditions changed, and they were no longer able to survive in the new conditions.

Life probably began in water, and the first plants were completely aquatic. During the evolutionary struggle, plants as well as animals have slowly emerged from the water to colonize the land.

What were these first plants like? Obviously we cannot study them, as they have been extinct for many millions of years. Their fossils are not very convincing because, unlike animals with bones and shells, they had no hard parts to be preserved. The best way of answering this question is to look at some of the simple plants growing in water, the home of the first plants.

8.2. The algae

Many of the simple aquatic plants now living have no roots, stems or leaves; nor do they have flowers or fruits. They form a vast group of plants which we call the **algae**. They are primary producers in many complex food-webs in lakes, rivers and oceans.

The gamete-producing structures of the algae consist only of a simple cell. This means that the developing gametes, the eggs and sperms, are only protected by a single cell wall. If these plants were exposed to the air they would rapidly dry out and the gametes would become desiccated and die. This is one reason why this vast group of simple plants, the algae, are largely restricted to life in water.

Investigation 8a. To examine a collection of freshwater algae

Take some jam jars and collect water containing green plant life from a number of localities, such as a small pond, a lake, a stream or ditch, a water butt, cattle trough and a gutter. Ignore the large, obviously rooted plants and those with flowers, but collect any 'slime' from the surface of the water and also 'green water' from puddles.

1. Back in the laboratory, examine the plants you have collected. In most cases you will need a microscope. Place a drop of 'green water' on a slide and put a cover-slip over it. Examine it under the low magnification ($\times 30$ or $\times 40$) and the medium magnification ($\times 100$) of the microscope.

   There are probably a number of free and fast-moving forms. You may need to slow them down. Place a few wisps of cotton wool between the microscope slide and cover-slip to confine them to a small area.

   If any of these organisms are green, they are minute, free-swimming plants—algae. Compare the organisms you can see with Figure 8.1 below. Are there any similar forms? Do not be surprised if there are not, as there are hundreds of different species —far too many to illustrate in this book. Observe them and try to work out how they move. One typical, free-living alga is called *Chlamydomonas*. It is shown in Figure 8.2 and is described in Section 8.3. It consists of just a single cell.

2. Place any 'slime' or green strands you may have collected on a microscope slide. Separate the individual strands with the aid of mounted needles until you have just one or two. Place a single

Figure 8.1 A selection of free-swimming, freshwater algae

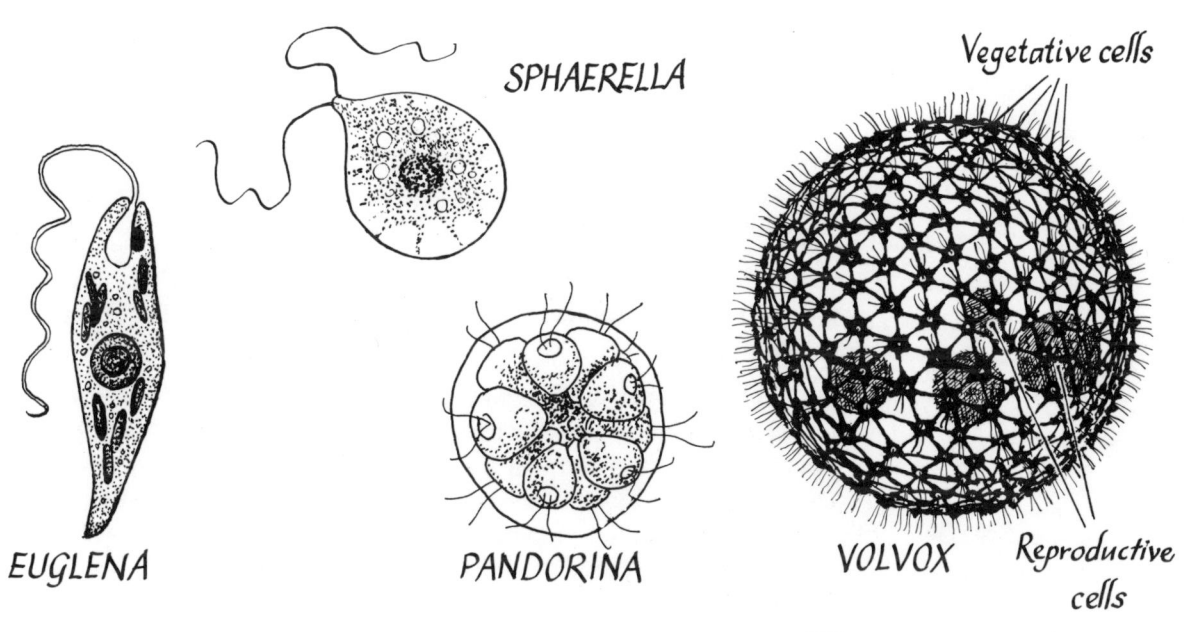

EUGLENA SPHAERELLA PANDORINA VOLVOX

Vegetative cells
Reproductive cells

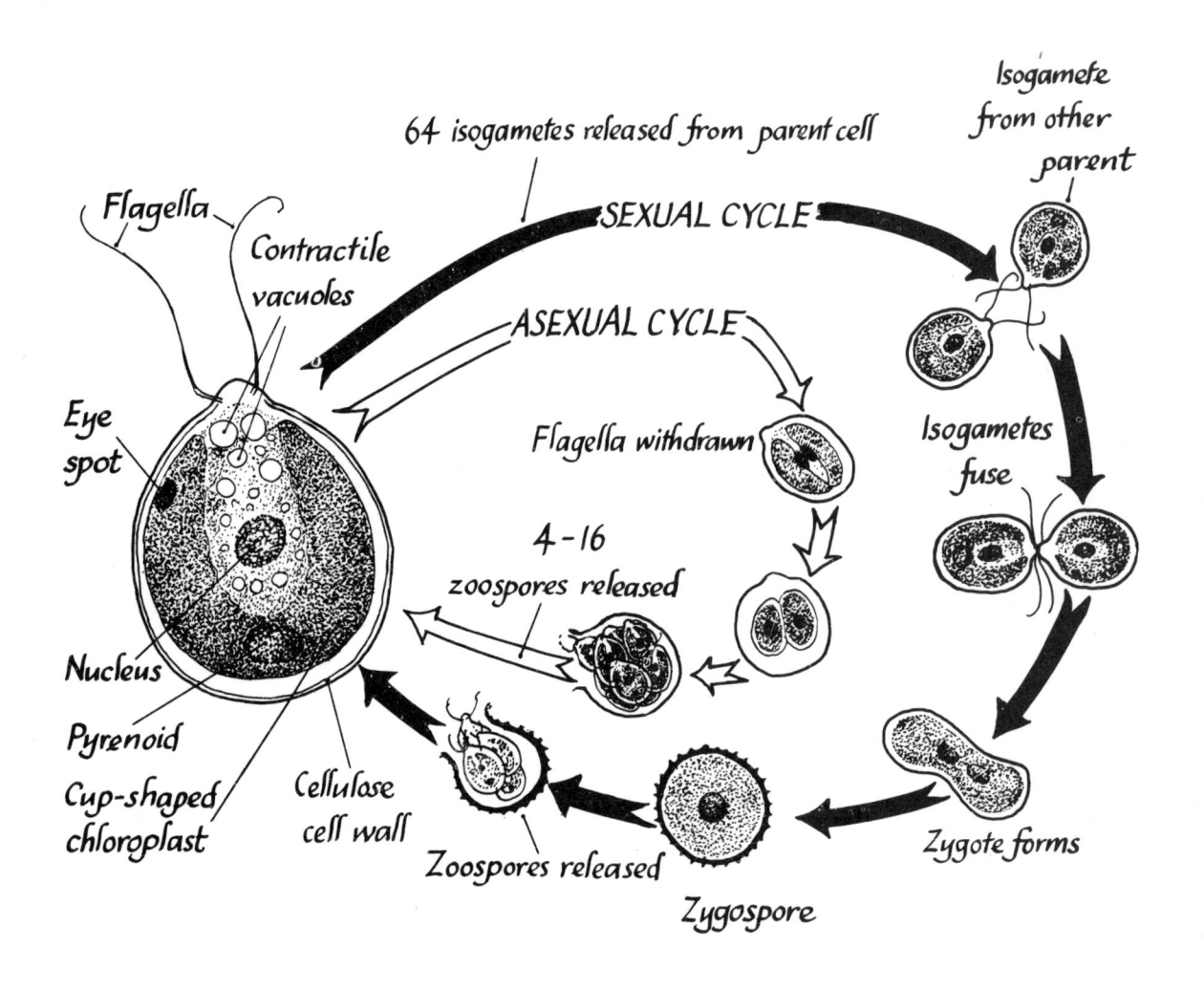

Figure 8.2 The structure and life-cycle of *Chlamydomonas*

drop of water on to the specimen on the slide and put a cover-slip over it. Examine the slide under the low power of the microscope. You have probably mounted a many-celled, filamentous alga, similar to *Spirogyra* shown in Figure 8.3 and described in Section 8.4.

8.3. Chlamydomonas: a free-swimming, unicellular, fresh-water alga

Chlamydomonas consists only of a single cell (less than 0·1 mm in diameter), within which all its life processes are carried out. This minute plant swims through the water propelled by the lashing of a pair of whip-like processes, called **flagella**, which are situated at its anterior end. Like all green plants, *Chlamydomonas* makes its own food by photosynthesis. It swims towards moderate light due to the sensitivity of the eye spot at the anterior end of the cell.

Chlamydomonas reproduces in two ways. The first method is *asexual*, which only involves a single organism. Up to sixteen **zoospores** are produced inside the parent cell. Eventually the zoospores escape and grow into mature plants. The second method, *sexual* reproduction, involves two organisms. The contents of the parent cells divide to form sixty-four **isogametes**. They are called isogametes as it is not possible to distinguish between the male and female. These gametes are much smaller than the parent cells and have no cell walls. When they are released, the gametes from one parent fuse with those from another to form zygotes. This may occur at the approach of unfavourable conditions. The zygotes are able to survive adverse conditions such as prolonged cold or drought. When favourable conditions return, they burst open to release a number of zoospores which eventually develop into adult organisms.

8.4. Spirogyra: a filament of similar cells

Spirogyra is a simple plant found in the slime on the surface of freshwater ponds. It is in the form of a filament composed of similar cylindrical cells joined at their ends (see Figure 8.3). There is no specialization or division of labour: like *Chlamydomonas*, each cell is able to carry out all the life processes. If you examine a filament of *Spirogyra* under the microscope you will see the spiral chloroplast which gives the plant its name.

If a *Spirogyra* filament becomes broken into pieces, each piece may become a new plant (asexual reproduction). *Spirogyra* also reproduces sexually by **conjugation**, as shown in Figure 8.3. Two filaments lie close together on the surface of the water and a conjugation canal develops between the cells of the two filaments. The contents of these cells lose water and become 'rounded off' to form isogametes. The isogametes from one filament (sometimes referred to as the 'male' filament) migrate through the conjugation canals to fuse with the isogametes in the other 'female' filament. The wall of the resulting zygote grows thick with stored food to form a **zygospore**, which falls to the bottom of the pond when the filament decays. The zygospore remains at the bottom of the pond until conditions are favourable, and then germinates to produce a new filament.

Spirogyra feeds, respires and gets rid of waste in the same way as *Chlamydomonas*. Materials in solution enter and leave the cells by the process of *simple diffusion*.

It is important to remember that these algae are the modern descendents of the earliest plants. In their level of organization, they may resemble their ancient ancestors of several hundred million years ago. *Chlamydomonas* and *Spirogyra* live in fresh water, but most algae are marine.

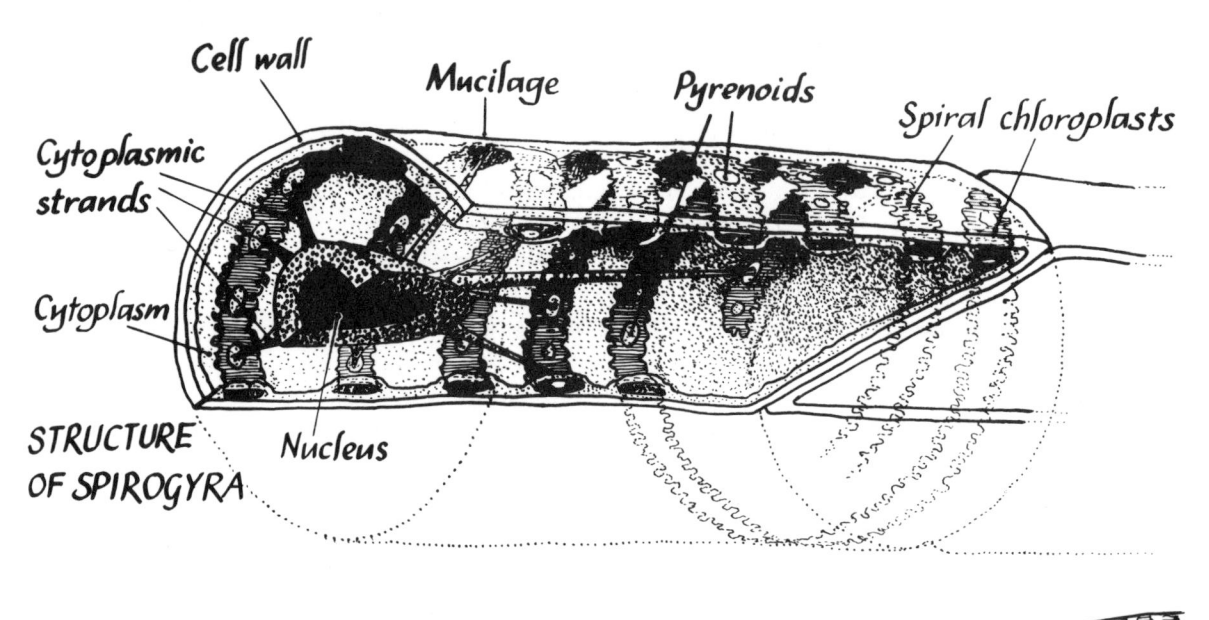

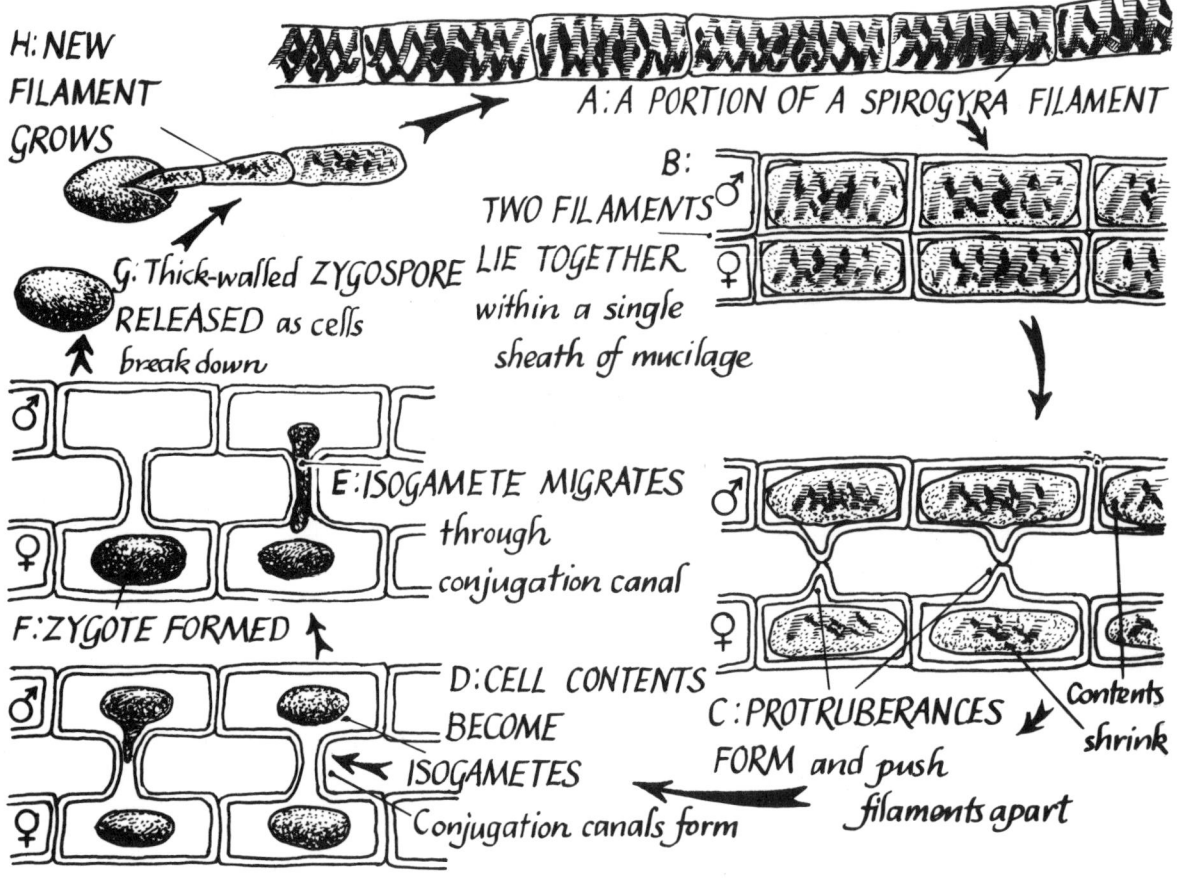

Figure 8.3 The structure and life-cycle of *Spirogyra*

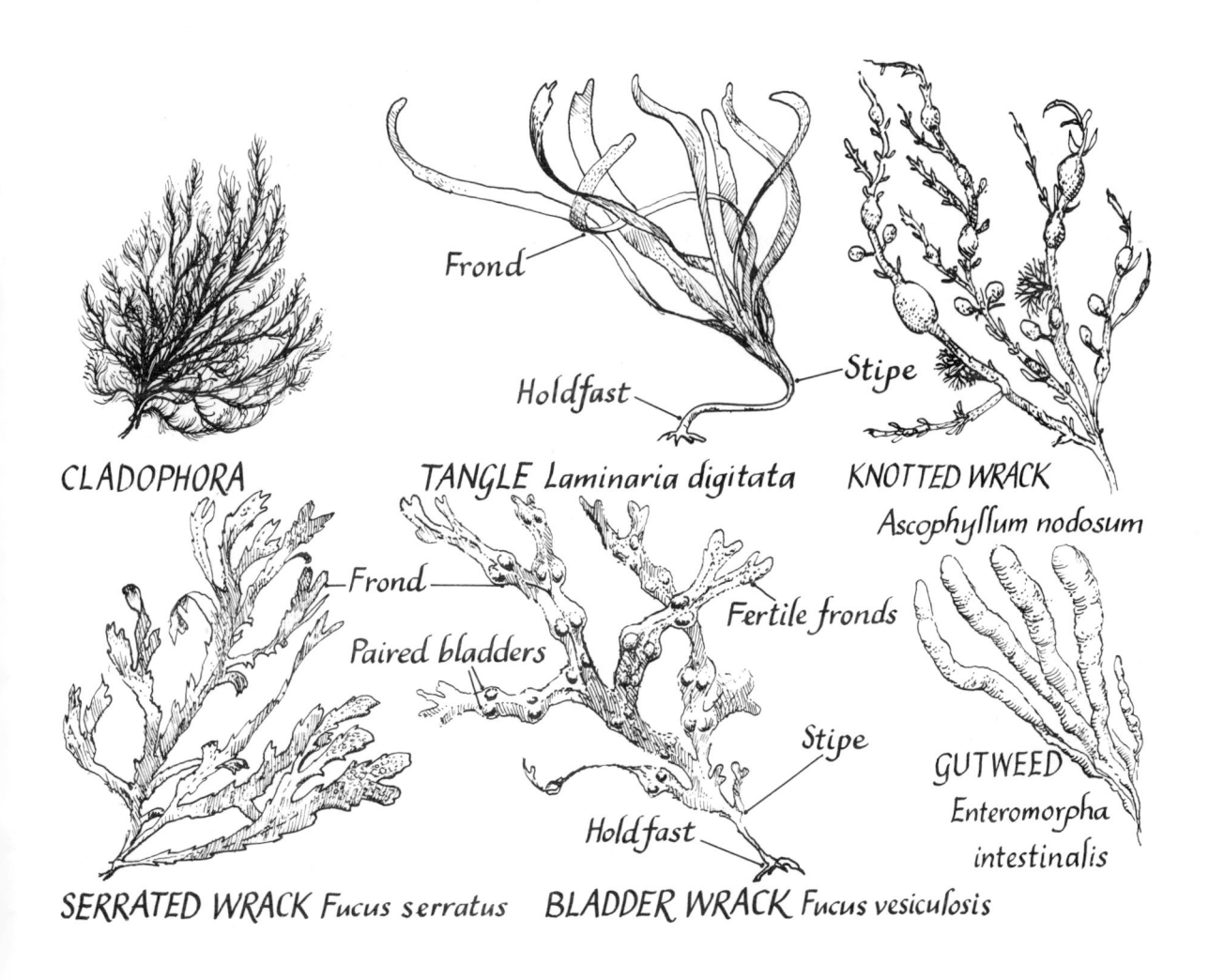

Figure 8.4 Some common marine algae

8.5. Marine algae: seaweeds

Investigation 8b. To examine a collection of marine algae

If you are fortunate enough to be able to visit a rocky shore, take some polythene bags with you. If possible, try to be there at low tide when you will be able to collect from low down on the shore. Most of the plants usually referred to as 'seaweeds' are marine algae (see Figure 8.4). Working up the shore from the sea, collect *one* example of each different plant as you go. Make a note of the order in which you find them.

Back in the laboratory, try to identify your collection using the following key. This key can only include a few of the very common marine algae, so do not be surprised if you find one that is not included.

Key for the identification of some of the commoner seaweeds found on the rocky shores around Britain

1a. Plant distinctly green .... green alga .... go on to 2
 b. Plant olive or brown .... brown alga .... go on to 4
 c. Plant red, purplish or pink .... red alga

2a. Bright green tubular seaweed 0·5 to 1 cm in diameter, occurring in rock pools .... ENTEROMORPHA (gutweed)
 b. If not, ... go on to 3

3a. A green seaweed forming a broad flattened sheet two layers thick (looking rather like a battered lettuce leaf) .... ULVA LACTUCA (sea lettuce)
 b. A rather dark, dull-green seaweed; moss-like with tufted branches attached by rhizoids .... CLADOPHORA

4a. Medium-sized, brown seaweeds 10 to 200 cm in length, attached to a rock by means of a holdfast .... a wrack .... go on to 5
 b. Very large, stalked brown seaweeds, up to 3 metres in length, attached to a rock by a stout holdfast; found near to or just below low tide level .... LAMINARIA (an oarweed) .... go on to 8

5a. A small wrack, about 10 cm long, with a channel-shaped stalk; found growing near high tide level .... PELVETIA (channelled wrack)
 b. If not, ... go on to 6

6a. Medium-sized seaweeds 20 to 150 cm in length, with a well-defined midrib .... FUCUS .... go on to 7
 b. A large brown seaweed with *no* midrib, but with large unpaired air bladders at intervals of about 5 cm; found on sheltered, gently sloping, rocky shores .... ASCOPHYLLUM (knotted wrack)

7a. A *Fucus* of the middle shore with paired air bladders on either side of the midrib .... FUCUS VESICULOSIS (bladder wrack)
 b. A *Fucus* of the lower part of the middle shore, *without* air bladders but with a toothed margin .... FUCUS SERRATUS (serrated wrack)
 c. A smaller *Fucus* of the upper middle shore, without bladders or serrations; fronds spirally twisted .... FUCUS SPIRALIS (spiral wrack)

8a. A massive oarweed with a broad frond divided into broad strips splayed like the fingers of a hand; found in very exposed situations .... LAMINARIA DIGITATA (tangle)
 b. A large oarweed consisting of a long undivided blade with frilled edges; found in slightly more sheltered situations .... LAMINARIA SACCHARINA (sea belt)

8.6. The fungi: simple plants without pigments

There is another great group of plants which have no roots, stems or leaves, and whose reproductive organs are unicellular—the **fungi**. The fungi, however, differ from the algae in having no pigments.

The absence of pigment means that they are unable to manufacture their own energy-rich carbohydrates. Unlike almost all other plants they are not producers, but resemble animals in being consumers, which means they must be provided with energy-rich food. For this reason, many scientists put the fungi in a kingdom by themselves or group them in a special kingdom together with those tiny plants we call bacteria.

Some fungi 'steal' their nourishment by living in, or on, another living organism; organisms which feed in this way are called **parasites**. Many plant diseases are caused by parasitic fungi. Rusts, smuts, mildew and 'damping off' are all examples. Perhaps the most notorious parasitic fungus is the potato blight fungus, *Phytophthora infestans*, which ruined the potato crops in Ireland in the 1840s, causing almost a million peasants to die of starvation because at that time the potato was their only food.

8.7. Pin mould: a saprophytic fungus

Fungi may also obtain food by digesting the dead and decaying remains of other plants and animals, and absorbing the energy-rich substances directly from them. Organisms which feed in this way are called **saprophytes**. Many bacteria are also saprophytes. Saprophytes carry out the processes of decay. This may seem rather unpleasant, but it is a vitally important job, as it releases all the material taken from the environment by an organism in its lifetime and enables it to be used again by other living organisms.

The commonest saprophytic fungi are the pin moulds, like *Mucor* and *Rhizopus*.

Investigation 8c. To discover the conditions under which pin moulds grow best

Take three petri dishes and three beakers or jam jars. Under the first beaker place a piece of lightly toasted bread, and under the second, a piece of damp bread. Leave the third beaker empty. Put the apparatus on one side for about four days (see Figure 8.5). The contents of the beakers should then be studied carefully under a powerful hand lens or a binocular microscope. Explain what happens in each beaker, giving reasons for any differences. You will probably get green and red moulds growing as well as the pin mould.

Investigation 8d. To examine the structure of a pin mould

Use the best colony of pin mould to study its structure. The plant body is called a **mycelium** and consists of a network of threads called **hyphae**. The hyphae form a network rather like cotton wool, which

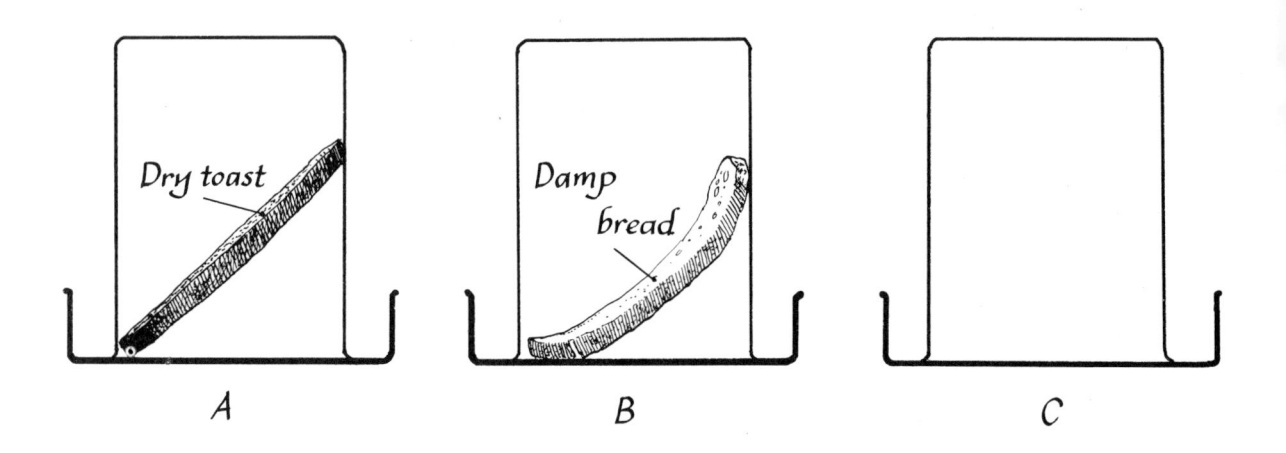

Figure 8.5 Growing pin mould

Figure 8.6 *Mucor* growing on bread and reproducing asexually

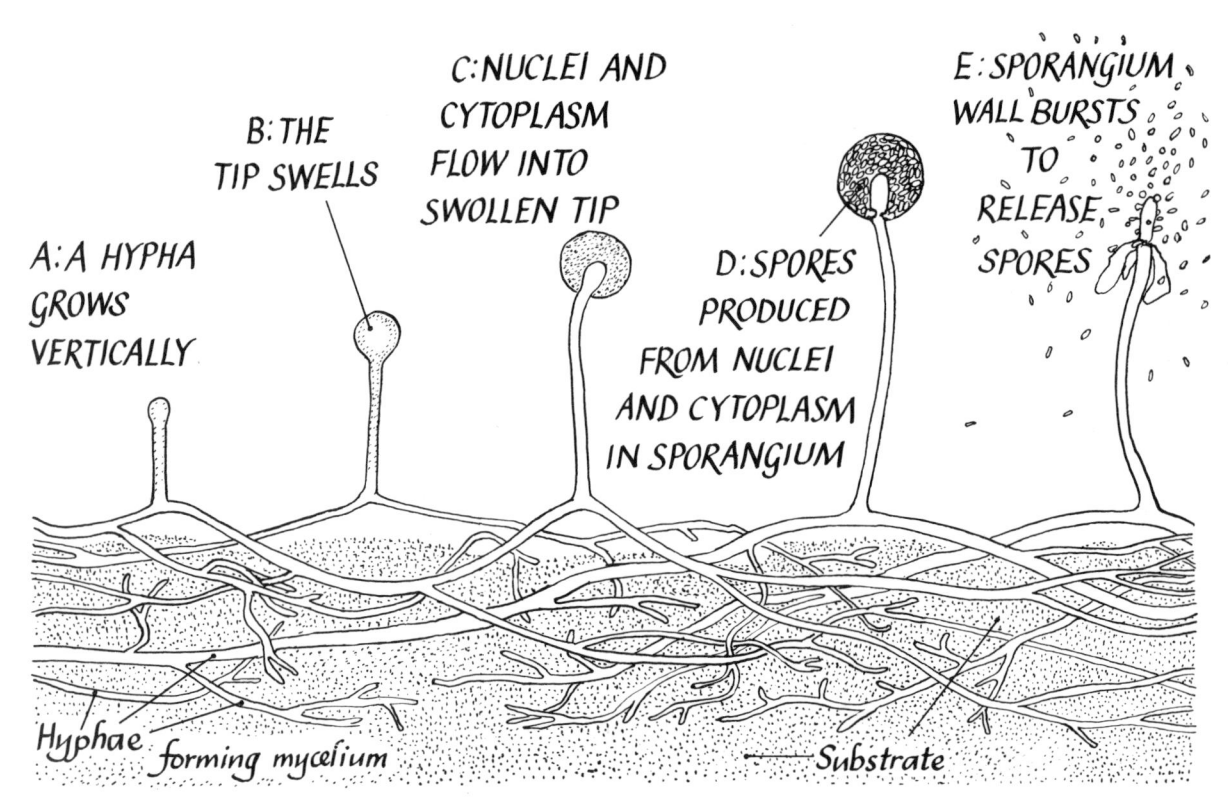

covers and penetrates the material on which the fungus is living (see Figure 8.6).

Examine a hypha carefully under a powerful microscope. It is not composed of discrete cells like other plants and animals that we have studied. Each hypha is a continuous tube comprising a cell wall lined with cytoplasm. The nuclei are embedded in the cytoplasm, and each nucleus controls the area of cytoplasm around it. This type of structure is called a **coenocyte**, and is found in many fungi and in some algae (see Figure 8.7).

Figure 8.7 A portion of the coenocyte of *Mucor*

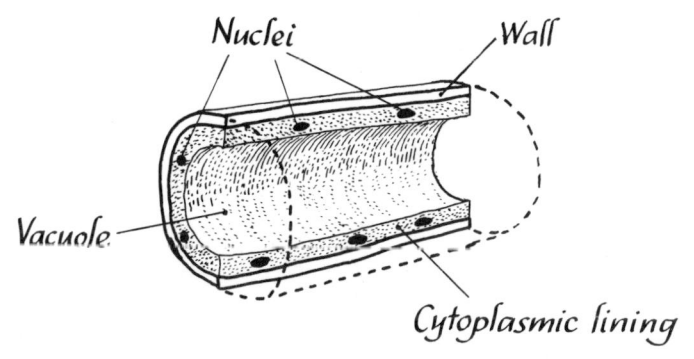

Asexual reproduction

If you leave a flourishing colony for a few days you will notice that the mycelium becomes covered with black dots like pinheads; hence the name pin mould. The fungus is now reproducing asexually by means of spores which are liberated when the spore-producing organs, the **sporangia** (the pinheads), burst (see Figure 8.6). The spores are very light and are carried by the air currents. Should they land on warm, damp food, they germinate to produce new mycelia. This method of reproduction is the most common, particularly when conditions are favourable and food abundant. If conditions are not favourable for germination, the spores may remain dormant but viable for several years.

Sexual reproduction

Sexual reproduction takes place when conditions become less favourable. Short branches arise from adjacent hyphae, and their tips become swollen and separated from the mycelium by the formation of cross walls (see Figure 8.8). These swollen tips are the gametes.

Figure 8.8 The stages of sexual reproduction of *Mucor*

A: HYPHAE TOUCH   B: BRANCHES GROW   C: GAMETES FORMED AT THE TIPS   D: GAMETES FUSE FORMING ZYGOSPORE   E: ZYGOSPORE GERMINATES

Figure 8.9 A bracket fungus growing on a tree

The walls between the two gametes dissolve, and they fuse to form a zygote. The wall of the zygote becomes thickened with stored food and dark in colour. The resulting zygospore can resist adverse conditions. Eventually when good conditions return, the zygospore germinates to produce a single sporangium, which liberates a large number of spores. Each spore, given damp, warm conditions and suitable food, will germinate and produce a new mycelium.

8.8. Mushrooms and toadstools: gill fungi

When you have previously used the word fungus you probably did not think of either potato blight or pin mould, but of mushrooms found in the fields and toadstools found in the woods. You may also have noticed the bracket fungi growing on the trunks and branches of living trees. These are all **gill fungi** (see Figures 8.9 and 8.10).

The mushrooms we gather in the fields are merely the reproductive portion of extensive underground mycelia. The mycelium is thought to feed saprophytically as the fungus flourishes in fields frequented by horses. Some scientists, however, think that the mushroom may obtain some of its food from the roots of grasses.

The woodland toadstools are also the reproductive structure of underground mycelia, but hyphae of toadstool mycelia actually penetrate the roots of trees such as beech, birch and pine, to form an association for mutual benefit. The tree is a green plant and is thought to provide the fungus with carbohydrate and vitamins. The fungus is able to convert humus to nitrates which the tree uses for building up proteins and which assist the absorption of water and nutrient salts. This type of association, where two organisms live together for mutual benefit, is another example of **symbiosis**. You will remember a similar association between the alga *Zoochlorella* and *Hydra*.

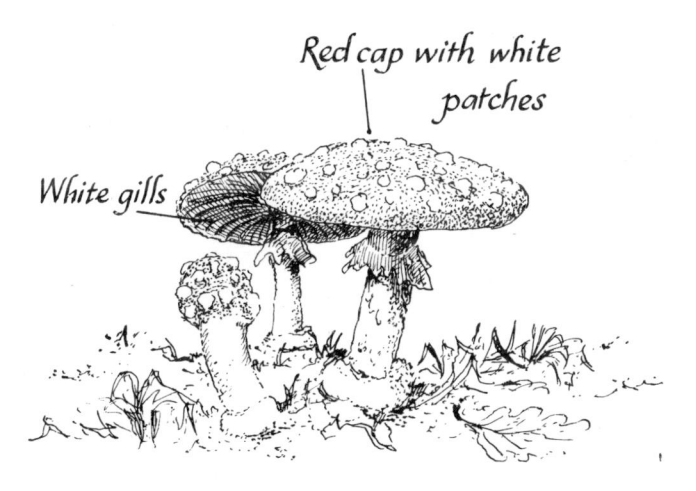

Figure 8.10 Fly agaric toadstool

An association between a fungus and a higher green plant is called a **mycorrhiza**. Scientists by no means fully understand how this relationship works.

All these gill fungi reproduce by spores born on their gills. The mushroom spore germinates to produce an underground mycelium. In autumn, the mycelium forms a clump of hyphae which develops into a mushroom with its stalk and its cap. At first the undersurface of the cap is covered by a white skin, the **velum**, but as the cap expands laterally it tears to expose the pink gills which radiate from the stalk to the periphery of the cap, like the spokes of a bicycle wheel (see Figure 8.11). When the spores ripen, the gills turn dark brown in colour. The ripe spores are shot away from the gill surface, and are dispersed by air currents.

Investigation 8e. To discover what fungi grow locally

If you have a suitable wood nearby you can easily go on a **fungal forage**. The most suitable time for this investigation is in October.

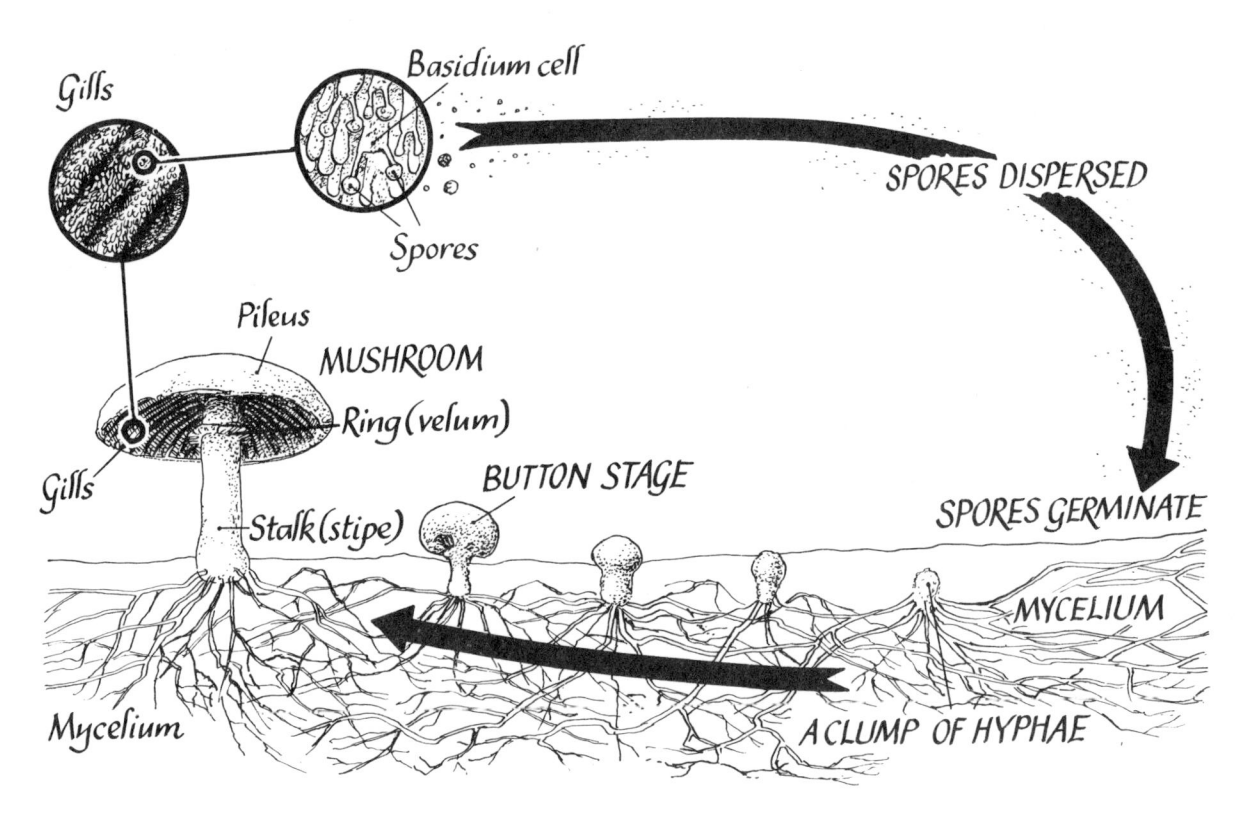

Figure 8.11 The life-cycle of the mushroom

Take a basket or some polythene bags and search your area, looking particularly at and under leaf litter. Collect one example of each fungus you find. Make a note of the position and conditions under which each was growing.

Back at school pool your collection and arrange it in some sort of systematic order. Why do you find a greater variety of fungi in the woods than in the fields?

(*Note.* If fungi are left around in the laboratory, they will soon become covered with a mass of insect larvae.)

8.9. The plant division Thallophyta: algae and fungi

The **algae** and **fungi** are both simple plants having no roots, stems, leaves, flowers or fruits, and whose sex organs consist of a single cell. These groups, together with the **lichens** and **bacteria**, are placed together to form the large group of simple plants, the **Thallophyta**.

8.10. The division Bryophyta: liverworts and mosses

The liverworts and mosses together form the second division of plants, the **Bryophyta**. They are more highly evolved than the Thallophyta but, even so, both the liverworts and mosses are fairly primitive plants. Simple stem and leaf-like structures occur. Although they are not aquatic like most of the algae, bryophytes do need water for fertilization, and they easily become dried up or desiccated. As a result they tend to live in damp places.

Figure 8.12 The liverwort *Marchantia*

The liverworts, such as *Marchantia* (see Figure 8.12), are even less advanced than the mosses, and tend to live in very damp conditions such as on the banks of streams or under the overhang of small waterfalls.

8.11. The mosses

Mosses can live in much drier situations than liverworts, but they are usually found in moist places. Moisture is again essential for fertilization.

Investigation 8f. To collect mosses and liverworts

Collect as many mosses and liverworts as you can find. Make a note of the situation you found each one growing in, for example on the top of a wall or on the bark of a dead tree. They can be kept for a short time in polythene bags, and even if they do become very brown and dried up, they can often be revived by soaking in water.

To grow your mosses and liverworts you need a container with a lid, such as a sweet jar, or other large screw-top jar, or a plastic refrigerator box with a transparent top. A small aquarium covered by a sheet of glass is also suitable. Lay your jar on one side and place a little damp peat along the bottom. Plant small but vigorous clumps of various mosses and liverworts on the peat and then replace the top of the jar (see Figure 8.13). Place your 'bryophyte garden' in a sunny position. Insect-eating plants, such as the sundew, can be planted in amongst the mosses with some success. If the moisture content is correct, the water will circulate within the container, and it will not need any maintenance.

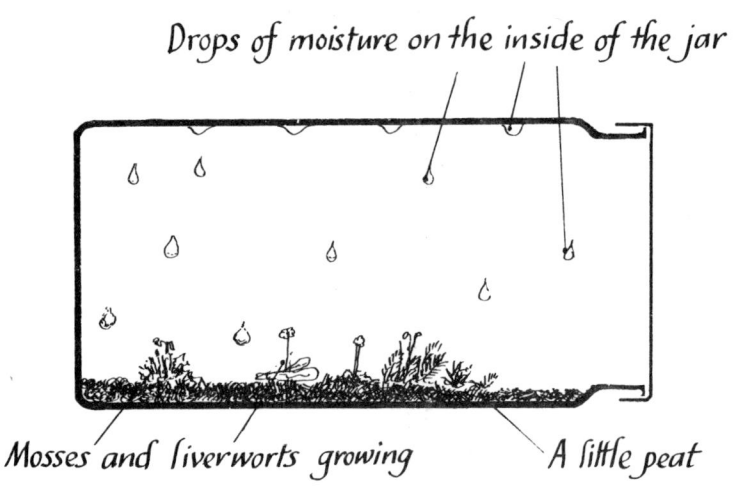

Figure 8.13 Mosses and liverworts growing in a jar

Investigation 8g. To examine the collection of mosses and liverworts

With the aid of a lens and a pair of dissecting needles, carefully examine a number of species of moss and, if possible, a liverwort as well. Carefully tease apart the individual moss plants from the cushion. Compare individual plants from what are obviously different species. Make a note of what features they have in common. If you are fortunate enough to have a liverwort, compare its features with those of the moss. Make a note of the characteristics which they share and the ways in which they differ.

Study the moss plants with the aid of a hand lens or binocular microscope. Notice whether your moss plant has a single main axis which is more or less erect (for example, *Funaria*) or whether it is branched, feathery and prostrate, that is, tending to lie on the ground (*Hypnum*) (see Figure 8.14). Detailed identification of mosses is not easy, for it requires detailed microscopic examination of the leaves.

Did either the liverwort or any of the mosses you examined bear a vertical stalk with a capsule at its tip? If so, remove a capsule, place it on a microscope slide with a drop of water and crush the capsule with the flat surface of a scalpel blade. Put a cover-slip over it and examine the preparation with the low power of a microscope. You will almost certainly see a mass of more or less spherical bodies. These are spores, the asexual reproductive structures of the moss. The spores are usually dispersed by air currents, and if they settle in a suitable position they germinate, and eventually develop into a new liverwort or moss.

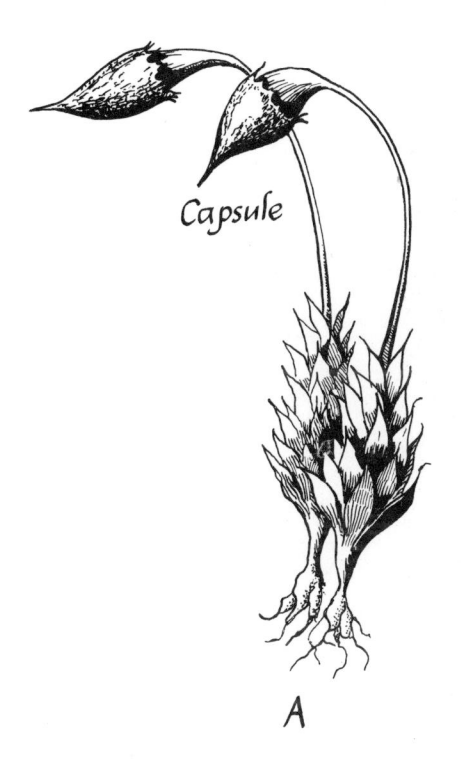

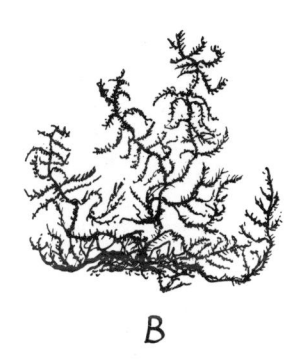

Figure 8.14 (a) An erect moss—*Funaria*. (b) A feathery moss—*Hypnum*

8.12. The division Pteridophyta

The third great division of plants, the **Pteridophyta**, includes the ferns, the horsetails and the club mosses. Stems, roots and leaves are present with a well-developed conducting system. You could probably recognize a fern at a glance, but you may not be quite so familiar with the horsetails and club mosses. The horsetail, as the name suggests, resembles the tail of a horse. Its leaves are reduced to small scales, but it has a large number of ridged and jointed branches arising from the main stem in regular whorls (see Figure 8.15). You will probably be able to find horsetails growing in ditches and other damp places. They grow to a height of about 1 metre.

You are not so likely to find club mosses, which grow in the grasslands of upland areas such as North Wales. They are much smaller and more compact than the horsetails. The leaves, bearing the reproductive structures, are grouped into a loose cone at the tip of the stem (see Figure 8.16). *Lycopodium* is the commonest club moss and its spores are used for some experiments in physics.

8.13. The ferns

Investigation 8h. To compare the male fern with the bracken plant

Both the male fern and bracken are true ferns. Examine the two plants carefully. Look at the underground parts of the plants first.

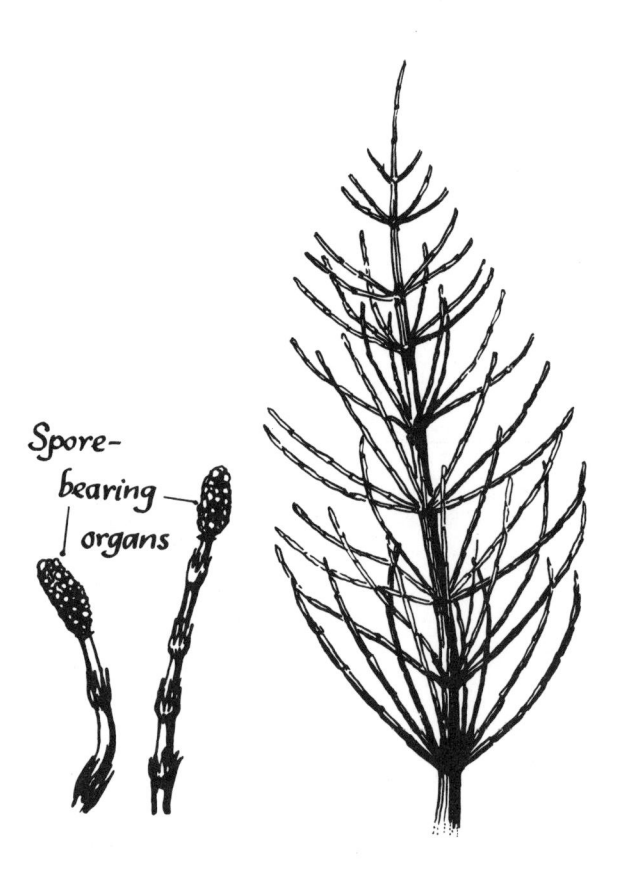

Figure 8.15 A horsetail

You will notice that there is an underground stem called a **rhizome**, from which the roots are given off. The large leaves or fronds arise from the growing anterior part of the rhizome, whilst the posterior part of the rhizome bears the bases of the old dead fronds and may even be decaying away (see Figure 8.17). Can you see the roots arising from the rhizome? The young fronds arise from the tip of the rhizome and at first are coiled up rather like a clock-spring, which unrolls as the frond opens.

Examine single fronds from the male fern and bracken. What is the most obvious difference? Follow the main axis of each frond and

Figure 8.16 A club moss

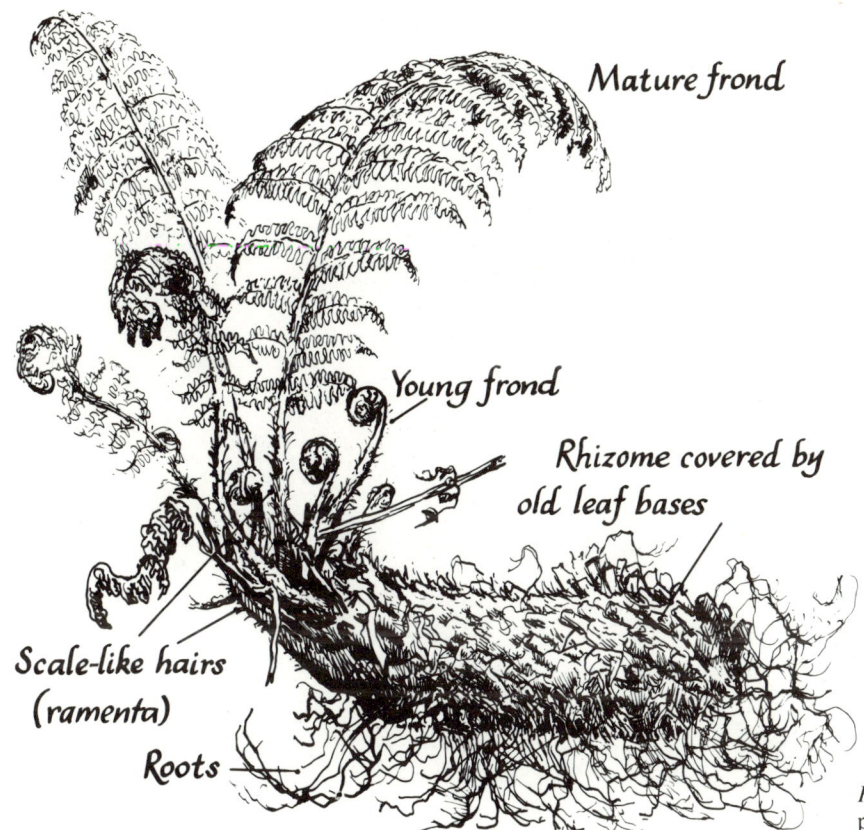

Figure 8.17 The male fern plant with its rhizome

see how many branches are formed. Draw the two fronds and compare them with Figure 8.18.

The frond of the male fern has opposite branches called **pinnae**. Each pinna bears oppositely arranged **pinnules**. How many times does the bracken frond subdivide? Now look very carefully at the undersurface of the pinnae near to the tips of the fronds. You will probably find reddish-brown areas on some of them. These are called the **sori**. Each sorus consists of a flap of tissue called the **indusium** which protects a cluster of sporangia, the spore-producing organs. Are the sori of the male fern the same as those of bracken? Compare the undersurface of your fertile pinnules with Figure 8.19.

When the sporangia are ripe the indusium withers away, exposing the sporangia whose capsules lose water and burst open scattering the spores far and wide. Remove a sorus from one of the fronds, mount it in water on a microscope slide and place a cover-slip over it. Squeeze the preparation to release the spores and examine them under the low power of a microscope. Compare your preparation with Figure 8.20, which is a diagram of a section cut through a sorus. Your preparation will not look much like this, but you should be able to see the sporangia with their stalks and capsules as well as the remains of the indusium and, of course, the spores. You would

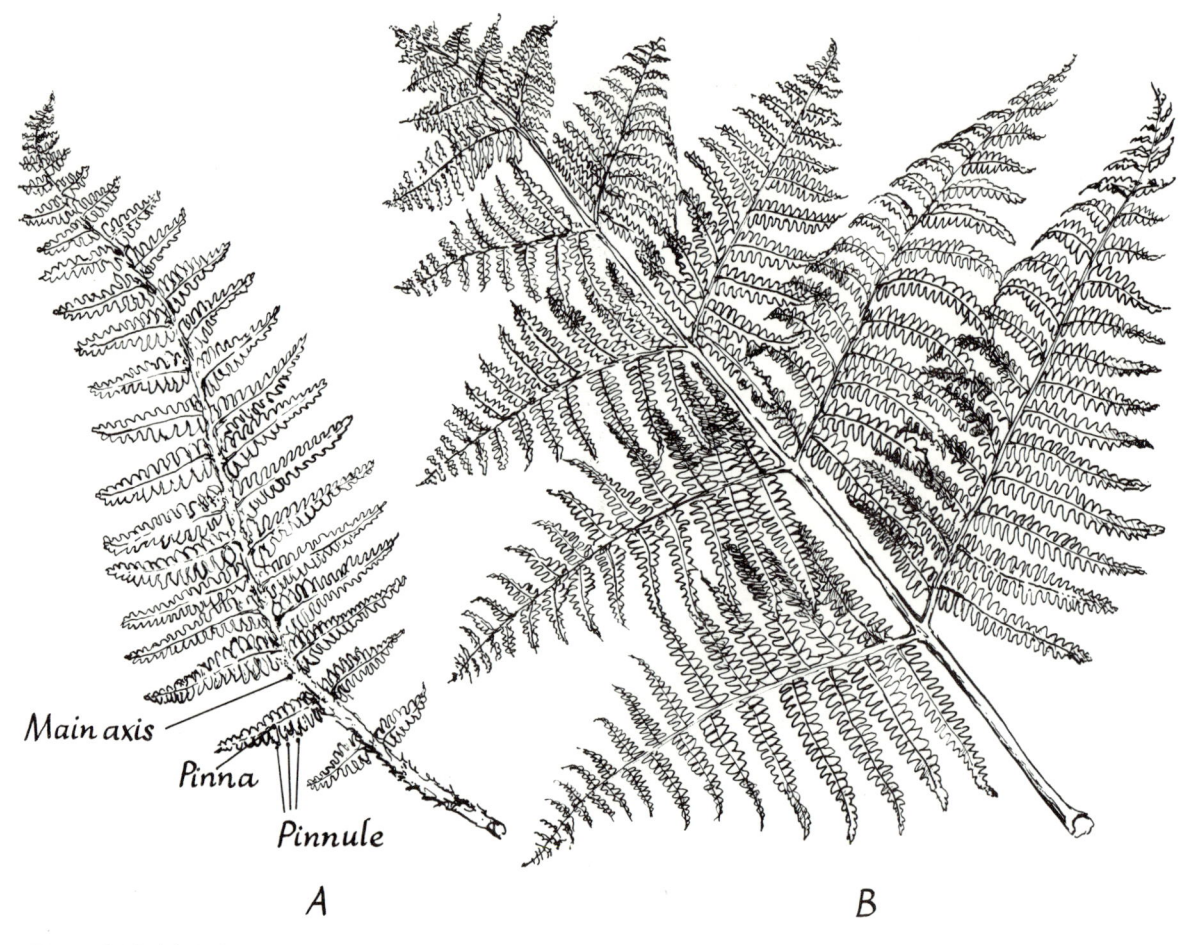

Figure 8.18 (a) A frond of the male fern. (b) A bracken frond

be able to see rather more if you have a prepared slide of a section through a sorus to examine under your microscope.

8.14. Reproduction in the ferns

The main part of the fern which you have just examined produces spores. This means that the fern plant is reproducing asexually and

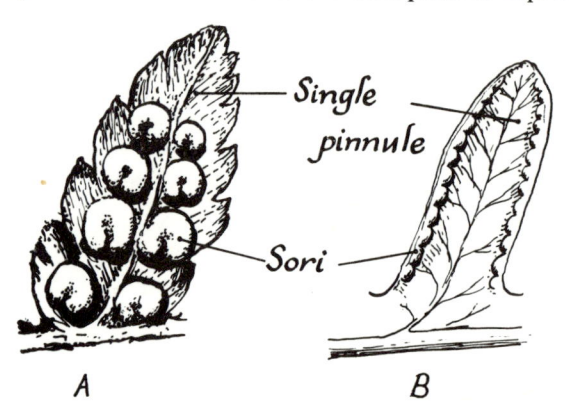

Figure 8.19 The arrangement of the sori (a) in the male fern and (b) in bracken

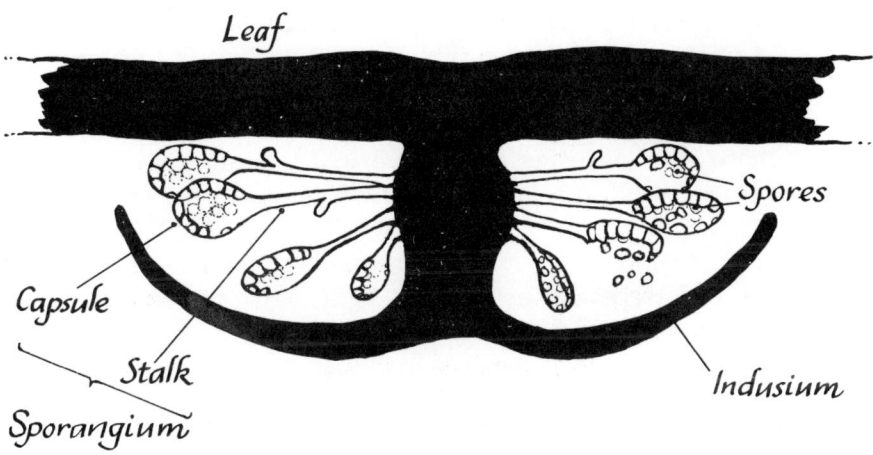

Figure 8.20 A section through the sorus of a male fern

is the spore-plant stage. The spores are carried away from the parent plant by air currents, and if they settle in a suitable position they germinate, *not* to produce a new fern plant but to grow into a very simple, heart-shaped structure just a few millimetres in diameter. This is the gamete-plant stage which is called a **prothallus** (see Figure 8.21). The prothallus bears both the male and female sex organs. It is small and delicate and is easily damaged by desiccation. The ripe egg cell releases malic acid which attracts the male gametes, the free-swimming sperm cells, which fertilize it. As fertilization in ferns is again by swimming gametes, moisture is again necessary for fertilization. The zygote thus formed eventually grows into the large fern plant, and the prothallus withers away.

8.15. Ancient ferns and coal formation

The division Pteridophyta is still a diverse and widely scattered group of plants which often still dominate damp and shaded situations, but 300 million years ago in the Carboniferous (coal-bearing)

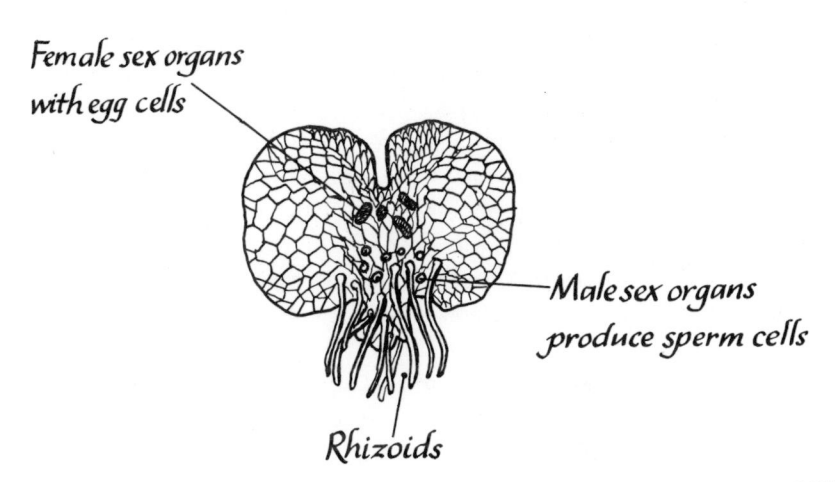

Figure 8.21 The underside of the prothallus fern

era, the earth was covered by great swampy forests composed of huge, tree-like ferns. Periodically, the level of the land fell and the seas swept over these forests, covering them with sand and mud. Throughout the ensuing ages, as more and more materials were deposited, the sand was compressed to form sandstone rock, and every metre depth of plant remains was crushed to form less than 1 centimetre of coal.

The burning of coal releases energy as heat and light, and carbon dioxide gas escapes up the chimney. This energy was captured from the sun by these large ferns all those years ago. The carbon in the carbon dioxide gas was removed from that ancient atmosphere when the fern absorbed carbon dioxide for photosynthesis.

You may occasionally see a leaf impression along the bedding plane of a piece of coal. This is an imprint of a fern from the ancient forests.

8.16. The division Spermatophyta: the seed-bearing plants

The division **Spermatophyta** includes all the higher or advanced plants. Most of these have flowers and are dealt with in Chapter 9, but members of the class **Gymnospermae** have no flowers and will, therefore, be studied in this chapter. The main advances shown are the development of the seed, and the tree form. The plants in this division are the first to be completely independent of water for the process of fertilization. The male sex cell is no longer a swimming gamete; it loses its flagella and has its own special tube, the pollen tube, to carry it to the female gamete.

8.17. The pine with its naked seed and tree form

The most familiar gymnosperms are the cone-bearing trees (conifers), such as the pine, cedar and spruce. It is true that they have no proper flowers, but they have special leaves, called **sporophylls**, which bear both the male and female spore-producing organs, the sporangia. These leaves are arranged to form the male and female **cones** which are a primitive type of flower. We shall see in a later chapter that a flower is composed of leaves which have become modified to do special jobs concerned with reproduction.

The pine tree is a woody perennial which continues to grow from year to year. It is a large plant with a large trunk which is able to store vast food reserves. It usually grows on well-drained soil, and is adapted to prevent excess water loss by having needle-shaped leaves which have a small surface area (see Figure 8.22). Like most conifers, it is an evergreen. This means that it does not shed all its leaves in the autumn, but sheds a few at a time throughout the year. Each leaf has a life of about three years.

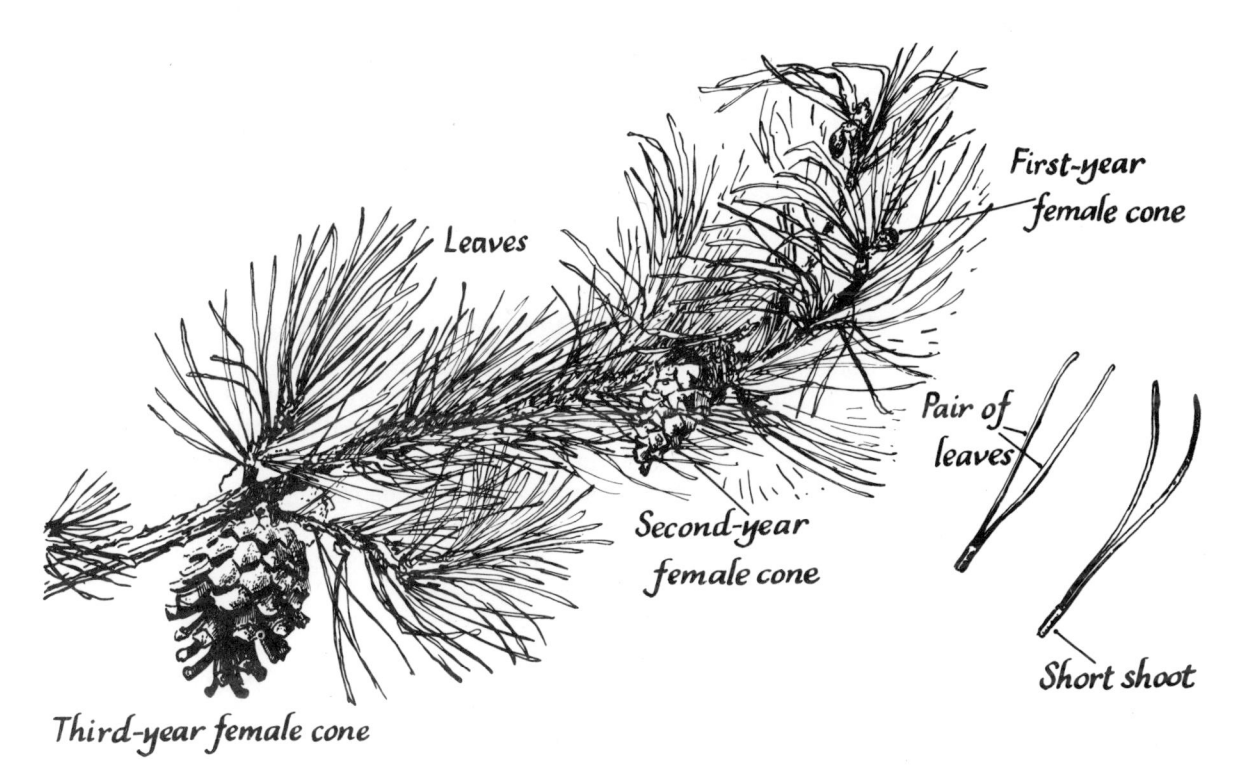

Figure 8.22 A shoot of a pine showing the leaf arrangement and first-, second- and third-year female cones

The **Scots pine**, our native pine, is sometimes used as a large Christmas tree, but it is another conifer, the **spruce**, which we normally use for this purpose. The needle leaves of the Scots pine are borne in pairs on short shoots which are shed with the leaves.

The male and female cones are borne on separate trees. The male cones are found in clusters at the tips of the branches and ripen in May to produce masses of yellow pollen grains (see Figure 8.23). The pollen grains contain the male gametes. The familiar cones of the pine tree are the female cones which produce the female gametes, the egg cells.

The pollen grains have air sacs which make them buoyant and easily blown about in the wind. When the young female cone is ripe the scales open, to allow the pollen grains to be blown inside, where they fertilize the egg cells. The scales then close.

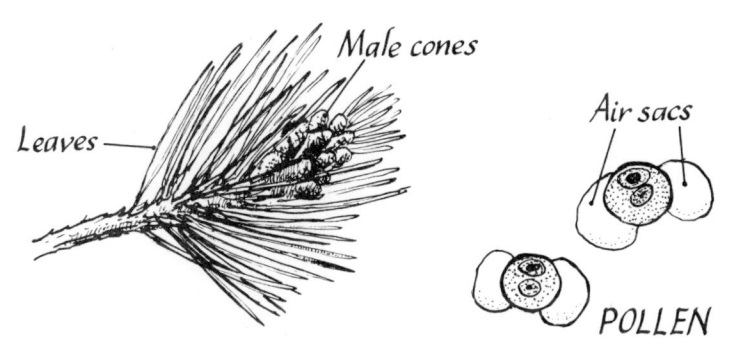

Figure 8.23 A cluster of male cones and some pollen

Two years later the scales open again to release the winged seeds which have developed from zygotes. The seed contains the embryo together with a supply of food which nourishes it. The pine seedling grows into a new pine tree, which may eventually reach a height of 30 metres. Why do you think the seeds of the pine trees have wing-like extensions of the seed coat?

Test your understanding

Copy and complete the following paragraph:

The division Thallophyta includes the simple plants that have no proper ....[1], ...[2] or leaves, ...[3] or fruits. There are two main classes, the ....[4], which live mainly in ....[5] and contain chlorophyll, and the ....[6], which lack ....[7] These plants which have no chlorophyll cannot feed by ....[8] but instead live as ....[9], obtaining their food from living plants and animals, or as saprophytes, digesting the remains of ....[10] plants and animals. The division Bryophyta includes the ....[11] like *Marchantia* and the ....[12] like *Funaria*. The ferns are members of the division ....[13], which also includes the ....[14] and the ....[15] The fern plant liberates asexual ....[16] to produce the heart-shaped ....[17] The division ....[18] contains the seed-bearing plants which are truly ....[19] because their gametes no longer have to rely on ....[20] for fertilization. Instead they have developed the ....[21] for conveying the male cells to the ....[22] The pollen grains and seeds of the pine tree are dispersed by the ....[23]

1. Name a plant that can move under its own power and describe its method of locomotion.
2. Mention three ways by which plants lacking chlorophyll are able to feed. Give the name of a plant which employs each method mentioned.
3. What are the three groups of algae which you are likely to find on a rocky shore? Name one representative from each group.
4. With reference to three different types of plant, explain the importance of spores to the simple plants.
5. What are the main differences between the mosses and the ferns?
6. Describe the process of reproduction in the pine.

Chapter 9

The Flowering Plant

9.1. Flowering plants

Most of the plants of the garden, field and hedgerow have flowers at some time during the year. These flowering plants form the largest and most important group of plants. The flowering plants are called **Angiosperms**, the second and larger class of the Spermatophyta (seed-bearing plants).

Investigation 9a. To examine the structure of a flowering plant, and to discover the functions performed by the different parts

Carefully dig (not pull) up a flowering plant such as shepherd's purse or groundsel. Hold the roots of the plant under a slow-running tap to wash any soil from the roots. Shepherd's purse is particularly suitable, as it is normally easy to find plenty of specimens with both flowers and fruit.

Examine your plant carefully and then draw it. Label the various parts with the help of Figure 9.1. Make notes about the parts you have labelled. What colour are they? Are they round or flattened? Are they smooth and shiny, or hairy? Try to suggest what tasks might be performed by these parts. Why do you think it is important to dig up the plants rather than just pull them up? The parts of the plant above the soil level form the **shoot system** and those parts below the soil level form the **root system.**

9.2. The shoot system

The shoot system consists of the stem, which links and supports the buds, the leaves, the flowers and the fruits. The flowers and fruits are concerned with sexual reproduction in the plant, and will be described in Chapter 12.

9.3. The stem

A stem can be recognized by the presence of leaves and buds which arise at regular intervals called **nodes**. The interval between

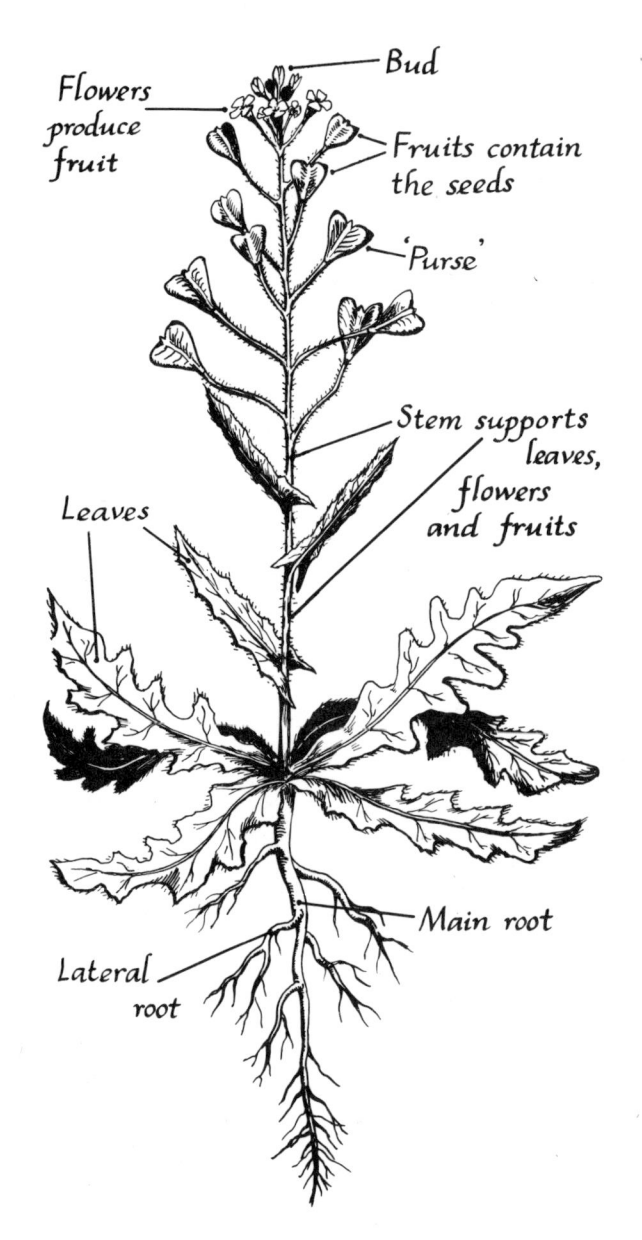

Figure 9.1 The parts of a flowering plant (Shepherd's purse)

adjacent nodes is called the **internode**. The length of the internode varies greatly from species to species, and even from plant to plant of the same species if they have grown under different conditions.

Investigation 9b. To compare the length of the internodes of plants growing under different light intensities

Examine a daisy or dandelion plant and two bean or pea plants. (One of the bean or pea plants has been grown in normal light conditions but the other, of a similar age, has been grown in darkness.)

Find the points at which the leaves are attached to the stems (the nodes) and measure the distance between them.

Where would you expect to find the daisy growing? Why should the length of its internodes be different from a plant like the bean or pea? Is there any difference in internodal length between the bean or pea plant grown in normal light and the plant grown in the dark?

Plants living in open situations where the light intensity is high may have very short internodes. This forms a **rosette** type of plant, close to the ground, like the daisy (see Figure 9.2) or the dandelion.

Figure 9.2 A daisy plant

Climbing plants or plants living in the shade may have long internodes, like the pea, bean (see Figure 9.3) or honeysuckle.

Investigation 9c. To examine the structure of a stem

Place some cut stems of a young herbaceous plant, such as buttercup or sunflower, in a beaker containing a solution of a dye such as **eosin**, and leave it for several hours before the investigation. Cut about 5 cm from one of the stems and hold it firmly between the thumb and first finger. Using a sharp, single-edged type of razor-blade, cut transverse sections from the stem as thinly as possible, as shown in Figure 9.4.

Use a small paint brush to pick the sections from the surface of the razor-blade, and put them into a watchglass containing water. When a number of sections have been cut, select the one which looks the thinnest and most transparent, and transfer it with the brush to a drop of water on a microscope slide. The section chosen need not be complete; parts of sections are often the thinnest. Carefully lower a cover-slip over the section and examine it, using the low power of the microscope. Compare your slide with Figure 9.5.

Figure 9.3 Part of a bean plant

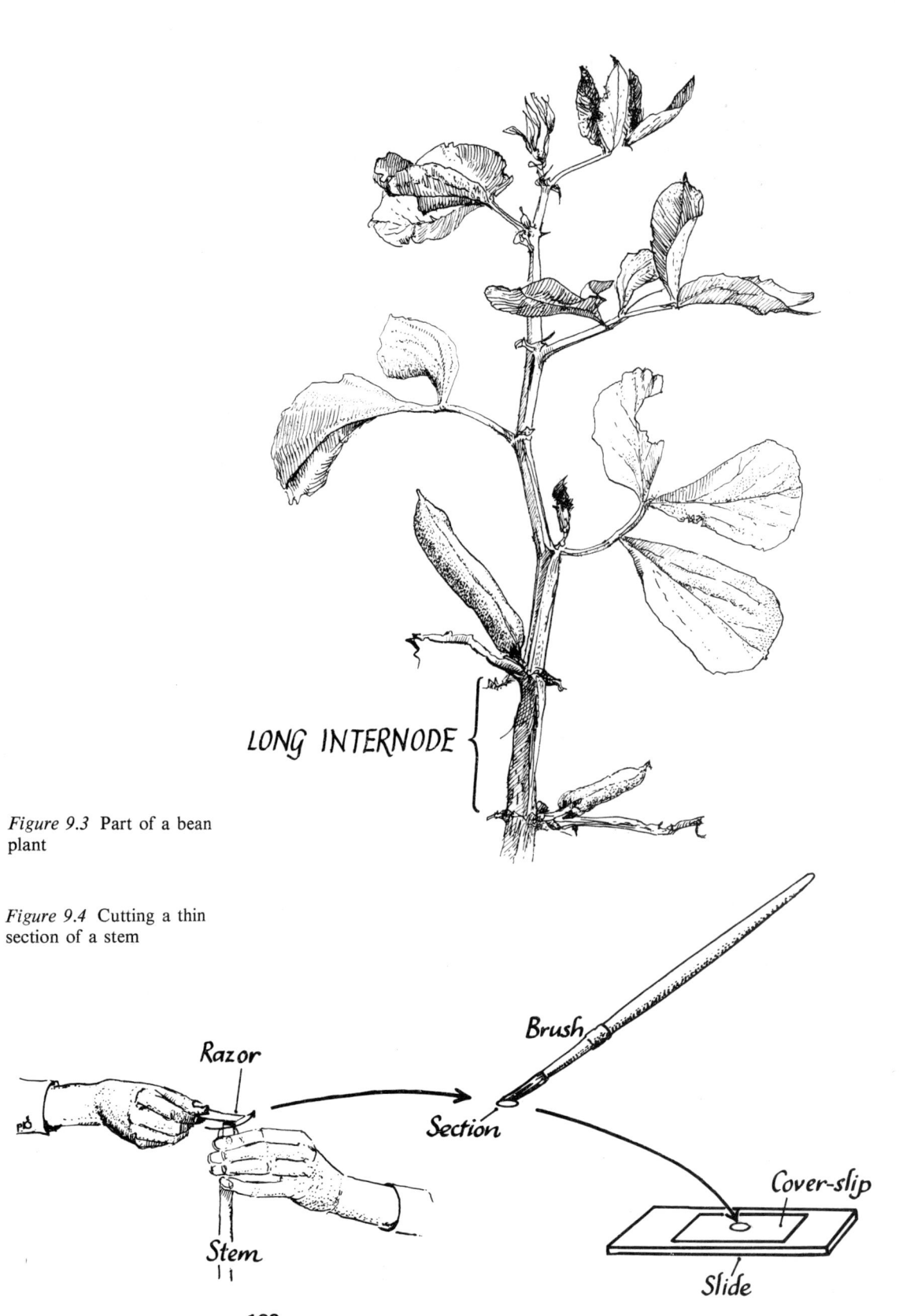

Figure 9.4 Cutting a thin section of a stem

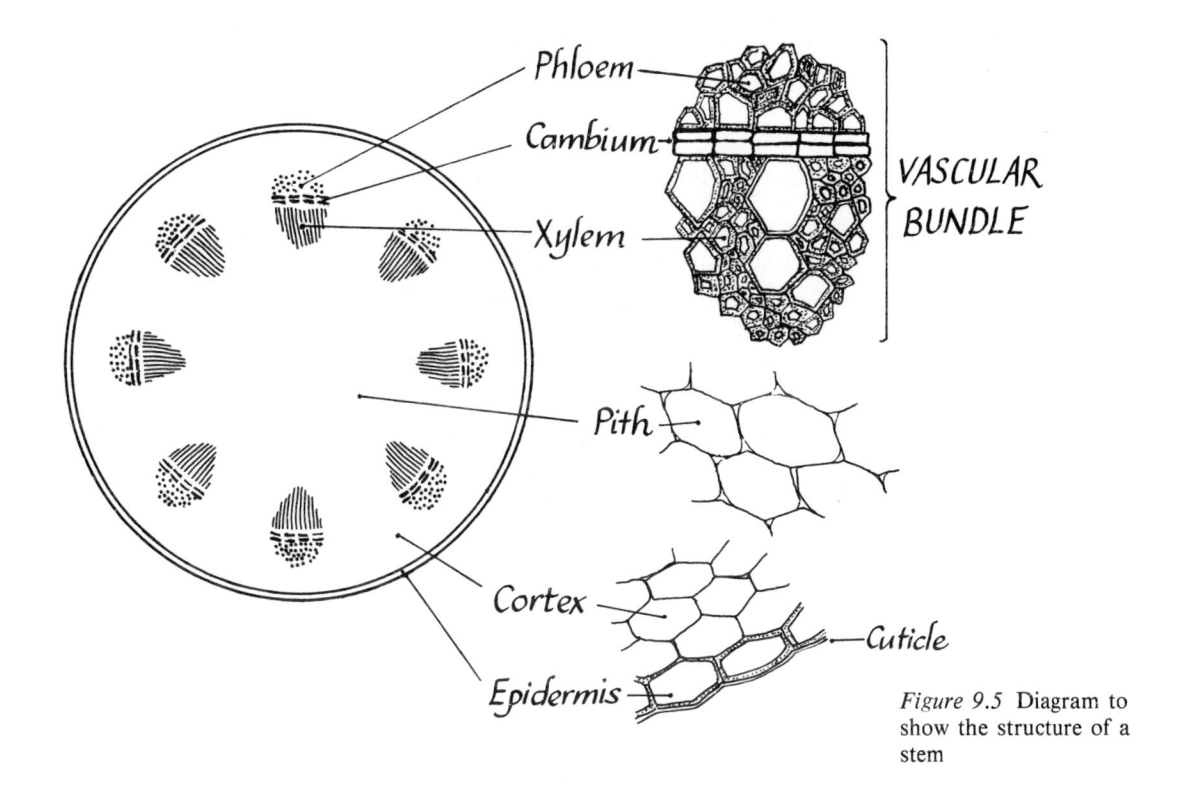

Figure 9.5 Diagram to show the structure of a stem

Examine the cells around the edge of the section. Can you see an outer, single layer of cells which is slightly different from the others and which forms a 'skin' around the stem? This 'skin' is called the **epidermis**. The cells of the epidermis fit closely together and are covered on the outside by a protective layer called the **cuticle**. Look at the cells just inside the epidermis. These are the cells of the **cortex**, used for storage and packing. In the centre of the stem are similar but larger cells forming the **pith**. The centre of some stems is hollow (pith cavity).

Can you see a ring of structures in your section? These are the **vascular bundles**. Examine a single vascular bundle using the high power objective of the microscope. Is any part of the vascular bundle stained? If so, what does this indicate? Why do you think the vascular bundles are arranged in a ring close to the periphery of the stem?

The vascular bundles are the transport system of the plant. The inner region of the bundle is stained red because the water, containing the dye eosin, passed through this tissue on its way up the plant. This tissue consists mainly of vessels and fibres and is called the **xylem**. Look at the part of the vascular bundle nearer to the epidermis; it is composed of different cells which form the **phloem**. The phloem is concerned with the transport of manufactured foods, such as sugars, from the leaves to other parts of the plant. Water and mineral salts travel up the xylem whilst manufactured foods pass down the phloem.

9.4. Secondary growth in stems

In herbaceous plants, which have no woody tissue and die back to ground level at the end of each growing season, the vascular bundles may only contain xylem and phloem. In trees and shrubs, however, whose stems persist from year to year, there is a third part of the vascular bundle called the **cambium** which is sandwiched between the xylem and the phloem. At first, the cambium is found only in the vascular bundles, but later grows to form a complete cylinder between the cortex and the pith. Unlike other plant cells which, once mature, are no longer capable of growth, the cells of the cambium retain the power of cell division to produce new phloem cells towards the outside of the stem and new xylem cells towards the inside, as shown in Figure 9.6. The xylem forms the wood of the tree. As the cambium produces more xylem than phloem, this process increases the girth, the strength and the transport capacity of the stem, and is known as **secondary thickening**.

As the girth of the stem increases, the epidermis splits. It is obvious that if the stem had no protection, it would lose water, insects would lay their eggs in it and it would rapidly become infected by fungi. To prevent this, there is a second layer of cambium just below the epidermis, called the **cork cambium**. The cork cambium produces the bark around the stem of the plant.

9.5. Spring and autumn wood: annual rings

The xylem forming the wood of the stem consists of both vessels and fibres, but it is not produced at the same rate throughout the year. Secondary growth occurs during the growing season when food and water are readily available. The rate of growth, therefore, becomes much slower during the autumn and winter. In the spring and early summer, the leaves unfold and need large quantities of water and mineral salts. The cambium responds by producing xylem with many, large, thin-walled vessels, thus increasing the conducting power of the stem. Only a few fibres are produced at this time. The tissue so formed is known as **spring wood**. As the season progresses, the additional weight produced by the season's growth needs support. The cambium therefore produces fewer vessels of smaller diameter and thicker walls, together with a large number of fibres to give the stem additional strength. This tissue is known as **autumn wood**.

The point at which the autumn wood of one season abuts on to

A - YOUNG STEM

B - CAMBIUM EXTENDS BETWEEN BUNDLES

C - THE CAMBIUM FORMS A COMPLETE RING

D - THE CAMBIUM PRODUCES A RING OF PHLOEM towards the outside of the stem AND one of XYLEM towards the inside of the stem

Secondary phloem
Secondary xylem

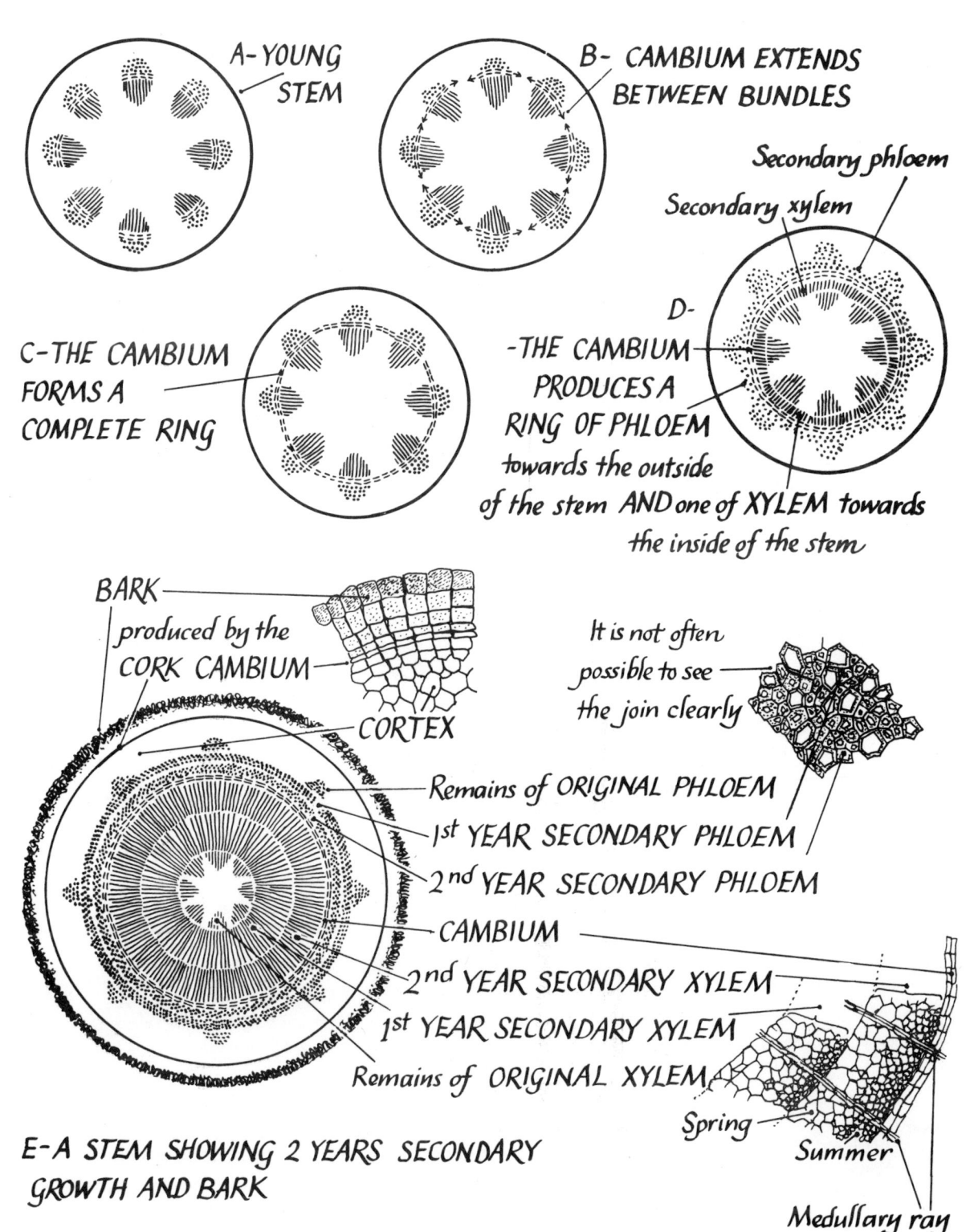

E - A STEM SHOWING 2 YEARS SECONDARY GROWTH AND BARK

BARK produced by the CORK CAMBIUM
CORTEX
Remains of ORIGINAL PHLOEM
1st YEAR SECONDARY PHLOEM
2nd YEAR SECONDARY PHLOEM
CAMBIUM
2nd YEAR SECONDARY XYLEM
1st YEAR SECONDARY XYLEM
Remains of ORIGINAL XYLEM

It is not often possible to see the join clearly

Spring
Summer
Medullary ray

Figure 9.6 Stages in secondary thickening of a stem

the spring wood of the following season forms a very distinct boundary between the growth of the two seasons.

Investigation 9d. To discover the age of a tree by counting the annual rings

Examine the end of a log cut from the trunk or branch of a tree. Try to distinguish between the spring and autumn wood. If the log has just been sawn you will have to sandpaper the end of the log

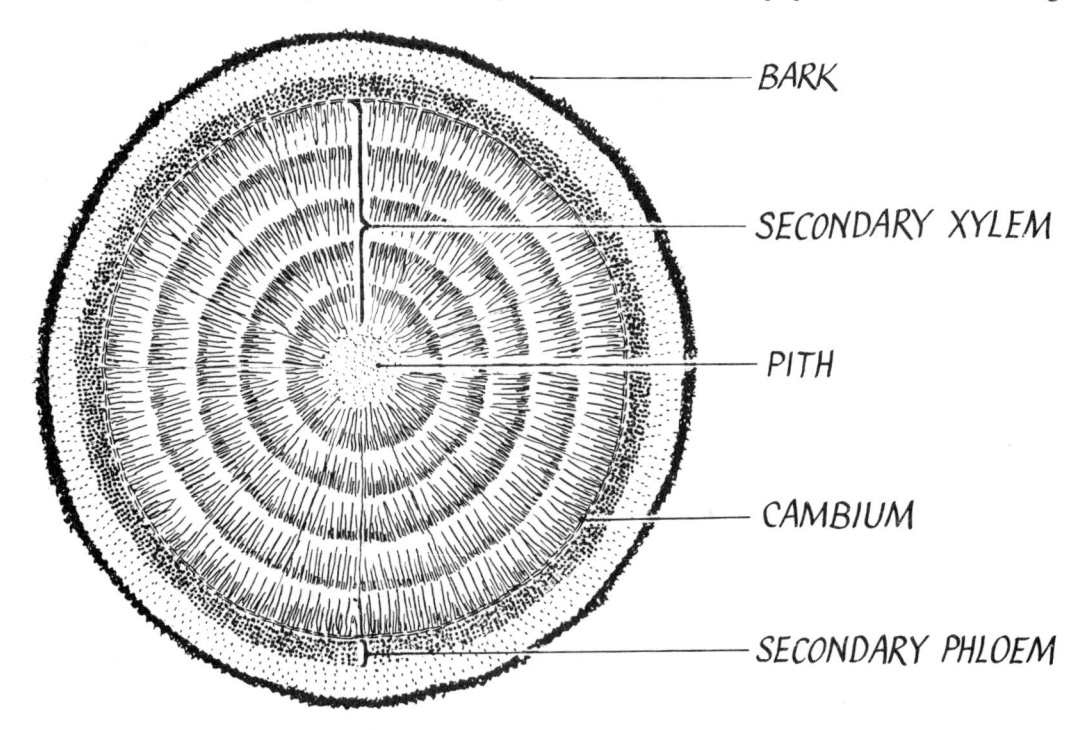

Figure 9.7 A section of a woody stem with annual rings. How old is it?

until it is fairly smooth; you should then be able to see the xylem produced in a single season as a ring. Each year's growth of xylem is called an **annual ring** (see Figure 9.7). Find the age of your particular log.

Devise a method of testing to determine which season's wood is the hardest. Do you get the result that you would expect?

9.6. The functions of the stem

The stem performs several functions. It provides a link between the roots and the leaves, along which raw materials and manufactured foods can pass. The stem also holds the leaves in a position where they may easily obtain plenty of light needed for photosynthesis. The stem supports the flowers in the best position for pollination and, later, the fruits for the dispersal of their seeds. In some plants, the stem may be modified or used as a food storage organ, to enable the plant either to survive unfavourable conditions such as winter (**perennation**) or to produce new plants without the production of flowers and seeds (**vegetative reproduction**). These two processes are described in Chapter 13.

9.7. Buds

At a node, the stem bears a bud in the leaf axil. If the leaves have been shed, the bud occurs just above the leaf scar.

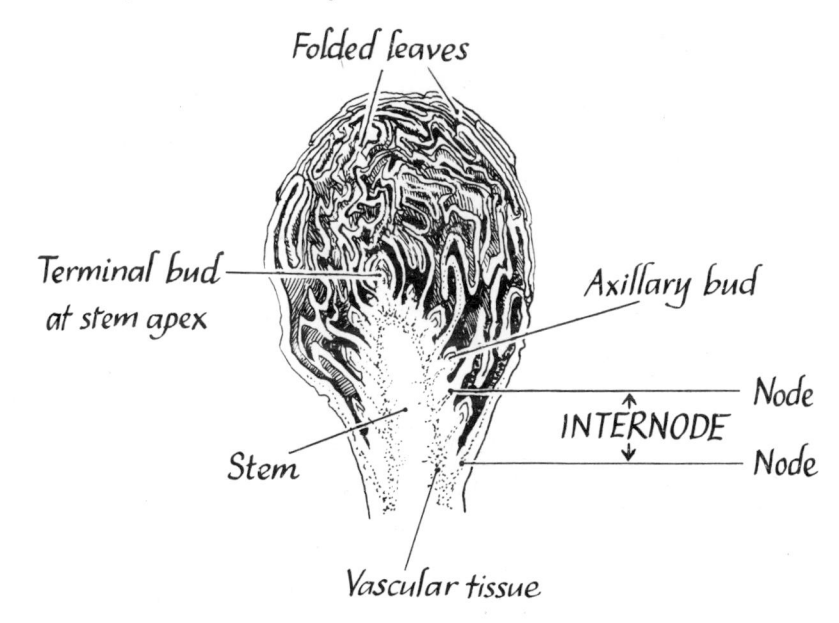

Figure 9.8 A Brussels sprout bud cut in vertical section

Investigation 9e. To examine a Brussels sprout bud

Hold a Brussels sprout between the thumb and forefinger, and with a sharp knife or scalpel cut it vertically in half through the stalk. Examine one half carefully. What does the bud consist of? Look at the main axis of the bud and carefully examine the attachment of the leaves. They arise in a regular manner at nodes, and in the axils of these leaves are small **axillary buds**. What does the presence of leaves and axillary buds tell us about Brussels sprouts? Notice how the green leaves are folded over the delicate growing point of the sprout to protect it (see Figure 9.8). Use 'iodine' to discover if any part of the bud contains starch.

The Brussels sprout is a bud which lacks any special protection other than its own folded leaves. A bud is a stem which is condensed due to greatly reduced internodes. As a result, the leaves are very close together. At the beginning of the growing season, the internodes elongate and the bud expands to form the new season's stem. All buds contain the next season's leaves, and some buds contain the flowers as well.

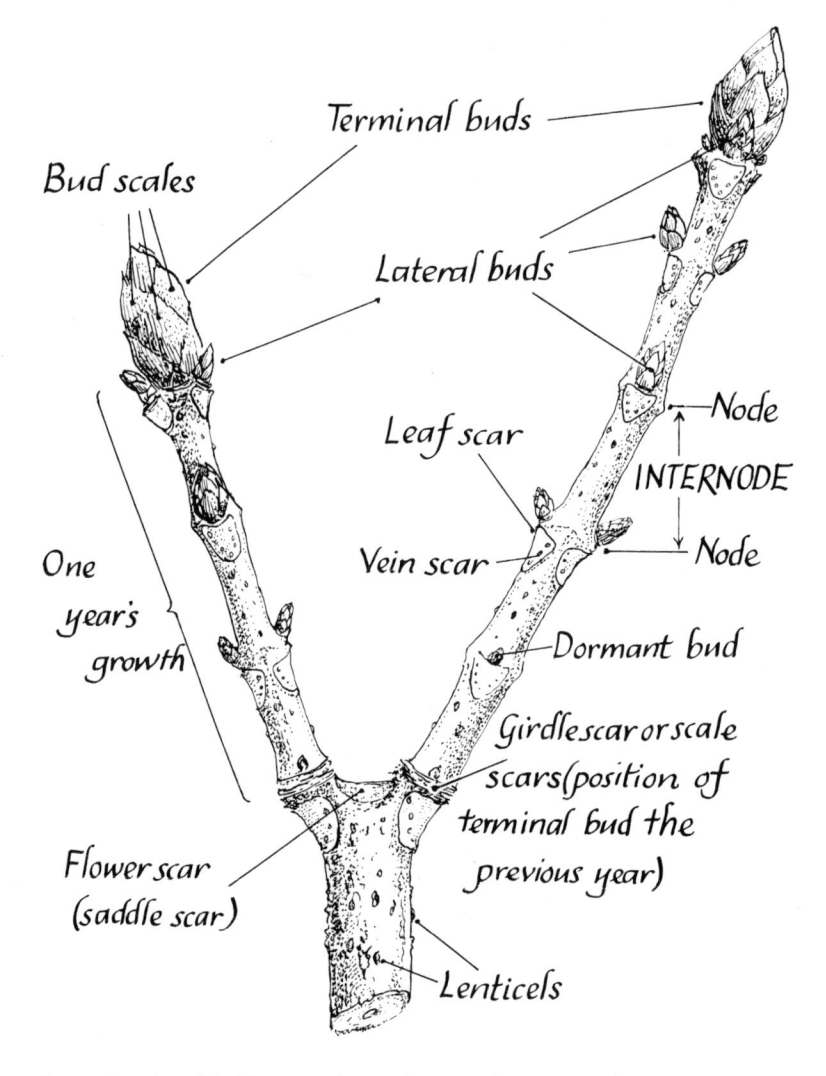

Figure 9.9 A winter twig of horse-chestnut

Investigation 9f. To examine a horse-chestnut twig

Examine a horse-chestnut twig and draw it carefully. Notice that it is woody, indicating that secondary growth has occurred. The epidermis has been replaced by the corky bark. Can you find slit-like pores in the bark? These are **lenticels**, which allow gaseous exchange to occur through the bark.

Look at the buds; there are two types. At the tip of each branch is a large **terminal bud**, which will open in the spring to produce the next year's growth. It may contain an immature flower, in which case, after the flower has withered and fallen, a saddle scar will remain on the twig. The lateral buds on either side of the terminal bud will then produce lateral branches (see Figure 9.9). The smaller buds lower down on the stem are axillary buds. Look beneath the bud and you will see the horseshoe-shaped leaf scar left by the leaf which was shed last autumn.

The development of these smaller buds is suppressed by a hormone which passes down the stem from the terminal bud. If, however, the terminal bud is removed, the flow of hormone will stop and the axillary buds will develop and open. When gardeners prune plants, they are making use of this fact.

Investigation 9g. To dissect a horse-chestnut bud

Dip the terminal bud of your twig into ether to remove the stickiness. Why do you think horse-chestnut buds are sticky? With the aid of a pair of forceps, remove the scales of the bud and arrange them on a white tile in the order that you remove them. How do the outer scales differ from those beneath? Carefully examine the scars left by the bud scales. Can you find similar scars on the twig? What does the portion of stem between two sets of scars represent? Continue until you have removed all the contents of the bud. How can you tell that the furry structures within are leaves? Does your bud contain a flower or just leaves? How does this horse-chestnut bud differ from the Brussels sprout bud?

★ WARNING. *All naked flames must be extinguished before the ether bottle is opened.*

The winter bud of the horse-chestnut is better protected than that of the Brussels sprout. The leaves within the horse-chestnut bud are densely covered by tiny white hairs. These can be removed by gently rubbing the immature leaves with the tip of a needle. The horse-chestnut bud is also protected by bud scales, which drop off when the bud opens. The bud scales leave behind scars which encircle the twig. These are called **girdle scars**, and if you look carefully you will find them at intervals along the twig. They indicate the former position of a terminal bud. The tissue between two adjacent girdle scars represents one season's growth. The sticky secretion of the horse-chestnut is added protection against attack by birds, insects or fungi. The structure of the horse-chestnut bud is shown in Figure 9.10.

Figure 9.10 A vertical section through a horse-chestnut bud

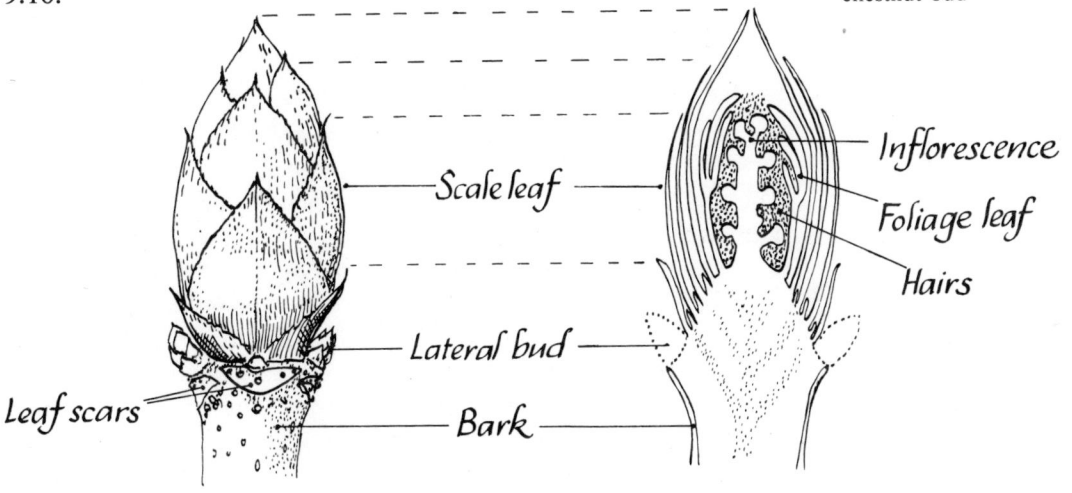

9.8. The leaves

The leaf has often been described as the plant's factory or laboratory. It is the centre of much of the work of the plant, particularly food manufacture or **photosynthesis,** described in Chapter 10. The leaf is also concerned with the loss of excess water from the plant by evaporation. This process is called **transpiration,** and is described in some detail in Chapter 11.

Leaves exhibit an almost infinite variety of shape, from the pitcher-shaped insect trap of the pitcher plant to the needle-shaped leaf of the pine trees, and of size, from the minute leaf of duckweed to the massive leaf of the banana plant.

Investigation 9h. To examine the main parts of a leaf

Hold a leaf up to the light and examine it with a hand lens. Can you see a fine network of white strands with green areas between them? The white strands are the **veins** of the leaf and contain vascular bundles. The veins are tougher than the green parts of the leaf. If you search through a pile of decaying leaves, you will almost certainly discover some leaves in which the green part has completely decayed, leaving a 'skeleton' of veins.

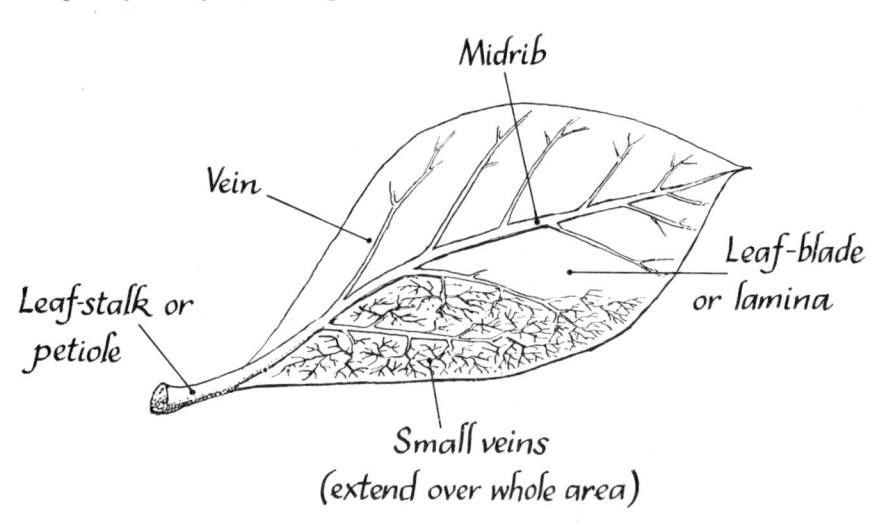

Figure 9.11 The main parts of a leaf

The leaf consists of the leaf-stalk, or **petiole**, and the leaf-blade, or **lamina** (see Figure 9.11). The petiole consists mainly of veins and supporting tissues. The lamina is supported by the central midrib from which the veins radiate. The flattened shape of the leaf provides a large surface area, allowing a large proportion of the chloroplast-containing cells to be exposed to sunlight. This enables the leaf to absorb the energy needed for photosynthesis. The large surface area of the leaf also allows water to evaporate freely during transpiration. Respiration occurs in the leaf cells—as it does in all living cells.

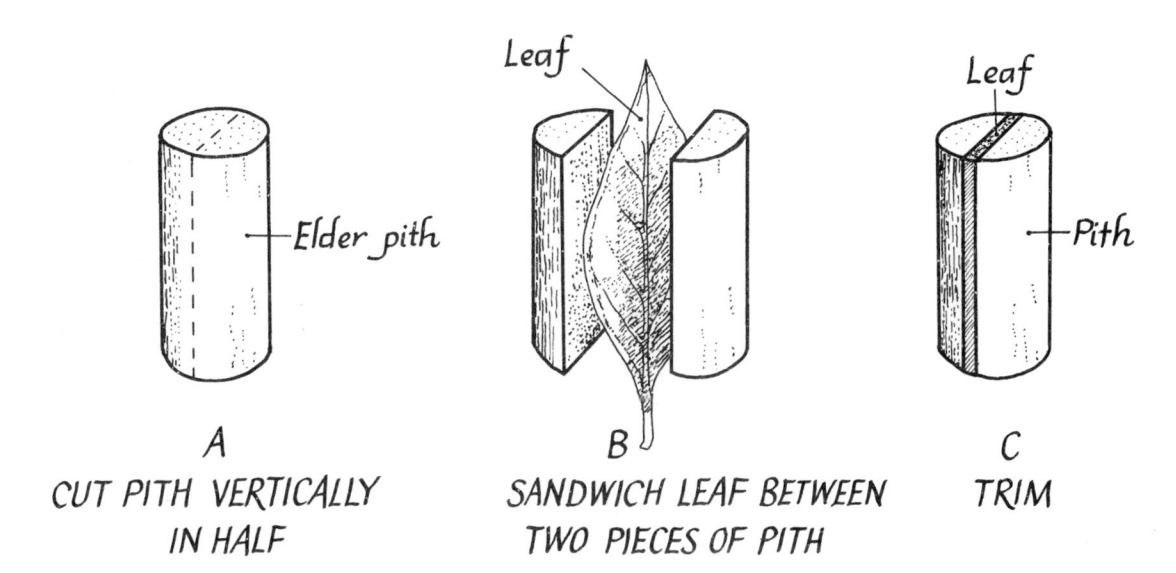

A
CUT PITH VERTICALLY
IN HALF

— Elder pith

B
SANDWICH LEAF BETWEEN
TWO PIECES OF PITH

Leaf

C
TRIM

Leaf
— Pith

Figure 9.12 Using elder pith to support the leaf whilst cutting a section

Investigation 9i. To examine the structure of a leaf

Examine with a microscope a prepared slide of a section through a leaf. If prepared slides are not available, you can attempt to cut a section of a leaf yourself, using the same method as in Investigation 9c. As the leaf is thin, it is easier to cut a section if the leaf is sandwiched between two pieces of elder pith, as shown in Figure 9.12.

Compare your slide with Figure 9.13. If you have a freshly cut

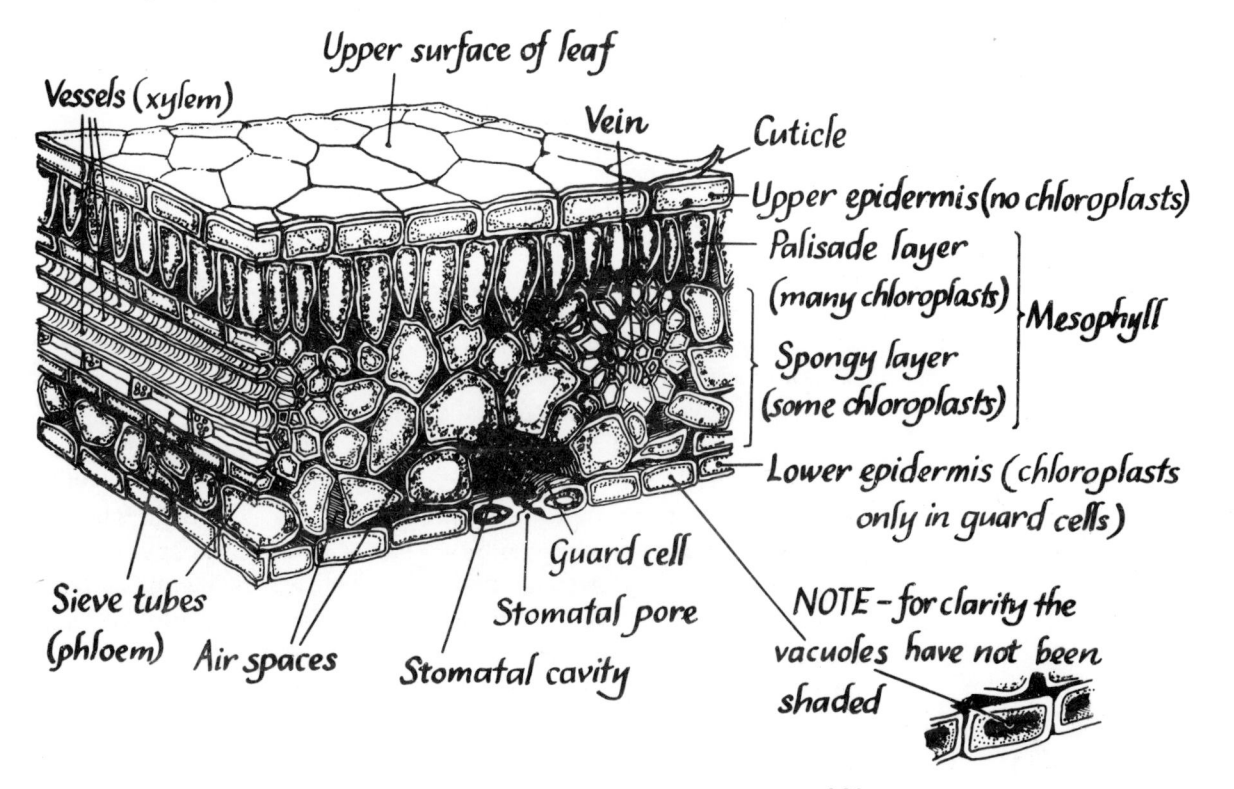

Figure 9.13 Diagram of the internal structure of a leaf

Vessels (xylem)
Upper surface of leaf
Vein
Cuticle
Upper epidermis (no chloroplasts)
Palisade layer (many chloroplasts)
Spongy layer (some chloroplasts)
Mesophyll
Lower epidermis (chloroplasts only in guard cells)
Sieve tubes (phloem)
Air spaces
Guard cell
Stomatal pore
Stomatal cavity
NOTE – for clarity the vacuoles have not been shaded

141

section, try to find out if the green colouring of the leaf is restricted to certain parts.

Examine the upper and lower surface layers of cells. Like the stem, the outermost layer of cells forms a 'skin', called the epidermis. Most of the epidermal cells do not contain green pigment.

The cells between the upper and lower epidermis of the leaf form the **mesophyll**. Look carefully at the mesophyll cells of your section. Are they all the same or can you distinguish two layers? From Figure 9.13 it is clear that the mesophyll cells nearer to the upper epidermis are more tightly packed and darker green in colour than those nearer to the lower epidermis. The upper layer is the **palisade** mesophyll, and is composed of tightly packed cylindrical cells arranged at right angles to the leaf surface. These cells contain the photosynthetic pigment **chlorophyll**, giving the upper surface of the leaf a deep-green appearance. Chlorophyll is found in discrete granules within the cell, called **chloroplasts**. Most of the photosynthesis takes place in the palisade layer of the mesophyll.

The lower layer of the mesophyll is called the **spongy** mesophyll because the cells are less regular in shape and are loosely packed. Between the cells is a network of intercellular spaces through which gases and water vapour can diffuse. The cells of the spongy mesophyll usually do not contain many chloroplasts, giving the lower surface of the leaf a light-green appearance. Extending through the mesophyll are the veins. These consist of vascular bundles containing both xylem and phloem cells.

The pores in the epidermis are called **stomata**. They open and close in response to changes in light intensity, thus regulating the

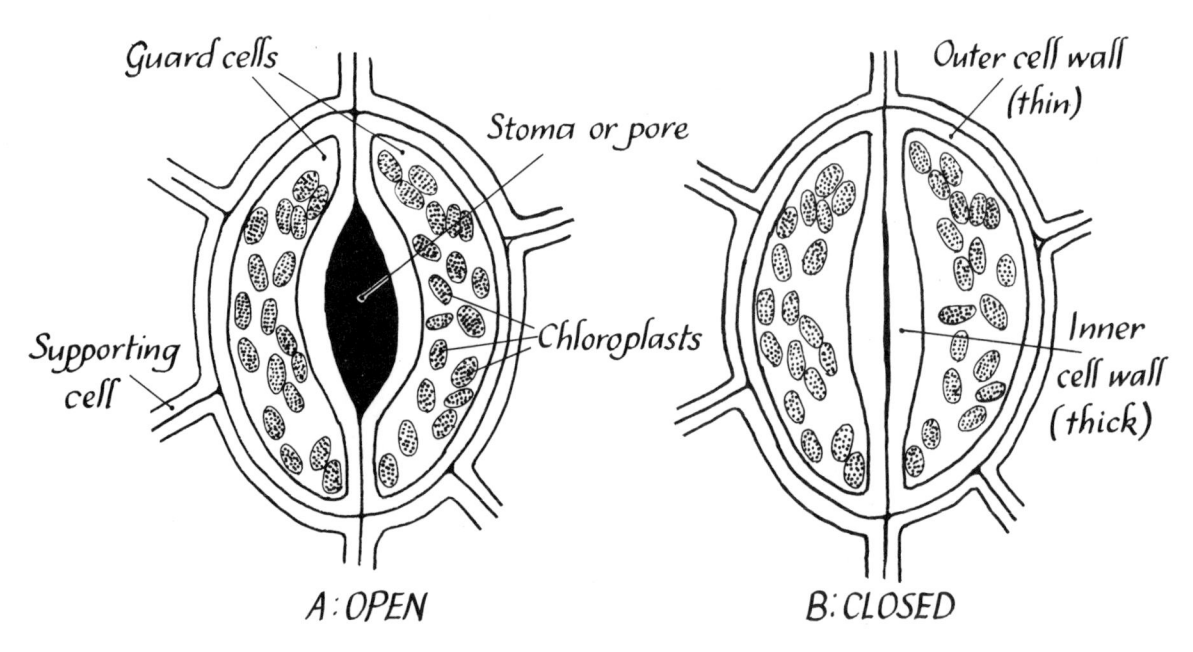

Figure 9.14 Surface view of stomata

passage of gases and water vapour. Are they found on both surfaces of the leaf?

Investigation 9j. To study the distribution of stomata on a leaf

Paint 1 cm² of the upper and lower surface of a privet leaf with nail varnish. When the varnish is perfectly dry, carefully peel it from each surface and mount the peels on a microscope slide. Make sure you know which peel came from which leaf surface. Examine the peels using the medium power of the microscope. The varnish peels act rather like plaster casts and take an accurate impression of the leaf surface. Can you see the impressions of the

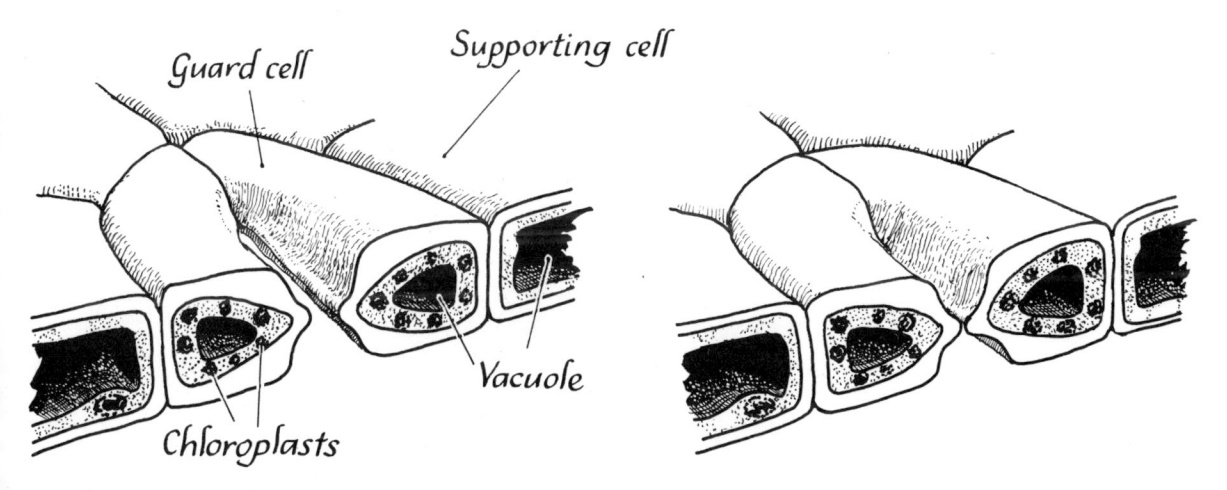

A: OPEN B: CLOSED

stomata and of the sausage-shaped guard cells (see Figures 9.14 and 9.15)? Are they fairly evenly distributed?

Figure 9.15 Stomata shown in vertical section

Compare the shape of the cells of the upper epidermis with those of the lower epidermis. Most plants have far more stomata on the lower than on the upper surface of the leaf. Exceptions are grass plants, which have more or less vertical leaves.

9.9. The root system

The parts of the plant below the soil level, which form the root system, may be almost as branching and as extensive below the ground as the shoot system is above the ground. If possible, have another look at the plant used in Investigation 9a, and estimate what proportion of the plant is root system and what proportion is shoot system. Why is the root system so extensive? Roots can always be distinguished from underground stems as they *never* bear leaves or buds, only smaller lateral roots.

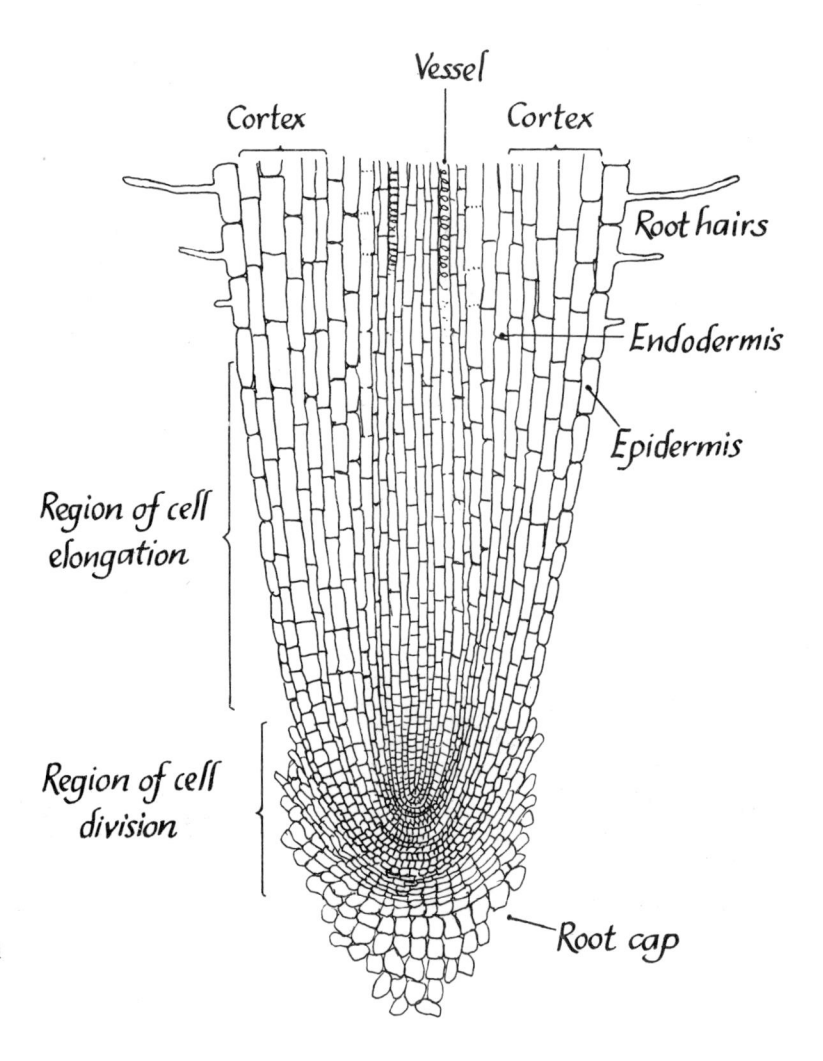

Figure 9.16 A longitudinal section of a young root tip

Investigation 9k. To prepare a squashed root tip slide

Examine the root of a mustard seedling that has been growing in a damp atmosphere. Can you see a mass of fine hairs covering part of the root? Cut the last centimetre from the root and place it in a drop of water on a microscope slide. Gently lower a cover-slip on to the drop of water and root tip. As the root tip is quite thick, the cover-slip will rest on it. Fold a piece of filter paper around the slide and cover-slip and then press the cover-slip gently with the first finger to squash the root tip. The space between the cover-slip and the slide will be completely filled with water and will appear transparent.

First examine the slide under the low power of the microscope. Move the slide about so that you can see all parts of the root tip. Start by examining the very tip and then work your way backwards. At the tip you will see the slightly elongated cells of the **root cap**. These cells are gelatinous and are rubbed off as the growing root pushes through the soil. The functions of the root cap are to protect the delicate root tip and to lubricate its passage through the soil. Look carefully just behind the root cap. Can you see a mass of small, tightly packed cells with dense contents? This is the region of cell division, where new cells are being produced (see Figure 9.16). These cells are more or less as long as they are wide. What about the cells a little further up? These are elongated. Behind this region of elongation, the outermost layer of cells, the epidermis, bears fine projections. This is the region where the root absorbs water. The projections are the **root hairs**, which greatly increase the surface area of the young part of the root so that it can absorb adequate supplies of water.

A root hair is a single cell. It develops from an epidermal cell just behind the region of elongation. The length to which the root hair grows will depend on the availability of water in the soil. If there is plenty of water in the soil the root hairs will be fairly short, but if the soil is very dry the root hairs will grow long, penetrating the spaces between the soil particles in the quest for water. Root hairs are only found on the young parts of the root. Their life is short; eventually, as the root gets older, they wither away. When the root hairs are lost, the outermost layer of the cortex is exposed. This layer becomes corky and waterproof and forms the **epidermis** of the older part of the root. One of the most important functions of the root is to absorb water and to pass it to those parts of the plant where it is needed. What part of the root conducts water to the shoot?

Investigation 9I. To examine the structure of a young root

Examine a prepared slide of a transverse section through a young root. Compare your slide with Figure 9.17. The conducting tissue is

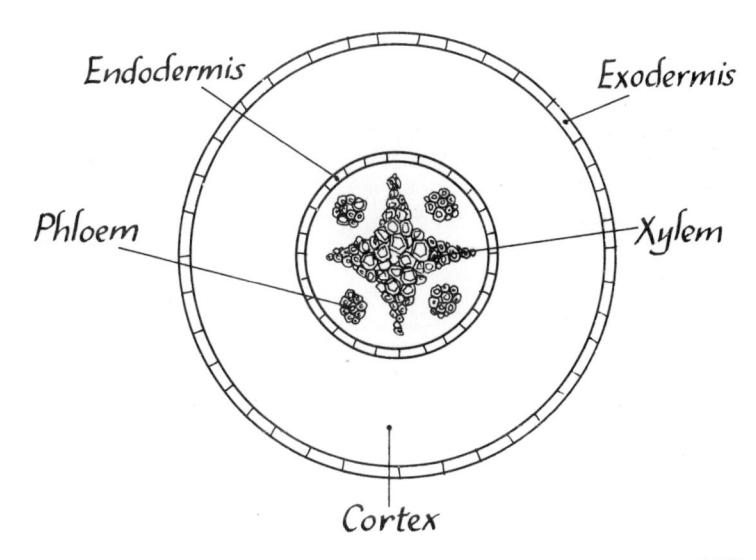

Figure 9.17 Diagram of a transverse section through a young root

situated in the centre of the root. It consists of groups of xylem tissue, frequently arranged in the form of a star, and groups of phloem which may be arranged between the points of the xylem 'star'. It is the xylem which is concerned with conducting water from the root to those parts of the plant where it is required. The phloem is concerned with the passage of manufactured foods, such as sugar, from the site of their synthesis to those parts of the plant where they are needed.

There are two main types of root system, the **tap** root and **fibrous** root systems. A tap root system has a single main root, as in the shepherd's purse (Figure 9.1). Lateral roots arise from a tap root, but these are always smaller. A tap root is usually deep, but is not particularly extensive. A fibrous root system is composed of a large number of fine roots of approximately similar size, which usually arise from the base of the stem. These fine roots are examples of **adventitious** roots, a name given to roots arising from any part of the plant other than a main tap root.

9.10. The functions of the root

The root system is extensive and branched, as it must anchor the plant firmly in the ground. In addition, it must be large enough to absorb all the water and mineral salts that the plant requires. In some plants the root system may be modified as a food storage organ, to assist either perennation or vegetative reproduction.

9.11. Comparison between stems and roots

The structures of stems and roots are compared in Table 9.1.

TABLE 9.1. DIFFERENCES BETWEEN STEMS AND ROOTS

Stems	Roots
1. Usually above ground.	1. Usually below ground.
2. Frequently green.	2. Rarely green.
3. Always bear leaves or leaf scars.	3. Never bear leaves or leaf scars.
4. Always bear buds.	4. Never bear buds.
5. Bear flowers and fruits.	5. Never bear flowers or fruits.
6. Vascular bundles arranged in a ring or scattered.	6. Vascular bundles towards the centre of the root.
7. Xylem and phloem in the same vascular bundle.	7. Xylem and phloem in separate vascular bundles.
8. Surface covered with cuticle.	8. No cuticle.
9. No root hairs.	9. Bears root hairs near tip.

Figure 9.18 (left) Wheat plant: a monocotyledon

Figure 9.19 (right) Daisy plant: a dicotyledon

9.12. Monocotyledons and dicotyledons

There are two groups of Angiosperms, or flowering plants. They are the narrow-leafed plants such as the cereals, grasses and 'spring bulbs', which form the group known as the **monocotyledons** (see Figure 9.18), and the broad-leafed plants (the others), which are known as the **dicotyledons** (see Figure 9.19).

Investigation 9m. To compare a monocotyledon with a dicotyledon

Examine a monocotyledon, such as a grass or cereal plant, or a tulip, crocus or bluebell, and compare it with a dicotyledon, such as a buttercup or wallflower. Be sure to examine the entire plant. First of all examine the leaves and make a note of any marked differences between those of each type of plant. Then compare the roots carefully. Count the number of sepals and petals in the flowers. If possible, examine the seeds and attempt to discover how many cotyledons or seed leaves they contain. Before you attempt this, pick out a large seed and soak it well in water first. Use a microscope to examine prepared slides of transverse sections through a stem of each type of plant. Look particularly at the arrangement of the vascular bundles. Make a list of the ways in which the types of plant differ and compare your list with Table 9.2.

TABLE 9.2. DIFFERENCES BETWEEN MONOCOTYLEDONS AND DICOTYLEDONS

Monocotyledons	Dicotyledons
1. Narrow leaves with parallel veins.	1. Broad leaves with a network of veins.
2. Usually have a fibrous root system.	2. Usually have a tap root system.
3. Sepals and petals in threes or multiples thereof.	3. Sepals and petals in fives or fours, or multiples thereof.
4. A single cotyledon in the seed.	4. Two cotyledons in the seed.
5. Vascular bundles scattered in stem.	5. Vascular bundles arranged in a ring close to the margin of the stem.

Figure 9.20 Some common deciduous trees

OAK   BEECH   ENGLISH ELM

Figure 9.21 Some common evergreen trees and shrubs

YEW   HOLLY   LAWSON'S CYPRESS

9.13. Deciduous and evergreen plants

Most woody plants in Britain respond to the onset of the unfavourable winter conditions by shedding their leaves to reduce water loss to a minimum. These are **deciduous** plants (see Figure 9.20).

Plants which retain their leaves throughout the winter months are called **evergreens**. These include all the coniferous trees except the larch (see Figure 9.21). Evergreens often grow in less favourable conditions and are usually adapted to reduce water loss without shedding their leaves. The pine has leaves with sunken stomata and the laurel has a thick waxy cuticle.

Test your understanding

Copy out and complete the following paragraph:

The parts of the plant above the soil level form the ....[1] system and those below form the ....[2] system. Stems always bear leaves and ....[3] The layer of cells covering the young stem is called the ....[4] The transport system of the plant consists of the ....[5] bundles which contain both ....[6] and phloem. The ....[7] is concerned with the upward transport of ....[8] and mineral salts. The ....[9] is concerned with the downward transport of manufactured foods, such as ....[10] The leaves are concerned particularly with the processes of ....[11] and ....[12] The root is concerned with ....[13] the plant firmly in the soil and the absorption of ....[14] and ....[15] Narrow-leafed plants are called ....[16], whilst dicotyledons have broad leaves with a ....[17] of viens ....[18] plants usually lose their leaves before winter, but ....[19] plants, such as ....[20], retain their leaves.

1. What are the main parts of the shoot system?
2. How do stems differ from roots?
3. What are the functions of the stem?
4. What is secondary thickening of a stem and why is it necessary?
5. Explain the functions of xylem and phloem. Where in the plant would you find them?
6. Why is it so important to dig up plants carefully when transplanting them?
7. What are the functions of the root system?
8. Why are leaves flattened structures?
9. What are the differences between monocotyledons and dicotyledons? Give an example of each.
10. Which plants lose their leaves in autumn? Why is this necessary? Why do evergreen plants not need to shed their leaves?

TOPIC C: THE WORKING OF THE PLANT

Chapter 10

Food-making by Plants: Photosynthesis

10.1. The need for food

Both plants and animals need food for growth and for the liberation of energy. It has been known for a very long time how animals obtain their food and to some extent what they use it for. Without food, animals do not grow, but instead waste away and eventually die. What about plants? They do not eat and yet they continue to grow. A seed may weigh a fraction of a gramme, but it may germinate and grow into a large tree, weighing several thousand kilogrammes.

The ancient Greek philosopher Aristotle suggested that the food of a plant was produced in the soil and that it entered the plant through the roots. This idea, although it had not been proved, was accepted until the seventeenth century, when a Flemish chemist, van Helmont, carried out a famous experiment, which is illustrated in Figure 10.1. In this experiment, he set out to prove that the plant was produced from water.

10.2. Van Helmont's experiment

Van Helmont filled a tub with 90·73 kg of oven-dried soil and planted in it a young willow tree weighing 2·27 kg. He covered the soil to prevent dust from getting into the tub. The soil was kept moist by adding only rain water or distilled water. Five years later he removed the tree, and found that it weighed 77·51 kg, a gain of 75·24 kg. He then dried and weighed the soil. The result was 90·67 kg, a loss of 60 g.

Van Helmont did not include the leaves shed in the four autumns in his calculations. Therefore, he thought 75·24 kg of wood, bark and root had arisen from water alone. He considered that the loss in weight of the soil of 60 g was due to experimental error. Why do you think Van Helmont dried the soil each time before weighing it? Can you suggest any reason for the difference in soil weight? Was van Helmont right to discount the loss of 60 g as experimental

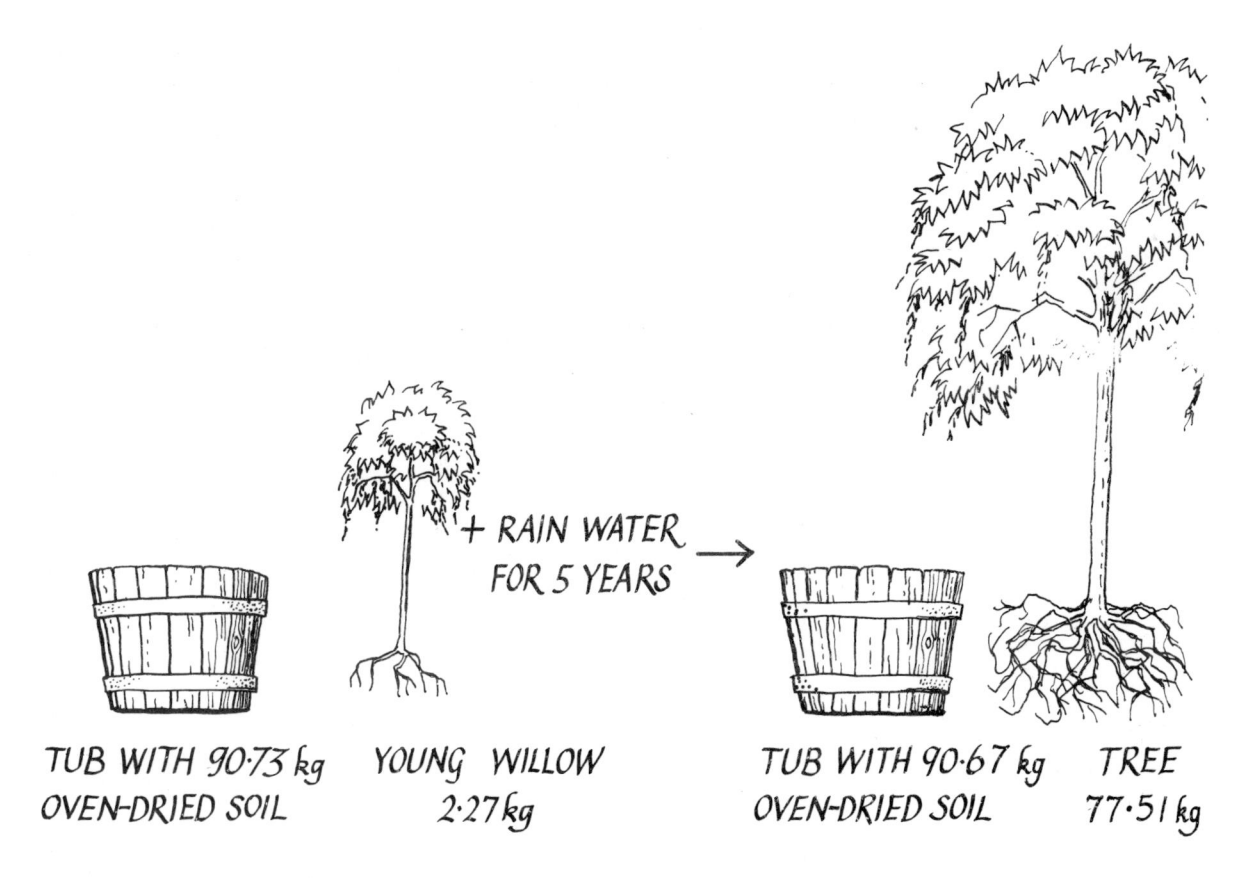

TUB WITH 90·73 kg OVEN-DRIED SOIL   YOUNG WILLOW 2·27 kg   + RAIN WATER FOR 5 YEARS →   TUB WITH 90·67 kg OVEN-DRIED SOIL   TREE 77·51 kg

error? Do these results support Aristotle's hypothesis that the food of a plant is produced from the soil? The weight of the tree did increase considerably. Do you agree with van Helmont that the increase was produced from the water? Can you offer an explanation?

Figure 10.1 Van Helmont's experiment

10.3. Gaseous exchange in plants

Energy is essential for the maintenance of life in all organisms. Living organisms derive their energy from the process of respiration. In almost all organisms, the gas oxygen is necessary for this process. Although living organisms are constantly removing oxygen gas from the atmosphere, the proportion of oxygen in the atmosphere does not diminish but remains constant at about 21%.

The gas carbon dioxide is constantly being produced by all living organisms during respiration. Even so, *on average*, the proportion of carbon dioxide in the atmosphere does not increase but remains constant at 0·03%. What do these observations suggest? Are there other processes in nature which, in turn, remove carbon dioxide from the atmosphere and add oxygen to the atmosphere? Let us carefully examine the carbon dioxide content of the air around an actively growing cereal crop, over a 24-hour period. Unfortunately, it is not possible to take these measurements very accurately in school, so we must rely on the secondhand results of scientists, which are shown in the graph in Figure 10.2.

The time of day is shown on the horizontal axis of the graph and the percentage of carbon dioxide in the air on the vertical axis. You will see from the horizontal line across the middle of the graph that the mean carbon dioxide concentration (the carbon dioxide concentration averaged over a twenty-four hour period) is constant at 0·03%. However, does the concentration fluctuate within the twenty-four hour period? If so, when is it at the maximum and when is it at the minimum concentration?

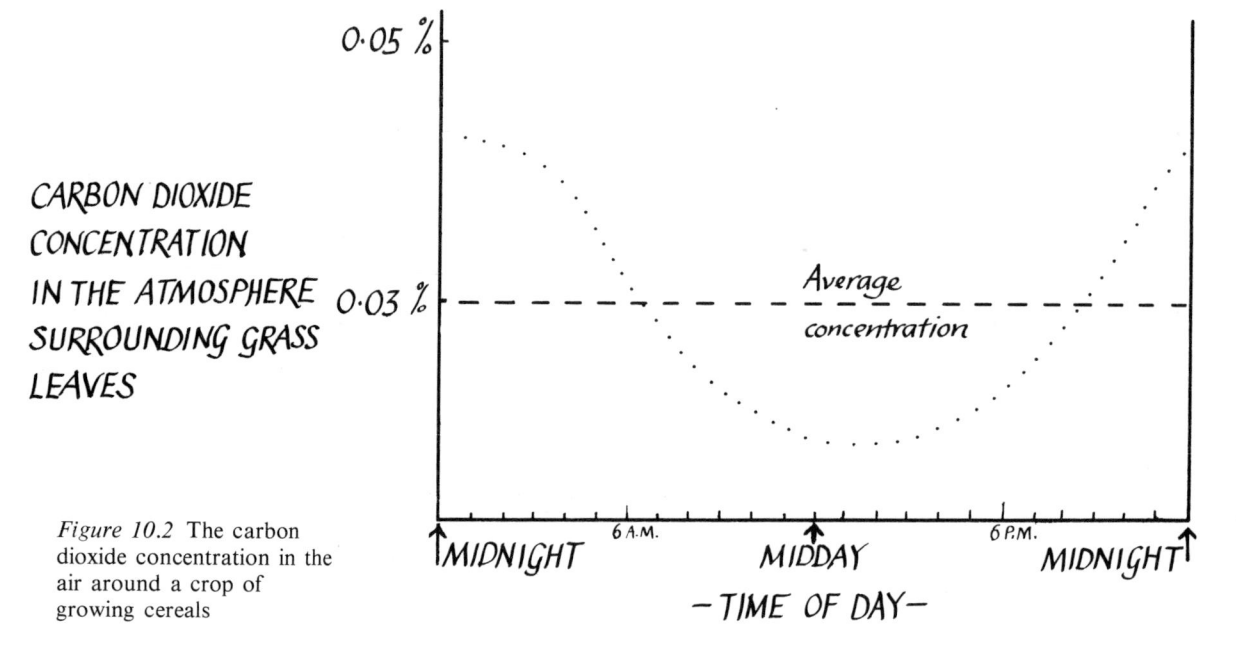

Figure 10.2 The carbon dioxide concentration in the air around a crop of growing cereals

Could the plants be removing some of the carbon dioxide from the atmosphere at certain times of the day and using it for making food? To test this suggestion, it is necessary to deprive the plants of carbon dioxide in order to discover if they can manufacture their food without it. How do we know whether or not the plant has made any food during the experiment? It is necessary to know what food the plant manufactures, and how it can be detected.

The green plant manufactures glucose sugar which it stores as starch. If, therefore, we can detect the presence of starch in a plant at the end of an investigation where none existed at the beginning, then we can conclude that the plant has manufactured starch during the investigation. If the plant does produce starch, then we can assume that the investigation was carried out under suitable conditions and that all the requirements for food manufacture were available.

Investigation 10a. To discover if a leaf contains starch

Take a leaf from a plant which has been exposed to sunlight for some hours. Submerge the leaf in boiling water for two minutes. Then soak it in hot methylated spirits in a test-tube which is in a water-bath, as shown in Figure 10.3. *Make sure that the bunsen flame is turned right down whilst the tube of methylated spirits is over the water-bath, and be sure to keep the tube and the bottle of methylated spirits well away from the bunsen flame.* The leaf loses its colour in

★ *This investigation should only be carried out under the supervision of a teacher.*

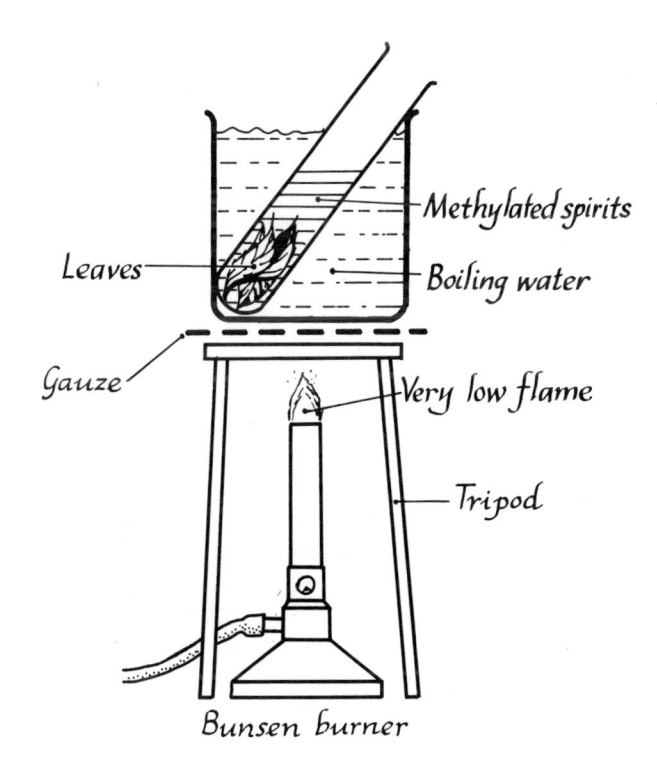

Figure 10.3 Removing the chlorophyll from the leaves

the methylated spirits and also becomes rather brittle. Soak the leaf in cold water for a few moments. What effect does this have on the leaf?

Finally, place the leaf in a shallow dish or watchglass and flood it with a solution of iodine in potassium iodide. If starch comes into contact with 'iodine solution' it turns a very dark blue (almost black) colour. How would you know whether your leaf has been manufacturing food or not?

You will use this test for starch in several investigations in this chapter, to help you decide if starch formation occurs under various conditions. *Be sure to observe the precautions with the methylated spirits each time you carry it out.*

We put the leaf in hot water to kill it and thus make the cells permeable to methylated spirits. The hot water destroys the protoplasm and bursts any starch grains present. The presence of chlorophyll in the leaf makes it difficult to observe the starch/iodine colour change, so it must be removed. Chlorophyll dissolves in hot methylated spirits, which it turns green. This causes the creamy-white appearance of the leaves. Methylated spirits also dehydrates the leaves, making them stiff and brittle. When the de-coloured leaf is dipped into cold water, it reabsorbs water and becomes supple again.

If we are to assume that the starch, found to be present in the leaf, was manufactured during the investigation, then we must be sure that the leaf was free from starch at the beginning of the investigation. This can be checked using the technique in Investigation 10a.

Investigation 10b. To discover if a leaf loses its starch during darkness

Take the plant in which you have demonstrated the presence of starch and place it in a dark place for 48 hours. After this time test two of its leaves for the presence of starch. What does this show?

10.4. Is carbon dioxide necessary for the plant to manufacture starch?

The results shown in Figure 10.2 indicate that the carbon dioxide concentration in the air around a cereal crop falls during daylight, reaching its lowest reading around noon when the light intensity is at its highest. A **control** experiment, in which similar readings were taken in the absence of plants, showed a constant concentration of 0·03%, with no daily fluctuations. It has been found that 13% of the dry weight of a plant is carbon. Van Helmont's willow tree could not have obtained its carbon from the water or from the soil. These observations suggest that the plant uses atmospheric carbon dioxide in the manufacture of its food.

Investigation 10c. To discover if carbon dioxide is necessary for a plant to manufacture starch

Take two de-starched plants, that is, plants which have been kept in a dark cupboard for 48 hours prior to the investigation. Test two leaves from each plant to make sure that all the starch has been removed.

To discover if a particular factor is essential to a process, the factor concerned is eliminated to see if the process will continue in its absence. In this investigation, carbon dioxide must be eliminated. Place one of the potted plants on a piece of glass and then cover it with a bell jar. Place an open dish of saturated potassium hydroxide solution (to absorb carbon dioxide from the air) under the bell jar beside the plant, and place a tube containing soda lime (to absorb any carbon dioxide entering from the air) in the neck of the bell jar (see Figure 10.4). At the same time set up the control experiment using the other plant (see Figure 10.5). The conditions for this plant are the same as for the first, except that potassium hydroxide solution and soda lime are not used. Thus, carbon dioxide is available

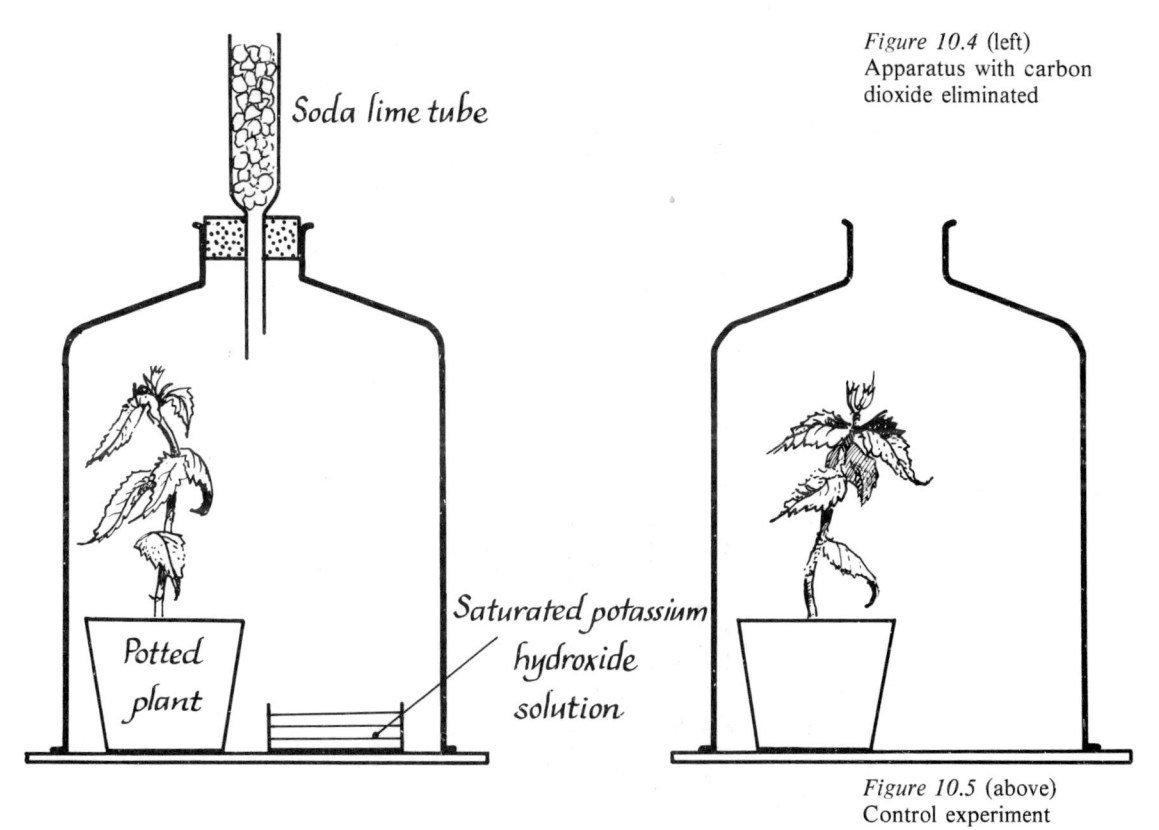

Figure 10.4 (left) Apparatus with carbon dioxide eliminated

Figure 10.5 (above) Control experiment

to this plant. Place both plants in a sunny position for several hours, and then remove a leaf from each of them and test for the presence of starch. When you test the leaves from the two plants for the presence of starch, do not forget to label them in some way so that you know which leaf is which. Write down your results. What conclusions can you draw from them?

10.5. Is oxygen given off by a plant during starch production?

In Section 10.3 it was mentioned that the overall oxygen concentration in the atmosphere remained constant, despite the fact that it was constantly being used by all living organisms for respiration. Could the green plants be putting some of it back as a by-product of food manufacture?

Investigation 10d. To collect any gas produced by a green plant, and to discover what it is

As it is difficult to collect gas from a land plant, an aquatic plant such as *Elodea canadensis*, the Canadian pondweed, is used. Place equal quantities of pondweed into three large beakers labelled A, B and C. Almost fill beaker A with a 1% solution of sodium bicarbonate. Add similar quantities of water to beakers B and C.

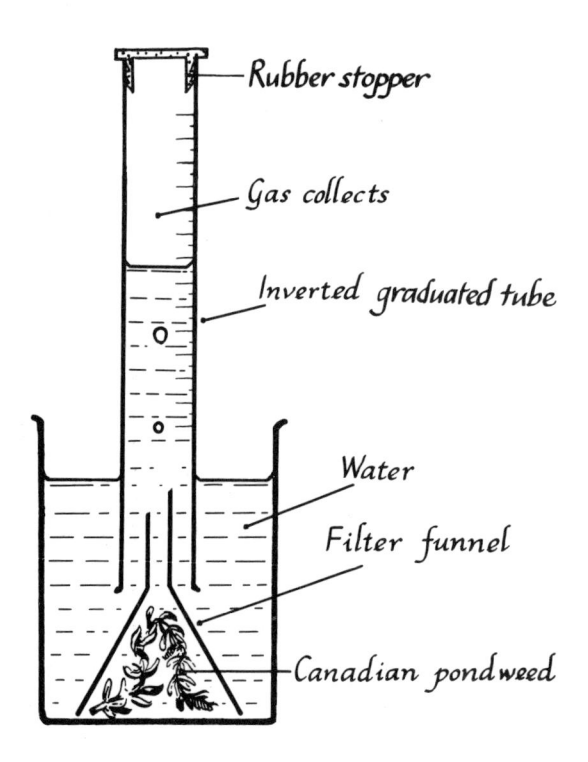

Figure 10.6 Collecting gas from water plants

Cover the pondweed with inverted funnels which have short stems. It is important that the funnel stems do not protrude above the water level in the beaker. Invert a test-tube full of water over each funnel. Alternatively, a graduated tube with a rubber stopper may be used, as shown in Figure 10.6. This will enable the volume of gas to be measured more accurately. Place beakers A and B in a sunny position, but keep beaker C in the dark.

Examine the beakers after two or three days. If you have used graduated tubes, record the volume of gas produced in each tube. What are the differences between the three sets of apparatus at the end of the experiment? Give reasons for these differences. Test the gas in the tubes to see if it is oxygen. Why do you think that sodium bicarbonate was added to beaker A? Did it make any difference to the result?

10.6. The importance of light

Investigation 10e. To discover if light is necessary for food manufacture in a plant

We must eliminate light from all or from part of a plant, to see if it will manufacture food in its absence. Take a de-starched plant, such as a geranium or nasturtium, and pin a few pieces of cork to one of the leaves, as shown in Figure 10.7, or fix a stencil bearing your initials to a leaf, as shown in Figure 10.8.

Figure 10.7 (left) Leaf with a cork mask

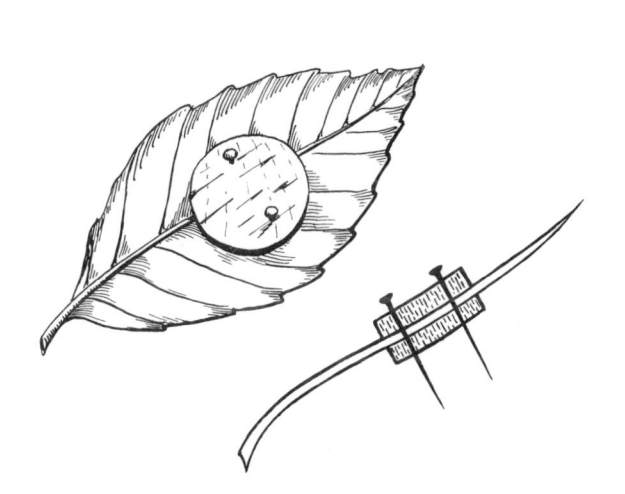

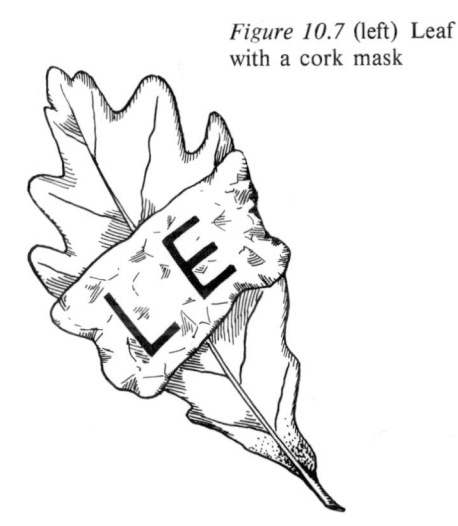

Figure 10.8 (above) Leaf with initials on a stencil

Place the plant in a sunny position for several hours. Then pluck the leaves bearing the cork or stencil and test them for the presence of starch. Which areas contain starch and which do not? Can you draw any conclusions from this investigation? Is it necessary to have a control?

10.7. Photosynthesis—the synthesis of food with the aid of light

The previous investigation indicates that light is essential for the production of starches and sugars in green plants. It is from this that the name **photosynthesis** is derived.

Green plants are the **producers** in nature. They harness the sun's energy and convert it into a form which living organisms can utilize (see Figure 10.9). All other organisms obtain their energy-containing compounds secondhand, either directly or indirectly from green plants. These other organisms are called **consumers.**

In Chapter 8 we learnt that the group of plants called the **fungi** were consumers, and unlike the green plants were not able to photosynthesize. What makes a green plant green?

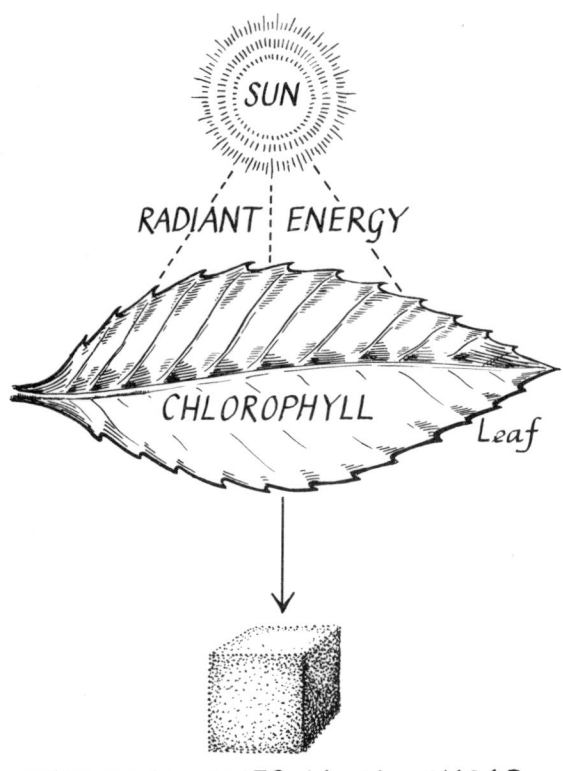

Figure 10.9 A leaf traps the sun's energy

10.8. Is chlorophyll essential for photosynthesis?

The fact that green plants are able to manufacture sugars and starches by photosynthesis, whilst the non-green plants cannot, suggests that the green pigment (chlorophyll) may be necessary for photosynthesis to occur.

Investigation 10f. To discover if chlorophyll is necessary for photosynthesis

We cannot deprive a leaf of its chlorophyll without killing it, but fortunately some species of privet, geranium, maple and other plants have what are described as **variegated** leaves. These normal, healthy leaves are partly green and partly white, as seen in Figure 10.10. If cells from the white area are compared with the cells from the green area under a microscope, it will be seen that the cells from the green area contain chloroplasts, whilst those from the white area do not.

Pick the leaf of a variegated plant which has been exposed to sunlight for some hours, and place it on a white tile or paper. Place a piece of ground glass, such as a gas jar lid, over the leaf. Trace the outline of the leaf on the ground glass and shade in the green areas.

Now test the leaf for starch as in Investigation 10a. Compare the pattern of the starch in the leaf (the black area) with the tracing on the glass. What conclusion can you draw? Does this investigation require a control?

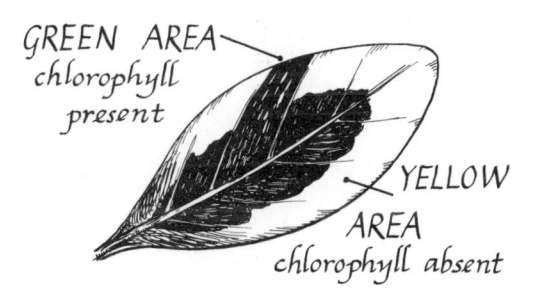

Figure 10.10 The leaf of a variegated privet

10.9. The overall process of photosynthesis

Let us now carefully examine the information that has been gained from the investigations in this chapter. It has been demonstrated that carbon dioxide, light and chlorophyll are essential for the process. Water and the enzymes of the living plant are also necessary. The process produces glucose, which is converted into starch. Oxygen, a by-product, is given off as a gas. To summarize:

$$\text{carbon dioxide} + \text{water} + \text{energy} \xrightarrow[\text{(trapped by chlorophyll)}]{\text{sunlight}} \text{glucose} + \text{oxygen}$$

10.10. The chemistry of photosynthesis

The chemical formula of a molecule of glucose is $C_6H_{12}O_6$, which means that one molecule of glucose contains six atoms of carbon, twelve atoms of hydrogen and six atoms of oxygen. One molecule of oxygen contains two atoms (and is written as O_2). A single molecule of water contains two atoms of hydrogen and one of oxygen. How many water molecules and carbon dioxide molecules are needed to make a single molecule of glucose? How many oxygen molecules will also be produced?

Remember that in a chemical equation there must be the same number of atoms of each type of element on each side of the equation. Try to balance the equation for photosynthesis, first in words and then in chemical formulae.

? carbon dioxide + ? water + light energy ⟶ 1 glucose + ? oxygen
? CO_2 + ? H_2O + energy ⟶ 1 $C_6H_{12}O_6$ + ? O_2

It is important to notice that the equation which you have just completed is the overall equation, and merely tells us the substances present before and after the reaction, and their relative proportions. There is, in fact, a series of chemical reactions involved. You might assume from the balanced equation that the oxygen released at the end of the process comes from the carbon dioxide, but this has been found to be incorrect. You might well ask how scientists can tell which oxygen atoms come from where. They use the same principle that you use to identify your school cap and scarf from those of your classmates, that is by putting tags or labels on them.

How can you label atoms? **Isotopes** are used. These are atoms which have the same chemical properties, but slightly different masses. For example, the normal oxygen atom has an atomic mass of 16 (O^{16}), but a small proportion of oxygen atoms have an atomic mass of 18 (O^{18}). The latter can be detected by sensitive instruments and their path can be traced through a chemical process, such as photosynthesis. If a plant is fed with water containing O^{18}, the 'labelled' oxygen appears in the oxygen which is given off. If, on the other hand, the plant is fed with carbon dioxide containing labelled oxygen, the labelled oxygen will be found in the glucose at the end of the process. This makes a difference to the overall equation which you have just balanced. If you have done this properly you will get this result:

$$6CO_2 + 6H_2O^* + \text{energy} \longrightarrow 1C_6H_{12}O_6 + 6O_2^*$$
$$(O^* = O^{18} \text{ or labelled oxygen})$$

By using labelled oxygen atoms scientists have shown that the oxygen given off comes entirely from the water. In our equation, we have only six labelled oxygen atoms on the left-hand side of the equation, but there are twelve labelled oxygen atoms on the right-hand side. So, to balance the equation, in the light of modern knowledge it is necessary to add six molecules of water to each side of the equation:

6 carbon dioxide + 12 water* + light energy $\longrightarrow$
$\qquad\qquad\qquad\qquad\qquad$ 1 glucose + 6 oxygen* + 6 water

$$6CO_2 + 12H_2O^* + \text{energy} \longrightarrow 1C_6H_{12}O_6 + 6O_2^* + 6H_2O$$

10.11. The site of photosynthesis

Photosynthesis takes place in the chloroplasts and will occur in any part of the plant containing them. However, the main organs of photosynthesis are the leaves. The chloroplasts are concentrated in the palisade layer in the upper region of the leaf (see Figure 9.13). This is why the upper surface of a leaf is much darker than the lower surface. How is the leaf adapted to carry out this process of photosynthesis?

As can be seen from Figure 9.13, the leaf is a thin flattened structure which has a very large surface area in relation to its volume. This enables it to expose as many chloroplasts as possible to the light. The large surface area also enables a large amount of carbon dioxide to diffuse into the leaf through the pores, or stomata, in the lower epidermis. The stomata open during the day to admit carbon dioxide when the plant is photosynthesizing. At night when it does not need carbon dioxide they close to prevent unnecessary evaporation of water.

The spongy layer of cells has large interconnecting air spaces which allow the gases to diffuse the short distance to the palisade layer. Carbon dioxide dissolves in the moisture on the surface of the cells and enters the cell in solution.

Test your understanding

Copy and complete the following paragraph:

Photosynthesis is a process carried out only by ....[1] It occurs mainly in the cells of the ....[2], which contain distinct bodies called ....[3] These bodies are coloured ....[4] because they contain the pigment ....[5], which traps the energy from ....[6] so that the plant can convert it into the ....[7] energy of ....[8] The raw materials needed are water and ....[9], which forms ....[10] per cent of the air and enters the leaf through pores, or ....[11], on the ....[12] surface of the leaf. The main product is ....[13] sugar, which in daylight is immediately converted into insoluble ....[14] Another product of the process is the gas ....[15] Green plants are the only organisms which can harness the sun's energy, and are called ....[16] This harnessed energy is vital to *all* other living things, animal and plant, these being called ....[17]

1. Explain why green plants are called producers.
2. Explain what mistakes van Helmont made in his experiment.
3. Explain why control experiments are so important in biology, and give an example of when you would perform one.
4. Explain how isotopes may be used in biological research.
5. 'All energy originates in the sun.' Explain this statement with reference to photosynthesis, coal and electricity.

Chapter 11

Plants and Water

11.1. The need for water

Water is essential to all forms of life. We know that plants will die if the soil becomes dry and parched, and that animals will perish if there is no water to drink or succulent plants to eat. Why is water so important to living things? About 80% of the bodies of most plants and animals consists of water. Water is a solvent in which many substances vital to the chemical activities of life are dissolved. It is important as a transport medium for dissolved materials. Water is an essential constituent of protoplasm. It is also a raw material for certain metabolic processes, such as photosynthesis, discussed in the previous chapter. Herbaceous plants depend upon water for support: cells full of water become firm, or **turgid**, and if a large number of such cells are turgid, then they give some rigidity to the plant.

11.2. Where do plants get their water from?

Many plants consist of about 80% water. Where does this water come from? How does it enter the plant? During a prolonged spell of dry weather, you probably water the plants in the garden. If you have house plants, you will certainly water them at regular intervals. You do not add the water directly to the plant, but saturate the soil around it. The plant takes the water it needs from the soil. In Investigation 16g you are invited to perform an experiment to discover if a particular sample of soil contains water, and if so, how much. You will probably be surprised at the quantity of water that the soil contains. It is from this 'reservoir' of soil water that the plant obtains the water it needs. Since a plant gets its water from the soil, and the root is the part of the plant that is buried in the soil, then it is reasonable to suggest that water enters the plant through the root.

Investigation 11a. To discover if a plant absorbs water through its root

Dig up a growing plant, such as groundsel, and carefully wash the soil from its roots. Take a conical flask or a jar and fill it two-thirds

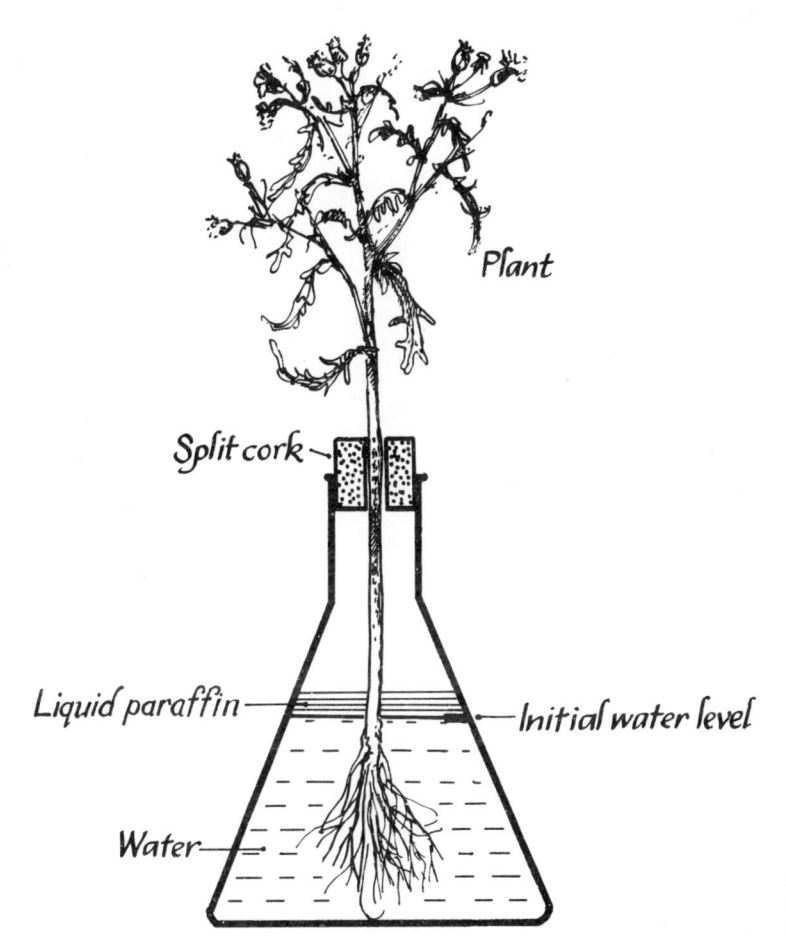

Figure 11.1 Apparatus to discover if roots absorb water

full of water. Place the roots of the plant in the water so that the plant is supported in such a way that the water level corresponds to the soil surface. Cover the surface of the water with liquid paraffin and carefully support the stem of the plant in the neck of the flask with cotton wool or with a split cork (see Figure 11.1).

Carefully mark the level of the liquid in the flask and place it in a light, airy position. Check and mark the level of the liquid in the flask each day. Is there any change? Where could the water have gone to? Why do you think the surface of the water was covered by a thin layer of liquid paraffin? Write down your conclusions.

11.3. How is the root adapted to absorb water from the soil?

Investigation 11b. To examine a young root

Germinate some mustard, cress or similar seeds on moist blotting paper or in damp sawdust. Place a single seedling on a microscope slide in a drop of water. Cover with a large cover-slip and gently press down to squash the seedling. Examine the preparation under

165

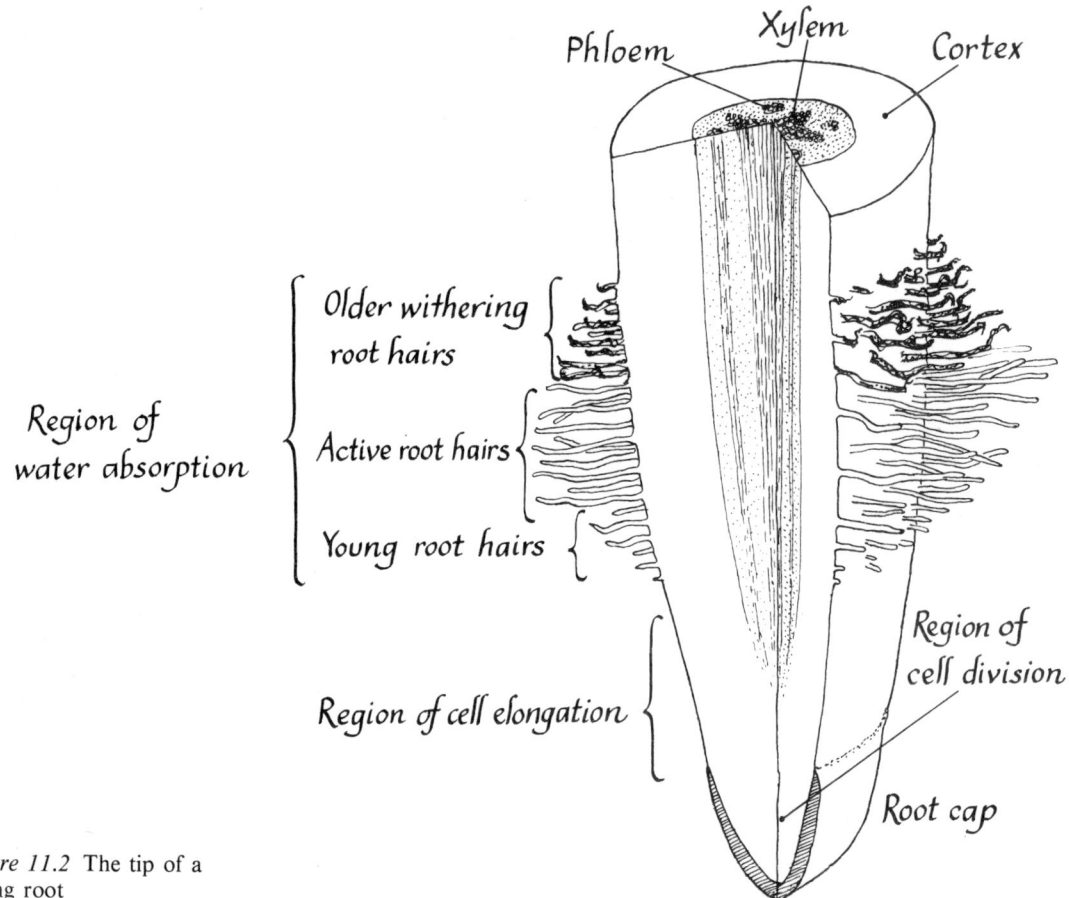

Figure 11.2 The tip of a young root

Figure 11.3 A single root hair cell

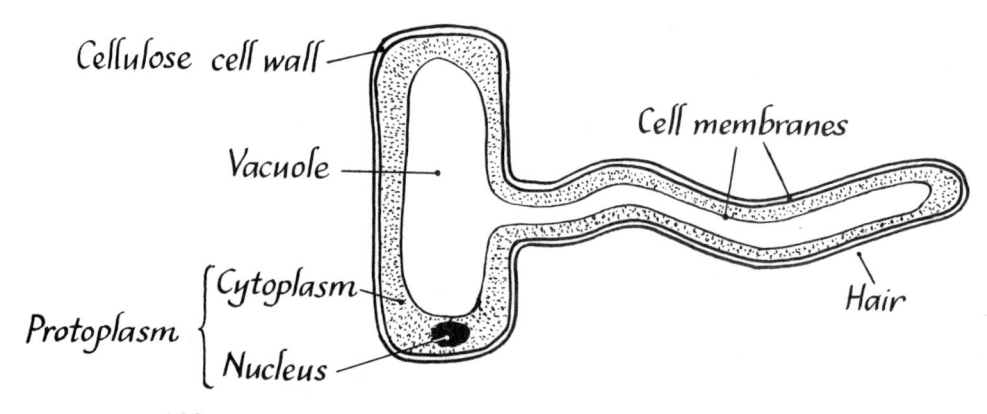

the *low* power of a microscope. You will probably have to move the slide about to see the entire root. Find the tip of the root first and then gradually move the slide along so that you can work your way up the root to the older parts. Compare your slide with Figure 11.2.

Did you notice the mass of fine hairs growing just a millimetre or so behind the tip of the root? These are called **root hairs**, and each consists of a single cell (see Figure 11.3).

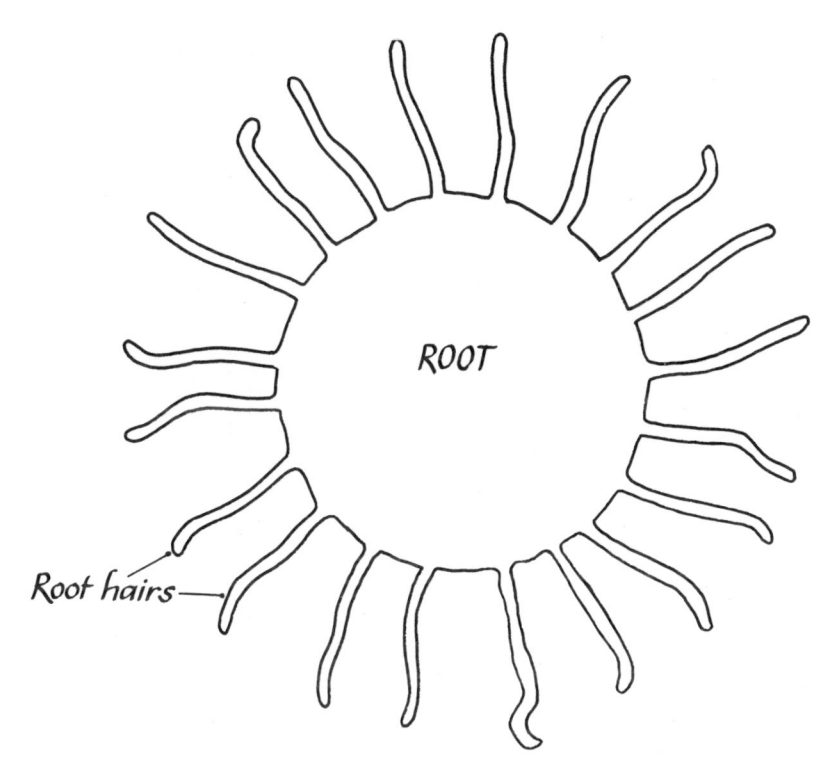

Figure 11.4 Diagram to show young root in transverse section

How do you think these hairs help the root to absorb water from the soil? Reference to Figure 11.4, a transverse section through the young root, may give you a clue.

Immediately behind the protective root cap lies the growing point. Here all new root cells arise by division of existing cells. Behind the growing point the cells undergo elongation, pushing the tip of the root further into the soil. After elongation the root cells become differentiated into various forms, according to their future functions. Some of the outermost cells develop into root hairs (piliferous layer). Root hairs are short-lived and once lost cause the underlying cortex to become exposed. This becomes corky and waterproof to form the exodermis, the outermost layer of cells in the older part of the root. This, of course, means that only the young part of the root, with the piliferous layer intact, is capable of absorbing water. This emphasizes the need for a greater surface area in the young region, achieved by the presence of abundant root hairs.

11.4. How does water enter the root hair cells?

Investigation 11c. To study the passage of water through a non-living membrane of parchment

Set up two pieces of apparatus as in Figure 11.5. Great care must be taken to ensure that the parchment membranes are completely

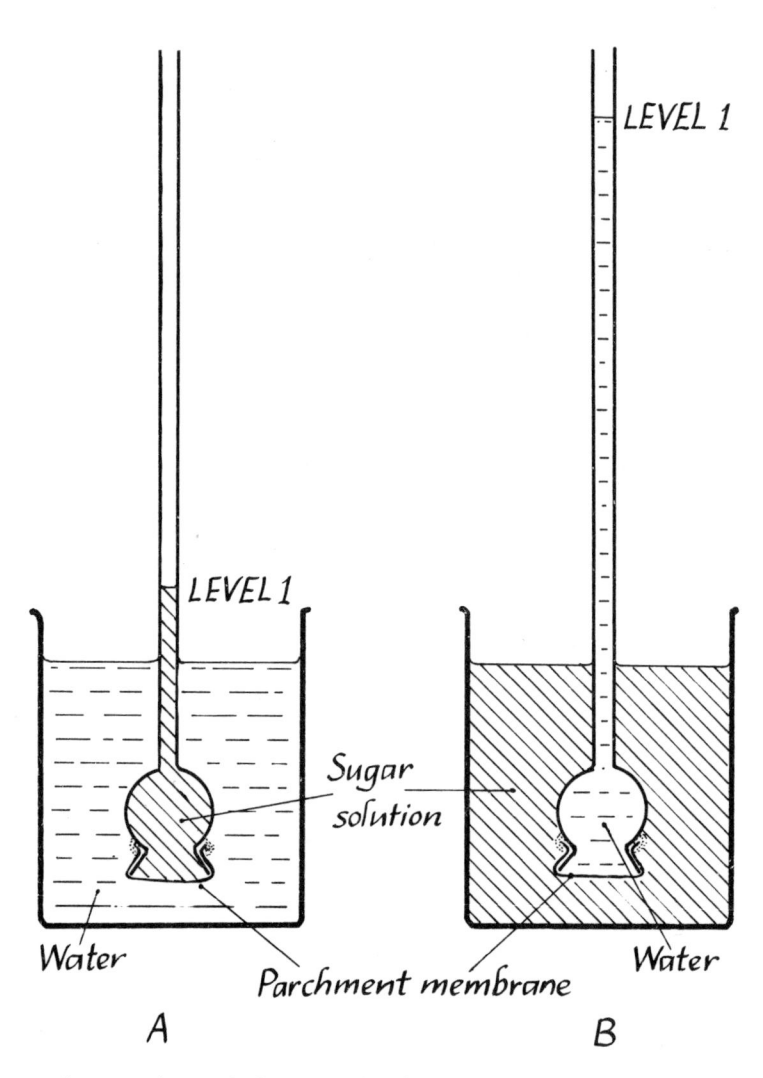

Figure 11.5 Two thistle funnel osmometers

and securely sealed on to the funnels. Thistle funnel A is partially filled with sugar solution up to the level indicated in the diagram. It is lowered into a beaker of distilled water and supported in position by a retort stand and clamp. Thistle funnel B is filled with distilled water and then lowered into a beaker containing sugar solution. The level of distilled water in the stem of thistle funnel B should be rather higher than the level of the sugar solution in A, as shown in the diagram. The original levels of the sugar solution and the distilled water should be marked on the stems of the thistle funnels.

Examine the apparatus after three or four hours and record any changes that have taken place. Leave the apparatus overnight and record any further changes. In which direction has the water passed through the membrane in each case?

Water is composed of relatively small molecules. It is a liquid in which certain solids will dissolve and is therefore called a **solvent**.

Sugar is a solid and consists of larger molecules. It is called a **solute** and it will dissolve in a solvent, such as water, to form a **solution**.

Parchment is an example of a non-living **semi-permeable membrane**. A semi-permeable membrane is one which will allow the passage of small solvent molecules, such as water, but not the large solute molecules, such as sugar. The level of the solution in the stem of thistle funnel A will rise considerably, but the level of the water in the stem of thistle funnel B will fall. In both cases, the solvent, water, passes through the semi-permeable membrane into the sugar solution. This process is called **osmosis** and is the way in which water enters the root hair cells of the plant.

11.5. A simplified explanation of osmosis

Osmosis is a physical process which occurs in both living and non-living systems. It is a complex process which can be thought of in the following terms. The parchment membrane stretched across the bottom of the thistle funnel can be thought of as having tiny holes which will allow the small solvent molecules to pass through, but not the large solute molecules (see Figure 11.6).

The molecules within a solution are in constant motion, due to the kinetic energy which they possess. They change direction only when they collide with other molecules or with the walls of their container.

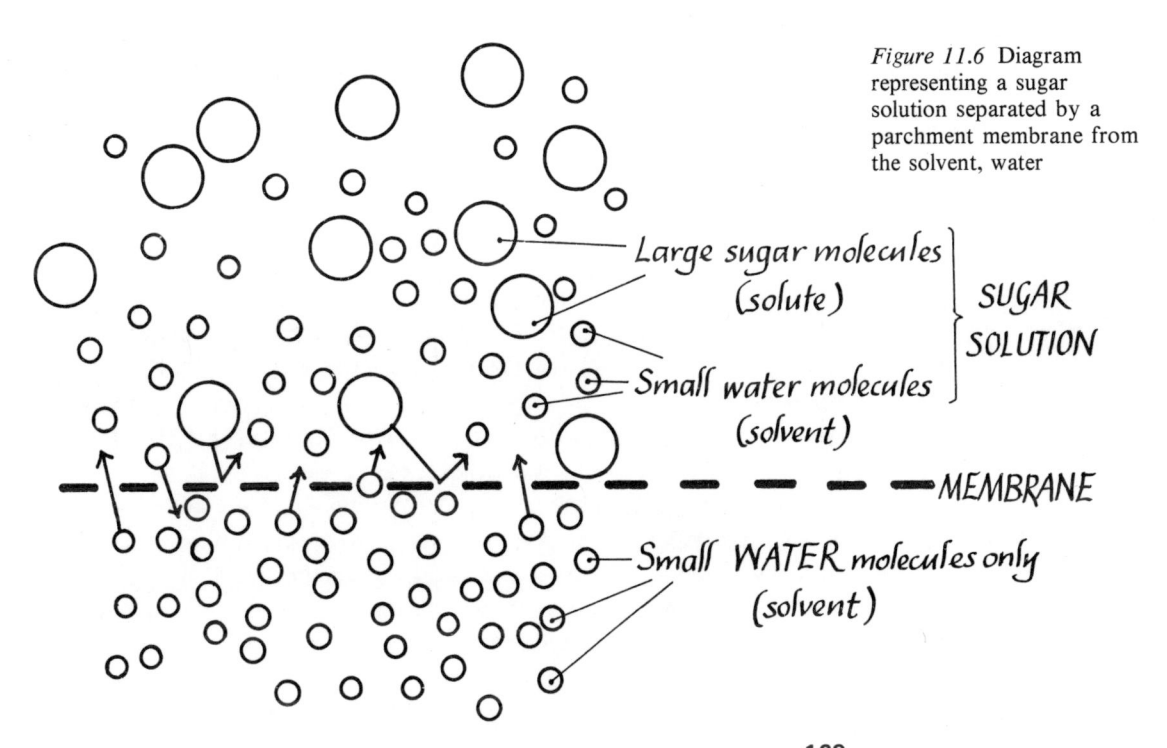

Figure 11.6 Diagram representing a sugar solution separated by a parchment membrane from the solvent, water

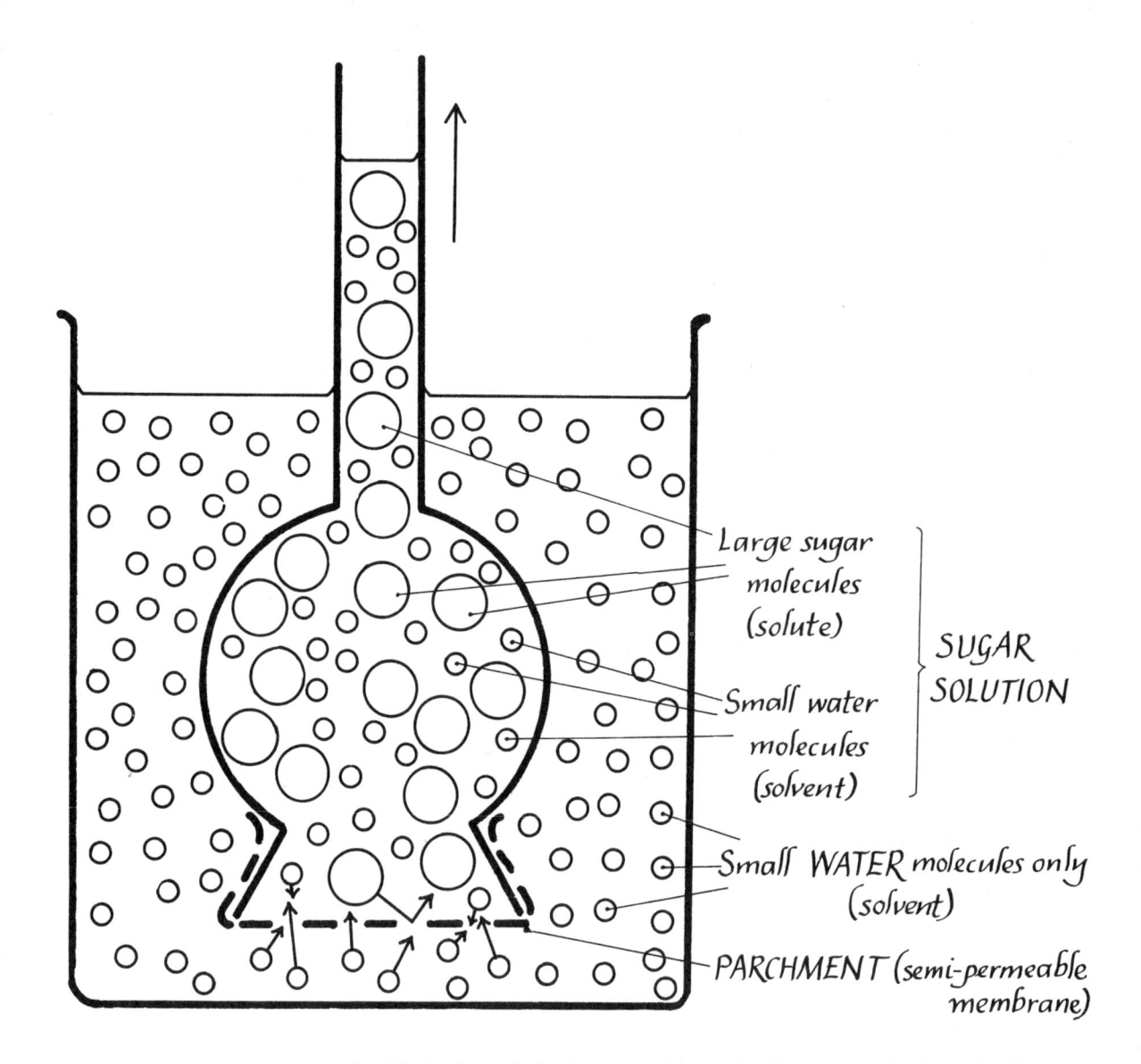

Figure 11.7 Diagrammatic representation of osmosis (Investigation 11c)

In thistle funnel A, shown enlarged in diagrammatic form in Figure 11.7, some of the molecules will collide with the semi-permeable membrane. If a small solvent molecule, such as water, happens to approach one of the 'tiny holes' in the membrane, it will pass through into the sugar solution, but if one of the large solute molecules, such as sugar, approaches one of the holes, it cannot pass through because it is too large and so bounces off the membrane and is retained within the thistle funnel. This means that there is a shift of water molecules into the thistle funnel but not of sugar molecules out of it. As a result, the water flows into thistle funnel A and the level of the solution in the thistle funnel stem rises. In thistle funnel B, water flows from the thistle funnel into the solution in the beaker, with the result that the level of the water in the stem of the thistle funnel falls.

The sugar solution, however, contains water molecules in addition to the sugar molecules, so some water molecules in the sugar solution approach the 'tiny holes' in the semi-permeable membrane and will pass through into the water. In the water, however, the concentration of the water molecules is at its maximum while in the solution the water molecules are at rather less than their maximum possible concentration. This being so, as with simple diffusion, the molecules will tend to pass from regions of high concentration where they are crowded together, to regions of lower concentration where they are less crowded. This means that water from the pure solvent will pass into the solution much more rapidly than water from the solution will pass into the pure solvent. Hence water enters thistle funnel A and leaves thistle funnel B.

Osmosis occurs when a more concentrated solution is separated from a less concentrated solution by a semi-permeable membrane. The solvent, usually water, flows from the dilute solution into the stronger solution. When will the osmotic flow of the water cease?

11.6. Plant and animal cells as osmotic systems

Investigation 11d. To study the effect of placing living plant cells in water and in strong sugar solution

An onion bulb is a good source of living cells, as sheets one cell thick can easily be peeled from the inside of the bulb scales (see Investigation 2b). If a red-skinned onion is used, the cell contents are coloured and are easy to observe, but a white one will do. Alternatively, this investigation can be carried out using algal filaments, such as *Spirogyra*, instead of onion epidermis. Do not let the cells dry out or they will die. Transfer them to the solution rapidly. Peel two sheets of cells, each of about 1 cm², from your onion epidermis. Mount one sheet in tap water on a microscope slide, and the other in a 50% sugar solution. Examine each of the slides for several minutes with the aid of a microscope. Draw the cells as seen on the two slides and compare them. Try to explain any differences.

Then, using a filter paper, draw the sugar solution from under the cover-slip of the second slide and replace it with distilled water. If you pipette a few drops of water on to one edge of the cover-slip and apply the filter paper to the opposite edge, the sugar solution will be removed from the preparation and the distilled water drawn in to take its place. Watch the cells on this slide carefully, and, with the aid of diagrams, write a careful account of what happens. Try to explain any changes you have observed in terms of osmosis.

Water enters and leaves the cells of plants and animals by osmosis.

The cellulose cell wall of a plant cell (see Figure 2.7) is **fully permeable** to both solute and solvent molecules; in other words, the pores between the molecules of the cellulose are large enough to allow the passage of both solute and solvent molecules. The layer of cytoplasm lining the cell wall, however, is not fully permeable. It is a semi-permeable membrane. The cell sap in the vacuole is a solution of sugars, salts and organic acids. When a plant cell is immersed in a very dilute solution, such as tap water, which is less concentrated

Figure 11.8 An onion epidermal cell

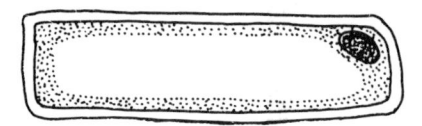

than the cell sap in the vacuole, water enters the cell vacuole by osmosis. This causes the cell contents to expand and push against the cell wall until the cell wall prevents further expansion. At this point, the cell stops taking in water as the pressure of the cell contents pushing against the cell wall equals the inward pressure of the cell wall. At this point, the cell is said to be **turgid** (see Figure 11.9).

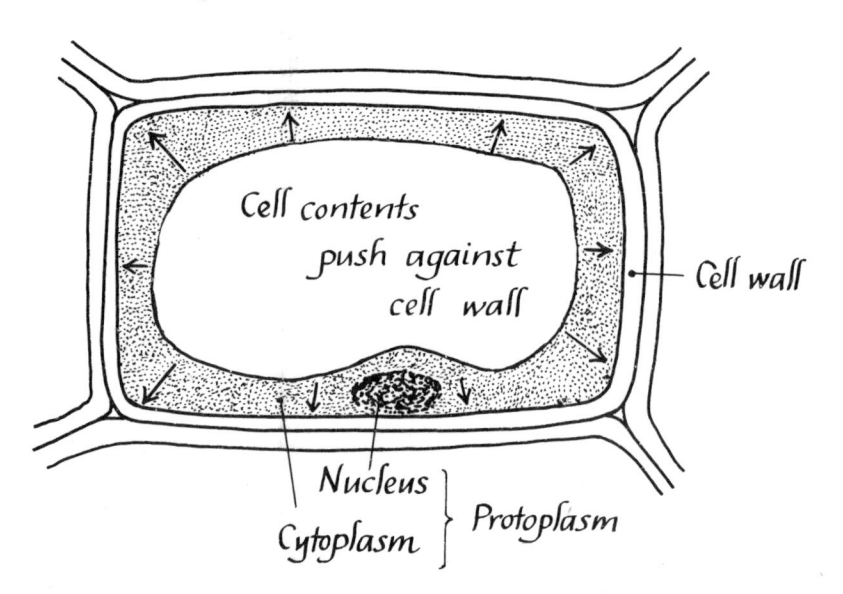

Figure 11.9 A turgid plant cell

It can be likened to a football, the leather case representing the cellulose cell wall, the bladder representing the cytoplasmic lining of the cell, and the air being pumped in representing the water. It is easy to blow up the football at first, but when it is nearly inflated further expansion of the bladder is strongly resisted by the case.

If the cell is immersed in a solution which is more concentrated than the cell sap, then water will leave the cell vacuole and the cytoplasmic contents of the cell will shrink away from the cell wall. The cell is then said to be **flaccid** (see Figure 11.10).

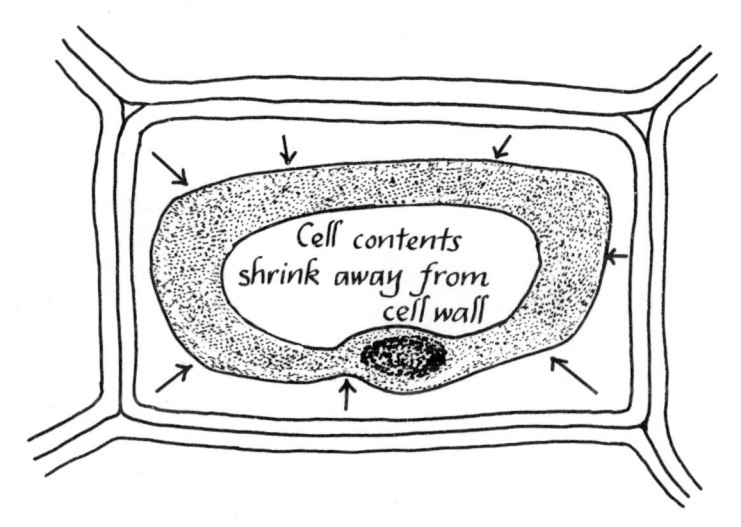

Figure 11.10 A flaccid plant cell

An animal cell such as a red blood cell (see Figure 11.11) has no cellulose wall. It is bounded by its semi-permeable membrane. What would happen to the red blood cell if it were to be immersed in distilled water? What would happen if the bladder of the football were taken from its leather case and blown up very hard indeed?

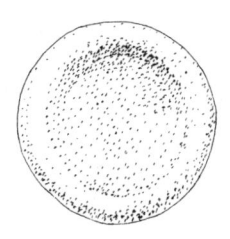

Figure 11.11 A red blood cell

11.7. Is live tissue necessary for osmosis?

Investigation 11e. Osmosis in potato tissue

Peel a potato and cut it in half (across the shortest diameter) so that it will stand on its cut surface. Carefully excavate a cavity in the rounded surface, taking care not to penetrate the base or the sides. This can be done with a stout cork borer. Two such potato cups can usually be made from one potato. You will need three cups, A, B and C. Cup C should be boiled for about ten minutes. Place each cup in a small dish of water (see Figure 11.12). Half of a petri dish is suitable. Note the level of the water in the dishes.

Place a little sugar in the cavities of cups A and C. Re-examine them after twenty-four hours. Note any changes and try to explain why they happen. Has osmosis occurred in any of the cups? What effect did boiling have on cup C? Why did water enter cups A and C but not B? Why did the level of the water in cup A rise so much that

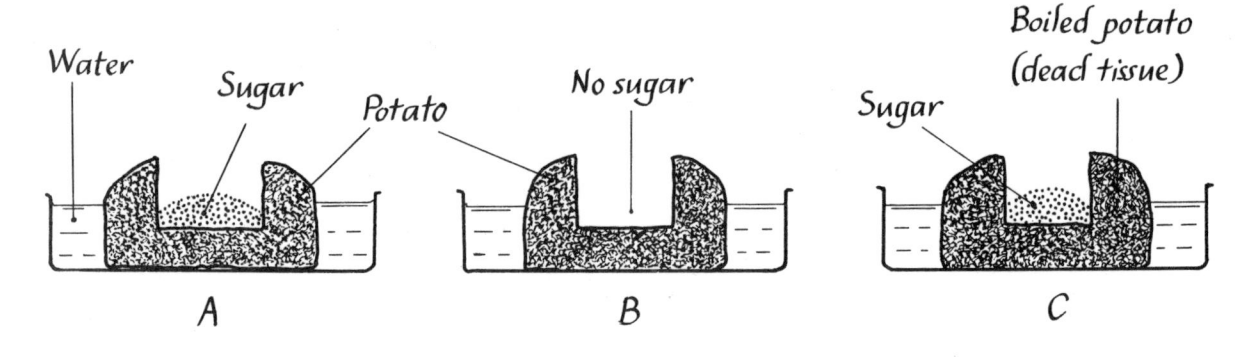

Figure 11.12 The three petri dishes set up for Investigation 11e

it overflowed, whilst in cup C it only rose to the level of the water in the dish? Does osmosis occur in dead plant tissue? If not, can you suggest why not?

11.8. The entry of water into the plant

Soil water does contain some dissolved mineral salts, but it is much more dilute (contains a far higher concentration of water molecules) than the cell sap of the root hair cells. These root hair cells, like all plant cells, are surrounded by a cell wall composed of cellulose. As the cellulose cell wall is fully permeable it does not influence the process of osmosis. It is the cytoplasmic lining of the cell which is semi-permeable. As the concentration of the cell sap is greater than the soil water, water passes by osmosis from the soil through the semi-permeable cytoplasmic lining of the root hair cell into the vacuole (A). This addition of water dilutes the cell sap in A which is now more dilute than the cell sap of the outermost layer of cortical cells (B). This results in water flowing by osmosis from the vacuole of cell A into the vacuole of cell B. This in turn dilutes the cell sap in B, making it more dilute than the cell sap in the vacuole of cell C. Hence water passes from cell B to cell C of the cortex, and so on. In this way water passes by osmosis right across the cortex of the root to the conducting tissues of the stele (see Figure 11.13). In the stele, the water enters the xylem, composed of vessels which have lost their cell contents. The xylem vessels form continuous tubes for the passage of water up the stem. The water passing into the xylem vessels sets up a hydrostatic pressure which is known as **root pressure.**

Investigation 11f. To discover if the membrane of an egg (a cell) and the skin of a grape are semi-permeable

Remove the shells from two hen's eggs by placing them carefully in dilute hydrochloric acid. The shell consists largely of calcium carbonate which dissolves in the dilute acid, leaving the egg enclosed

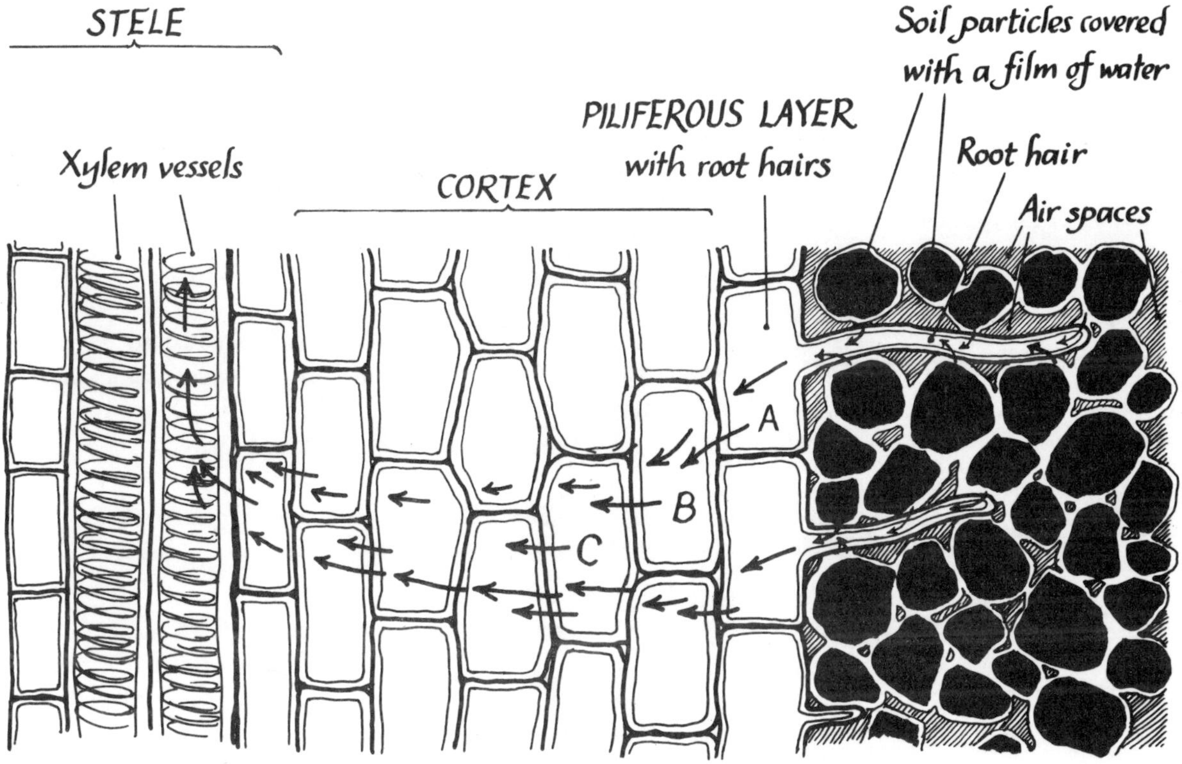

Figure 11.13 Part of a longitudinal section of a young root showing the passage of water into the root

in its membrane. Place one egg in distilled water and the other in a strong salt solution. Observe the eggs carefully, record what happens and account for any changes.

Take two fresh grapes. Place one in distilled water and the other in a strong sugar or salt solution. Again observe any changes which occur over the next twenty-four hours and explain them.

11.9. The loss of water from the plant: transpiration

In Chapters 9 and 10 we learnt how the leaf was adapted for the process of photosynthesis. It is designed to allow gaseous exchange between the living cells of the leaf and the atmosphere. Because gases enter and leave cells in solution, the leaf has a large internal surface which is moist. In addition, the leaf surface is pierced by numerous stomata, through which the atmosphere communicates with the internal surface of the leaf. This structure suggests that the loss of water in the form of water vapour is almost inevitable.

Investigation 11g. To discover if the leaf of a growing tree loses water

Place a dry boiling-tube over a leaf or a leafy twig of a vigorous, growing plant. Secure the tube with cotton wool packing and leave

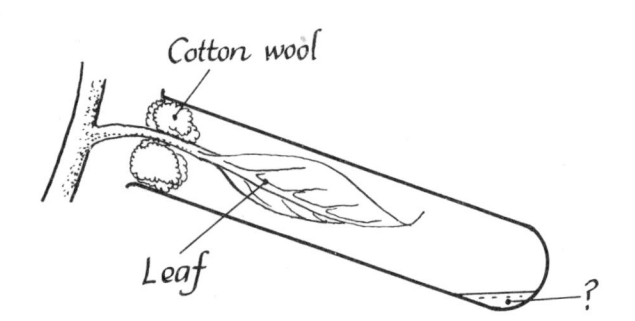

Figure 11.14 The tube secured to the twig with cotton wool

for twenty-four hours (see Figure 11.14). What do you notice when you re-examine the tube? Use white anhydrous copper sulphate to help you to determine the nature of any liquid which may have collected in the tube. What conclusion can you draw?

Investigation 11h. To discover the mass of water given off by the leaves of a potted plant in a given time

Set up two bell jars as in Figure 11.15. The plant in bell jar B has no leaves and the leaf scars and stems are covered with Vaseline to prevent evaporation of water from them. A dish of calcium chloride (which absorbs water from the air) of known mass is placed in each bell jar. These are re-weighed after a given period, such as twenty-four hours. Compare the changes in mass of the calcium chloride in each bell jar. Any increase is due to water absorbed. Draw what conclusions you can regarding the site of water loss.

Figure 11.15 Apparatus for Investigation 11h

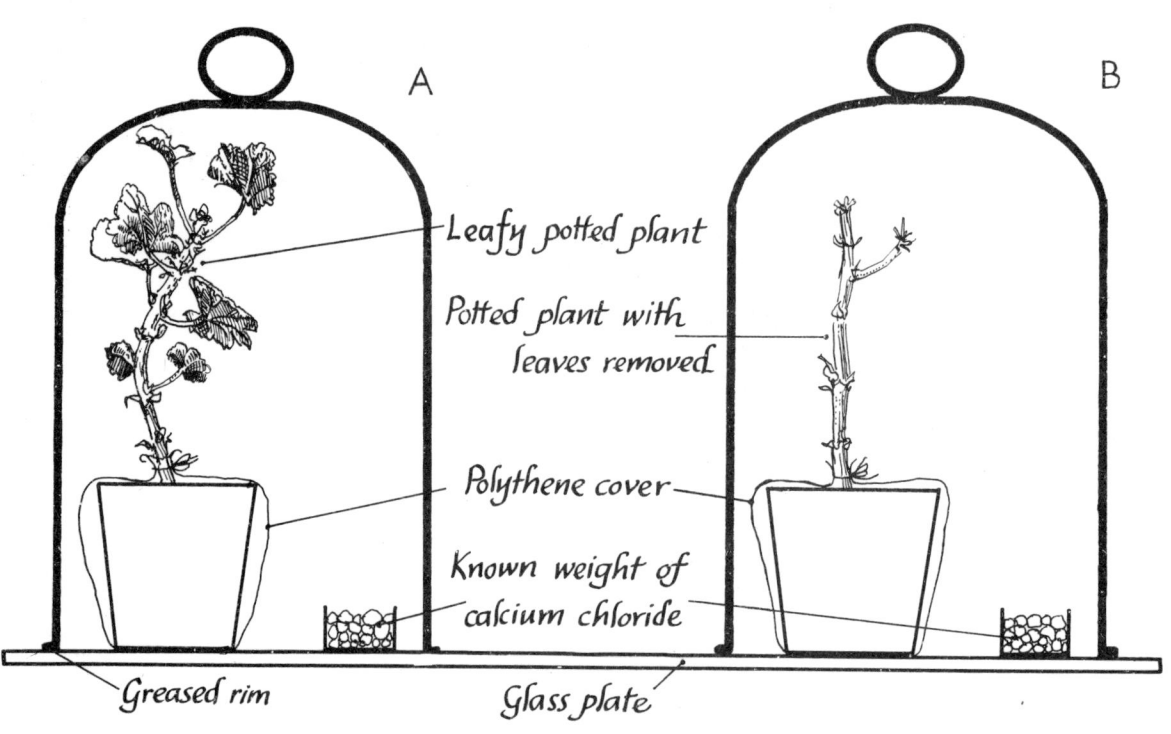

Investigation 11i. An alternative investigation to measure the loss of water by mass from a potted plant

Take a well-watered, potted plant and enclose the soil and pot in a polythene bag so that only the stem and leaves are exposed to the air. Carefully seal the polythene bag around the stem of the plant. Place the plant on a balance as in Figure 11.16, and make a note of

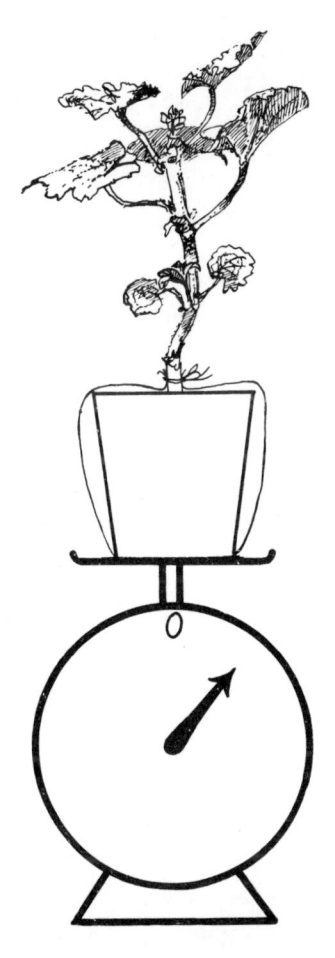

Figure 11.16 Potted plant on a balance

the total mass. Place the plant in an airy, sunny place and keep careful records of the total mass at regular intervals over the next few days. Explain any changes in mass. Why are the pot and the soil enclosed in a polythene bag?

Investigation 11j. To find out which surface of the leaf loses water most rapidly

Using a sharp blade, cut a number of leaves from an ivy, lilac or laurel plant. Cut the leaves cleanly through the petiole and stand them in a beaker of water until they are needed. Divide the leaves into five groups, A, B, C, D and E.

Do nothing to the leaves in group A. Smear the *upper* surface of the leaves in group B with a thin layer of Vaseline. Smear the *lower* surface of the leaves in group C with Vaseline, and *both surfaces* of the leaves in group D. Leave group E in the beaker of water. Hang each group of leaves from A to D from string stretched between two retort stands in an airy part of the laboratory. The leaves can be attached to the string by a loop of fuse wire as in Figure 11.17. Weigh the leaves before they are attached to the string by hanging them from the beam of a balance with the fuse wire loop.

Examine and weigh the leaves each day and record the order in which the leaves dry up, become brittle and lose mass. From your results can you suggest which surface of the leaf loses water most rapidly?

Gaseous exchange between the leaves and the atmosphere takes place through the stomatal pores. It is through the stomata that the plant loses water vapour during transpiration. The result of this investigation indicates that water is lost most rapidly from the lower surface of the leaf. This suggests that the stomata are more numerous on the lower surface of the leaf than they are on the upper surface. This idea is supported by the results of the nail varnish peel experiment in Chapter 9.

Figure 11.17 The Vaselined leaves experiment

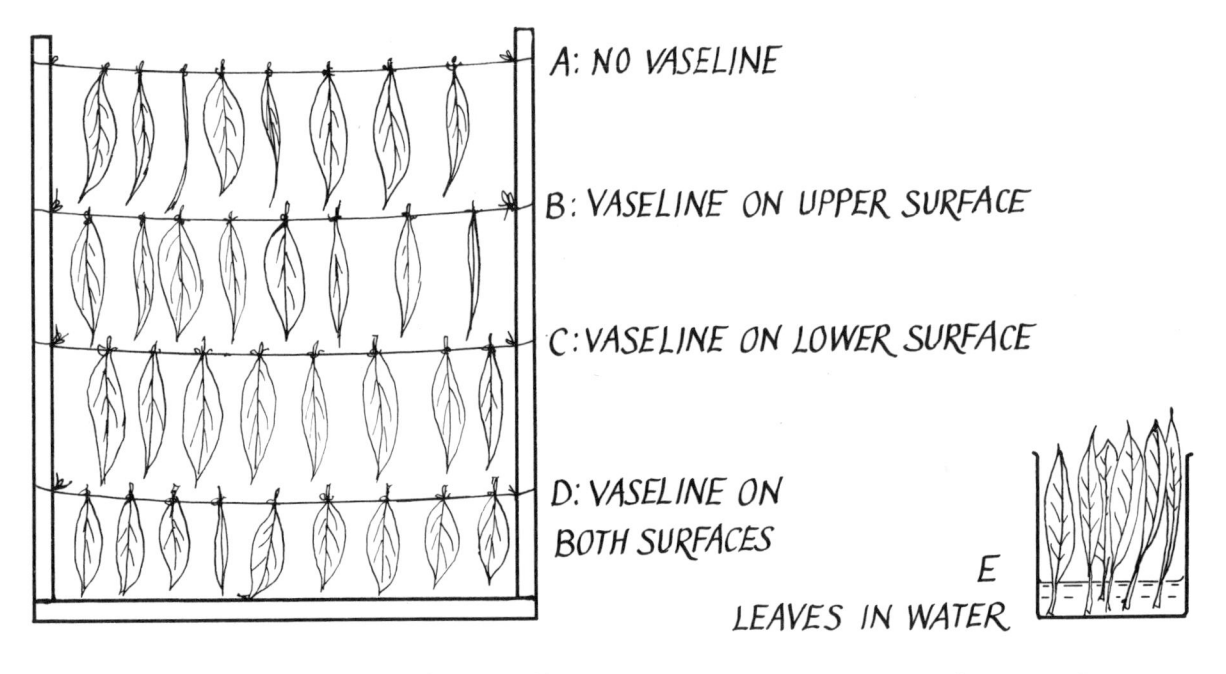

A: NO VASELINE

B: VASELINE ON UPPER SURFACE

C: VASELINE ON LOWER SURFACE

D: VASELINE ON BOTH SURFACES

E LEAVES IN WATER

11.10. The effect of external conditions on the rate of transpiration

An instrument called a potometer consists of a tube to which a leafy twig can be fitted, a reservoir of water controlled by a spring clip, or a stop-cock, connected to a piece of capillary tube mounted on a scale. When the spring clip is opened water flows into the capillary tube and pushes out any air (see Figure 11.18).

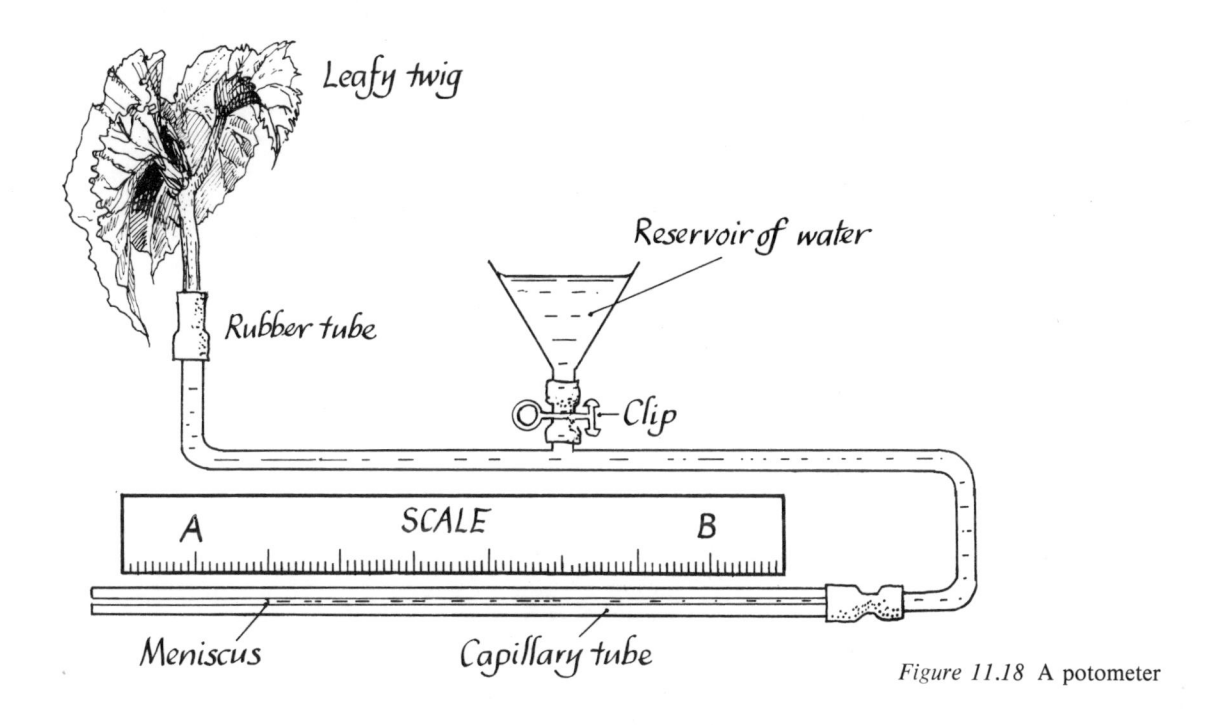

Figure 11.18 A potometer

Investigation 11k. To discover how external conditions influence the rate of transpiration

First of all, the potometer must be filled with water and all air bubbles must be excluded. This is best done by filling a sink with water and submerging the entire apparatus. The leafy twig should also be cut with a sharp knife whilst being held under the water. This prevents any air bubbles from entering the xylem. As the leaves of the twig transpire, they lose water and water is drawn from the potometer. As this happens the water surface, the meniscus, is drawn along the capillary tube from A to B. The meniscus can be returned to point A by opening the spring clip a little and allowing water to enter the apparatus.

Measure the time taken for the meniscus to pass from A to B (a) in the laboratory, (b) near a radiator, (c) near to a window, (d) in the dark and (e) in humid conditions. Humid conditions can be achieved by supporting a damp towel over the apparatus by means of a retort stand. Repeat the experiment in a draughty situation (either outdoors, or indoors in front of a fan).

The results should be recorded carefully, and the effect of air currents, temperature, humidity and light intensity on the rate of transpiration should be noted. Leaves lose water through the stomata by evaporation and this water is replaced by water drawn from the petiole and thence from the stem. The apparatus in Figure 11.18 actually measures the rate of water absorption rather than the rate of transpiration, but for our purpose we may take these to be equal.

The rate of transpiration increases when conditions favour the physical process of evaporation, and when conditions are such that the stomata are open. Rises in temperature, light intensity and wind velocity tend to increase the rate, whilst darkness, an increase in humidity and a fall in temperature will tend to decrease the rate.

11.11. The transpiration stream

Plants lose considerable quantities of water from the leaves. This loss must be made good by water entering the plant by osmosis.

Investigation 11I. To discover by what path water passes through the plant

Place a fresh stick of celery, white dead-nettle or other suitable plant material into a solution containing the red dye **eosin**. After several hours, cut transverse sections at various points and examine them with a magnifying glass or using the low power of a microscope. Is the whole section stained red, or is the red stain confined to certain areas which are concerned with the transport of water up the plant?

On a dry, windy summer's day, an oak tree may lose as much as a thousand litres of water. A single maize plant may take in 200 litres of water during its life, but loses 198 litres of it by transpiration. During a single growing season a crop of cotton will lose 250 kg for every square metre.

In daylight, the guard cells of the stomata become turgid and the stomatal pore opens. As you can see from Figure 9.13, the atmospheric air can now diffuse freely into the air spaces within the leaf and the air from the leaf spaces can diffuse freely into the atmosphere. Water vapour will also diffuse out of the leaf whenever the stomata are open. This water is replaced by water from the cells of the leaf surrounding the stomata. As a result, the cell sap of these cells becomes more concentrated and takes water from neighbouring cells by osmosis. These cells then take water from the xylem elements of the tiny veins in the leaf. Water is drawn up the xylem in this way, assisted by root pressure. The water entering the xylem in the young part of the root has passed from cell to cell across the cortex after

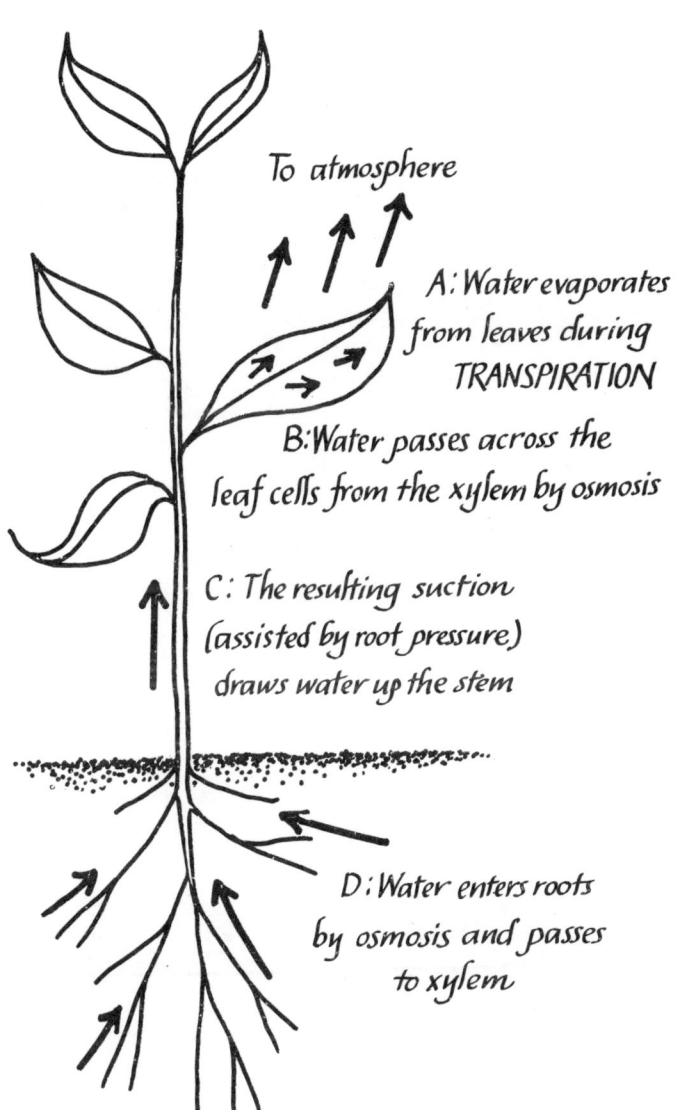

Figure 11.19 The transpiration stream

A: Water evaporates from leaves during TRANSPIRATION

B: Water passes across the leaf cells from the xylem by osmosis

C: The resulting suction (assisted by root pressure) draws water up the stem

D: Water enters roots by osmosis and passes to xylem

entering the root hairs by osmosis. Thus water enters the roots of plants to be carried by the xylem vessels and ultimately some is lost through the leaves. This flow of water is called the **transpiration stream** (see Figure 11.19).

Remember that the **xylem** vessels carry water up the plant from the root to the leaves and the **phloem** tubules carry manufactured food such as sugars from the leaves usually down the plant to regions where it is used for growth and respiration or is stored. These vessels and tubes form the 'pipelines' of the plant.

11.12. Plants and water availability

Many plants have become adapted to live in extreme conditions. Some plants are even found growing in deserts. Plants which are

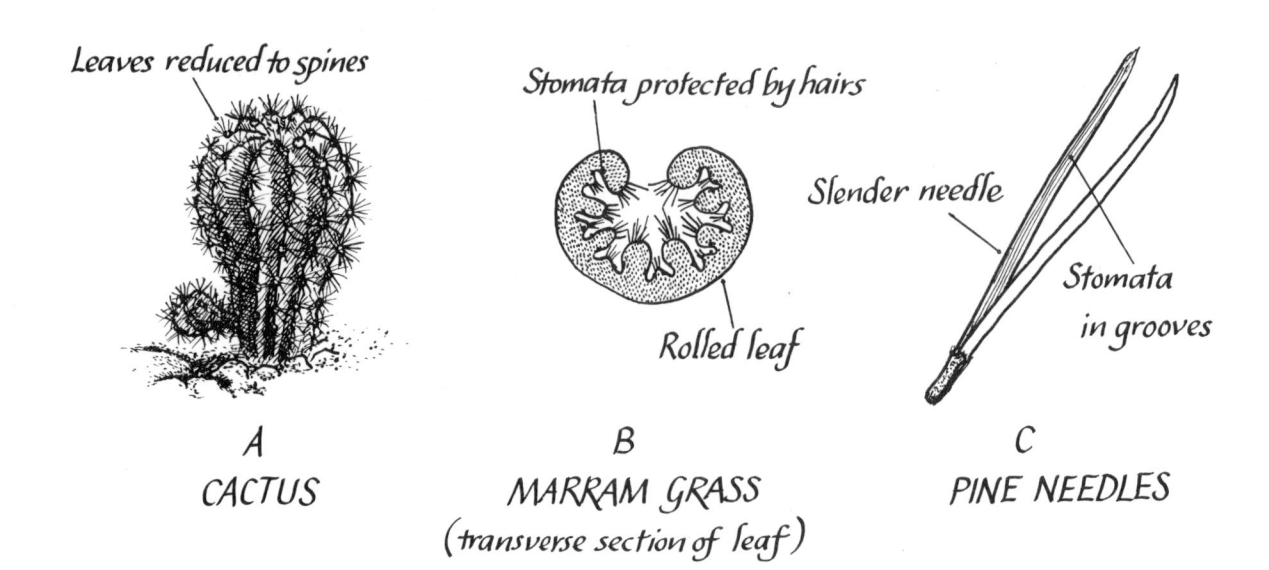

A	B	C
CACTUS — Leaves reduced to spines	MARRAM GRASS (transverse section of leaf) — Stomata protected by hairs; Rolled leaf	PINE NEEDLES — Slender needle; Stomata in grooves

Figure 11.20 Methods of reducing water loss from leaves

adapted to thrive under conditions of water scarcity (for example, desert plants) are called **xerophytes**. In most cases they are able to reduce water loss, or, in other words, to slow down the rate of transpiration. This is done by reducing the leaf surface area: the leaves of many cacti are reduced to spines, the leaves of the pine tree are needle-like, and the leaves of marram grass are curled up to maintain moist air around the enclosed stomata (see Figure 11.20).

Plants living in very damp conditions are called **hydrophytes** (see Figure 11.21). These include the water-lilies and also the submerged plants. The buoyancy of the water lessens the need for support, so there is little strengthening tissue. The submerged leaves of plants like water-milfoil and water-crowfoot are finely dissected to increase the efficiency of light capture and gaseous exchange, and also to help the leaves to withstand the water currents without tearing.

Figure 11.21 Some hydrophytes

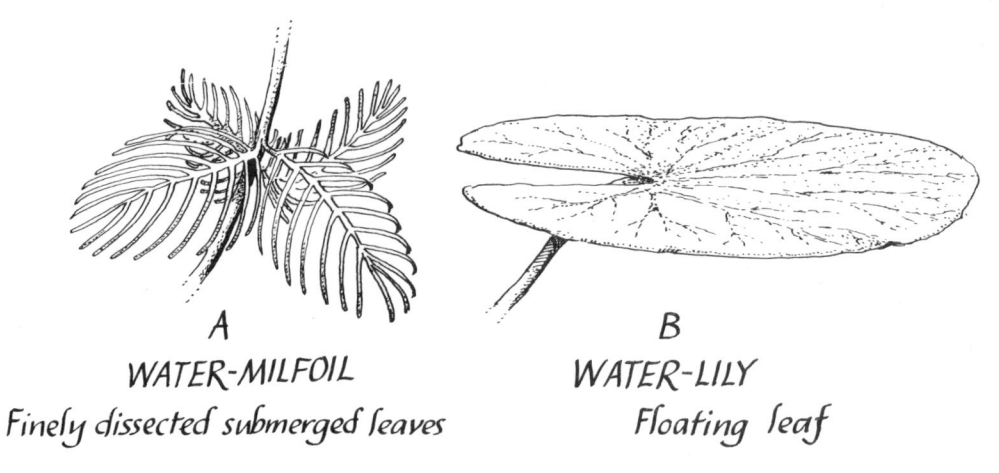

A
WATER-MILFOIL
Finely dissected submerged leaves

B
WATER-LILY
Floating leaf

A third group of plants are adapted for living in conditions of high salinity (salt content). These plants are called **halophytes** and are found in coastal areas, particularly on salt marshes. These plants do not wilt when submerged in salt water because their cell sap is very concentrated, even more so than the sea water which covers them at high tide.

Test your understanding

Copy and complete the following paragraph:

The surface area of a young root is greatly increased by the presence of thousands of ....[1] A large surface area is necessary for the plant to obtain enough ....[2] from the ....[3] by the process called ....[4] This occurs when a concentrated solution is separated from a ....[5] solution by a ....[6] membrane. In this process ....[7] flows through the membrane from a ....[8] solution into a ....[9] solution. In a plant cell such as a root hair the ....[10] is the semi-permeable membrane. The soil water acts as the ....[11] and the cell sap as the ....[12] solution. The plant is constantly losing water from its ....[13] by the process of ....[14] This water is replaced by water drawn up by the ....[15] vessels of the stem by the ....[16] stream. When a cell can take up no more water it is said to be ....[17], but if the cell loses a great deal of water it becomes ....[18] If a large proportion of the cells in a plant lose water, the plant will ....[19]

1. Describe an experiment to demonstrate osmosis.
2. Explain how water passes across the cortex of a root.
3. Why does water only enter through the young part of the root?
4. Explain what is meant by root pressure.
5. What external factors influence the rate of transpiration?
6. Describe how you would compare the transpiration rate under different conditions.
7. Explain why transpiration should be an inevitable consequence of leaf structure.
8. What are the main factors which maintain the flow of water through the plant?
9. What are the effects of water shortage in a plant?
10. How is the distribution of stomata related to water loss?
11. Distinguish between xerophytic plants and hydrophytic plants, naming an example of each.
12. Describe, with examples, ways in which plants have become modified to restrict water loss.

Chapter 12

Reproduction in the Flowering Plant

12.1. Sexual reproduction

In both plants and animals sexual reproduction is fundamentally similar. It involves the fusion of a male gamete with a female gamete. This process is known as **fertilization**, and results in a single cell called a zygote.

In earlier chapters, you have learnt how the amoeba and *Chlamydomonas* split into two, and how the hydra produce buds. Many lowly organisms seem to manage with asexual reproduction. What then is the advantage of sexual reproduction with its problem of making sure that fertilization occurs?

Although sexual reproduction appears to present a lot of problems, without it **evolution**, the gradual development of more complex forms of life, would have been a much slower process. Sexual reproduction allows variation, for the genes of one parent may be complemented by those of the other to produce vigorous offspring. Any inherited defects passed on to succeeding generations by asexual reproduction are rapidly eliminated by sexual reproduction.

12.2. The problem of fertilization

It is a fact that almost all animals, except the very simple ones, have the male and female gamete-producing organs on different individuals, the male animal and the female animal. They are said to be **dioecious.** During the breeding season, the males are attracted to the female. This is brought about by some colour change, secretion or mode of behaviour. As animals move freely under their own power, two individuals of different sexes can approach each other, and the male gametes can then be transferred to the female and fertilization take place. Flowering plants differ from animals in that they are firmly rooted into the ground and cannot approach another plant to bring about fertilization. How then does it occur? There must obviously be some external agent for transferring the male gametes to the female. The two most important agents are **wind** and **insects.**

Figure 12.1 A diagrammatic section of a flower

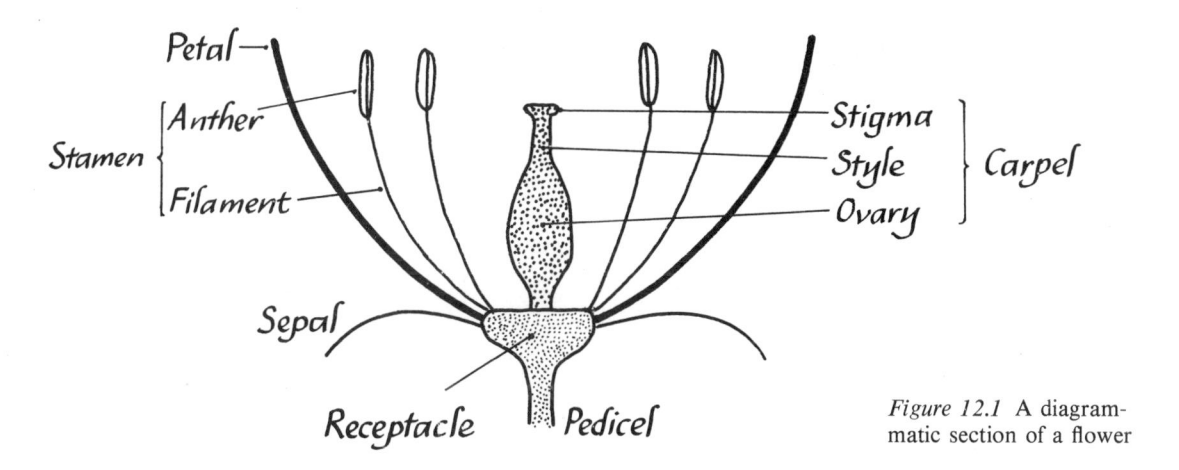

12.3. The structure of a flower

The flower is the reproductive structure of the higher plant. It has evolved from a leafy shoot in which spirally arranged leaves have become modified to perform special functions concerned with reproduction (see Figure 12.1).

Investigation 12a. The parts of the flower and their uses

Take a white tile or a piece of white paper, a needle, a pair of forceps and a hand lens. Obtain a flower, such as a buttercup or a wallflower. Starting from the outside of your flower, carefully remove the outermost parts with the aid of your needle and forceps. Arrange these parts in a large ring around your white tile. These structures are usually green, resembling the leaves from which they have developed. These modified leaves are called the **sepals** and together they form the **calyx**. The function of the calyx is to protect the flower and the gametes it produces, particularly whilst it is in bud. In some cases, it also provides support when the flower is open. The modified leaves next removed are the **petals**, which together form the **corolla**. The function of the corolla in insect-pollinated flowers is to attract insects to the flowers; such flowers are therefore large, brightly coloured and conspicuously situated. Arrange the petals in a circle on your tile, just inside the ring of sepals. If you are investigating a buttercup flower, look carefully at the base of the petals. Do you see a delicate flap of tissue? Lift it carefully with the tip of your needle. Beneath is the **nectary** which secretes the sugary fluid called **nectar**. Can you suggest a reason for the presence of the nectary? In what sort of flowers would you expect to find nectaries? The sepals and petals together form the **perianth**, which is the part of the flower not directly concerned with reproduction.

The next modified leaves are the spore-bearing leaves, called the **stamens**. The stamens collectively form the **androecium**, the male part of the flower. Arrange the stamens inside the ring of petals on your tile as you remove them. If you examine a single stamen with your hand lens you will notice that it is composed of two parts, the stalk, or filament, and the pollen-producing **anther** at its tip (see Figures 12.2 and 12.3). The anther usually consists of four pollen sacs. Examine a prepared slide of a transverse section of an anther under the low ($\times 30$) or medium ($\times 100$) power of a microscope.

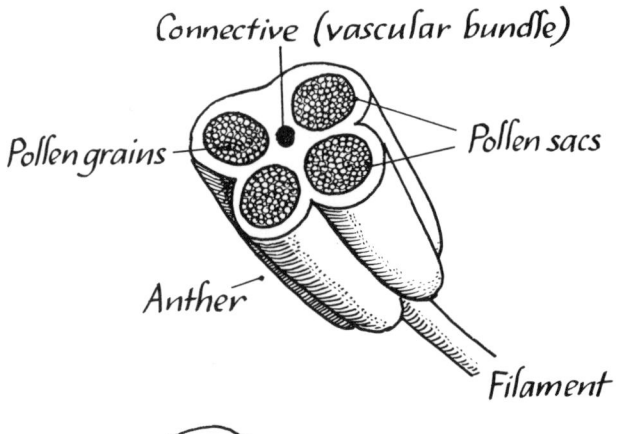

Figure 12.2 An anther cut to show the transverse section

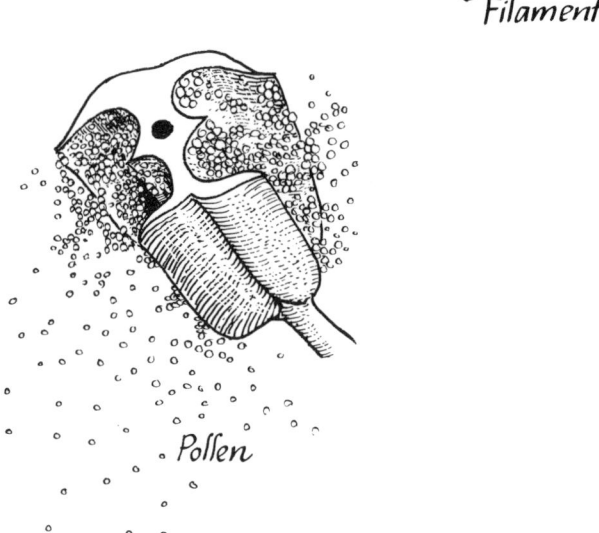

Figure 12.3 A ripe anther cut in the same way

You are now left with the last set of specialized leaves, the **carpels**, which are attached to the **receptacle**, the swollen tip of the flower stalk or **pedicel**. Collectively, the carpels form the female part of the flower, the **gynaecium** or **pistil**. Each carpel is formed from a modified leaf which becomes folded, the free edges then fusing. This encloses a cavity in which the **ovules** develop. Each carpel consists of three regions: at its tip is the **stigma**, on which the pollen grains are deposited; below is the **style**; and at the base, the **ovary** (see Figure 12.4). If you are examining the buttercup flower you will have a large number of separate carpels which can be counted, but the wallflower and tulip have more than one carpel fused together to form a single pistil (see Figures 12.5 and 12.6). How can you tell how many are fused together in the pistil? Cut the gynaecium transversely and study the section. If your flower has a single pistil, cut it in trans-

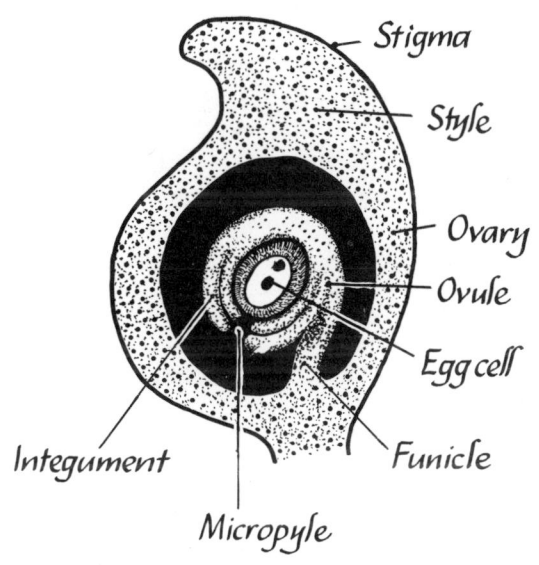

Figure 12.4 A single buttercup carpel cut in vertical section

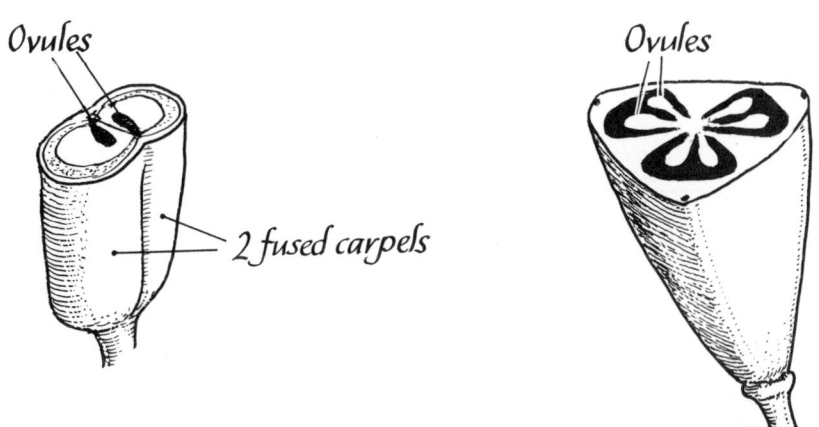

Figure 12.5 (left) A wallflower ovary cut in transverse section to show the two carpels

Figure 12.6 (right) A tulip ovary cut in transverse section to show the three carpels

verse section to discover how many carpels it is composed of, and place the carpels in the centre of the tile.

Draw what you see on the tile, label all the parts and make notes on the functions they perform. Compare your results with Figure 12.7.

Investigation 12b. To cut a flower in vertical section and examine its parts

Take a flower and cut the pedicel very close to the receptacle. Hold the flower between the thumb and first finger and with a sharp

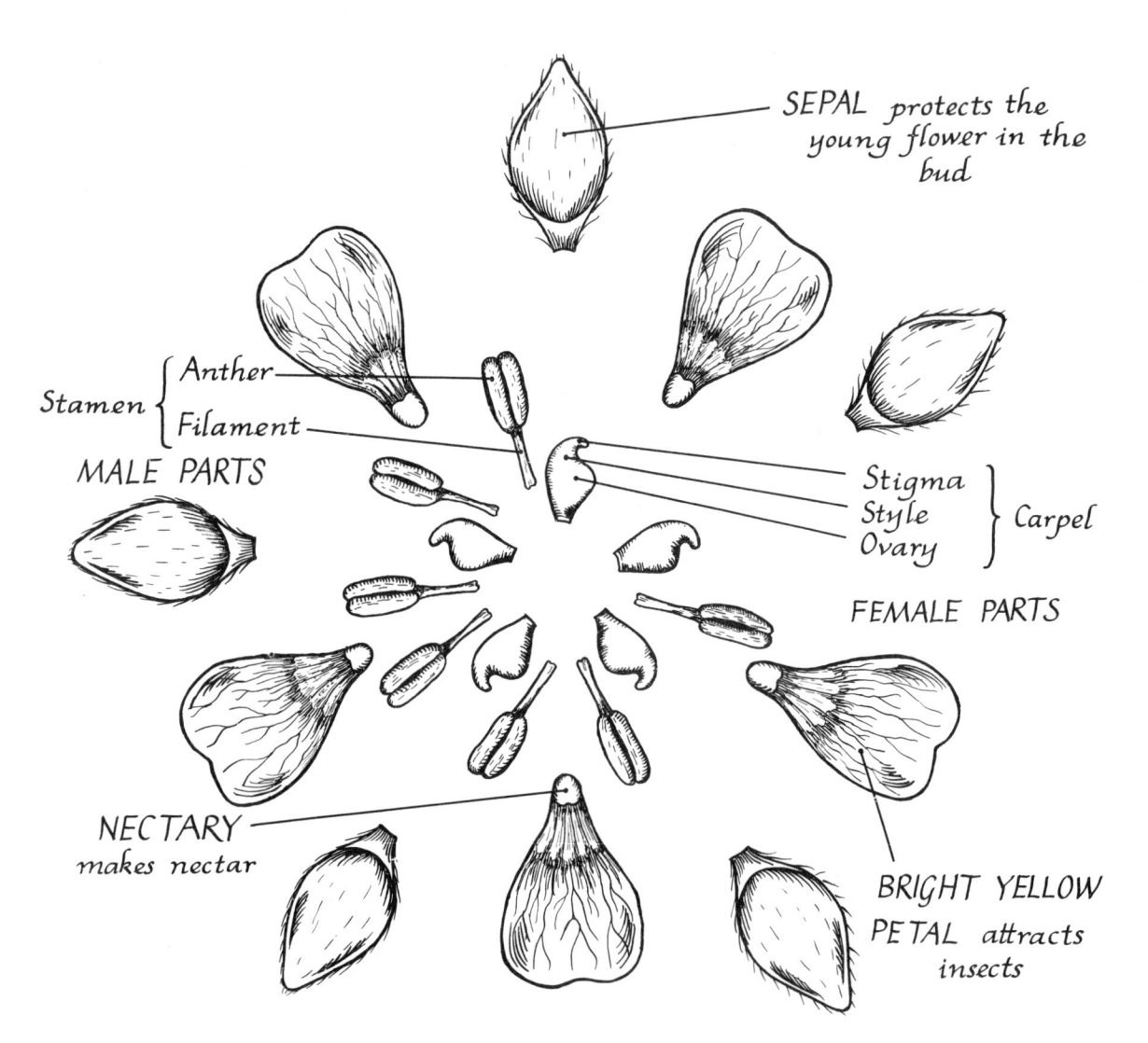

Figure 12.7 The dissected parts of a buttercup flower

knife or scalpel cut the flower through the stalk into two similar halves. Make a large clear drawing of half of your flower and label the different parts. Check your drawing against Figure 12.8.

You will have noticed that the two flowers studied have both the male and female organs in the same flower. This is the **hermaphrodite** condition, and is the case in most, but not all, flowering plants.

12.4. The gametes of the flowering plant

Inside the ripe pollen grains are three nuclei: the **tube nucleus**, which controls the growth of the pollen tube but plays no part in fertilization, and the two male **nuclei** (see Figure 12.9). These arise from the generative cell shortly before, or immediately after, pollination.

In the ovule of the ovary, one cell has become the **embryo sac** containing two very important nuclei: the egg nucleus, which is the

Figure 12.8 A wallflower cut in vertical section

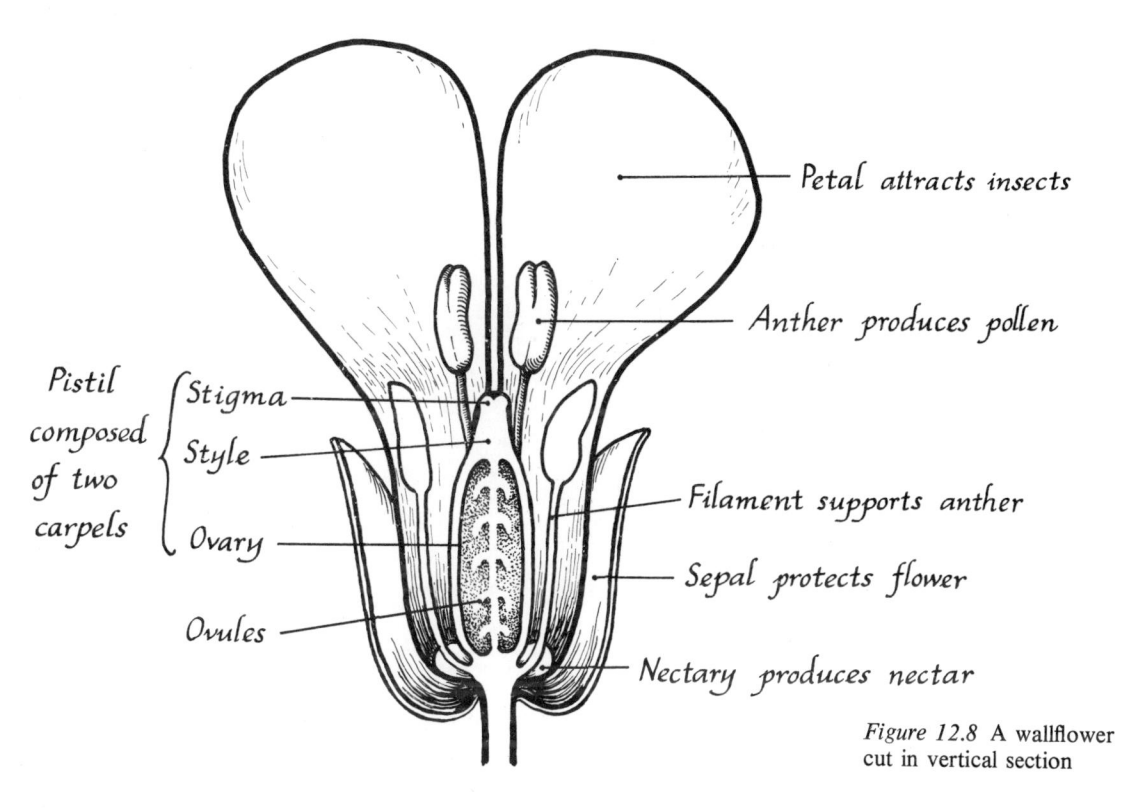

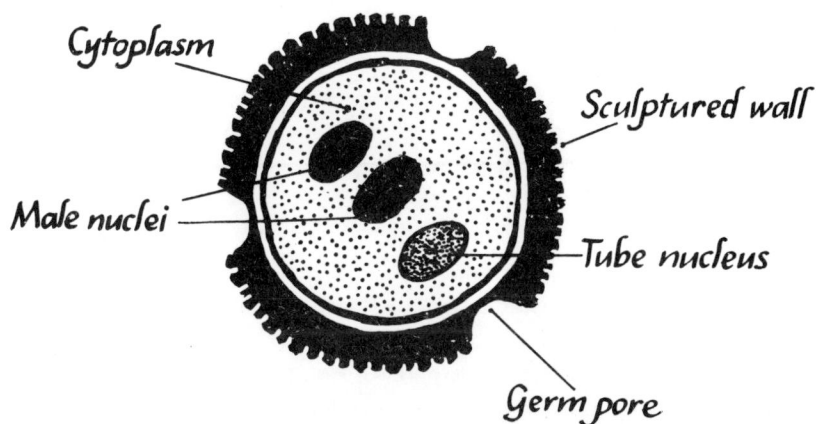

Figure 12.9 A pollen grain and its nuclei

female gamete and forms the zygote after fertilization, and the endosperm nucleus, which, when fertilized, produces the food reserves of the seed (see Figure 12.10).

Before fertilization can occur the pollen grain must reach the stigma.

12.5. Pollination

Pollination is the transfer of the pollen grain from the anther to the stigma of a flower of the same species. The normal method is

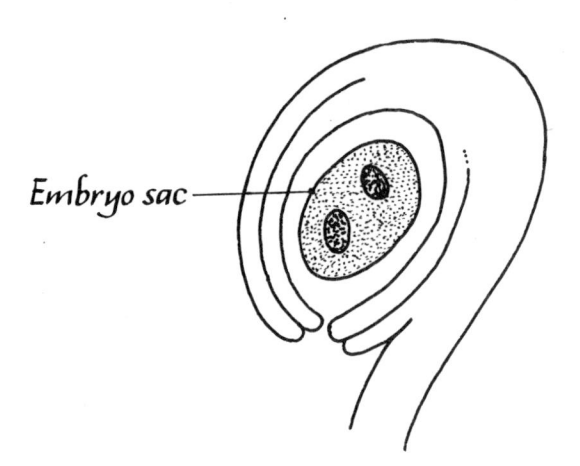

Figure 12.10 The embryo sac within the ovule

cross-pollination, in which pollen is transferred from the anther of the flower of one plant to the stigma of a flower of another plant. Sometimes **self-pollination** occurs when the pollen from a flower is transferred to its own stigma.

12.6. Why not self-pollination?

Self-pollination would appear to be the easiest method and would seem to solve several problems. Why then is it not the method normally employed? The famous naturalist, Charles Darwin, experimented with cabbages—some self-pollinated, others cross-pollinated. The cabbages resulting from self-pollination averaged 1 kg in mass whilst those resulting from cross-pollination weighed on average 3 kg. Thus cross-pollination appears to result in heavier crops. It also results in vigorous plants which are more resistant to disease. Any weak characteristic tends to be eliminated in plants resulting from cross-pollination.

Most flowers have quite elaborate devices to prevent self-pollination, but occasionally cross-pollination fails to take place. When this happens these devices break down and the flower is allowed to self-pollinate, as a last resort, to ensure the continuation of the species.

12.7. Insect pollination

Flowers pollinated by insects usually have large colourful petals and are scented, both of which advertise the presence of nectar to nearby insects such as bees. A bee collecting nectar from a young flower becomes liberally dusted with ripe pollen. When it then visits another flower which has ripe egg cells, the pollen from the bee's

Figure 12.11 Pollination by an insect

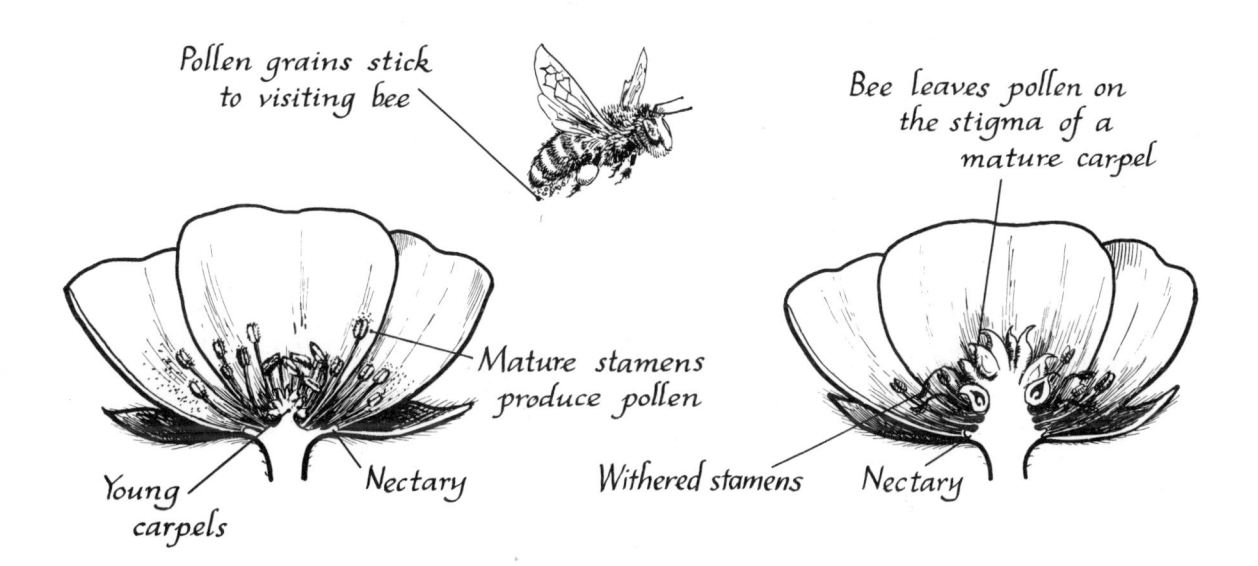

body sticks to the stigmas as the bee collects the nectar. The bee then flies away to convert the nectar into honey and to feed to its larvae some of the pollen which it has collected. It has unwittingly pollinated the flower (see Figure 12.11).

12.8. Pollination of the buttercup flower

The buttercup has a radially symmetrical flower, that is one which can be cut into two similar halves through any vertical plane. It is hermaphrodite, bearing the stamens and carpels in the same flower (see Figure 12.12). It is not a very specialized flower and can be

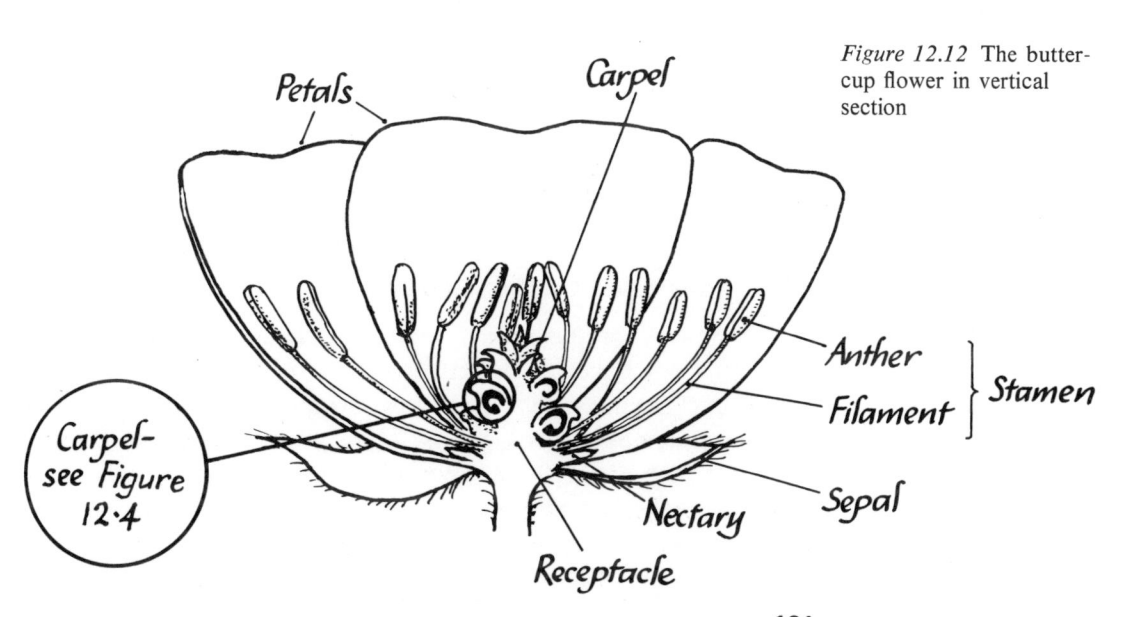

Figure 12.12 The buttercup flower in vertical section

191

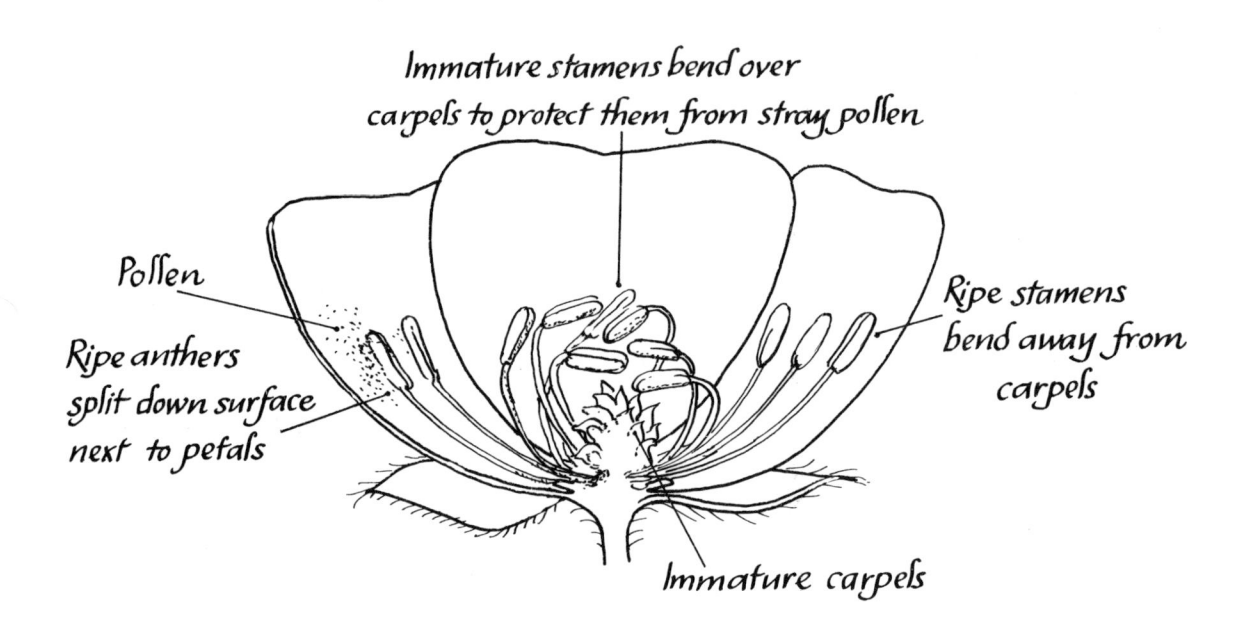

Figure 12.13 Diagram of a buttercup flower showing the mechanisms for preventing self-pollination

pollinated by a wide range of insects, from tiny flies and beetles to large bees, which are attracted by the colourful corolla and the nectar. On the petals are lines called **honey guides**, which lead visiting insects to the nectary at the base of the petals. As the insect makes its way to the nectary it crawls under the stamens and becomes covered with pollen. If the insect now visits an older flower with ripe carpels whose stamens have by now withered, it brushes against the stigma and pollination occurs.

The buttercup avoids self-pollination in the following ways:

a. The carpels do not ripen until the stamens are spent and withered.

b. The anthers split down the outside and shed their pollen to the outside of the flower, away from the stigma.

c. The outermost stamens nearest to the petals ripen first, and as they ripen they bend outwards towards the petals and away from the stigmas (see Figure 12.13).

12.9. Pollination by the wind

The flowers of the grasses, plantains, docks and many of our common trees have no brightly coloured petals. These flowers do not produce scent or nectar, but they do produce a large number of very light, smooth, pollen grains. The stamens have long filaments which trail out of the flower so that the wind can easily carry away the pollen. The stigmas of these flowers are often very branched and feathery, so that they can easily pick up pollen grains from the wind (see Figure 12.14).

Pollen grains blown by the wind

SINGLE GRASS FLOWERS

Pollen settles on feathery stigma

Pollen grains produced by stamens

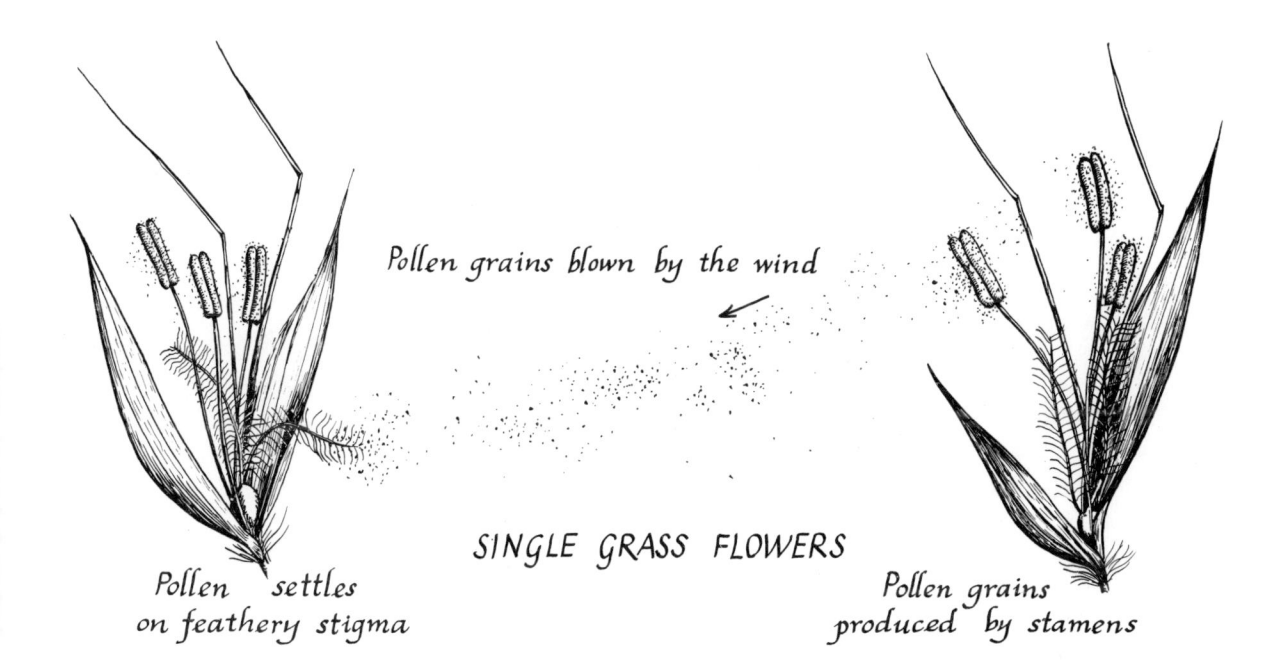

12.10. The wind-pollinated flower of the oat plant

Figure 12.14 Pollination by the wind

The oat is a monocotyledon, or narrow-leafed plant, so we shall expect the flower parts to be in threes. The flower is still hermaphrodite. The flower head, or inflorescence, is called a **panicle**, and consists of a collection of **spikelets** borne on stalks or **pedicels** (see Figure 12.15).

Investigation 12c. To discover the structure of the oat flower

With the aid of a tile, a needle, forceps and a hand lens, remove the parts of a single spikelet, starting from the outside. If oat flowers are not available, tall oat grass is a good substitute. Each spikelet is an individual flower and is enclosed in two scales called **glumes**. Remove the glumes from one of the spikelets. Inside you will find another pair of scales. The outer scale is called the **lemma**, which may bear a bristle. The inner scale is shorter and narrower and is called the **palea**. If the lemma and palea are now prised apart with the tip of a needle, the actual flower may be seen. You will need a hand lens to see the parts clearly. The flower consists of three parts: two scales called **lodicules**, which are the reduced petals; three stamens with long filaments; and a hairy ovary containing a single ovule and bearing a pair of feathery stigmas on short styles. Draw as much as you can see, and then compare your drawing with Figure 12.16.

12.11. A comparison of wind pollination and insect pollination

TABLE 12.1. THE DIFFERENCES BETWEEN INSECT- AND WIND-POLLINATED PLANTS

Insect-pollinated	Wind-pollinated
1. Brightly coloured conspicuous corolla.	1. Corolla greatly reduced.
2. Nectar and scent produced.	2. No nectar or scent produced.
3. A moderate quantity of relatively large and heavy pollen grains produced.	3. A vast quantity of very light pollen grains produced.
4. Sculptured pollen grains.	4. Smooth pollen grains.
5. Stamens within flower.	5. Stamens protrude from flower.
6. Compact stigma with surface sculptured complementary to pollen grains.	6. Feathery stigma.
7. Flowers open after the leaves.	7. Flowers open before the leaves.

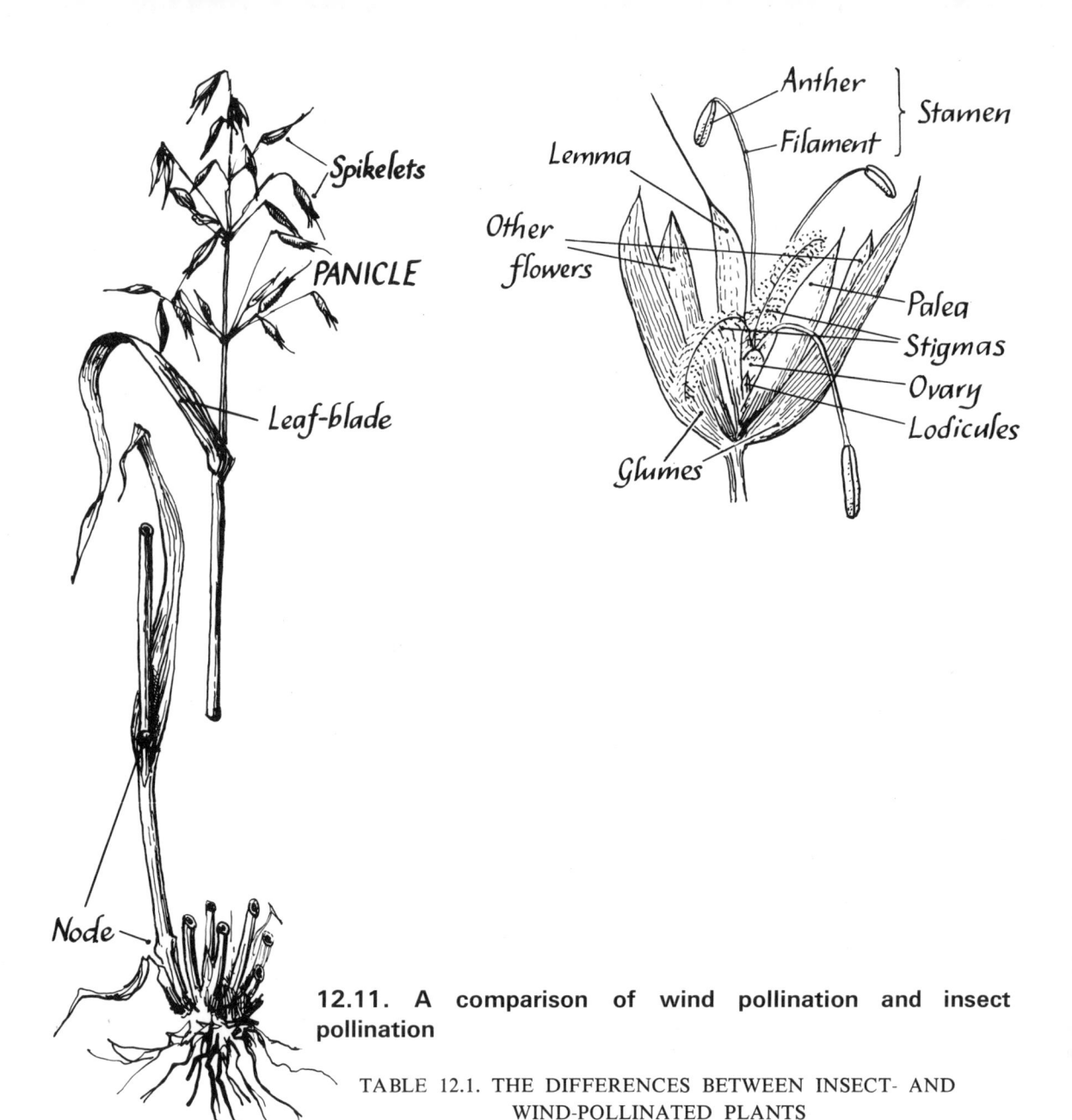

Figure 12.15 (above) The common oat plant

Figure 12.16 (above, right) A single spikelet of the oat flower

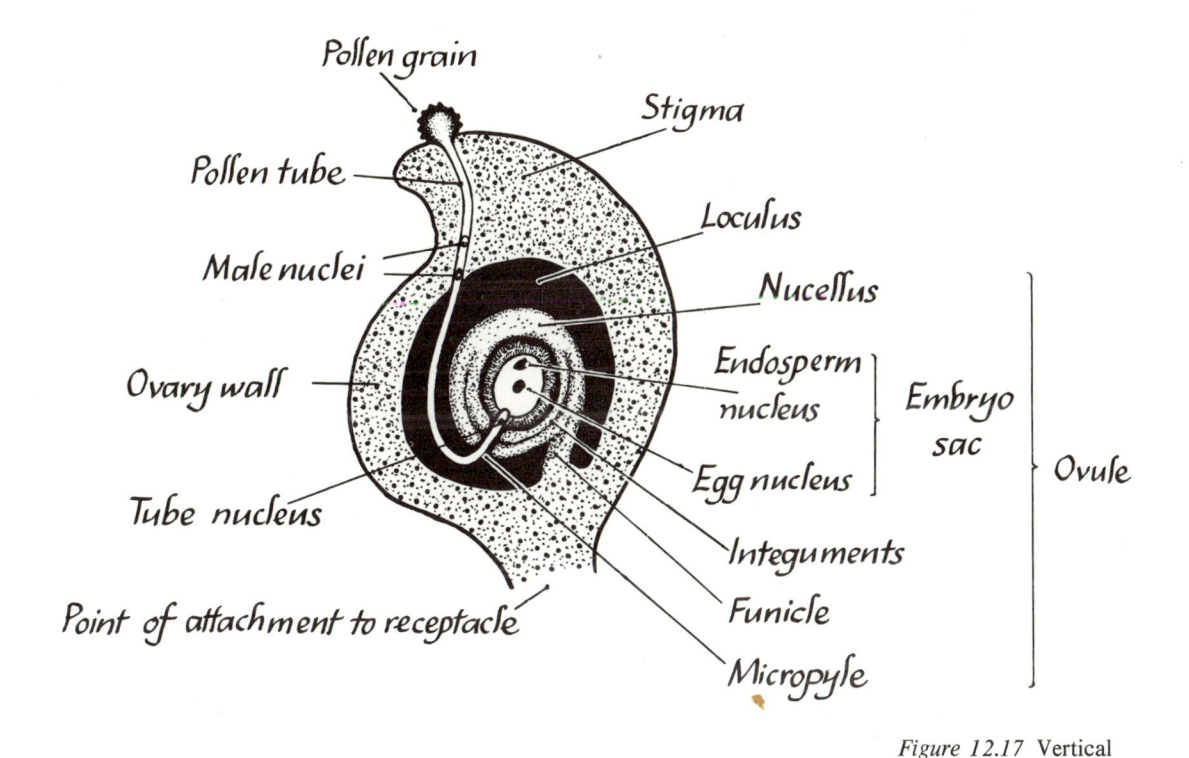

Figure 12.17 Vertical section of a single buttercup carpel at fertilization

12.12. Fertilization

When the pollen grain arrives on the sticky surface of the stigma, it absorbs water and sugar from the style and a pollen tube emerges through a thin region in the wall of the pollen grain called the **germ pore**. The pollen tubes are attracted by a substance secreted by the ovule. The pollen tube grows through the tissue of the style, partly by digestion and partly by tearing the tissues. At the tip of the pollen tube is the tube nucleus, which withers away as soon as the pollen tube penetrates the **micropyle** of the ovule. Meanwhile, within the ovule, one cell becomes enlarged to form the large embryo sac. The embryo sac nucleus divides to produce two gametes, the egg nucleus and the endosperm nucleus (see Figure 12.17).

When the tip of the pollen tube bursts, the two male nuclei are liberated in the embryo sac and a double fertilization takes place. One of the male nuclei fertilizes the egg nucleus to form the zygote which subsequently develops into the embryo of the seed, whilst the other male nucleus fertilizes the endosperm nucleus, the resulting fusion nucleus eventually forming the food reserves of the seed.

Investigation 12d. To study the growth of pollen grains

Warm a little agar until it melts and then add some sugar. When the sugar has dissolved, pour the agar into two petri dishes and allow it to set. Sprinkle a few pollen grains from a flower with ripe anthers on to the agar in each dish. Cover the contents of one dish with the top. Into the second dish, put a piece of the carpel of the same flower and then cover it. Place both dishes in a warm situation. After a few days examine the two dishes under a binocular, or very low power, microscope. Note the behaviour of the pollen grains in the two dishes and draw any conclusions you can.

12.13. The formation of the seed

The fertilized ovule becomes the seed. Inside the ovule, the fertilized egg nucleus divides to form the embryo, which is a young plant. The embryo consists of three parts: firstly, the **plumule**, which eventually develops into the shoot system of the new plant; secondly, the **radicle**, which gives rise to the root system; and thirdly, either one or two seed leaves, or **cotyledons**. The cotyledons may come above the ground at germination to form the first photosynthetic leaves or they may become packed with food reserves and remain below the ground.

The fertilized endosperm nucleus develops into the food storage tissue of the seed. The endosperm may be packed around the embryo in seeds such as castor oil. These seeds are called **endospermous seeds** and their cotyledons remain thin and leaf-like. In other seeds, such as the broad bean, the endosperm is absorbed into the cotyledons which become thick and fleshy. These seeds are called **non-endospermous seeds**.

The outer layers of the ovule form the **integuments** which become hardened to form the seed coat, or **testa**. The micropyle of the ovule persists to form the micropyle of the seed, and the funicle remains attaching the seed to the old ovary wall (see Figure 12.18).

Figure 12.18 Vertical section through a single buttercup carpel after fertilization

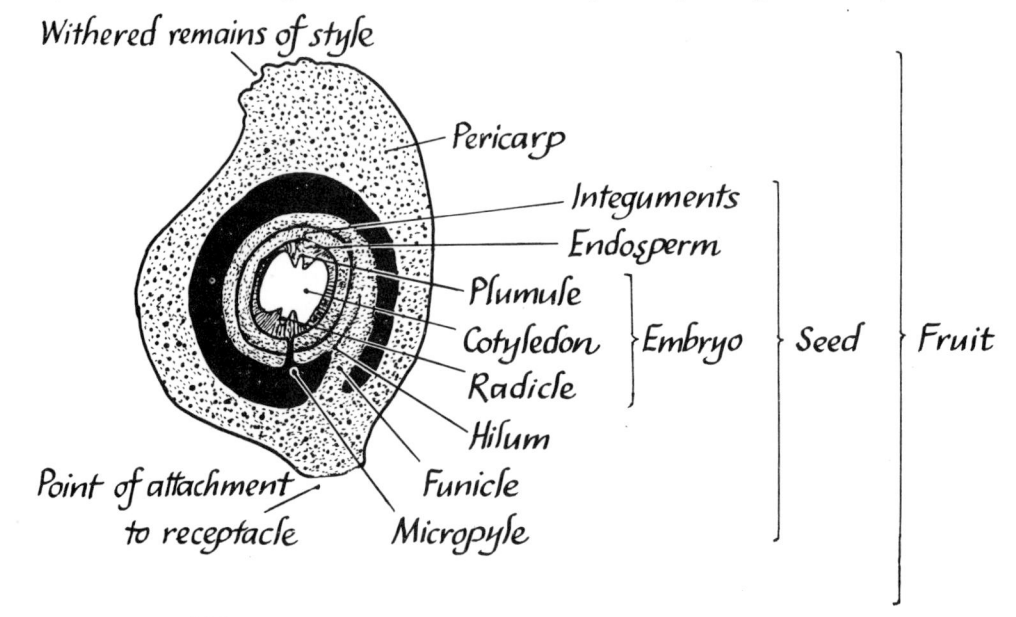

12.14. The formation of the fruit

Whilst these changes from ovule to seed have been taking place, the entire gynaecium has become modified to form the fruit. A fruit is a fertilized gynaecium, so its nature will largely be determined by the nature of the gynaecium from which it has developed. The ovary wall has been modified to form the **pericarp**. The nature of the pericarp is related to the way the fruit, and the seeds it contains, is dispersed.

12.15. The dispersal of fruits and seeds

It has been said that the pericarp of a fruit is often modified to assist its dispersal. Why is it necessary for the fruits and their seeds to be scattered at some distance from the parent plant? Remember a single plant produces many fruits, each of which may contain many seeds. Each seed has the potential to grow into a new plant. What would happen if all the seeds from a single plant were to fall to the ground immediately beneath that plant? It would result in overcrowding and severe competition for light, space, water, oxygen and mineral salts—competition which the parent plant would win at the expense of its own offspring. This would defeat the whole object of reproduction, which is to propagate and continue the species.

Fruits and seeds must therefore be dispersed or scattered away from the parent plant to situations where the young seedlings will have adequate space, light, water, oxygen and mineral salts.

There are *five* main methods of dispersal, namely by wind, by water, by being eaten by animals, by being carried on the fur of animals, and by explosion.

12.16. The dispersal of fruits and seeds by wind

Wind is a very efficient agent for scattering fruits and seeds. Fruits scattered in this way are produced in very large numbers and are usually very light with a large surface area. The large surface area may be achieved by the formation of a wing-like extension of the pericarp or by the formation of a parachute of hairs; both these modifications make the fruits very buoyant and easily carried in the air currents (see Figure 12.19).

The fruit of the clematis is an **achene** which has a persistent hairy style, while the fruits of ash and elm are **samaras** which have wing-like extensions of the pericarp. Both of these structures assist wind dispersal. The fruit of the dandelion is a **cypsela**, a dry, indehiscent, one-seeded fruit, with a pappus of hairs forming a parachute-like structure which enables the fruit to be carried great distances by the

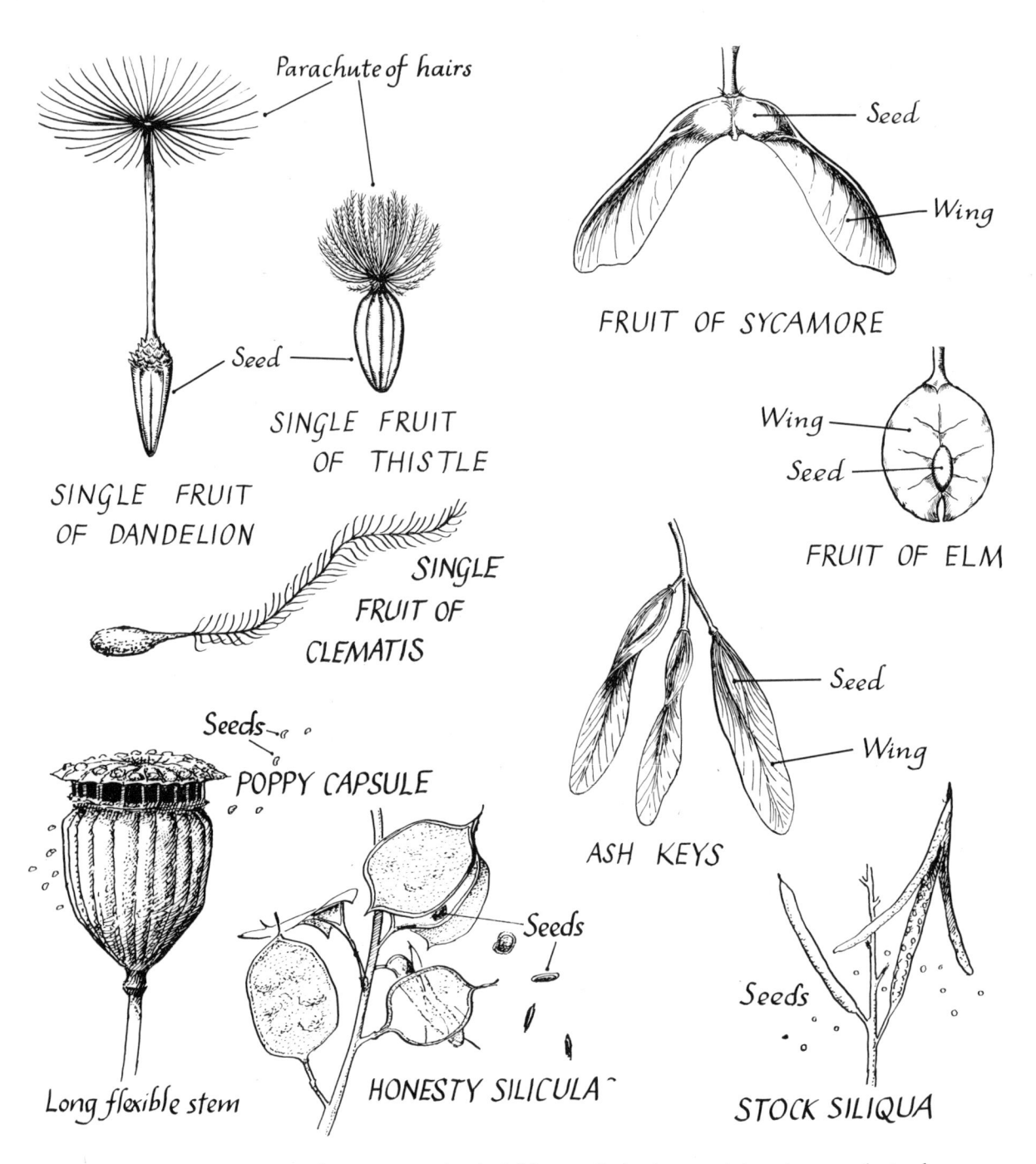

Figure 12.19 Fruits dispersed by the wind

air currents. An indehiscent fruit does not burst open, but releases its seeds when the pericarp decays.

Some seeds are light, but flattened to present a large surface area to the air currents. Two fruits which have large, light seeds are the **siliqua** of the stock and wallflower and the **silicula** of honesty and shepherd's purse.

Another method of dispersal dependent upon the wind is the

198

pepperpot or censer mechanism, which is characteristic of the capsule of the poppy. The capsule is borne at the tip of a long, 'whippy' stalk. When the capsule is blown by the wind the light seeds are scattered far and wide through the pores of the capsule. Seeds liberated as soon as they are ripe may be dispersed during conditions which are unfavourable for their germination and survival. Many plants therefore have a mechanism for timing their seed dispersal. Pine cones open in dry conditions but remain closed while the air is very humid, and the openings of the poppy capsule are closed during wet conditions, thus preventing dispersal.

12.17. The dispersal of fruits and seeds by water

Water is obviously a convenient agent for aquatic plants. The fruit of the water-lily is a **follicle**, formed from a single carpel containing many seeds. The seeds are liberated when the fruit splits down one axis. The seeds of the water-lily have a spongy testa which is full of air spaces. When the light seeds are liberated by the bursting of the follicle they float away downstream. Gradually water enters the air spaces of the testa, which eventually becomes waterlogged. This causes the seed to sink into the mud at the bottom of the stream, where it germinates.

A coconut is an example of a **drupe** with a fibrous pericarp which makes it buoyant. Coconuts which fall from the palm trees on to the beaches float away out to sea at very high tides. Eventually they may be cast on to the beach of an island some miles away, where

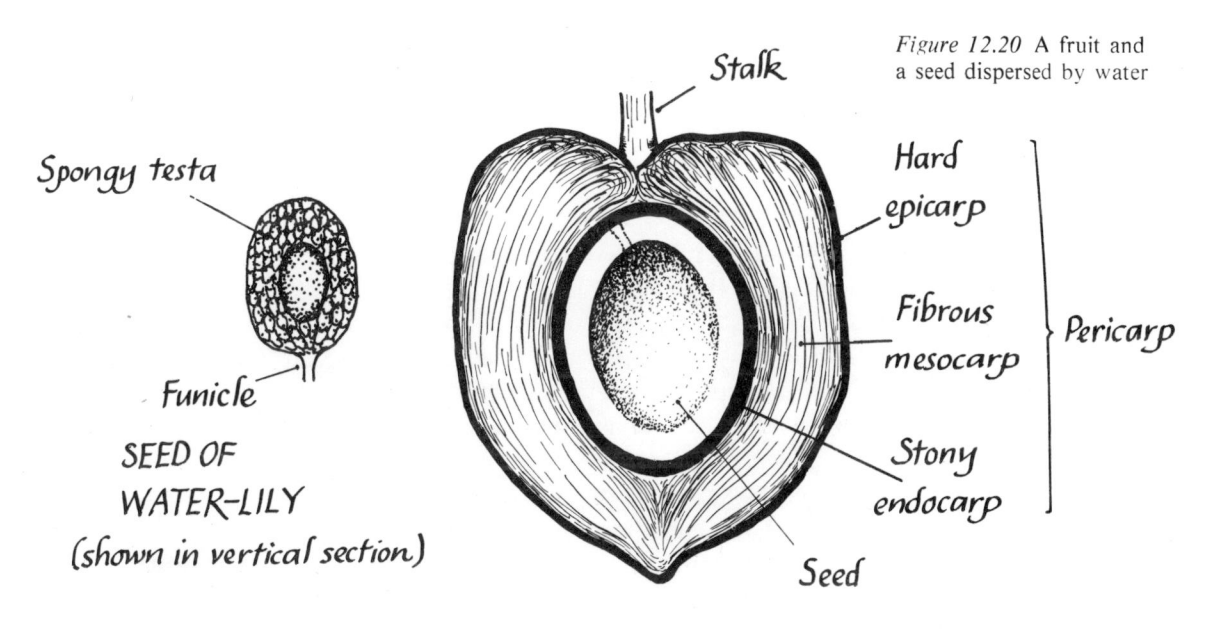

Figure 12.20 A fruit and a seed dispersed by water

they may germinate. The coconuts which you win at the fair are only the seeds of the coconut—the fibrous pericarp, used in the manufacture of coconut matting, has been removed (see Figure 12.20).

12.18. The dispersal of fruits and seeds by animals

The pericarps of many fruits are juicy and fleshy. This makes them very attractive food for birds and animals (see Figure 12.21).

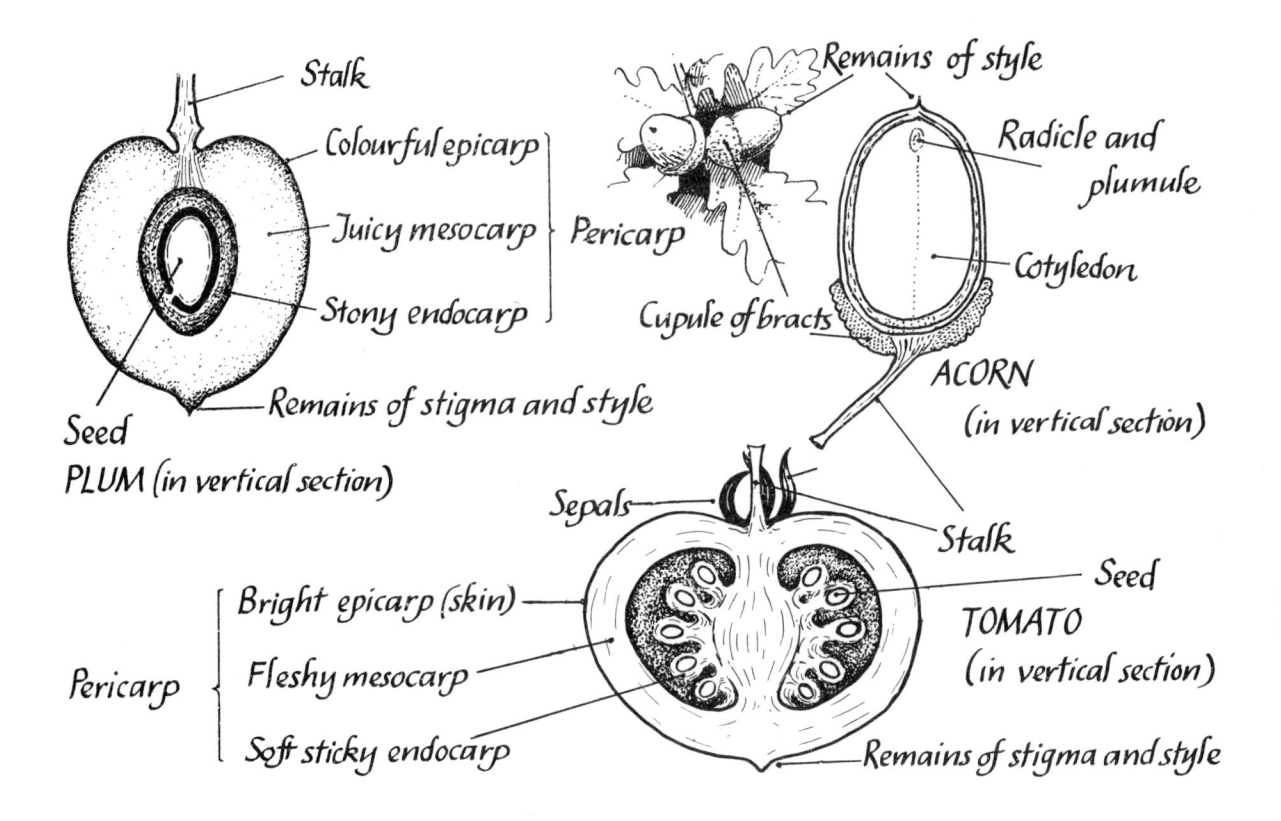

Figure 12.21 Fruits dispersed when they are eaten by animals

The **drupe** of the plum is a good example. A drupe is a succulent, one-seeded fruit which develops from a single carpel. The pericarp has three regions. The outer **epicarp** forms the skin of the fruit and is usually very brightly coloured. Can you suggest why? The fleshy portion of the pericarp is called the **mesocarp** and the hard inner region which forms the stone around the seed is called the **endocarp**. When the drupe is eaten by an animal or bird it may be carried some distance before the stone is rejected. The seed is released by the decay of the endocarp.

Another example of a succulent fruit dispersed by animals is the **berry**. The berry is usually eaten whole and the seeds are swallowed. As the seed testa is tough and resists the action of the digestive juices, the seed passes unharmed through the digestive system of the animal or bird, to be deposited in its droppings some distance from the parent plant. Note that tomato plants grow wild on many sewage farms! Other examples of berries are the orange, the marrow, cucumber, grape and in fact any succulent many-seeded fruits.

Nuts are the food of many woodland creatures which may carry them away to a secret store some distance from the parent plant. If the nut is not needed, or is forgotten, then it will germinate to produce a new tree. An acorn, the fruit of the oak tree, is a good example.

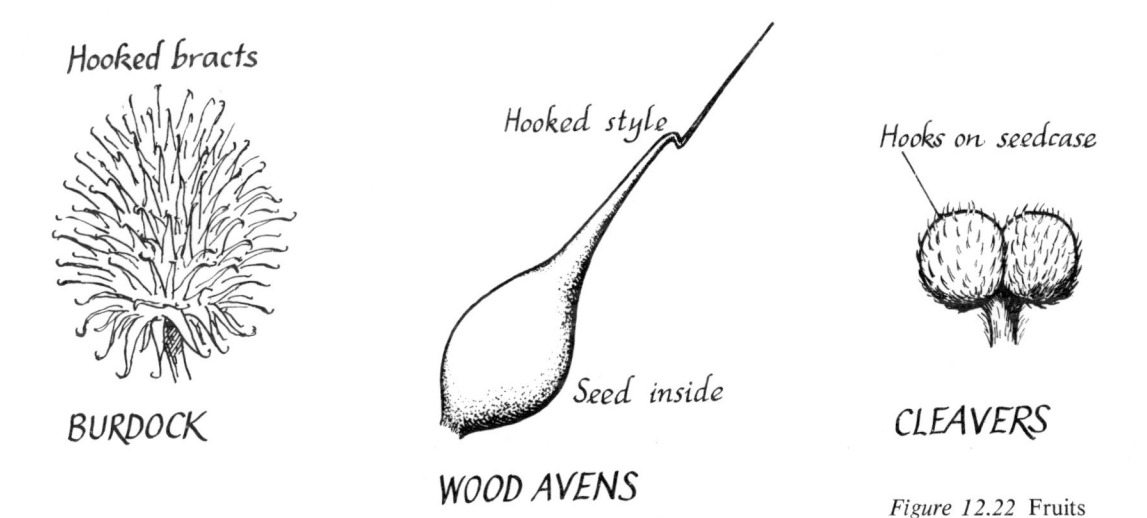

Figure 12.22 Fruits dispersed on the coats of animals

12.19. The dispersal of fruits and seeds by contact

Many fruits have hooks or similar devices on their pericarp, which easily become entangled in the fur or wool of passing animals (see Figure 12.22). Later on these fruits may fall to the ground when the animal has travelled some distance from the parent plant. The fruits of wood avens, or geum, are achenes with a persistent hooked style, and the fruits of cleavers and enchanter's nightshade have hooks developed on the pericarp.

It is an interesting exercise to remove and identify all the fruits and seeds from one's clothing after a country walk.

12.20. The dispersal of fruits and seeds by explosion

Some fruits burst open with almost explosive violence, scattering their seeds far and wide (see Figure 12.23).

There are two mechanisms which cause fruits to burst open:

a. The first is due to unequal drying of the pericarp. This sets up stresses and strains, which are released when the pericarp tears down a line of weakness. Legumes, such as gorse, sweet pea and clover,

SWEET PEA

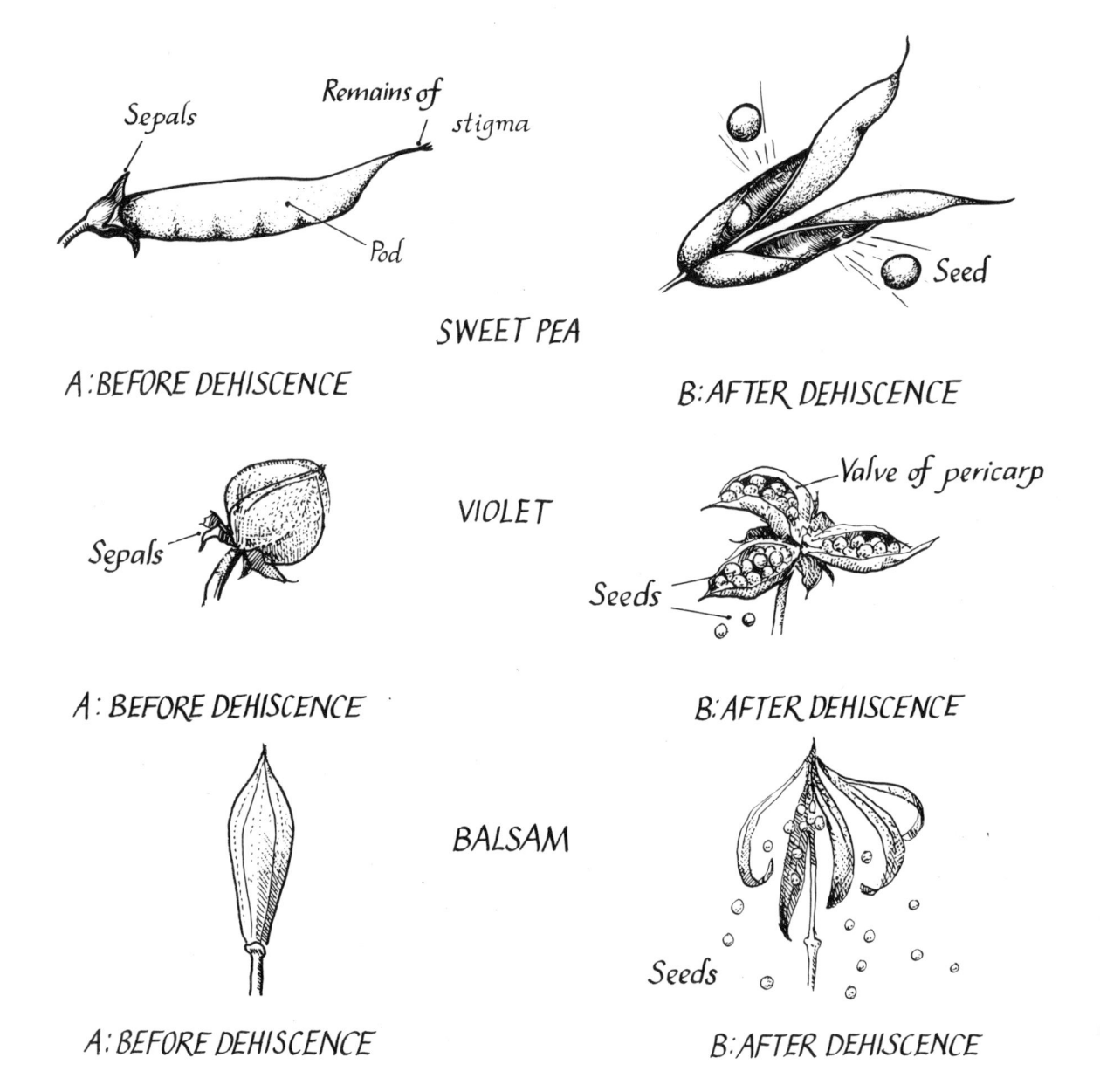

A: BEFORE DEHISCENCE   B: AFTER DEHISCENCE

VIOLET

A: BEFORE DEHISCENCE   B: AFTER DEHISCENCE

BALSAM

A: BEFORE DEHISCENCE   B: AFTER DEHISCENCE

Figure 12.23 Fruits and seeds dispersed by explosion

have such fruits. The seeds are hard and shiny. As the pod bursts open, the two valves twist and squeeze the shiny seeds, propelling them violently from the plant.

b. The second explosive mechanism is due to the turgidity or the pressure of water within the pericarp. Certain cells take in water by osmosis, causing some of the pericarp tissues to swell. This sets up stresses and strains in the pericarp, which cause it to tear along lines of weakness when the plant is disturbed. The fruits of the balsams are dispersed in this way. The large 'policeman's helmet', found by streams, and the woodland 'Noli me tangere' are two. Try to pick the flowers and you will be violently bombarded by seeds from the mature fruits.

12.21. False fruits: pseudocarps

False fruits develop from some part of the flower other than just the gynaecium. The receptacle is frequently involved (see Figure 12.24).

The apple is a **pome**, which is really a capsule embedded within a swollen receptacle. It is dispersed by animals attracted to the succulent receptacle, which they eat before rejecting the capsule containing the seeds (the core).

The strawberry fruit is also a pseudocarp and consists of a much swollen, juicy receptacle bearing a collection of achenes. Animals and birds are attracted by the brightly coloured juicy receptacle which they eat. The achenes resist the digestive juices of the animal and are deposited unharmed in its droppings.

Figure 12.24 Some false fruits

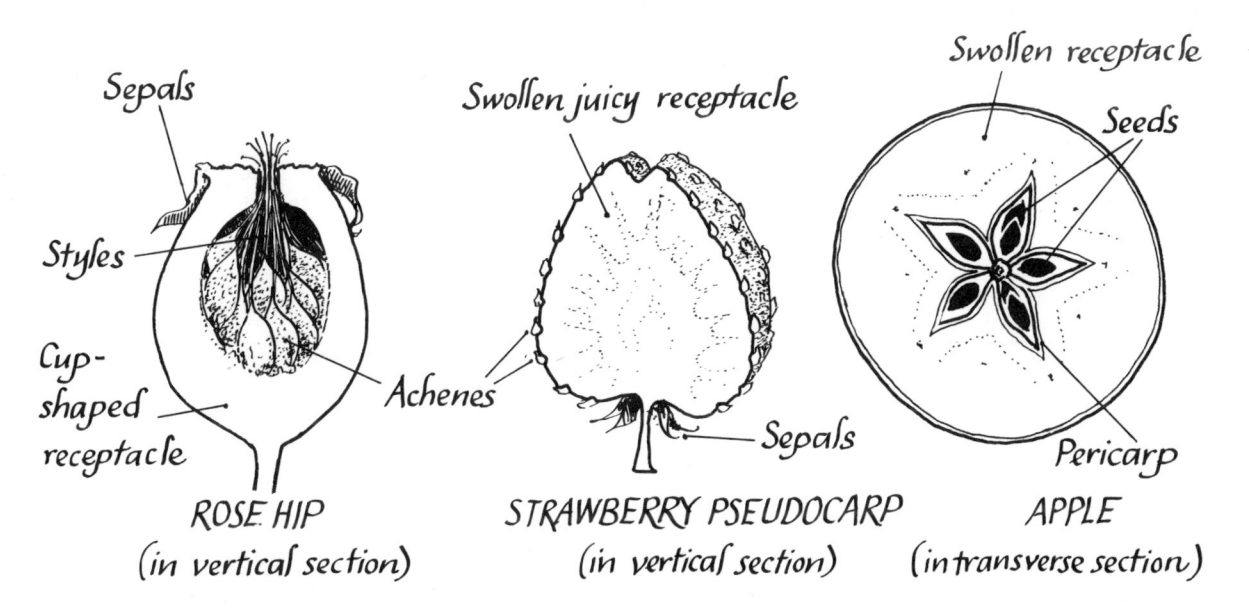

12.22. Classifying fruits

Investigation 12e. To classify a collection of fruits on their structure and to display them

During the summer or early autumn, collect as many fruits as you can from the fields, hedgerows and your garden. Do not forget that every plant which flowered in the summer now bears fruit. Identify the plant and decide the type of fruit by referring to Table 12.2.

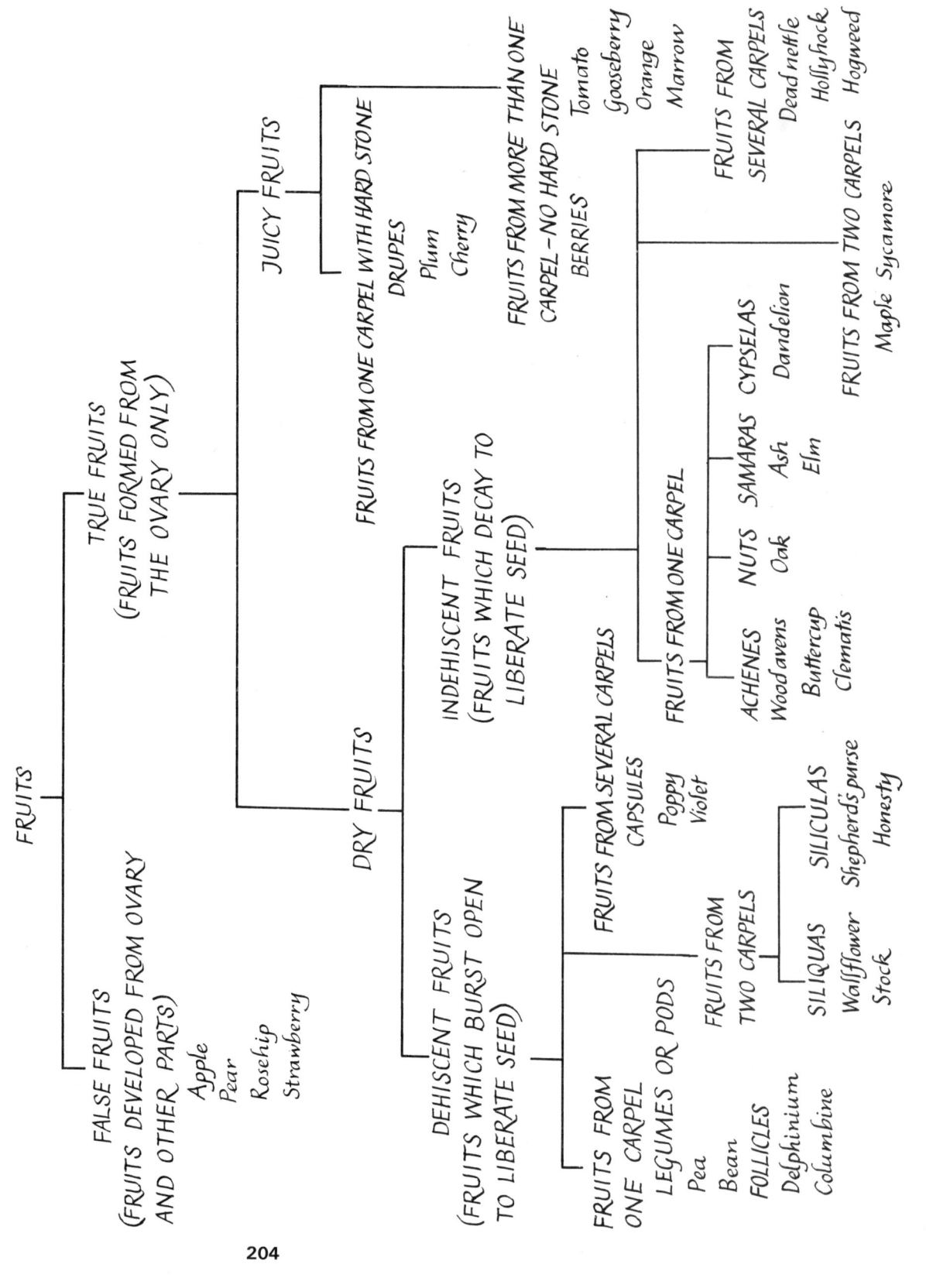

TABLE 12.2. CLASSIFICATION OF FRUITS BY STRUCTURE

```
FRUITS
├── FALSE FRUITS (FRUITS DEVELOPED FROM OVARY AND OTHER PARTS)
│       Apple
│       Pear
│       Rosehip
│       Strawberry
│
└── TRUE FRUITS (FRUITS FORMED FROM THE OVARY ONLY)
    │
    ├── DRY FRUITS
    │   │
    │   ├── DEHISCENT FRUITS (FRUITS WHICH BURST OPEN TO LIBERATE SEED)
    │   │   │
    │   │   ├── FRUITS FROM ONE CARPEL
    │   │   │   ├── LEGUMES OR PODS
    │   │   │   │     Pea
    │   │   │   │     Bean
    │   │   │   └── FOLLICLES
    │   │   │         Delphinium
    │   │   │         Columbine
    │   │   │
    │   │   └── FRUITS FROM SEVERAL CARPELS
    │   │       ├── CAPSULES
    │   │       │     Poppy
    │   │       │     Violet
    │   │       └── FRUITS FROM TWO CARPELS
    │   │           ├── SILIQUAS
    │   │           │     Wallflower
    │   │           │     Stock
    │   │           └── SILICULAS
    │   │                 Shepherd's purse
    │   │                 Honesty
    │   │
    │   └── INDEHISCENT FRUITS (FRUITS WHICH DECAY TO LIBERATE SEED)
    │       │
    │       └── FRUITS FROM ONE CARPEL
    │           ├── ACHENES
    │           │     Wood avens
    │           │     Buttercup
    │           │     Clematis
    │           ├── NUTS
    │           │     Oak
    │           ├── SAMARAS
    │           │     Ash
    │           │     Elm
    │           └── CYPSELAS
    │                 Dandelion
    │
    └── JUICY FRUITS
        │
        ├── FRUITS FROM ONE CARPEL WITH HARD STONE
        │   └── DRUPES
        │         Plum
        │         Cherry
        │
        └── FRUITS FROM MORE THAN ONE CARPEL – NO HARD STONE
            ├── BERRIES
            │     Tomato
            │     Gooseberry
            │     Orange
            │     Marrow
            ├── FRUITS FROM SEVERAL CARPELS
            │     Dead nettle
            │     Hollyhock
            │     Hogweed
            └── FRUITS FROM TWO CARPELS
                  Maple
                  Sycamore
```

Group similar fruits together and stick them on cardboard to make a chart illustrating structure.

Investigation 12f. To classify and display a collection of fruits according to their method of dispersal

Make your collection as in Investigation 12e, but this time when you have identified your fruits group together those fruits which are dispersed in a similar way. Display them on a chart.

There are many ingenious ways of presenting your collection. If all the completed charts are displayed on the classroom wall, perhaps you can judge the best ones. Do not forget that clarity, attractiveness and scientific accuracy must all be considered.

12.23. Seed structure

A seed develops from the ovule after fertilization. It consists of a plant embryo and a supply of food to nourish it until it is able to make its own food. It is enclosed in a tough seed coat, or testa.

Investigation 12g. To examine the structure of a large seed such as a broad bean

Soak your seeds in water for about two days before examining them. In addition to soaked seeds you will need a white tile, a scalpel, a needle, a pair of forceps and a hand lens.

Examine the soaked broad bean or other seed carefully and make two large drawings, one from the flat side and the other from the narrow end. Note the pale brown testa and the long black scar, or hilum, where its seed was attached to the inside of the pod. Note also the position of the young root or radicle. Squeeze the seed between your thumb and first finger. Do you see a drop of water ooze from the tiny hole near the radicle tip? This hole is the micropyle, where water first enters the dormant seed (see Figure 12.25). Using the

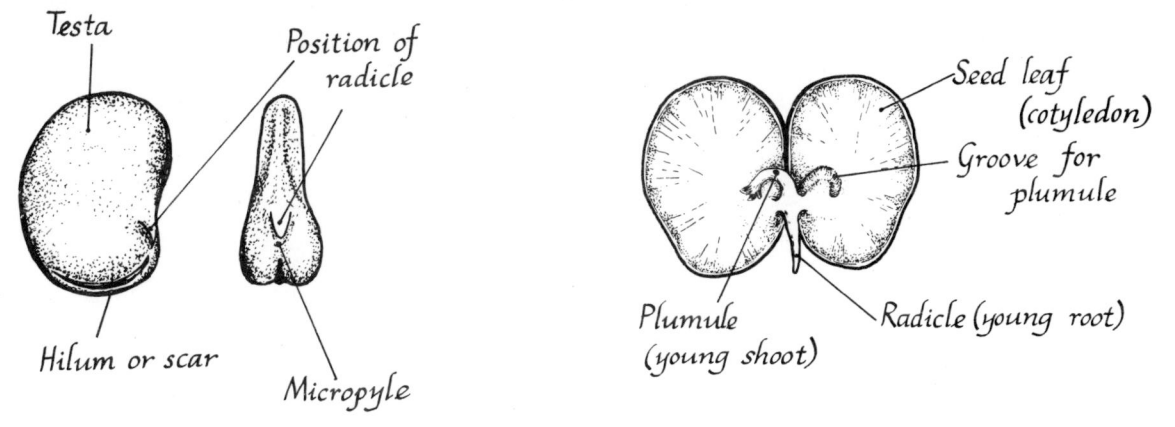

Figure 12.25 Diagrams to show the structure of the broad bean seed: (left) external views; (right) internal view after separation of the cotyledons

scalpel, cut round the curved edge of the seed and carefully remove the testa to examine its inner surface. Do you notice a little pocket? What do you think fitted into this pocket? What is the tiny hole at the bottom of the pocket? What is it there for?

In the broad bean, the embryo fills the entire testa. Carefully separate the two halves of the seed and examine the embryo. Notice the radicle or young root lying at the side. The plumule, or young shoot, is curved and fits into a hollow in the right-hand seed leaf, or cotyledon. If the embryo entirely fills the testa, where is the food supply or endosperm? Look carefully at the cotyledons or seed leaves. Do you notice how thick and unleaf-like they have become? This is because the endosperm has been absorbed by the cotyledons which store it until it is needed. This type of seed, which has no endosperm but instead has thick cotyledons, is called a **non-endospermous seed**. At germination, this type of cotyledon remains below the soil level and gradually shrivels as its food is used up. The broad bean seed has two cotyledons (dicotyledonous) and produces a broad-leafed plant. Do not discard the fragments of the dissected seeds: use them for Investigation 12h.

Investigation 12h. To find out what types of food are stored in these seeds

For this experiment you will need iodine solution in potassium iodide, Fehling's solutions A and B or Benedict's solution, Millon's reagent, a bunsen burner, an asbestos mat, a filter paper, a few small test-tubes in a rack and a test-tube holder.

Carry out the following tests on the seed fragments and record your results as in Table 12.3:

1. Test for simple sugar (for example, glucose)

Into a test-tube place 2 cm^3 of Benedict's solution. Add a few of the seed fragments, shake and heat the tube gently in a bunsen flame. A change in colour from blue to green/red indicates the presence of sugar. If there is no change in colour, then sugar is absent from the seed.

Alternatively, the test may be carried out using Fehling's solution (a mixture of equal volumes of Fehling's solutions A and B). The colour change is from blue to brick-red, if sugar is present.

2. Test for starch

Place a few fragments of seed in a small dish or watchglass and add a few drops of iodine solution (iodine dissolved in potassium iodide solution). A colour change from orange to blue/black indicates the presence of starch.

3. Test for protein

Into a test-tube place 2 cm³ of Millon's reagent. Add a few fragments of seed and heat gently in a bunsen flame. A change from colourless to red indicates the presence of protein.

4. Test for fat

Rub the fragments of seed on to a piece of filter paper. If the seeds contain fat a grease mark will be produced. If held to the light the mark will be seen to be translucent.

TABLE 12.3. RESULTS OF THE FOOD TESTS ON SEEDS

Type of Seed	Test Procedure	Result	Conclusion
Broad bean	Simple sugar test (fill in details)		
Broad bean	Starch test (fill in details)		
Broad bean	Protein test (fill in details)		
Broad bean	Fat test (fill in details)		

12.24. Germination

How do seeds become plants? The food stored in the seed nourishes the embryo until it is a self-supporting seedling. How does the seed develop? Germination is the name given to the earliest stage of plant growth, when the dormant seed begins to sprout.

Investigation 12i. To study the changes which occur during the germination of a seed such as broad bean or castor oil

Take a jam jar, three sheets of blotting paper and several seeds of each type. The seeds should be well soaked before starting the investigation. Line the jam jar with the blotting paper, and pack the centre with moist sawdust. Trap the seeds between the glass and the blotting paper, as shown in Figure 12.26. Add enough water to the sawdust to keep the blotting paper moist, but not soaking wet. Place the apparatus in a light, fairly warm position. Observe the daily progress of the seeds and draw one seedling of each at least twice a week to record their progress. Do not forget to keep the sawdust watered. Compare your drawings with Figure 12.27, and use these to complete the labels on your own drawings.

The germination of the broad bean is described as **hypogeal** because the food-laden cotyledons remain below the ground. The seed stores starch and protein. The germination of the castor oil seed is described as **epigeal** because the cotyledons come above the ground to form the first photosynthetic organs. The castor oil seed stores oil and protein.

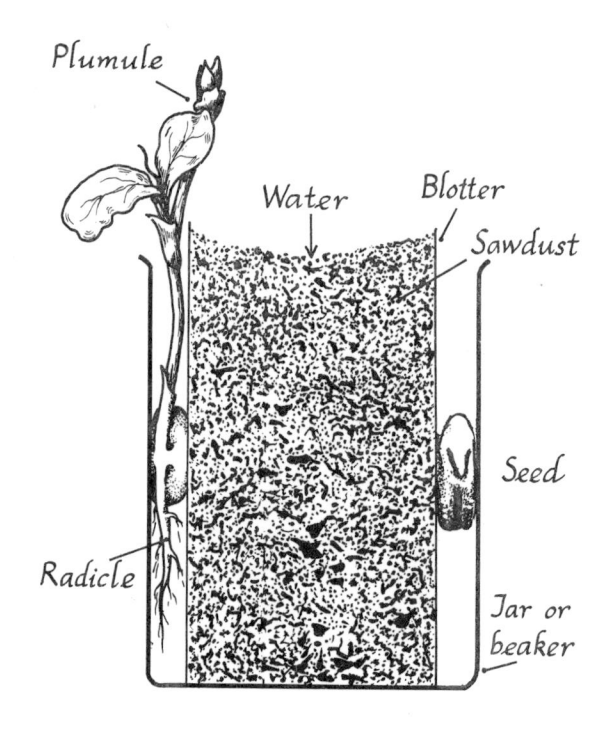

Figure 12.26 Apparatus set up to study the changes in a seed during germination

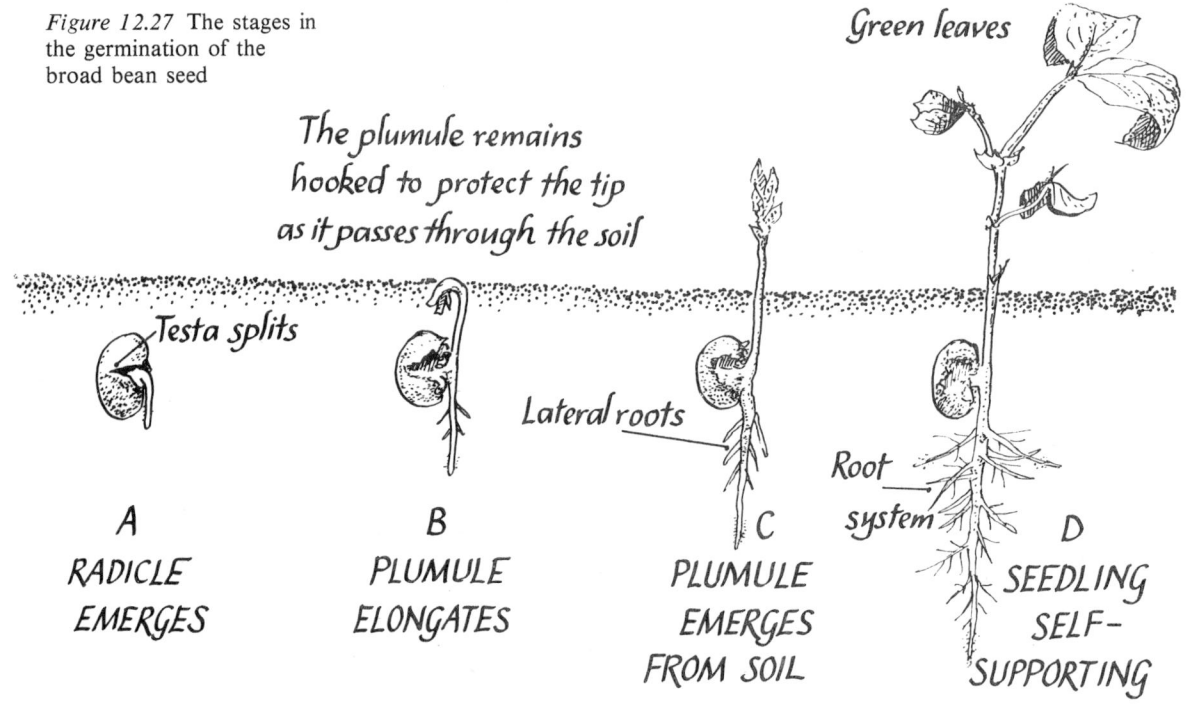

Figure 12.27 The stages in the germination of the broad bean seed

The plumule remains hooked to protect the tip as it passes through the soil

A
RADICLE EMERGES

B
PLUMULE ELONGATES

C
PLUMULE EMERGES FROM SOIL

D
SEEDLING SELF-SUPPORTING

12.25. The conditions needed for germination to take place

Your mother may have some dried peas in a jar in the pantry; these are seeds. You will have seen the packets of seeds in the nurseryman's shop. Let us carry out an investigation to find out why these seeds do not germinate in their packets.

Investigation 12j. To discover what conditions are necessary for seeds to germinate

Take a rack of five test-tubes labelled A, B, C, D and E. Place a little cotton wool into the bottom of each tube.
1. To tube A add a few cress seeds.
2. To tube B add a few cress seeds and enough water to soak the cotton wool and seeds.
3. To tube C add a few cress seeds and cover with cold boiled water. Then pour a layer of oil on the surface of the water to keep out air.
4. To tube D add a few cress seeds, and just enough water to soak them, placing the tube in a dark but fairly warm place to exclude any effect of light.
5. To tube E add a few cress seeds and just enough water to soak them, placing the tube in a very cold place such as a refrigerator to exclude any effect of warmth.

When you have set these tubes up, draw them as in Figure 12.28. Place tubes A, B and C in a light, warm and airy place.

Figure 12.28 The test-tubes set up at the beginning of the investigation

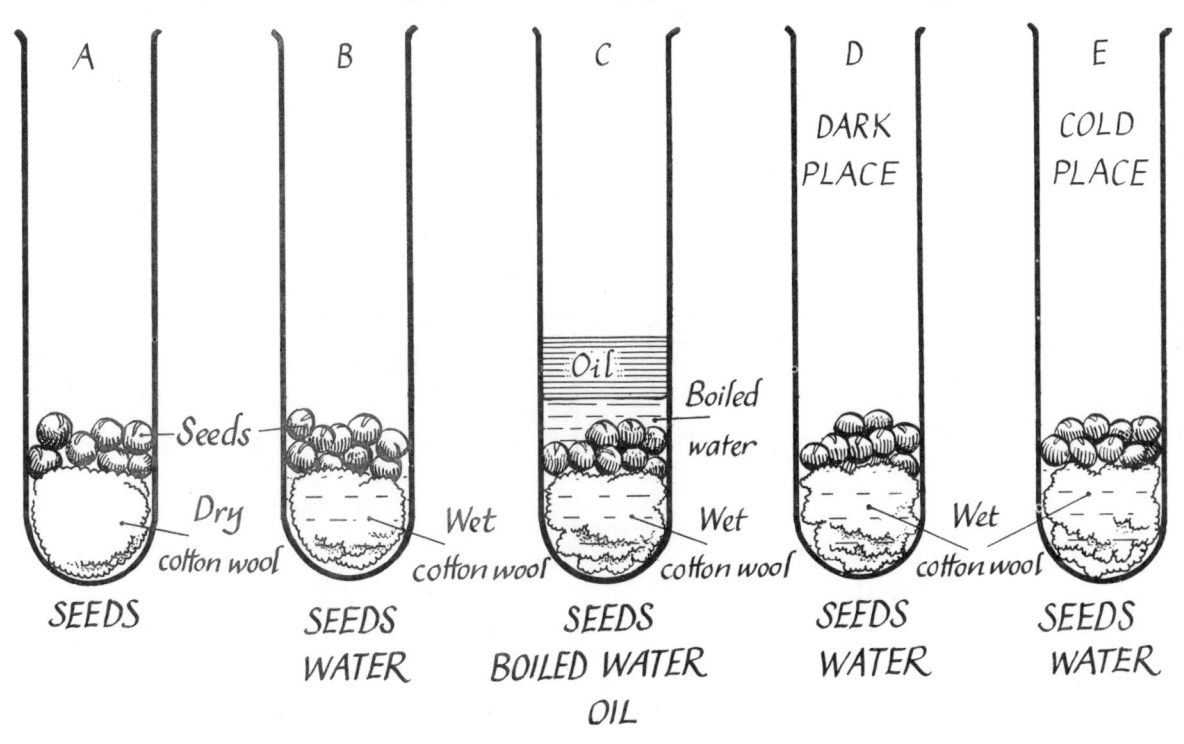

Leave the tubes for about five days, re-examine, and carefully record any changes which have taken place. Why have some of the seeds germinated, but not others? Why have some of the seeds germinated into vigorous green seedlings whilst others have produced sickly, spindly yellow seedlings? What conditions have produced healthy seedlings? Write down which conditions, if any, are lacking in each of the tubes. Why is it necessary to set up tube A? Which is the control experiment? Write down the conditions which you consider are necessary for a seed to germinate.

Test your understanding

Copy and complete the following paragraphs:

Flowers pollinated by ....[1] are usually bright and colourful, and produce a sugary solution called ....[2] which visiting ....[3] collect and make into ....[4] During this process ....[5] are transferred from the stamens of one flower to the ....[6] of another flower of the same ....[7] The pollen grain contains the ....[8] sex cell, which passes through the pollen tube to the ....[9] where it joins with the ....[10] cell, or female sex cell, during the process called ....[11] The resulting cell develops into an ....[12] or baby plant which becomes surrounded with a tough coat, or ....[13], and a supply of stored food to form a ....[14]

A fertilized ....[15] becomes a seed. A fertilized pistil or carpel becomes a ....[16] Inside a fruit are always found ....[17] It is important that fruits and seeds should be scattered away from the parent plant to prevent ....[18] and ....[19] Fruits scattered by the ....[20] are very light and have a large ....[21] Examples are ....[22] and ....[23] Fruits such as ....[24] have hooks so that they can cling to ....[25] Fruits dispersed by water are able to ....[26] such as the ....[27], while the fruits of the pea family are dispersed by ....[28]

The early development of a seed is called ....[29] For this to take place a seed must have an adequate supply of ....[30], a suitable ....[31], a supply of ....[32], and if the seedling is to make its own food it must have ....[33]

1. What are the advantages of sexual reproduction over asexual?
2. Compare insect pollination with wind pollination.
3. Describe how a seed is formed.
4. Why is dispersal of seeds and fruits desirable?
5. Why are so many fruits edible?
6. Describe how five named fruits are adapted for wind dispersal.
7. What conditions are necessary for germination to occur?
8. How could you test a seed for the presence of protein?

Chapter 13

Surviving the Winter

13.1. The problems facing a plant in winter

In our British climate, conditions favourable for plant growth alternate with unfavourable conditions. The favourable conditions form the growing season from spring, through the summer to the early autumn. During this period, the light intensity is high, the temperatures are moderate and adequate supplies of water are available to the plant. In late autumn and winter, however, the light intensity falls, thus slowing the rate of photosynthesis. The temperatures fall below the level at which the plant enzymes work efficiently and the soil water is cold, or may even be frozen, and so cannot be absorbed by the plant. A plant must 'pack' all its growth into the relatively short period of favourable conditions, and yet be able to survive the unfavourable conditions of winter.

13.2. The annual plant

The annual plant solves this problem by not attempting to live through the winter, but spends this time as a dormant seed. It germinates from seed in spring, and rapidly produces foliage leaves. In the summer, the plant flowers and pollination occurs. This results in fruits containing seeds, which are dispersed in the autumn of the same year. During the winter the species is only represented by the dormant seed. The sweet pea is a familiar example (see Figure 13.1).

13.3. The ephemerals

As their name suggests, they are short-lived. Ephemeral plants are annuals which complete several life-cycles, from germination to seed dispersal, within a single growing season. Many of the common garden weeds, such as groundsel and chickweed, are ephemeral plants.

13.4. The biennial plant

The biennial plant completes its life-cycle in two growing seasons. It germinates from seed in the spring of the first season and makes

Figure 13.1 The life-history of an annual plant, for example, sweet pea

Figure 13.2 The life-history of a biennial plant—the carrot

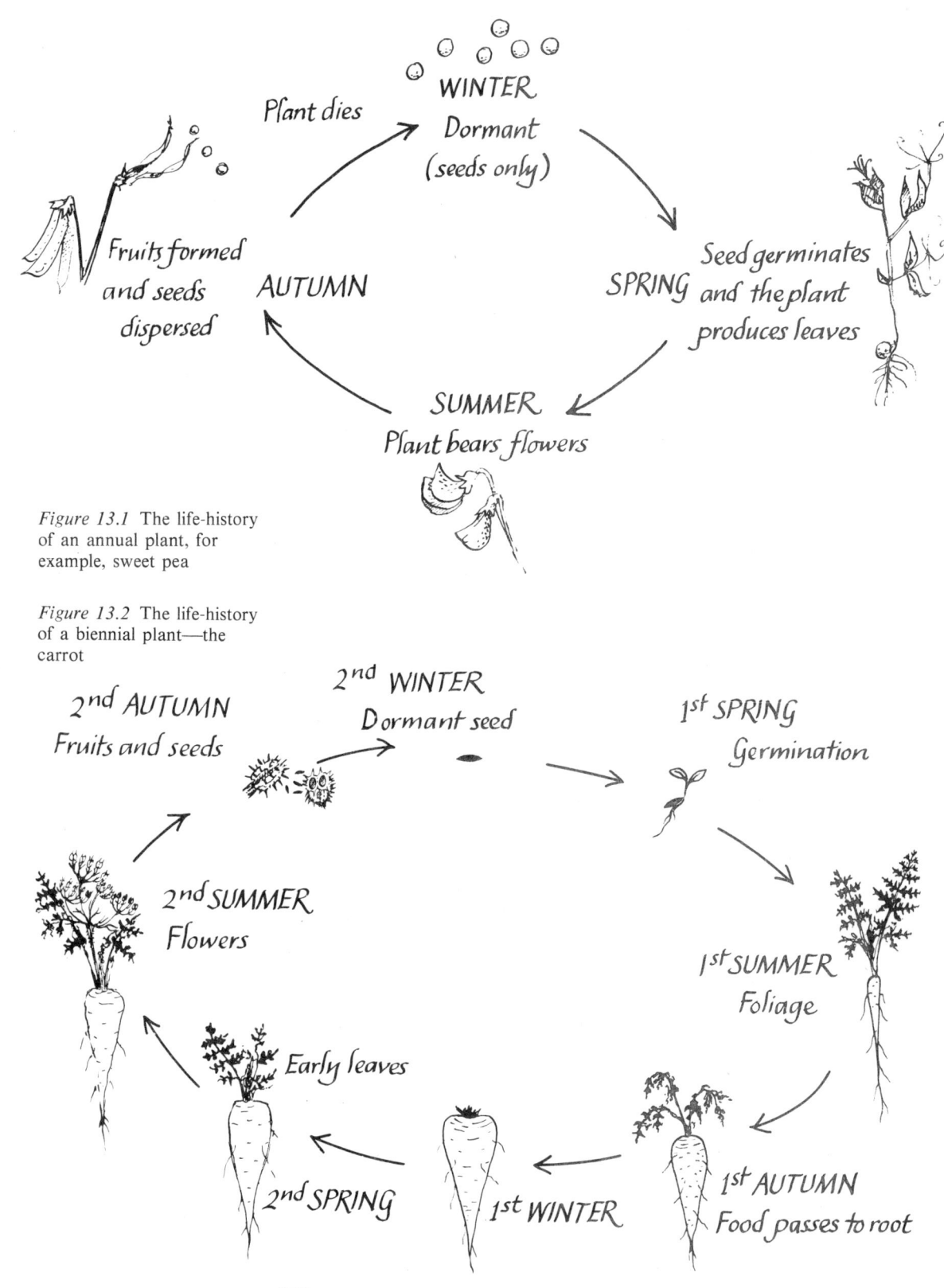

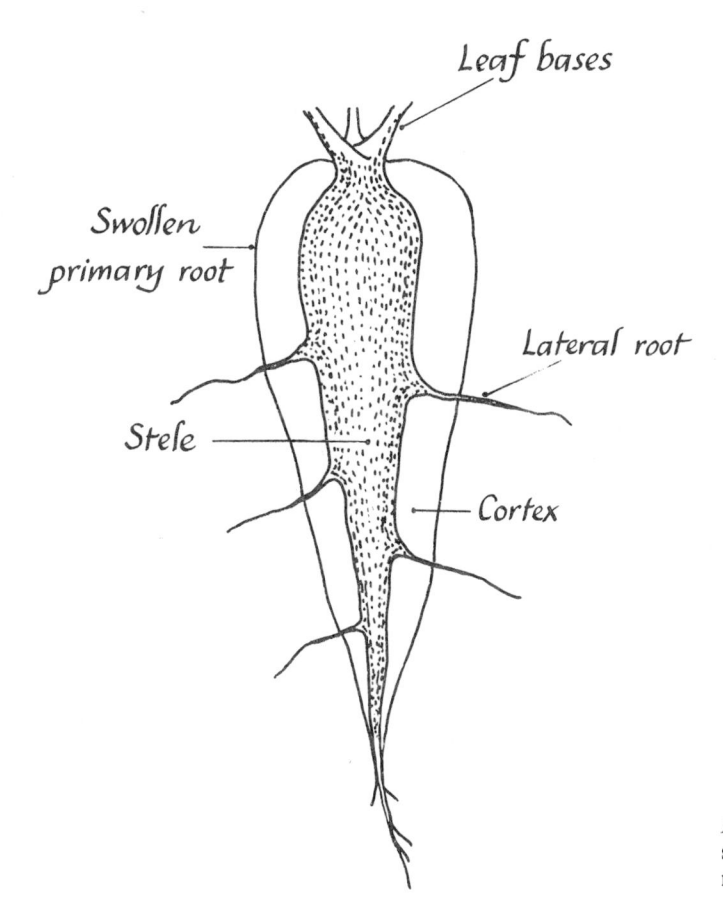

Figure 13.3 Vertical section of the swollen tap root of a carrot

vigorous foliage growth during the first summer. The materials produced by the leaves are passed usually to the root, which swells to form an underground storage organ. As winter approaches the foliage dies back to ground-level, leaving the storage organ protected beneath the soil. The following spring, buds at the tip of the storage organ burst forth early in the season, getting their food and energy from the storage organ. Flowers are produced during the second summer. These produce fruits which are dispersed in the autumn, when the plant dies and withers away. Many of our root crops are examples of the storage organs of biennial plants. The carrot is a biennial storage organ which has developed from a swollen tap root (see Figures 13.2 and 13.3). The sugar-rich food is stored in the root cortex.

13.5. The perennial plant

A perennial plant lives for a number of years and produces flowers, fruits and seeds each season (see Figure 13.4). It follows that it must face the problem of withstanding adverse conditions each

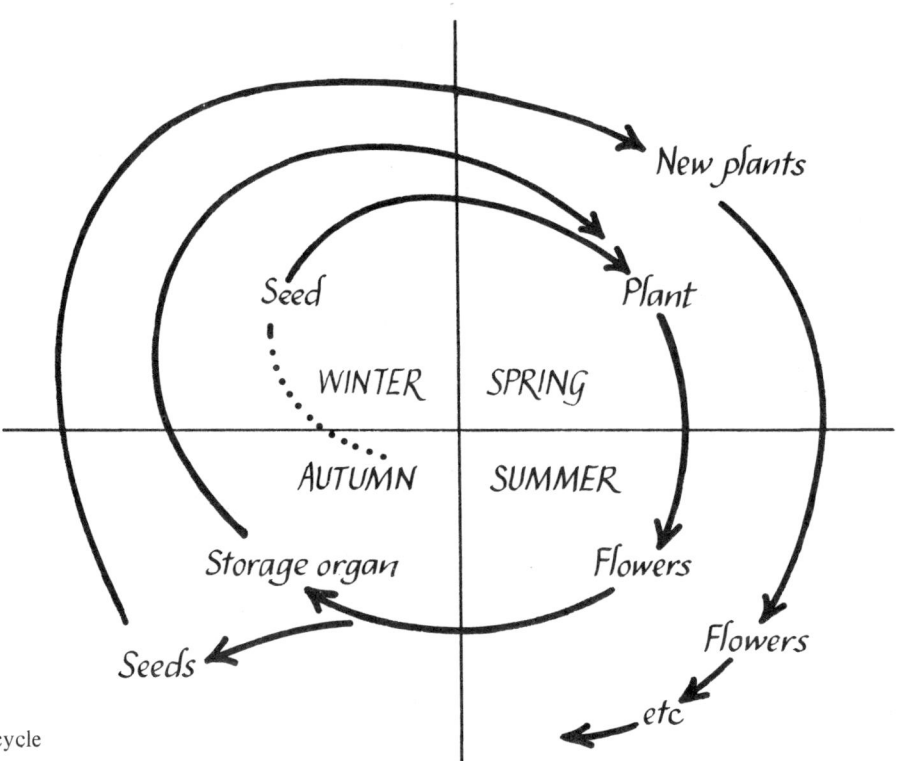

Figure 13.4 The life-cycle of a perennial plant

year. The process whereby a plant overcomes the adverse conditions of winter is called **perennation**. Perennials do this in two main ways:

a. The entire shoot system, the stem and foliage, may die back to ground level at the onset of adverse conditions. During the summer, these plants store the products of photosynthesis in some underground structure which becomes swollen. Below the ground, the storage organ can survive the adverse winter conditions. The following spring, buds produce new foliage and flowers very early in the season, at the expense of the stored food. Only herbaceous plants, with no woody growth, can perennate in this way, and are, therefore, called **herbaceous perennials**.

b. The second method of perennation is employed by trees and shrubs, plants which have a persistent, woody shoot system; this system is added to each year. These plants are called **woody perennials**. They usually lose their leaves at the end of the growing season to prevent the loss of water which is difficult to replace in the winter. They also protect next season's growth with winter buds. The delicate young flowers and leaves inside the bud are protected by the tough bud scales. Sometimes the bud is packed with tiny hairs to prevent frost damage. The horse-chestnut bud secretes a sticky substance to prevent infection by fungi or insect eggs.

13.6. Herbaceous perennials

Herbaceous perennials have organs of perennation which are either modified stem, root or leaf structures. Stem structures can be recognized by the presence of buds and leaves, or at least traces of scale leaves. Some structures may be derived from stems or leaves, even though they are buried in the soil. We shall examine a number of underground perennation organs and attempt to discover from what part of the plant they are derived.

13.7. The crocus corm

Investigation 13a. To discover the structure of a crocus corm

Take a crocus or montbretia corm, and a sharp knife. Cut the corm vertically through the terminal bud into two similar halves. Examine the contents of the terminal bud. Can you see the leaves and the immature flowers? Remove the scale leaves from the body of the corm. Notice the axillary buds in the leaf axils. These occur at the nodes. Notice the short internodes. Draw your section and compare it with Figure 13.5a. What part of the plant is modified to form the corm? Give reasons for your answer.

Investigation 13b. To trace the life-cycle of the crocus corm

Take six crocus corms in September and plant them with the tip of the terminal bud just below the surface of the moist bulb fibre. Keep the fibre just moist to touch, but not wet enough to allow water to be squeezed out of it. Dig up one corm every two months and preserve it either dry or in spirit. After ten months, the corms at different stages of development can be mounted or displayed in sequence. Compare the various stages with those shown in Figure 13.5.

A corm is a vertically condensed section of stem with short internodes. It is packed with stored food, and is covered by scale leaves which are the dried bases of the previous season's foliage leaves. At the tip is the terminal bud which contains the foliage leaves and flowers of the coming season. The stages in the life-cycle are as follows:

a. The dormant corm is usually planted in autumn. Later in the year it grows adventitious roots.
b. In early spring the terminal bud grows at the expense of the stored food and produces a flower.
c. Later in the spring the flower withers but the leaves persist and photosynthesize. The carbohydrate produced passes down the leaves and collects in the stem of the terminal bud which swells.
d. In summer the foliage leaves die down. The stem of the terminal bud has become swollen to form next season's corm. Contractile roots pull the new corm into the soil.

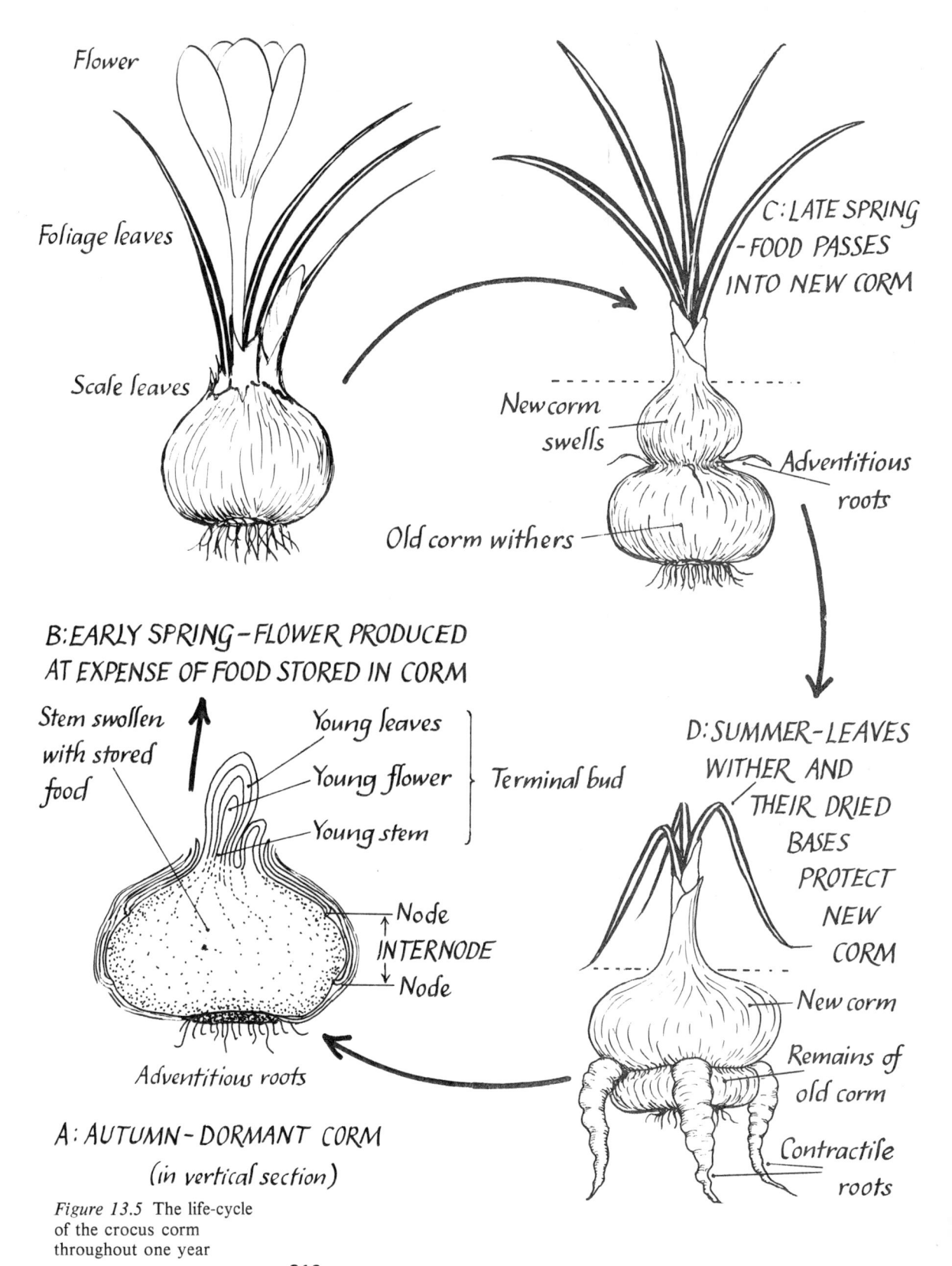

Figure 13.5 The life-cycle of the crocus corm throughout one year

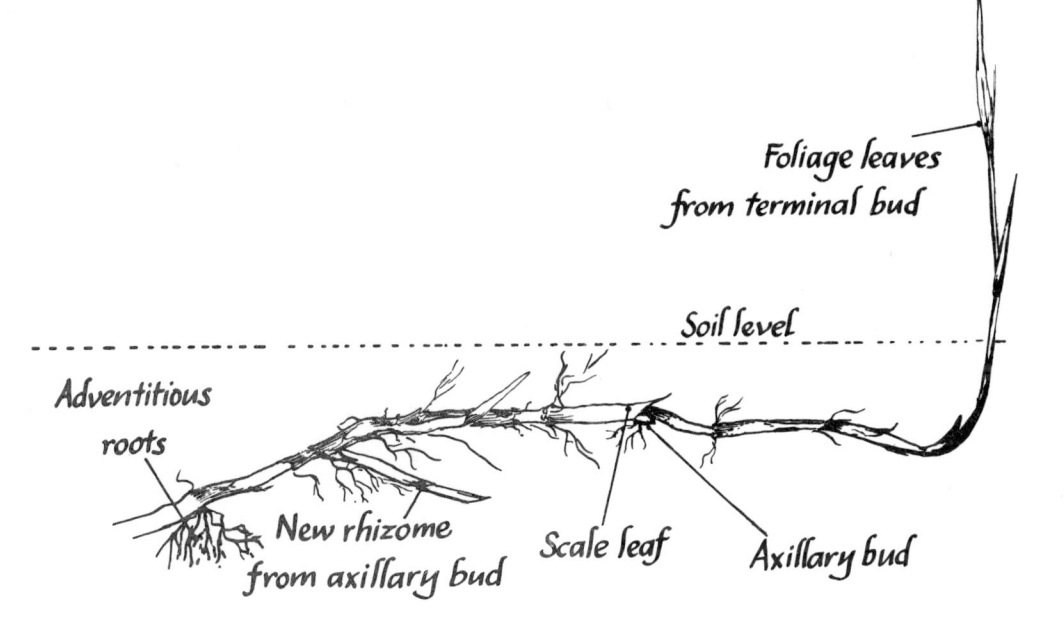

Figure 13.6 A couch grass rhizome contains little stored food

13.8. Rhizomes

Investigation 13c. To examine some rhizomes

Carefully examine and draw a number of rhizomes of such plants as couch grass, mint and iris. Label the different parts on your drawing. Compare your drawings with Figures 13.6 and 13.7. Use the figures to help you finish labelling your own drawings. What part of a plant is modified to form a rhizome?

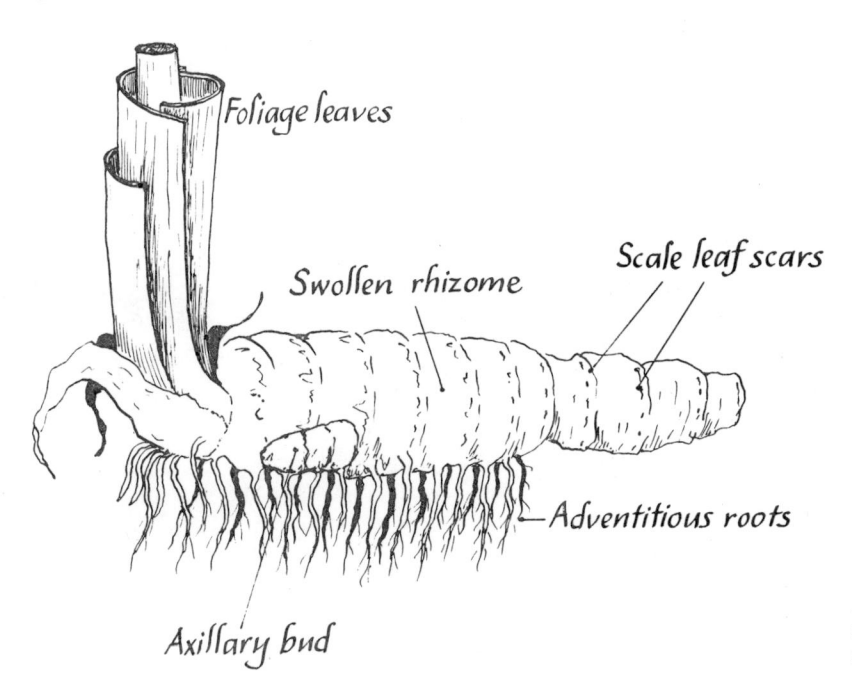

Figure 13.7 An iris rhizome, swollen with stored food

Did you find the axillary buds on the rhizomes? They lie close to the side under the dry, papery, scale leaves. These are the remains of the last year's foliage leaves.

A **rhizome** is a horizontal underground stem bearing scale leaves or leaf scars. At the tip of the rhizome is the terminal bud, and in the axils of the scale leaves are axillary buds. The terminal bud produces flowers and leaves early in the season, at the expense of the stored food. The food, produced by the leaves after flowering, passes to the axillary buds, which produce new rhizomes. These branch from the original rhizome, which may persist for several years. The rhizome may become very swollen, as in the iris, or remain unthickened, as in couch grass.

13.9. The potato tuber

Investigation 13d. To examine a potato tuber

Wash the soil from a potato tuber and examine it carefully. Can you see the scar where it was attached to the plant? Carefully examine the opposite end of the tuber. Can you see a large 'eye'? This is the terminal bud. Examine the other 'eyes'. In each case, three small buds lie just below a ridge. This ridge represents the remains of a leaf scar. The largest of the three buds is an **axillary** bud, and the two very tiny buds on either side are **accessory** buds. Note the lenticels piercing the corky bark of the potato. From what part of the plant is the potato tuber derived? What are your reasons? Make a drawing of your potato and refer to Figure 13.8 for help with labelling.

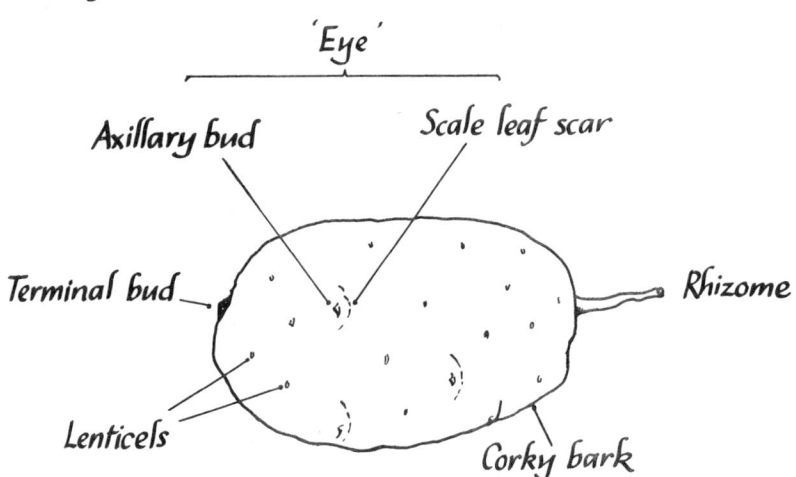

Figure 13.8 A potato tuber

Investigation 13e. To study the life-cycle of the potato tuber

In March, plant about ten good seed potatoes. At intervals of about a fortnight, dig up and examine a plant which has grown from

Figure 13.9 The life-cycle of the potato

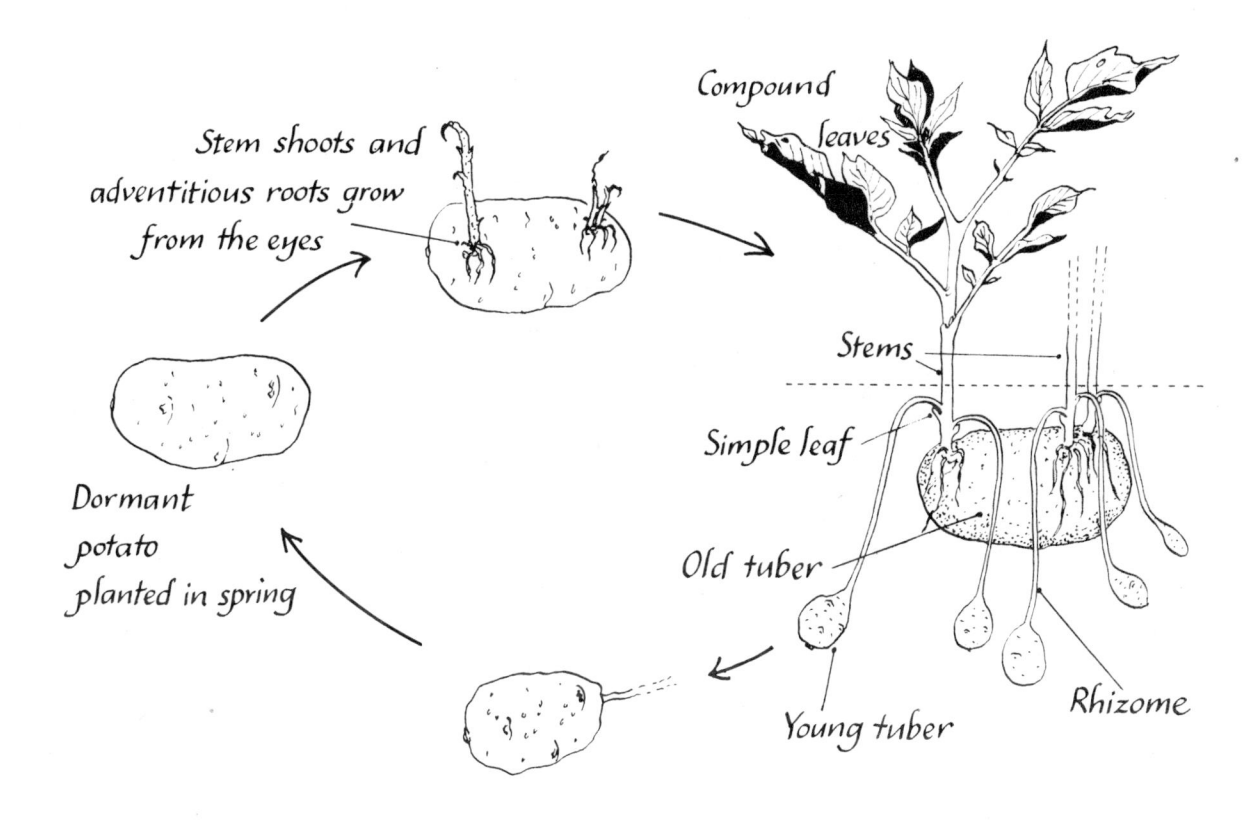

one of the tubers. Draw each stage carefully and compare it with the stages shown in Figure 13.9.

The potato tuber is planted in spring. The axillary buds soon produce shoots which have two kinds of leaf. The uppermost are compound leaves which photosynthesize, but near to the soil level, the stem produces very tiny, simple leaves. From the axils of these simple leaves arise rhizomes, which at first grow horizontally and then down into the ground. The gardener encourages the development of these rhizomes by 'earthing up' the potato plant in early summer. The carbohydrate produced by the large, compound leaves passes down the stem into the tips of these rhizomes. New tubers arise as the tips swell with starch stored in the pith. The old tuber then shrivels and dies. Each new stem tuber will produce a new potato plant next season, so the potato tuber is an organ both of perennation and propagation. The potato is an example of a **stem tuber**, the swollen tip of an underground stem.

13.10. Bulbs

Investigation 13f. To examine the structure of a bulb

Take two daffodil bulbs or two onions. (Daffodil bulbs sold by weight for naturalizing are suitable and cheap.) Cut one in vertical section and the other in transverse section. Notice the scale leaves, the swollen leaf bases and, in the centre, the terminal bud. If you have been fortunate in your section, you may see next year's terminal bud at the base of the flower bud. In the axils of the swollen leaf bases you can probably see axillary buds which develop into new bulbs.

Draw the two sections of your bulb, and then take one vertical half to pieces. Identify and note the function of each part, and state what it will become next season.

A **bulb** is an underground bud which is surrounded by thick fleshy leaves packed with stored food. You will remember that a bud is a condensed shoot with internodes so short that the leaves overlap. In most bulbs, including the daffodil, the fleshy storage leaves are the bases of the previous season's foliage leaves. The bulb is usually covered by brittle, papery scale leaves which were the swollen leaf bases of the previous season and whose food has now been used.

Bulbs are usually planted in autumn when they are in a dormant condition. In winter a few adventitious roots may grow from the base (Figure 13.10a). In the following spring, leaves and flowers grow rapidly from the terminal bud at the expense of the food stored in the bases of last year's foliage leaves (Figure 13.10b). The flowers wither in early summer, but the leaves continue to photosynthesize. The food produced is stored in the bases of the foliage leaves which become swollen (Figure 13.10c). The old leaf bases shrivel to become the dry scale leaves and an axillary bud in the axil of the swollen leaf bases becomes next year's terminal bud (Figure 13.10d).

13.11. Root tubers

Towards the end of the growing season, the fibrous roots of the dahlia and the lesser celandine become swollen with food passed down the stem from the leaves (see Figures 13.11 and 13.12). The swollen fibrous roots form root tubers. Buds arise from the tubers and in the following season develop into new stems with foliage leaves and flowers.

13.12. The materials in storage organs

Investigation 13g. To discover the nature of the food reserves in storage organs

Preserve fragments from the dissected storage organs and test for food materials, using the same methods as in Investigation 12h. Record your results in the same way.

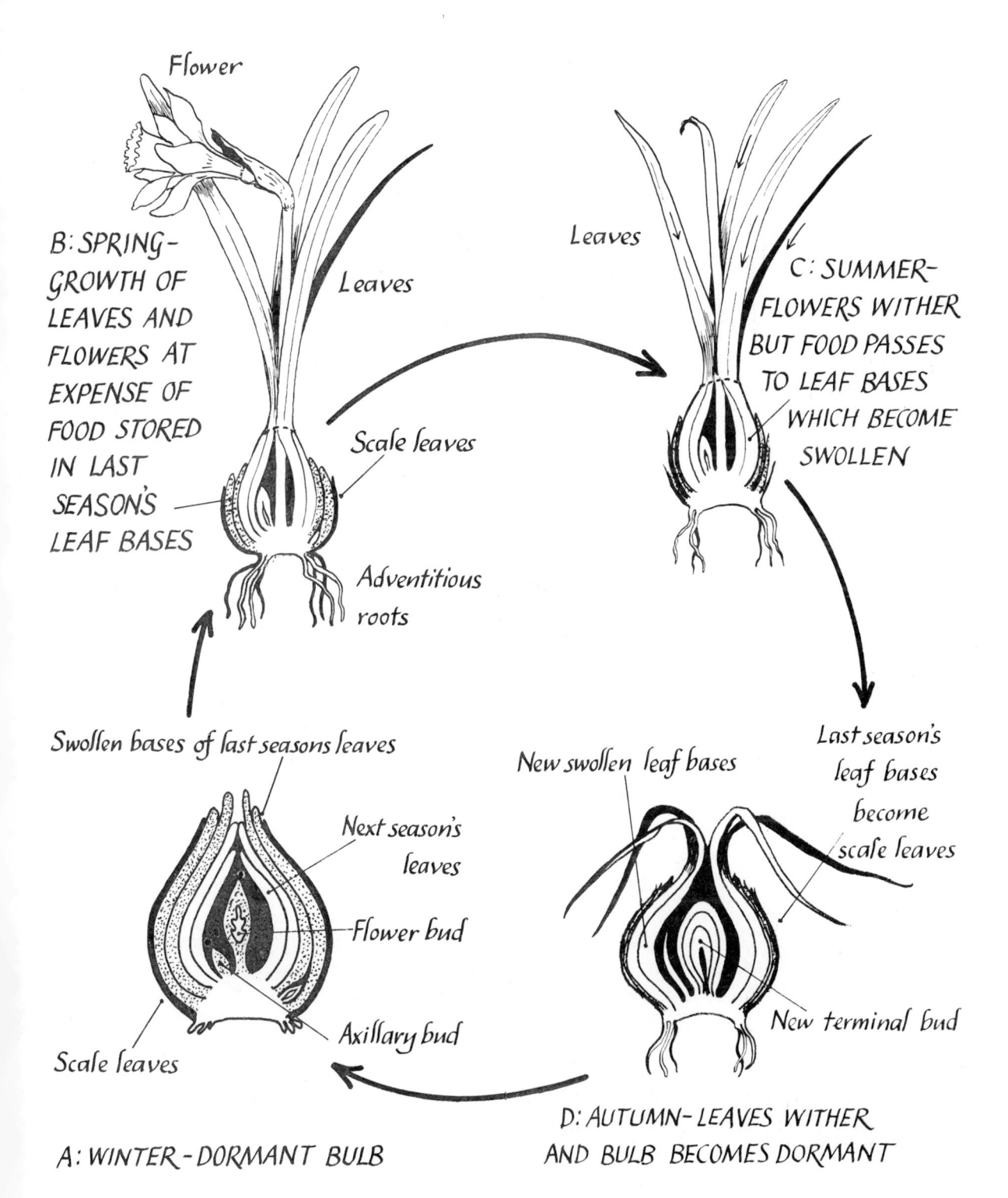

Figure 13.10 The life-cycle of the daffodil bulb

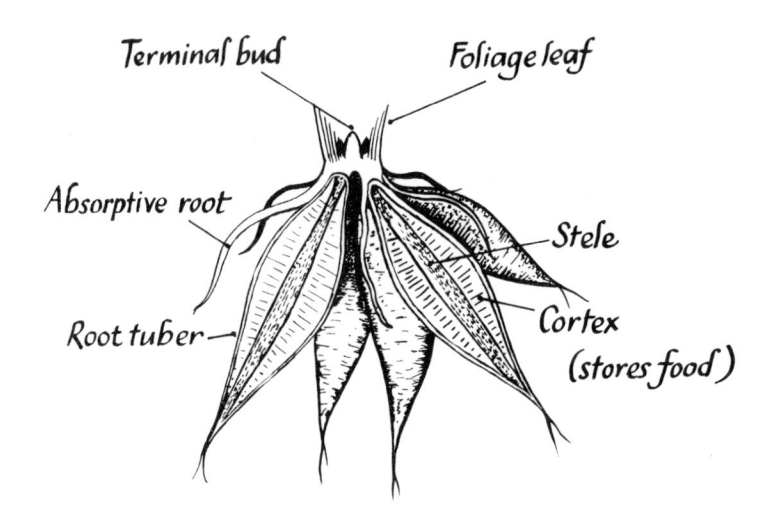

Figure 13.11 The root tubers of dahlia in vertical section

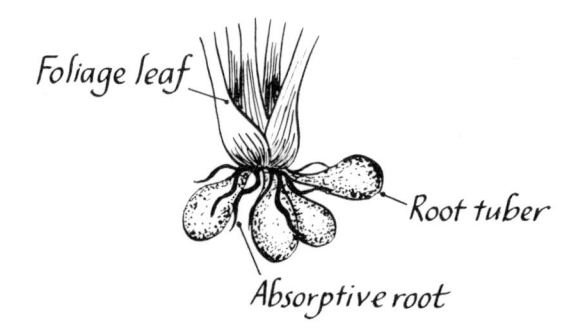

Figure 13.12 The root tubers of lesser celandine

13.13. Vegetative reproduction

You will have noticed that the storage organs of the examples mentioned acted both as organs of perennation and as organs of propagation, so that a single plant gave rise to several without the production of flowers, fruit and seeds. The ability of a piece of a plant to form a new, fully independent plant without the production of seeds is called **vegetative reproduction**.

Many plants have special methods of vegetative reproduction other than storage organs.

13.14. Natural methods of vegetative reproduction

a. The **runner** is an overground, horizontal stem which arises from an axillary bud on the stem of the parent plant. The runner has a terminal bud and axillary buds in the leaf axils. If the terminal bud or one of the axillary buds comes into contact with the damp soil, adventitious roots develop and a daughter plant is formed. Eventually, the runner shrivels away and the daughter plant is independent. An example which can be readily observed is the strawberry (see Figure 13.13).

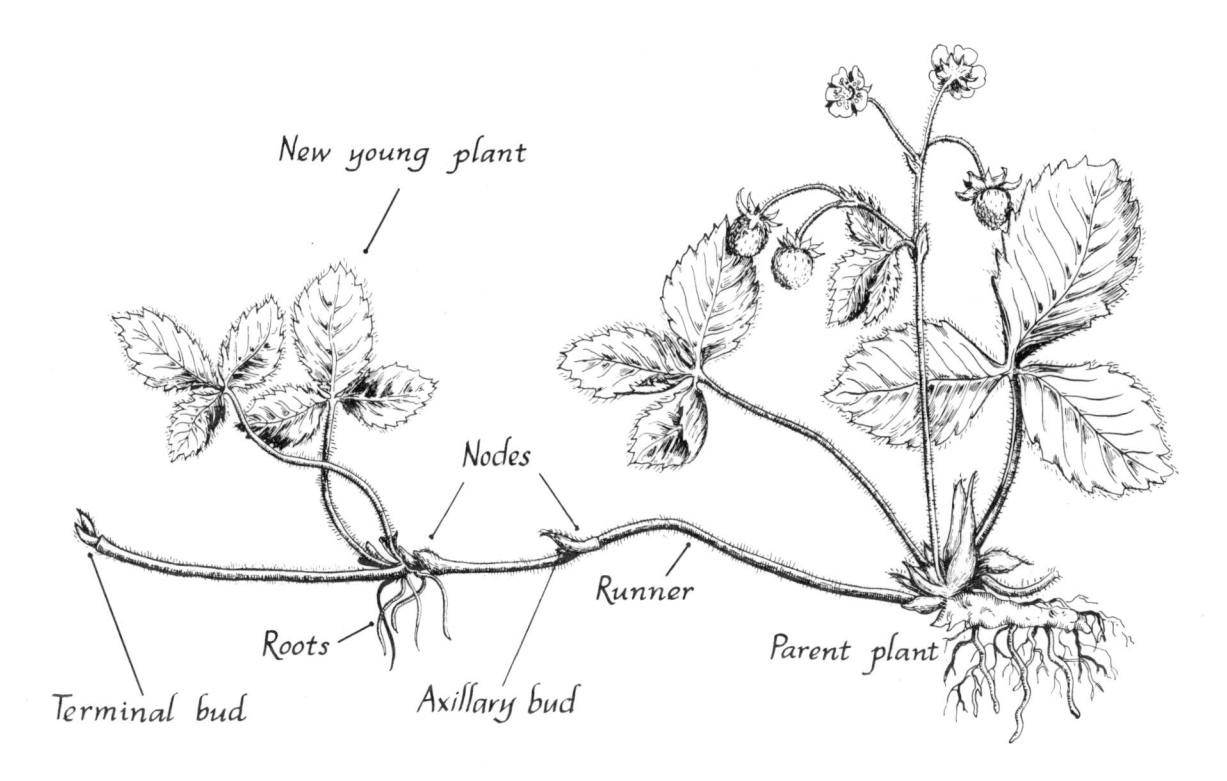

Figure 13.13 The strawberry runner

b. The **stolon**, which is so typical of the blackberry, is really a special kind of runner formed from the main stem which bends over to touch the ground. The terminal bud then develops adventitious roots and grows into a new plant (see Figure 13.14).

c. A **sucker** is a short runner which develops from an underground axillary bud. Eventually, the terminal bud of the shoot grows

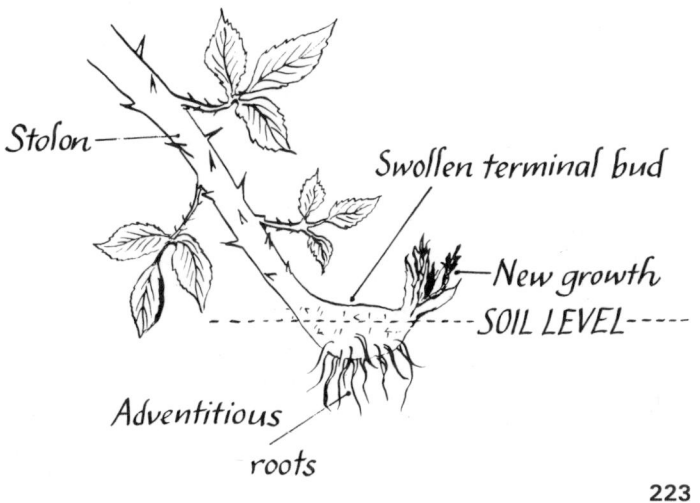

Figure 13.14 A blackberry stolon

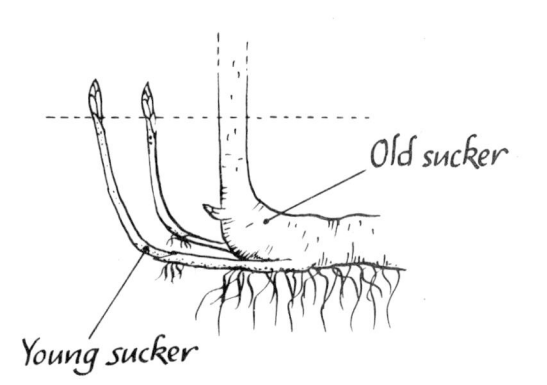

Figure 13.15 (above) A sucker

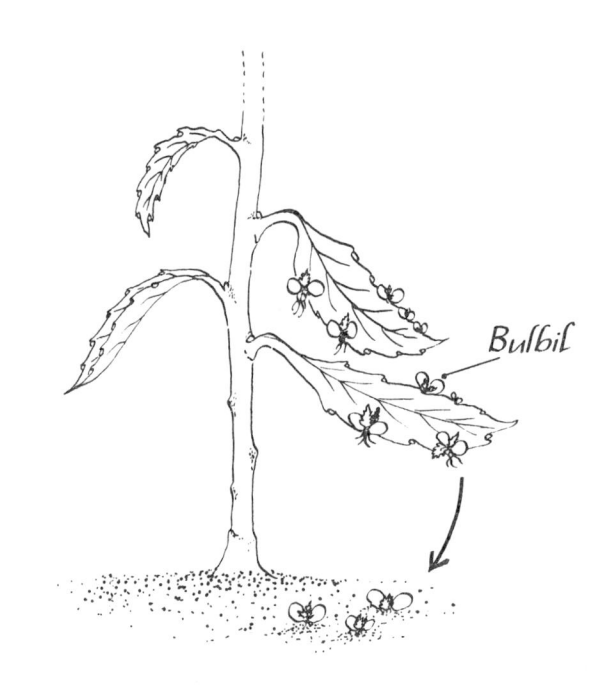

Figure 13.16 (right) Bryophyllum plant with bulbils on the leaves

to the surface and produces a new plant (see Figure 13.15). Suckers may be seen growing from the ground around the trunks of established trees. Suckers of propagated roses can be particularly troublesome, as they persistently arise from the root-stock of the wild rose on which the propagated rose was budded or grafted.

d. A **bulbil** is a bulb-like structure found growing on the aerial parts of the plant. When mature, it drops off and develops into an independent plant. The houseplant *Bryophyllum* is a good example (see Figure 13.16).

Runners, stolons and suckers do not store food, but conduct it from the parent to the daughter plant, until it is well established.

13.15. Artificial methods of vegetative reproduction

Gardeners frequently propagate plants artificially in the following ways:

a. **Cuttings** can be used to propagate a wide range of plants, including pelargoniums, carnations and practically any shrub. A vigorous shoot between 6 and 30 cm long is removed from the parent plant and placed in light, well-aerated but moist soil. A little heat may help, so the cuttings should be placed in a warm position. The formation of adventitious roots may be assisted by making 'nicks' near the base of the cutting to expose the cambium or by dipping the cutting in a hormone rooting powder, the purpose of which you will discover in the next chapter.

Figure 13.17 Layering carnations

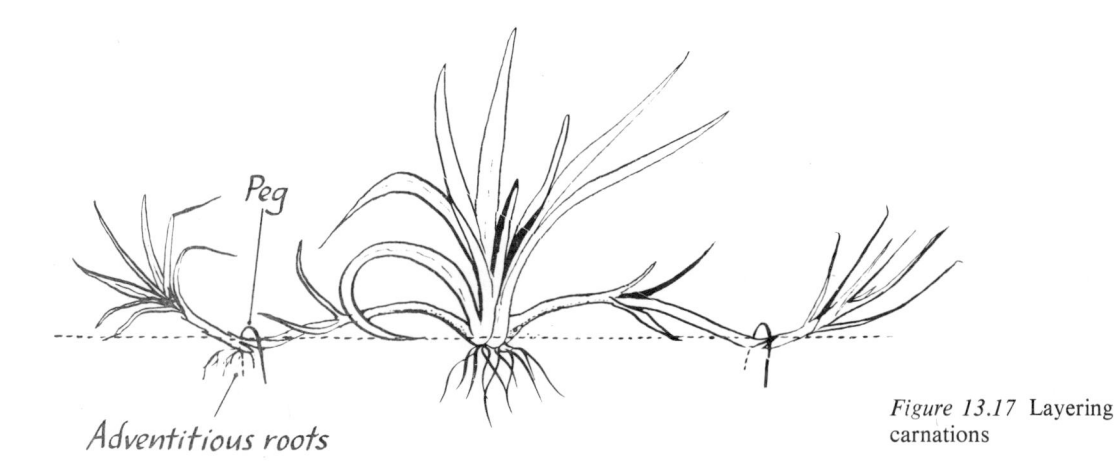

b. **Layering** is used to propagate carnations in about July. A healthy shoot is 'nicked' at an internode which is then pegged into the soil with a U-shaped peg. Adventitious roots develop from the cambium exposed by the incision and, when the new plant is established, it can be severed from the parent plant (see Figure 13.17).

c. **Budding** is used in rose, peach and plum cultivation. An established root-stock of a wild variety, of little commercial value, is taken. This is called the **stock**. A T-shaped incision is made near the top of the stock, exposing the cambium. A shield-shaped piece of bark, bearing a bud, is then cut from a plant of the variety to be propagated. This is called the **scion**. The scion is then slipped into the T-shaped slit on the stock, so that the cambium of the stock is in contact with the cambium of the scion (see Figure 13.18). The two are then bound together with thread, and the incision is covered with wax to prevent infection by fungi or insect eggs. Suckers that arise from the root-stock are of the wild variety. These should be cut off below ground level.

d. **Grafting** is used to propagate fruit trees. The stock is a well-established root-stock of a wild crab apple in which a V-shaped slit is cut. The scion is a vigorous shoot of the variety of plant desired,

Figure 13.18 Budding roses

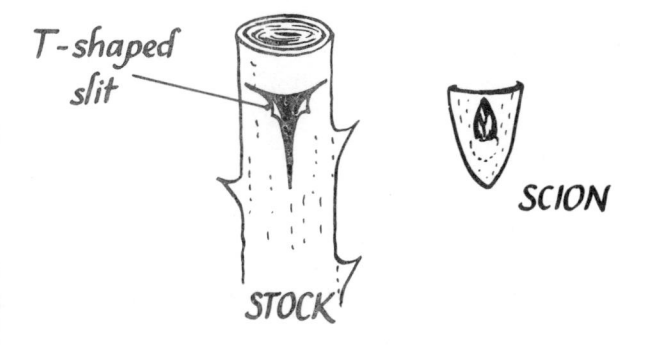

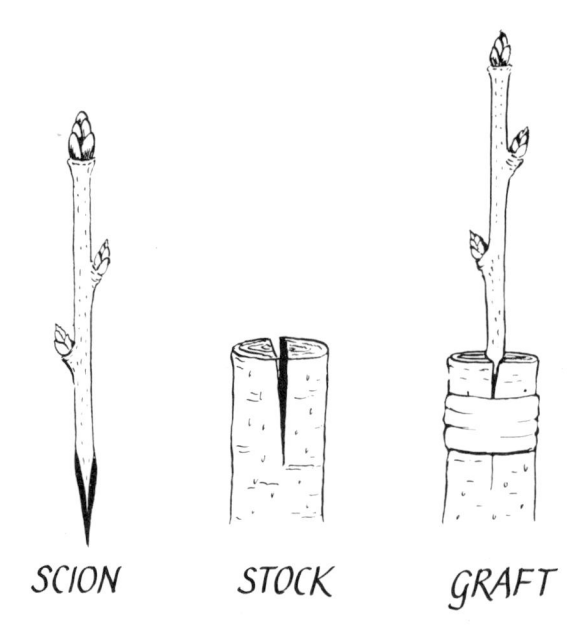

Figure 13.19 Grafting   SCION   STOCK   GRAFT

but it must be a closely related plant to the stock. Apples, pears, melons and quinces can be mutually grafted, as can plums, peaches, apricots and almonds, but it is not possible to graft an apple on to an oak. The scion is V-shaped to fit the stock, and must be carefully inserted to make sure that the cambium is in contact with that of the scion (see Figure 13.19). The two are then bound together with thread and the exposed surfaces covered with wax.

e. **Division** is used to propagate many plants in October and November or in March and April. The plant is divided with a sharp knife. The old stems should be cut away and a portion of the plant with strong crowns is then replanted.

13.16. The advantages of vegetative reproduction

Plants produced in this way are not dependent on the rather 'hit and miss' processes of pollination, fertilization and seed dispersal. The precarious process of germination is eliminated, as are the very vulnerable early seedling stages. Food can be obtained from the parent, so the plant does not have to wait until it can photosynthesize. In addition, the gardener is sure that he will get the variety of plant he wants. The new plant resembles the parent, as there is no chance of the variation which might result from cross-pollination. The gardener does not risk losing a proportion of his plants during germination, and he does not have to care for the delicate seedlings. The fruit producing plants are available years sooner than if they had been grown from seed.

Test your understanding

Copy and complete the following paragraphs:

An ....[1] plant is one which completes its life-cycle within a single growing season. On the other hand, a ....[2] plant requires ....[3] years to complete its cycle, the flowers and fruit not being produced until the ....[4] year. Plants which continue growing year after year are called ....[5].

The food stored in a storage organ enables the plant to survive the ....[6] and commence ....[7] in the ....[8] In the ....[9], stem tuber and ....[10], the food is stored in a modified ....[11], whereas in a bulb it is stored in ....[12] The dahlia and carrot both store food in the ....[13] Storage organs also act as organs of ....[14] A runner is a horizontal ....[15] which creeps along the surface of the ground, producing ....[16] roots and a new plant where a ....[17] touches the ground. Vegetative reproduction is a frequent practice in horticulture, as, for example, in the growing of roses by ....[18] and of fruit trees by ....[19] One important advantage of this method of reproduction to the gardener is that the new plant is ....[20]

1. What problems does a plant face in winter?
2. By what methods do plants overcome those problems?
3. With reference to named examples, explain the difference between a biennial and a perennial.
4. How does a bulb differ from a corm?
5. How does a potato tuber differ from a dahlia tuber?
6. Explain how vegetative reproduction differs from sexual reproduction.
7. Describe two methods of natural vegetative reproduction.
8. Distinguish between budding and grafting.
9. What are the advantages of artificial propagation?

Chapter 14

Plants and their Senses

Animals are able to respond to changes in their surroundings in such a way that they are able to benefit from them. This behaviour is brought about by the co-ordinated activity of the sense organs, effector organs, endocrine organs and nervous system. But what of plants? They are immobile. Can they respond to changes in their surroundings? Plant responses are not usually dramatic, but there are exceptions. If you touch the 'sensitive plant' *Mimosa pudica*, the leaves will immediately fold up. When a fly lands on the upper surface of a leaf of Venus' fly-trap, the leaf folds to enclose it.

14.1. Plant responses

Most plant responses, however, are gradual. You have probably noticed that the stems of pot plants grown indoors tend to lean towards the window and that when the stems of chrysanthemum plants are blown to the ground, their tips soon turn upwards. We take it for granted that stems grow up, roots grow down and that leaves turn towards the light. Some flowers close up at night and others turn with the movement of the sun. Can you think of any other plant responses? With every response, we must ask ourselves how the plant benefits from it, and what causes it.

Investigation 14a. The response to light

Label three small pots of wet sand A, B and C, and sow about ten oat grains in each, about 5 mm deep. (Ice cream or yoghurt tubs or disposable drinking cups make suitable pots.) Keep the pots in a warm, *dark* place for about four days, when the shoots will be about 10 mm long.
1. Place pot A inside a light-proof box, painted black on the inside.
2. Place pot B inside a similar box which has a slit cut in one end to admit light from one direction.
3. Place pot C in a position where it will receive even lighting from above (see Figure 14.1).

Figure 14.1 Oat seedlings with varied illumination

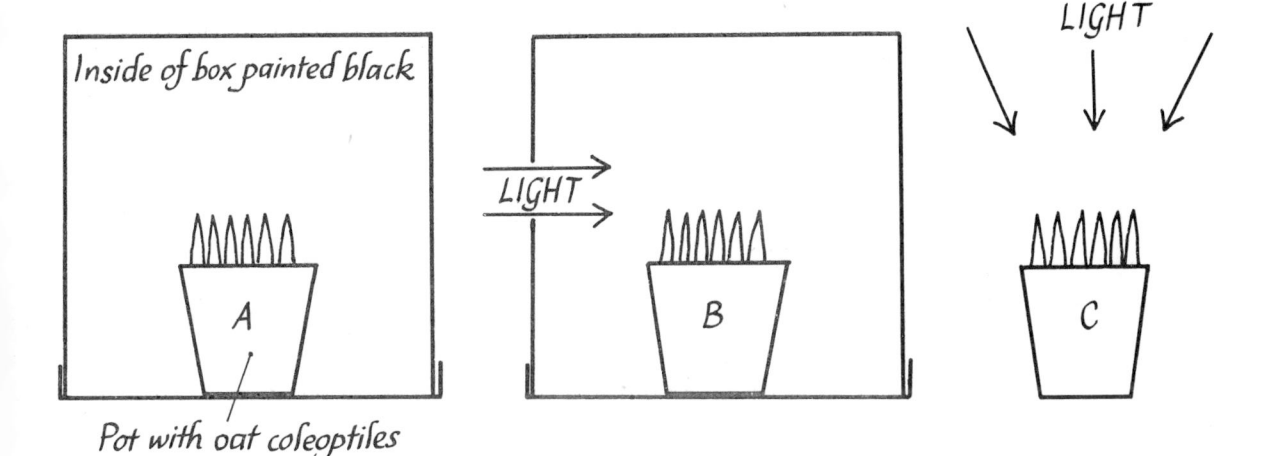

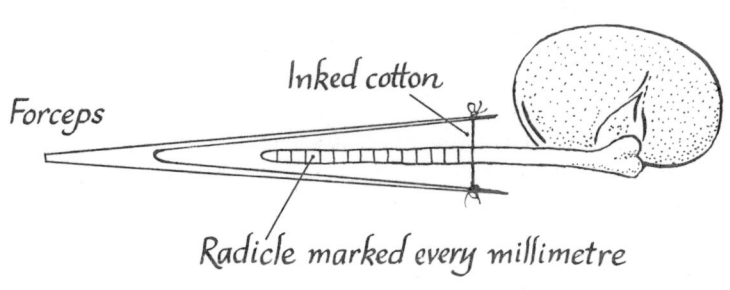

Cress seedlings can be used instead of oat. Sow a few cress seeds on a pad of moist cotton wool in a petri dish base or lid and germinate in the dark for three or four days.

Place the boxes in a moderately warm position. Make sure that light can enter box B. Use a lamp if necessary, but be careful not to place the lamp too close to the seedlings or its heat may influence their growth.

Examine the three pots of seedlings after a few days. Have any of them changed the direction in which they were growing? If so, what stimulus do you think caused the response? How does it benefit the plant? Does this experiment need a control?

14.2. The nature of a plant response

Investigation 14b. The nature and region of a response

Soak some broad bean seeds for twenty-four hours and then germinate them on moist sawdust for about five or six days. Select a seed with a straight radicle about 3 cm long. Tie a piece of silk or cotton between the tips of a pair of fine forceps and dip it into Indian ink. Starting from the tip, carefully touch the radicle with the cotton at millimetre intervals, so that when the ink is dry the radicle is marked along its length with lines 1 mm apart (see Figure 14.2).

Figure 14.2 Marking the radicle

229

Then, using a long, fine pin, fix the bean to the cork of the apparatus with its radicle horizontal, as shown in Figure 14.3. The apparatus consists of a gas jar or similar wide-mouthed jar with a tightly fitting cork. The jar has a little water in the bottom and is lined with moist blotting paper. It is covered with black paper. Place the apparatus in a moderately warm position, taking care to ensure that it is kept moist.

Figure 14.3 (below) Fixing the bean to the apparatus

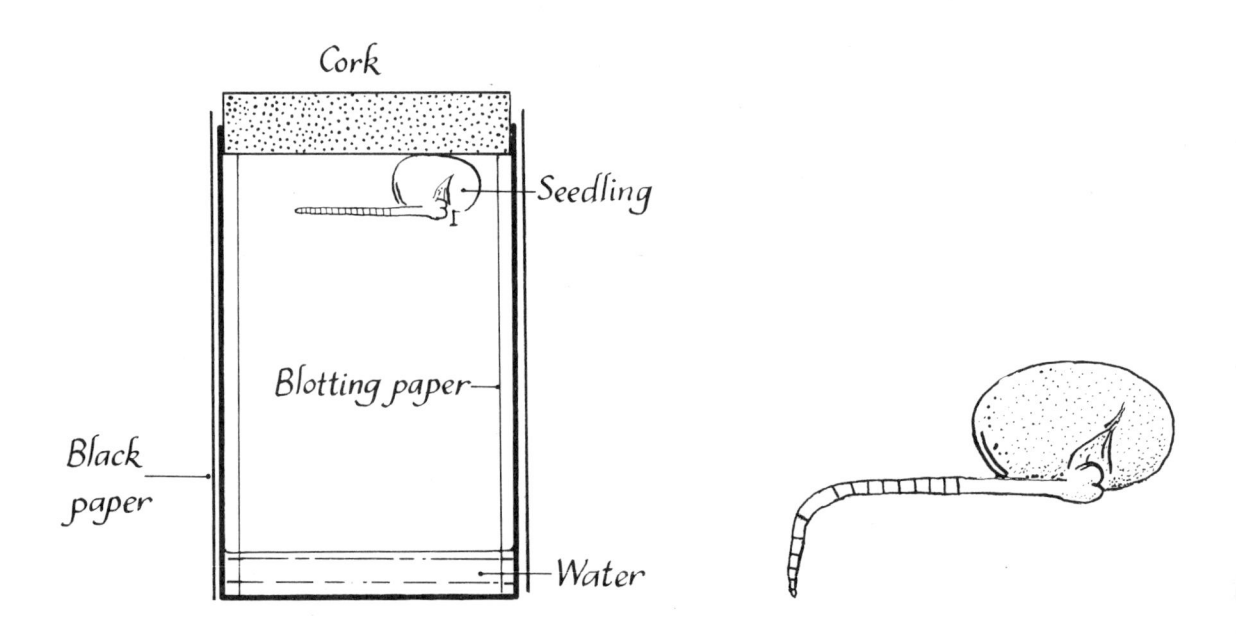

Figure 14.4 (right) The bean plant after the experiment

After a few days, carefully remove the cork and examine the bean radicle (see Figure 14.4). Has there been a change in its pattern of development? Note the direction of any bending. What is the response due to? How does it benefit the plant? Carefully measure the distances between the ink marks on the radicle. In what region does the most rapid growth take place? In what region does the bending response occur? Can you suggest what mechanism might bring about such a response?

Notice that the tip of the radicle has bent downwards and that the ink marks are no longer evenly spaced. The widest-spaced marks coincide with the bend in the radicle, suggesting that the mechanism of the response is **growth** and that the bending is due to more rapid growth on one side of the radicle than on the other. A bending growth movement in response to a **directional** stimulus is called a **tropism**. If the plant organ grows *towards* the stimulus it is a **positive** tropism, and if it grows *away* from the stimulus it is a **negative** tropism.

Tropisms are further described by using a prefix to indicate the stimulus. In Investigation 14a the seedlings in the dark, in pot A, show no response, those with even illumination from above, in pot C, grow normally, whilst those illuminated from one side only, in pot B, grew *towards* the light. As the seedlings with no light and even light do not respond, the cause of the response is the directional stimulus of light. This is described as a **positive phototropism.**

In Investigation 14b the radicle grows downwards. This suggests that the stimulus is gravity, but since we have not shown that a root *not* subjected to gravity fails to grow downwards, we cannot be sure that gravity is the stimulus.

Investigation 14c. To test the suggestion that the bean radicle grows downwards due to the directional stimulus of gravity

To be sure that the bending growth of the radicle in Investigation 14b was due to gravity, we must try to eliminate its effect on the bean radicle. This is done by stimulating all sides of the radicle evenly with gravity, using a **clinostat**. A clinostat is a cork disc mounted on the spindle of an electric or clockwork motor. The motor is geared down so that the cork disc revolves very slowly, about three or four times every hour.

Pin bean seedlings to the cork disc with their radicles horizontal, as in Figure 14.5. Line the Perspex cover of the clinostat disc with moist blotting paper to keep the air inside very moist and to prevent the delicate radicle tips from drying up. The Perspex cover should be covered on the outside with black paper. Can you suggest why? Switch on the motor and leave it running for several days.

Figure 14.5 Bean seedlings on a clinostat

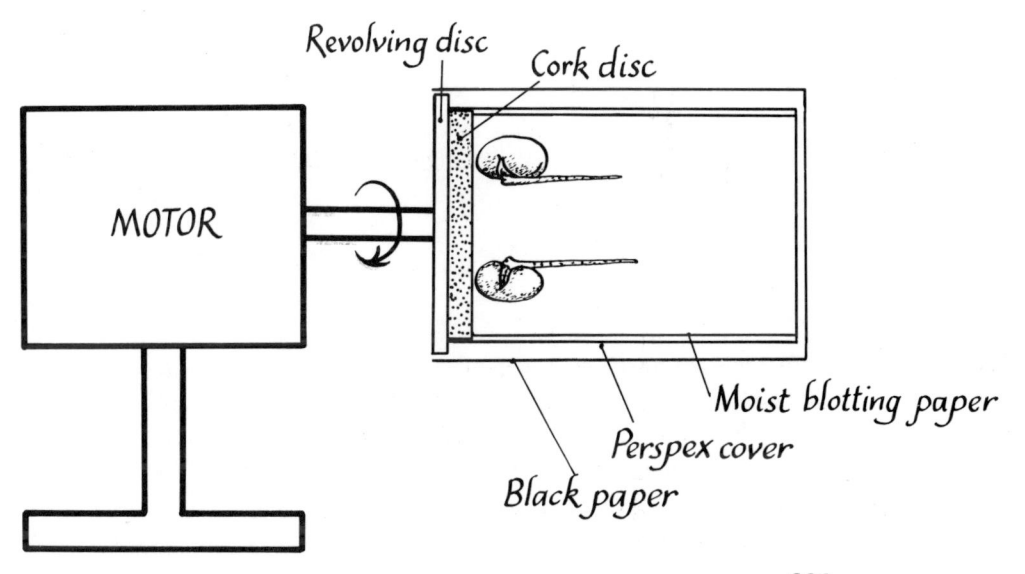

The effect of the clinostat is that, as the radicle revolves, all points on its surface are equally affected by gravity. Check from time to time that the seedlings still have adequate moisture.

Examine the seedlings after several days and record what has happened. What is the result? Does it support the suggestion that the bending is caused by the stimulus of gravity?

A bending growth movement in response to the directional stimulus of gravity is called **geotropism**. The behaviour of the bean radicle is positively geotropic. What benefit is this to the plant?

14.3. Perception of the stimulus

In order to carry out the behaviour we have observed, an organism needs a mechanism for detecting a stimulus, and also a mechanism for responding to it. These two mechanisms must in some way be linked within the organism. Unlike animals with their sense organs, plants do not seem to possess special organs for detecting changes within or around them.

Investigation 14d. The region of perception of the stimulus

Use the same apparatus as in Investigation 14b. Germinate two bean seedlings as before. With a very sharp razor, cut off the end of *one* radicle 3 mm from the tip. Mount both seedlings on the cork with their radicles in a horizontal position, as in Figure 14.6. Make sure that the seedlings have sufficient moisture. After several days remove the seedlings and examine their radicles carefully. Make a note of any changes. Can you draw any conclusions about the region of reception of a geotropic stimulus in the bean radicle?

Figure 14.6 (a) Bean seedling with entire radicle. (b) Bean seedling with decapitated radicle

Investigation 14e. Stimulus perception in oat coleoptiles

Germinate three batches of about ten oat grains in small pots labelled A, B and C (as Investigation 14a). The young shoot of oat is protected by a leaf sheath called a **coleoptile**. After about a week, the coleoptiles will be about 50 mm high.

1. Place pot A into a box which has a slit cut in one end to admit light. The inside of the box is painted black.

2. Make tiny 'dunces' caps from silver paper by twisting it around a pencil tip, and place the caps over the tips of the coleoptiles in pot B. Then place pot B in the box.
3. With a very sharp razor, cut about 5 mm from the tips of the coleoptiles in pot C and place the pot in the box (see Figure 14.7).

After a few days, examine the plants and make notes of any changes. Can you draw any conclusions about where the oat coleoptiles perceive the stimulus of light? Does this experiment need a control?

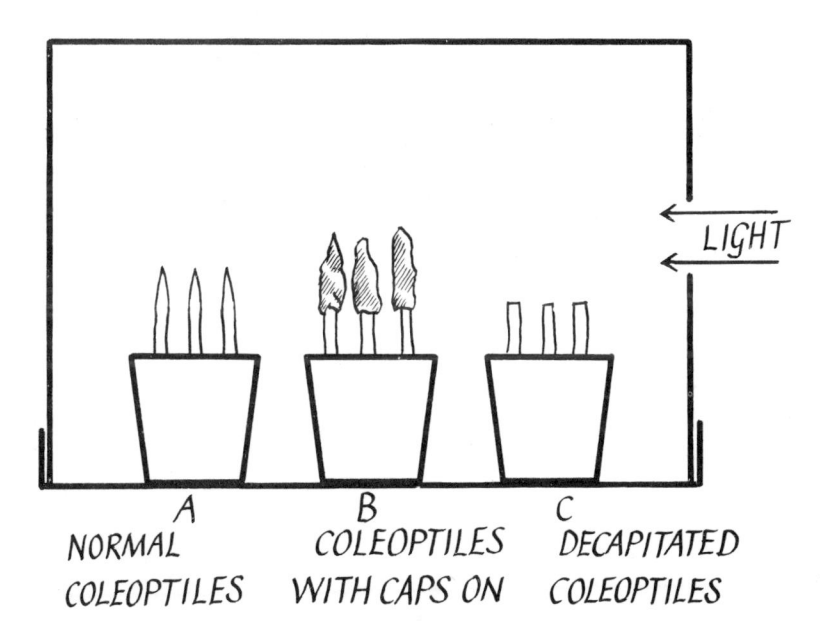

Figure 14.7 The three sets of seedlings

A NORMAL COLEOPTILES   B COLEOPTILES WITH CAPS ON   C DECAPITATED COLEOPTILES

14.4. Response to water

Investigation 14f. The response of roots to water

Take a large glass vessel such as a very large beaker or storage jar, or better still a wormery with a flat glass surface. Fill it with fine soil and place a porous pot in the centre of the vessel. Plant two well-established bean seedlings close up against the glass on either side of the porous pot (see Figure 14.8). Fill the porous pot with water, and then cover the glass of the wormery or the vessel with black paper or cloth. Keep the porous pot topped up with water, and observe periodically. After about a fortnight draw the root systems of the seedlings. Can you draw any conclusions about the response of roots to water?

Can you suggest why it was advisable to cover the glass with black cloth or paper? Does this experiment need a control? If you think so, set one up, draw it and describe what happens. The bending

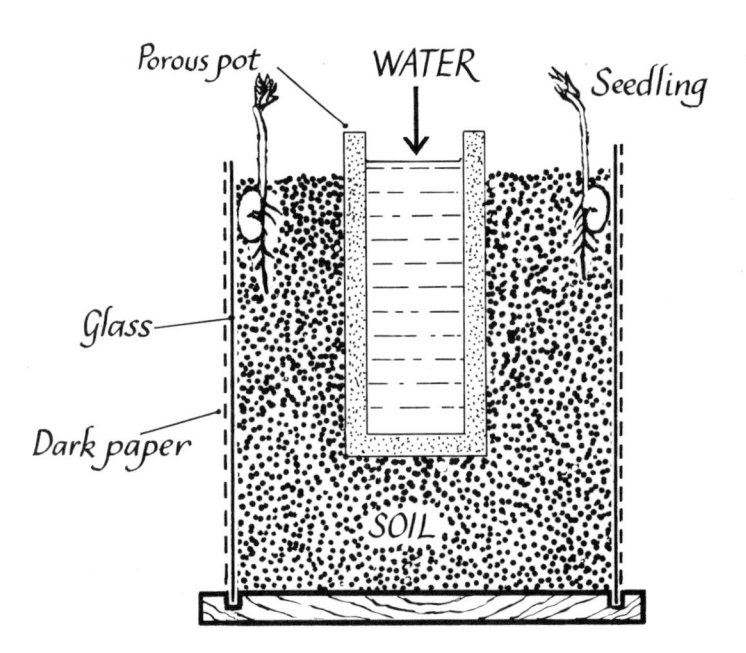

Figure 14.8 Apparatus to investigate the response of roots to water

growth movement of plants in response to water is known as **hydrotropism**. How does this response benefit the plant?

14.5. The adaptive nature of the responses

All the responses you have observed in the course of your investigations have been in the plant's interest. Can you suggest why plant stems are positively phototropic and negatively geotropic? Why are roots negatively phototropic and positively geotropic? From your own observations, does a root respond more readily to the stimulus of gravity or to the stimulus of water? Explain your answer.

14.6. The mechanism of tropic responses

It has been established that plant organs respond to directional stimuli with bending movements. The direction of these movements is determined by the direction of the stimulus. The movements are due to plant growth, for we have seen that the response takes place in the rapidly growing region of a plant organ. How does growth bring about bending of an organ? It is due to different rates of growth on opposite sides of a plant organ. If growth rate on, say, the left side of a root becomes faster than the growth rate on the right side, then the root will bend to the right (see Figure 14.9).

What causes the speed-up in growth rate in a particular region of a plant organ? About ninety years ago, **Charles Darwin** carried out an experiment similar to Investigation 14e, from which he deduced that the very tip of an oat coleoptile was able to sense the light and

FASTER GROWTH

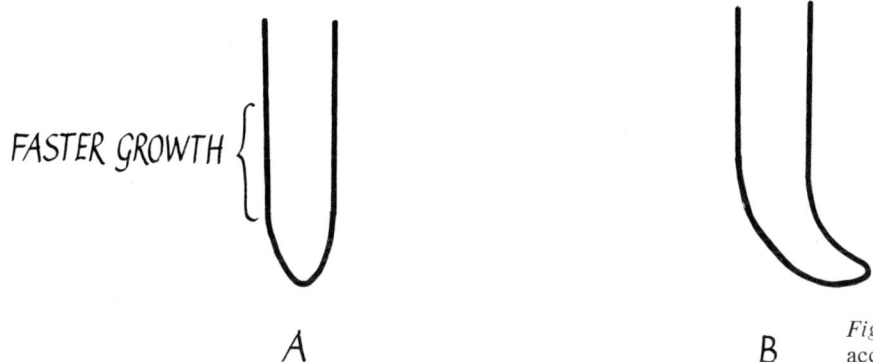

A   B

Figure 14.9 The result of accelerated growth on one side of a plant organ

was, in some way, able to send 'instructions' to the growing region just below.

Plants, however, have no sense organs, no nervous system and no well-defined pathways along which information and instructions can be transmitted. In 1910, a Danish scientist, **Peter Boysen-Jensen**, suggested the hypothesis that information about the light must be transferred from the dividing cells at the very tip to those of the growing region just behind by some **chemical substance**. He then carried out the following series of investigations to test his hypothesis.

a. He stimulated an oat coleoptile with a beam of light from one side only. The coleoptile responded and grew towards the light (see Figure 14.10).

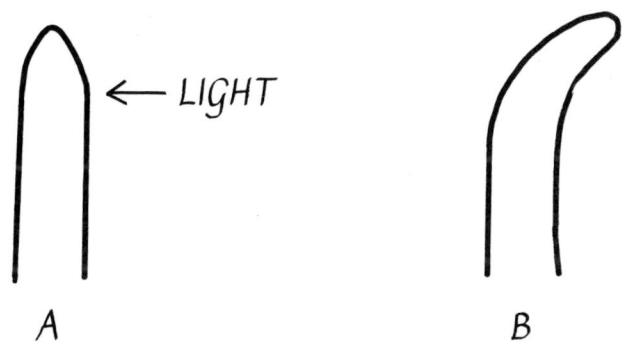

← LIGHT

A   B

Figure 14.10 The entire coleoptile responds when stimulated

b. He decapitated a coleoptile and stimulated it in the same way, but it did not respond (see Figure 14.11).

c. Next he stimulated a coleoptile and *then* decapitated it. This one

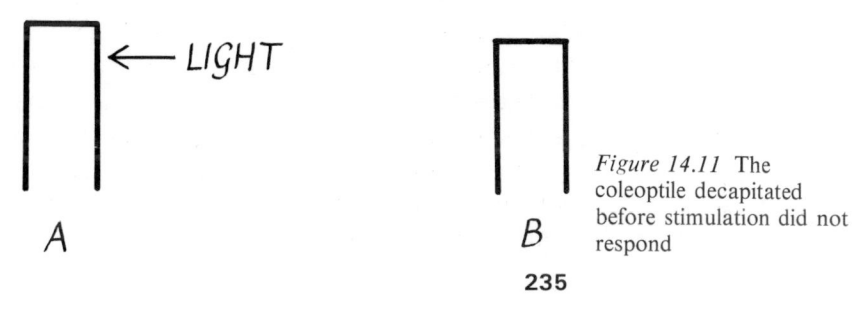

← LIGHT

A   B

Figure 14.11 The coleoptile decapitated before stimulation did not respond

Figure 14.12 The coleoptile stimulated before decapitation did respond

did respond (see Figure 14.12). Does the evidence support his hypothesis? If you think so, explain how.

d. He then decapitated a coleoptile, and placed a small block of gelatine between the coleoptile and its tip. The coleoptile was then stimulated in the usual way, and responded (see Figure 14.13).

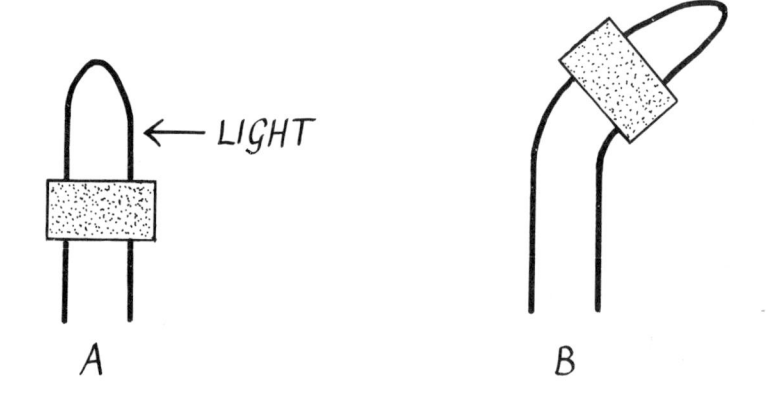

Figure 14.13 The coleoptile separated from its tip by a block of gelatine did respond

Investigations (a) and (b) show that the very tip of the coleoptile must be present at stimulation if a response is to occur. We can conclude that the tip is the sensitive region. Investigation (c) shows that, although the tip must be present when stimulated, it is not necessary for the actual response. Investigation (d) indicates that a response occurs if the coleoptile and its tip are joined by gelatine. Gelatine is mostly water, and substances can pass through it in much the same way as they can pass through water. This indicates that some non-living substance produced in the tip as a result of stimulation passes down the coleoptile to the growing region where it produces the response.

Boysen-Jensen then did a further set of experiments. He inserted a thin piece of mica part-way through the stem, between its tip and growing region, and then stimulated the coleoptile, first from the side in which the mica was placed and then from the opposite side. The results are shown in Figures 14.14 and 14.15.

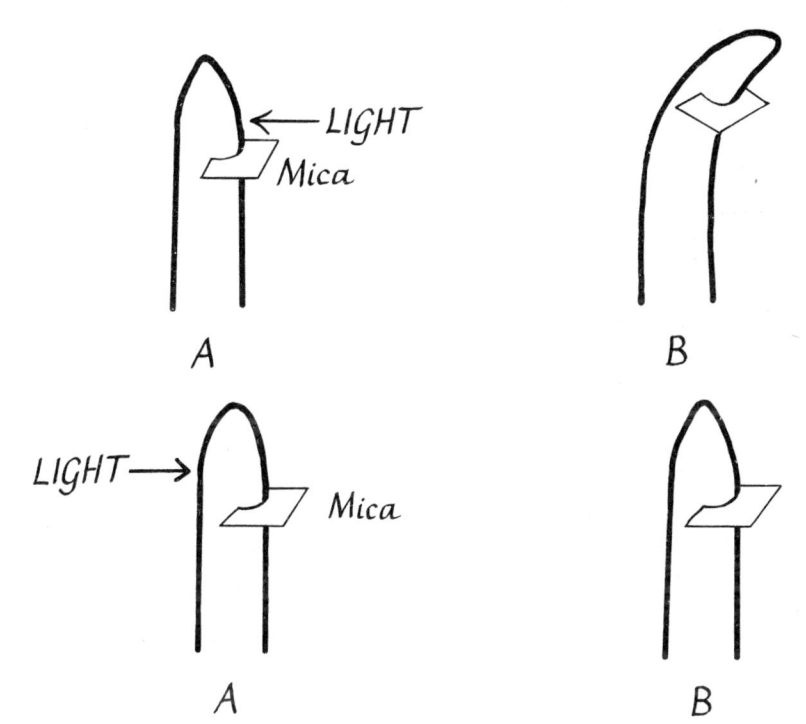

Figure 14.14 The coleoptile stimulated from the side in which the mica had been inserted did respond

Figure 14.15 The coleoptile stimulated from the opposite side did not respond

As the chemical stubstance was unable to pass through the mica, he concluded that it moved down the non-illuminated side of the stem. As the coleoptile bends towards the light, increased growth must take place on the side away from the light stimulus and, as the chemical passes down that side, he concluded that it was the presence of this substance that caused the increase in growth rate in that region. The chemical substance is a plant hormone called **auxin**.

Friedrich Went, a Dutch scientist, collected auxin by placing decapitated coleoptile tips on blocks of gelatine. The auxin diffused from the tips into the gelatine blocks. He then replaced a coleoptile tip with a block of this auxin-containing gelatine, and stimulated it with a beam of light. The coleoptile responded just as if the tip had been present (see Figure 14.16).

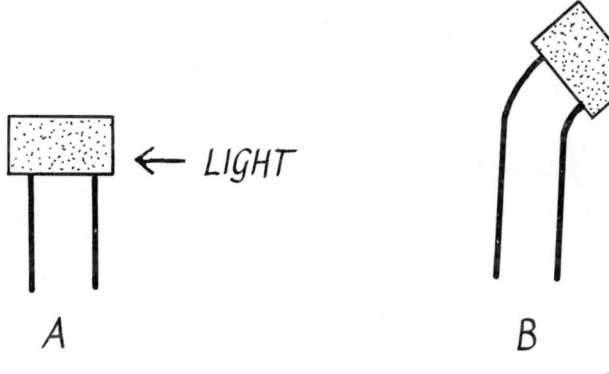

Figure 14.16 The coleoptile with the auxin-charged gelatine block behaved as if the tip were present

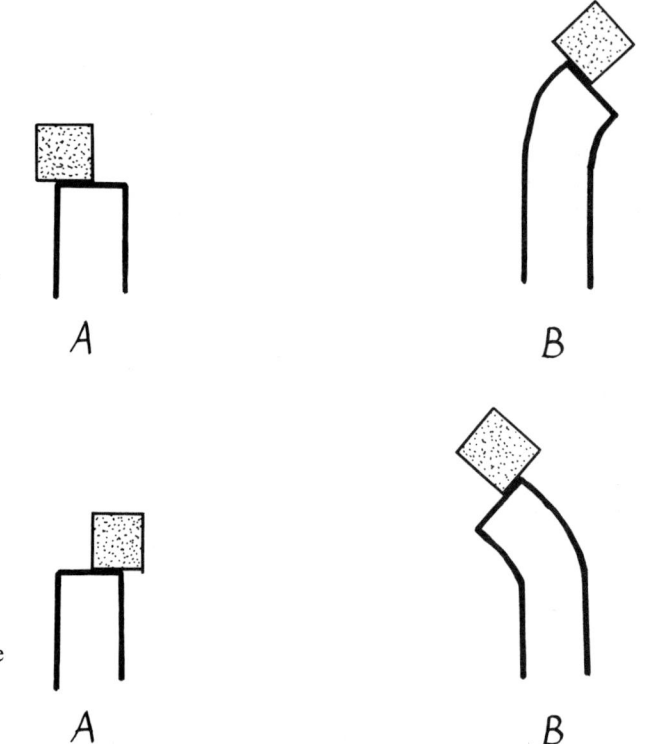

Figure 14.17 The coleoptile bent away from the side to which the auxin block was applied

Figure 14.18 The distribution of auxin in non-stimulated and in stimulated coleoptile tips

Went then placed his auxin-charged blocks on one side only, but *did not* stimulate them. The results are shown in Figure 14.17.

These experiments support the view that an increase in auxin concentration in a particular region of a growing coleoptile causes increased growth in that region. The stimulus of light causes the auxin to accumulate in the opposite side of the coleoptile. Analysis of non-stimulated and stimulated coleoptile tips shows the results in Figure 14.18.

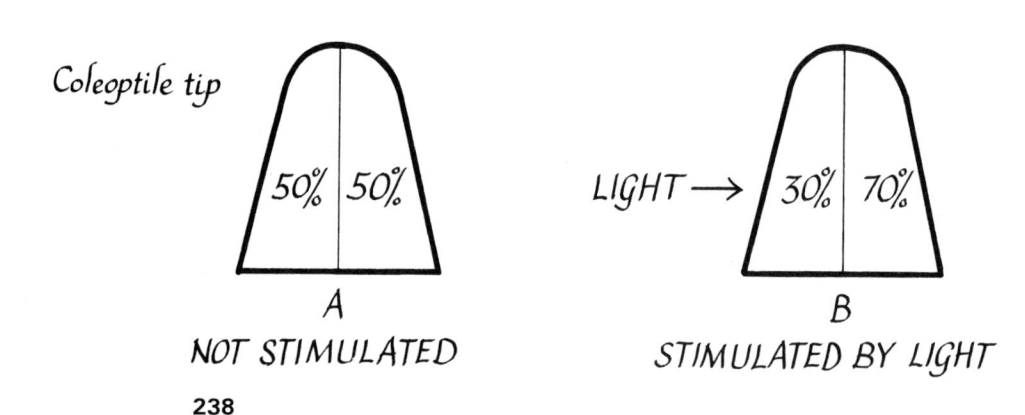

Roots respond differently. Increased auxin concentration causes retarded growth in roots. The auxin appears to slow down the growth rate. Gravity causes the auxin to collect on the lower side of a horizontal root. This retards growth and the root bends downwards (see Figure 14.19).

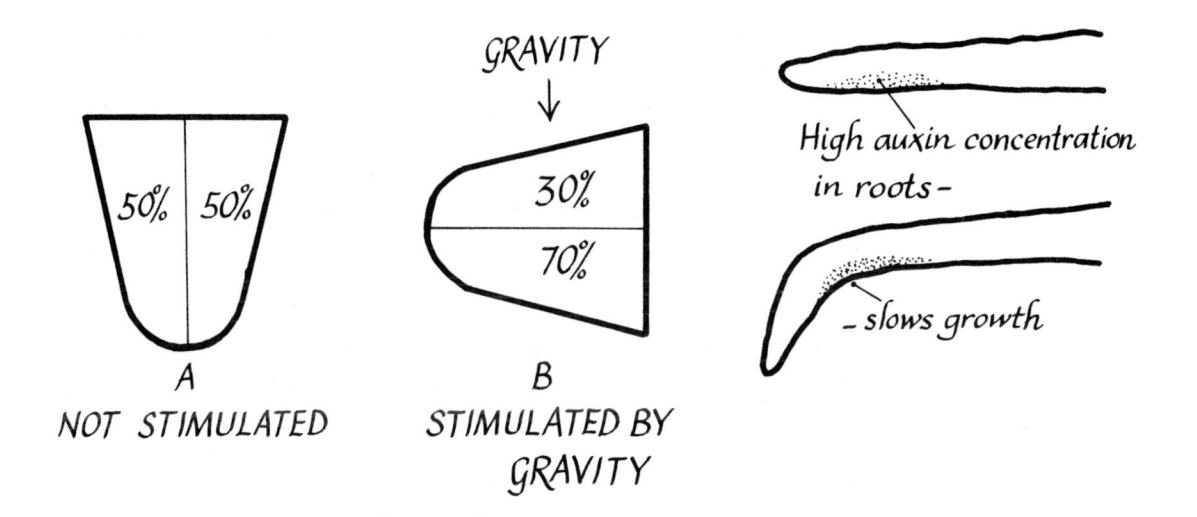

Although it is not yet completely understood, the auxin is thought to control the elongation of the cells by influencing the plasticity of the cell walls. A cell with a more plastic wall will elongate more readily than one with a less plastic cell wall.

Figure 14.19 The distribution of auxin in a vertical and a horizontal root tip, and the effect of an accumulation of auxin in a root tip

14.7. Plant hormones

There are three groups of plant hormones. The **auxins**, which were discovered by Friedrich Went and his fellow workers, are concerned with growth in plant cells and tissues. The **kinins** induce cell division, and the **gibberellins** promote cell enlargement, but only in the presence of auxin. Chemists have produced a synthetic growth substance similar to auxin which gives rise to the same sort of behaviour when applied to plants. It is called **indolylacetic acid (IAA** for short) or heteroauxin.

Investigation 14g. The effect of heteroauxin

Germinate three small pots of oat seedlings, as you have done previously, and label the pots A, B and C. You will need two small containers of lanolin cream, one containing pure lanolin and the other containing lanolin to which a dilute solution of IAA has been added. The lanolin and lanolin with IAA must be kept warm or they will become hard and difficult to smear. This can be done by placing the containers in a water-bath at about 45 °C.

When the oat coleoptiles are about 30 mm tall, treat the pots as follows:
1. Transfer pot A directly to a dark cupboard.

2. Gently smear *one* side of the coleoptiles in pot B with a thin layer of pure lanolin and transfer to the dark cupboard.
3. Gently smear *one* side of the coleoptiles in pot C with a thin layer of lanolin and IAA and transfer to the dark cupboard.

Examine the oat coleoptiles after about five hours or certainly no later than the next day. Comment on any changes that have occurred. This investigation is best carried out in subdued light. Can you suggest why?

Plant hormones are comparable to the hormones secreted by the endocrine organs of animals. They control a whole range of growth and developmental processes including, of course, the growth responses described in this chapter. Plant hormones influence the onset of flowering, wound healing, the development of roots, the inhibition and development of lateral buds, seed and spore germination, fruit development, cell division and cell enlargement. It is not surprising, therefore, that horticulturists have made great efforts to synthesize chemicals which have similar effects on plants and so boost crop production. Heteroauxin rooting compounds are used to encourage root formation when taking cuttings (see Chapter 13). The use of such compounds has made it possible to propagate many valuable ornamental plants which were otherwise difficult to grow.

Some hormones inhibit growth, like the hormones produced by terminal buds. These diffuse back down the stem and inhibit the development of the lateral buds. If the terminal bud is removed, as in pruning, the flow of hormone ceases and the lateral buds become lateral branches. A synthetic growth substance that acts as an inhibitor is **naphthalene acetic acid**, which prevents potatoes in store from sprouting, so that they can be stored in good condition for as long as three years. Apple trees are also sprayed with it to prevent early fruit drop, thus increasing the number of fruit which reach maturity.

Other man-made chemicals which have similar effects to heteroauxin include 2,4-dichlorophenoxyacetic acid (happily abbreviated to 2,4D). This is used as a selective weed-killer on lawns because it destroys the broad-leafed plants (dicotyledons) which are weeds in a lawn, but doesn't affect the grasses or other narrow-leafed plants (monocotyledons). In low concentrations 2,4D stimulates growth, but in high concentrations it causes the plants to grow so rapidly that they become large and twisted and soon wither and die. The broad, horizontal leaves of dicotyledons appear to absorb 2,4D more readily than the narrow, vertical leaves of monocotyledons.

The **gibberellins** were first discovered in Japan when it was noticed that certain rice plants in a crop grew very much taller than the others. On examination, these tall plants were found to be infected by a fungus, *Gibberella fujikoroi*. Substances extracted from these plants were found to stimulate the stem growth in large numbers of plants. The gibberellins are concerned with cell enlargement in shoots and coleoptiles only, and will not function in the absence of auxin. The two substances seem to be complementary to each other.

14.8. Types of response in plants

a. The tropism is perhaps the most important plant response and for this reason we have discussed it in some detail in the early part of this chapter. It is important to remember that a tropism is a *bending growth movement* by a *part* of the plant in which the direction of the bending response is determined by the direction of the stimulus. The stem of a houseplant performs a positive, phototropic response when it grows towards a window. The tip of a stem blown to the ground performs a negative geotropic response when it grows upwards.

b. A **taxis**, or tactic response, is a response by an *entire* motile organism, such as *Chlamydomonas*, or by a swimming gamete. *Chlamydomonas* swimming away from a very bright light performs a negative **phototactic** response, and the sperm cells of moss swimming towards the source of sucrose secreted by the egg cell exhibit a positive **chemotactic** response. In a taxis, as in a tropism, the direction of the response depends upon the direction of the stimulus.

c. A **nasty** is the response by a plant organ to a non-directional stimulus, such as a temperature change or a change in the intensity of a diffuse stimulus, such as daytime/night-time. The closing of the daisy flower at night is in response to changes in both light and temperature. This 'sleep' movement response is called a **nyctinasty**.

14.9. Differences between plant and animal responses

If both animals and plants are to behave sensibly, that is in a way that will ensure their *survival*, they must be able to detect stimuli and respond to them. In addition, they must have some method of linking up the mechanism for the detection of stimuli with the mechanisms of response.

In animals the sense organs detect the stimuli and the effector organs, the muscles and glands, produce the response, while plants usually detect stimuli in the tips of the roots and shoots, but have no special sense organs. The sense organs and effector organs in animals are linked up by two complementary systems. The nervous system conducts information in the form of impulses to the brain or spinal cord which then transmits 'instructions' in the form of impulses to the appropriate effector organ. Some stimuli cause the endocrine system of an animal to secrete hormones directly into the blood stream, which carries them to the part of the body where they produce the appropriate response. Plants have no nervous system; the detection and response mechanisms are linked by hormones which are produced in the region of the plant that detects the stimulus. The hormones then diffuse through the tissues to the region where the growth response occurs.

In animals the impulses travel along definite pathways (the nerves) very rapidly, and the response is almost instantaneous. The response is frequently a movement, such as the bending of the elbow. This is a temporary change which can easily be reversed. Since plant hormones simply diffuse through the tissues, and there is no definite pathway, the conduction is much slower than that of nerve impulses. Most plant responses are *growth* responses, and for that reason, the changes are much slower than, say, muscle contraction. Moreover, they cannot be reversed.

The conduction of animal hormones by the blood stream is a slower process than the conduction of nerve impulses, but rather faster than the conduction of plant hormones. The changes influenced by animal hormones are concerned with growth and development.

Test your understanding

Copy and complete the following paragraph:

There are three main types of plant response:....[1],....[2] and tropisms. A tropism is a bending ....[3] movement by a part of a plant, in which the direction of the ....[4] is determined by the direction of the application of the ....[5] A ....[6] is a bending growth response to the stimulus of light, and geotropism is a bending growth response to the stimulus of....[7] Main stems are positively ....[8] and negatively ....[9] Roots are positively ....[10]

1. Describe how you would show that a tropism is a growth movement.
2. How would you show that the tip of a shoot perceives the stimulus of directional light?
3. How can the effect of gravity on a plant be eliminated?
4. Explain the experiments of Peter Boysen-Jensen.
5. How does auxin appear to affect plant tissues?
6. Do roots and shoots respond in the same way to a given concentration of auxin?
7. What are the three main types of plant hormone?
8. Why is 2,4D described as a selective weed-killer?
9. What are the advantages of (a) rooting compounds and (b) pruning?
10. Explain the main differences between animal responses and plant responses.

TOPIC D: LIVING TOGETHER—THE COMMUNITY

Chapter 15

The Economy of Nature

15.1. The materials of life

Living things get their energy from the sun and their matter (substance) from the earth and the air. What are living things made of? Table 15.1 shows the results of analyses of an animal (man), a plant (wheat) and the earth's crust to show the chemical elements they contain.

TABLE 15.1. THE CHEMICAL COMPOSITIONS OF ANIMALS, PLANTS AND THE EARTH'S CRUST

Element	Symbol	Mass in Animals (%)	Mass in Plants (%)	Mass in Earth's Crust (%)
Oxygen	O	65	75	49
Carbon	C	18	13	0·09
Hydrogen	H	10	10	0·88
Nitrogen	N	3·3	0·45	0·03
Calcium	Ca	1·5	0·07	3·4
Phosphorus	P	1·0	0·6	0·12
Potassium	K	0·35	0·28	2·4
Sulphur	S	0·24	0·05	0·05
Sodium	Na	0·24	trace	2·6
Chlorine	Cl	0·19	0·04	0·19
Magnesium	Mg	0·05	0·06	1·9
Iron	Fe	0·005	0·03	4·7
Manganese	Mn	0·00003	0·01	0·08
Silicon	Si	trace	0·36	25

other elements to 100%

Are the proportions of the elements found in animals and plants similar to the proportions in which they occur in the earth's crust? If not, then organisms must select those chemicals which they need to build up their tissues.

Certain of the elements, such as nitrogen, carbon and phosphorus, are needed by animals in much higher proportions than they occur in nature. This presents a potential problem, namely that there is a danger that all these elements might become used up. Each year, green plants remove 0·4% of all the carbon dioxide in the atmosphere, during photosynthesis. This suggests that plants undergoing photosynthesis will remove all the carbon dioxide from the atmosphere in 250 years and that there will be none left. Happily, this is not the case, as these vital elements circulate in nature, moving from the non-living to the living world and back again. In this way, a balance is maintained and the vital elements are always available for life.

Investigation 15a. To find out if plant and animal tissues contain carbon

Place a piece of plant or animal tissue in a crucible and put the lid on. Heat the crucible strongly for several minutes and then allow it to cool. Examine the contents. What colour is the residue? What do you think this residue consists of? Do both plant and animal tissues leave the same sort of residue when heated strongly? What do you think will happen if you continue to heat this residue strongly? Will anything be left in the end? If so, what?

★ WARNING. *This investigation should be carried out in a fume cupboard if possible.*

15.2. The carbon cycle

The circulation in nature of carbon from the environment into living organisms and back into the environment is known as the **carbon cycle** (see Figure 15.1). We discovered, from Investigation 15a, that when plant and animal tissues are heated strongly, a black deposit is left in the crucible. This is carbon; if heated very strongly it disappears, as it combines with oxygen in the air to form carbon dioxide. Carbon forms a considerable part of both animal and plant tissue.

The carbon cycle has no beginning and no end, but it is convenient to start with the reservoir of carbon dioxide gas in the atmosphere and in solution in the waters of the earth. Carbon dioxide in solution is used in photosynthesis by the aquatic algae which, in fact, carry out about 90% of all the photosynthesis occurring on the earth. Similarly, the atmospheric carbon dioxide is taken into the green leaves of land plants and is converted into carbohydrates by photosynthesis. Aquatic and terrestrial plants are, of course, **producers**, harnessing the radiant energy of the sun and converting it into their own substance. In due course, some of the plants will be eaten by herbivores, such as rabbits; herbivores are the primary **consumers**. Much of the plant carbon becomes incorporated into the tissues of the rabbit. Some of these carbon-rich compounds consumed by the rabbit may be used to provide energy, in which case the carbon is converted to carbon dioxide gas and returned to the atmosphere.

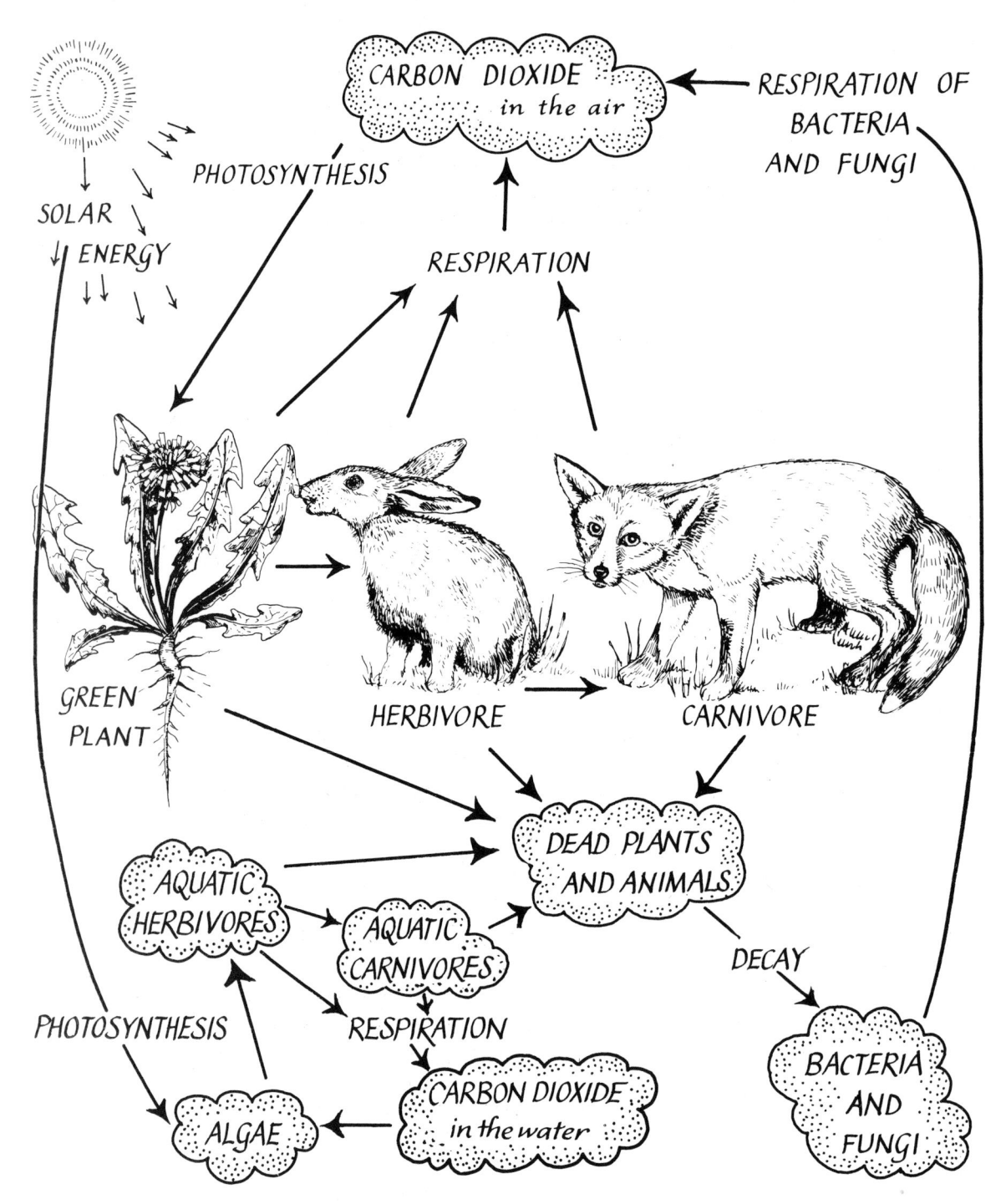

Figure 15.1 The carbon cycle

The rabbit, however, is a plentiful creature, and is eaten by a number of carnivores (meat-eating animals) and by man. These are the secondary consumers. Some of the carbon from the rabbit becomes incorporated into the substance of the secondary consumer and again a proportion returns to the air, as a result of respiration. Both producers and consumers may discard their carbon-containing wastes and, when they die, their bodies represent an accumulation of organic carbon compounds. These are attacked by a special group of consumers, the **decomposers**, which include bacteria and fungi. These convert organic carbon compounds back to inorganic carbon compounds by the process of decay. This process may sometimes be extremely slow. Carbon compounds may become incorporated into coal and petroleum, both of which may be eventually converted into gaseous carbon compounds which are released into the atmosphere. The main pathway, however, is from the earth's atmosphere or waters into living things, and then back again.

15.3. The nitrogen cycle

From Table 15.1, we see that nitrogen is another element which is present in relatively large quantities in animals (3·3%) and plants (0·45%), but only in small quantities in the earth's crust (0·03%). Nitrogen is an essential element of the proteins which form the basis of protoplasm, or living matter. Nitrogen is present in the meat and vegetables we eat. Whatever we eat, we can trace the food back to plants, which get their nitrogen from the soil. Again, there appears to be the danger that all the nitrogen in the environment will be used up and be incorporated into living organisms. That this does not occur is due to the fact that certain processes ensure the return of nitrogen from living things to the environment. Thus there exists a **nitrogen cycle** in nature (see Figure 15.2).

Four types of process occur in the nitrogen cycle: (a) nitrogen fixation, (b) nitrification, (c) denitrification and (d) decomposition.

a. Nitrogen fixation

This is the conversion of the gaseous nitrogen of the atmosphere into a form which can be used by organisms. There are three main ways in which this occurs: two of them depend on the activity of nitrogen-fixing soil bacteria, and the third on the effect of lightning on the gases of the atmosphere.

Investigation 15b. To examine root nodules

Carefully dig (not pull) up a leguminous (pod-fruiting) plant such as a lupin, clover, sweet pea or bean. Carefully wash the soil from the roots under a gently running tap. Can you see any lumps attached to the roots? These are the **root nodules**, which are so characteristic of the leguminous plants (see Figure 15.3). Examine a prepared microscope slide of a section through a root nodule. If you examine the cells in the central part of the nodule using the high-power objective,

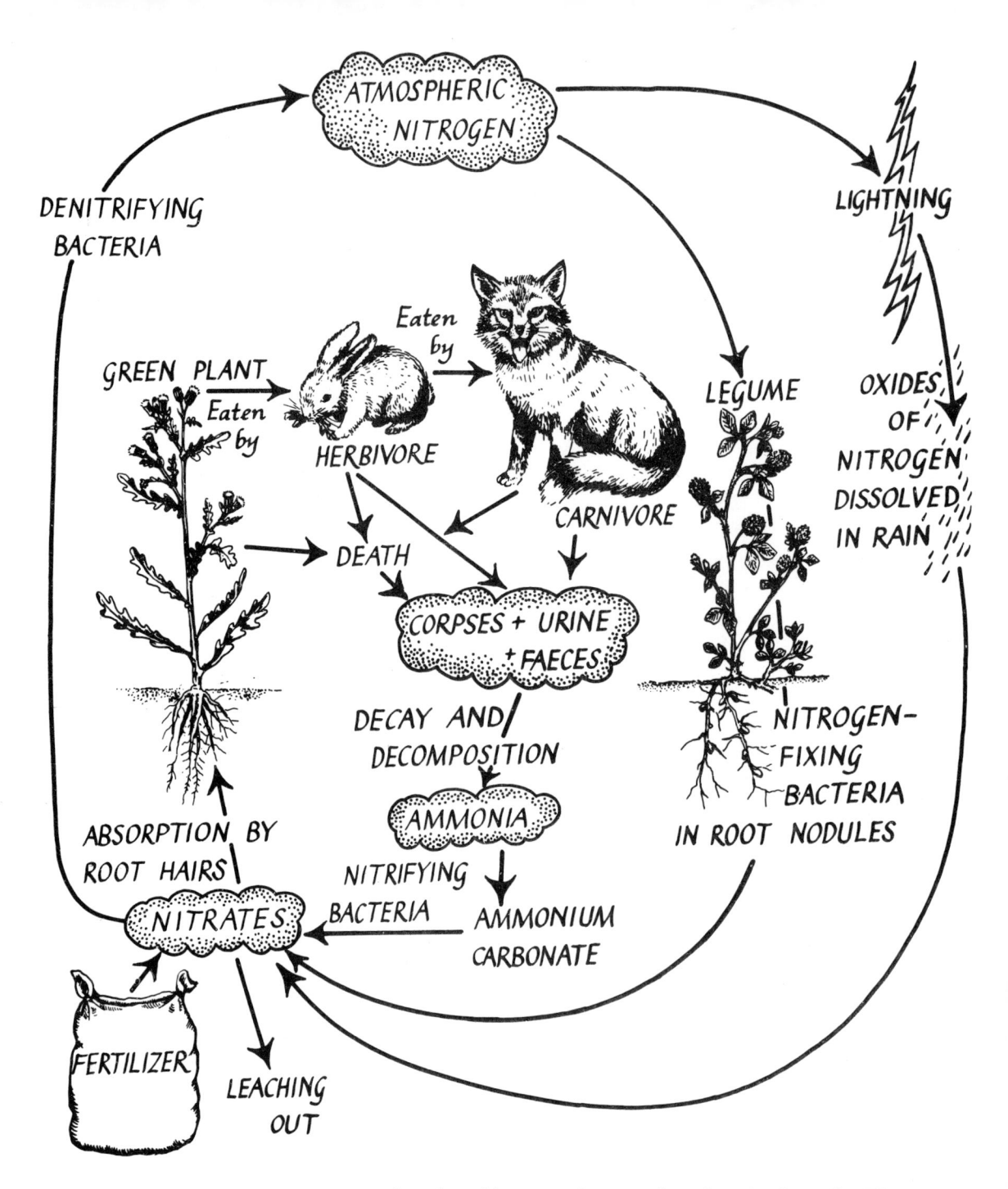

Figure 15.2 The nitrogen cycle

you may just be able to make out tiny dots in the cells. These are bacteria.

We know that 79% of the atmosphere consists of the rather inert gas, nitrogen. In this form, it cannot be used by animals or plants. The root-nodule bacteria are able to convert the gaseous nitrogen of the atmosphere into their own protein (**nitrogen fixation**). The

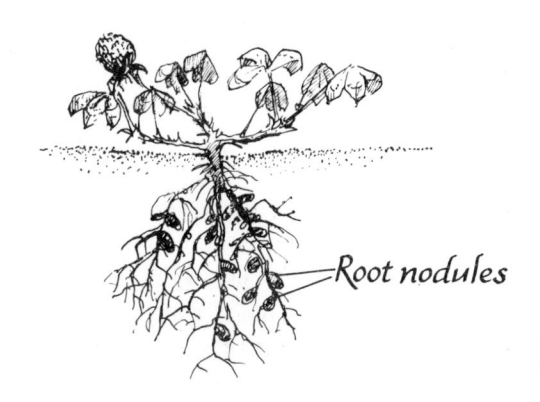

Figure 15.3 The root nodules of clover

bacteria fix more nitrogen than they need for their own use, and the excess is available to the leguminous plant which, as a result, thrives. In return, the green plant provides the bacteria with a supply of carbohydrate for respiration. Thus the two organisms benefit one another. This is another example of **symbiosis**—the association between two organisms in which each partner confers an advantage on the other. Can you think of two other examples of symbiosis which we have discussed? (See Chapters 4 and 8.)

Investigation 15c. Does the soil contain micro-organisms?

Weigh out 1 g of soil and place it in a bottle of 100 cm^3 of sterile distilled water. Let it stand for a few minutes and then close the stopper and shake vigorously. Loosen the cap of a McCartney bottle containing nutrient agar (for example, blood agar) and heat it in a pressure cooker for fifteen minutes to melt and sterilize it. Allow it to cool to about 50 °C, when it will still be liquid. Take 1 cm^3 of the soil water sample, and place it in a sterile petri dish. Pour the melted agar from the tube into a petri dish and quickly replace the top. Allow it to cool to 30 °C, when it will be set. Invert the petri dish to prevent condensation from affecting the agar, and incubate at 37 °C for about four days. After incubation, examine the contents of the petri dish carefully. Can you see spots on the surface of the agar? These are colonies of micro-organisms which normally live in the soil. Can you see any colonies which are feathery and composed of threads? These are probably soil fungi. The more compact colonies are probably bacteria. Incubate the dish for a further week and re-examine.

When plants and bacteria die, their nitrogen-rich remains are available for other organisms to convert into **nitrates**, the form in which nitrogen is most readily absorbed by the roots of the green plant. Land on which a crop of leguminous plants has been grown shows a considerable increase in fertility.

In addition to the symbiotic, nitrogen-fixing bacteria of leguminous plants, there are nitrogen-fixing bacteria living freely in the soil. These incorporate the atmospheric nitrogen into their own proteins, and after death they are converted into nitrates by other micro-organisms.

The third method of nitrogen fixation is due to the action of lightning on the gases of the atmosphere. Oxygen and nitrogen combine to form oxides of nitrogen which dissolve in the rain to form a very dilute solution of nitrous and nitric acids. As the rain soaks into the ground these acids react with bases to produce nitrites and nitrates which can then be absorbed and utilized by the plants.

b. Nitrification

This is carried out by another group of soil bacteria, the **nitrifying bacteria.** These convert unusable nitrogen-containing compounds like ammonia, resulting from the activity of the decomposers, into nitrites and then into nitrates. There are two types of nitrifying bacteria, one which converts ammonium compounds to nitrites, and a second which converts nitrites to nitrates. These bacteria work in the presence of atmospheric oxygen, so remember that it is a good idea to turn over a compost heap, from time to time, to encourage their activity.

c. Denitrification

This is carried out by denitrifying bacteria whose activities are not in the interest of the plant or the farmer. They convert the useful nitrates of the soil into useless nitrogen gas. The fact that these work only in the absence of oxygen is another good reason for keeping the soil and the compost heap well aerated. Denitrifying bacteria undo the work of the two previous groups of bacteria.

d. Decomposition

The **decomposers** are a vital group in maintaining the circulation of nitrogen and carbon. The organic material of the soil, which consists of the remains of dead plants and animals, is called humus. The decomposers release the nitrogen and carbon which has been incorporated into the organic world by previous generations of plants and animals. The nitrogen and carbon are then available for the use of living animals and plants. This vital work of the decomposing organisms is often considered harmful, because it causes the rotting of man's fabrics, dwellings or food. The decomposers consist of the soil fungi, which are saprophytes (like the moulds discussed in Chapter 8), and certain soil bacteria. In grassland soils the bacteria are the chief decomposers, whilst the soil fungi are the chief decomposers in woodland soils. If you turn the top few inches of woodland soil, you will probably see the white thread-like hyphae of these soil fungi. These fungi reproduce by spores, and often, in the autumn, the spore-forming bodies of these soil fungi appear above the ground as toadstools and puffballs. The fungi are particularly useful in breaking down cellulose.

The addition of inorganic fertilizers by man

In modern agriculture, tractors have almost completely replaced animal power, with the resultant loss to the soil of the rich nitrogenous materials from urine and dung. To compensate for this loss, and to achieve ever-increasing soil fertility, man is adding tremendous quantities of nitrogen-containing chemicals to the soil as artificial fertilizers (for example, ammonium sulphate, potassium nitrate).

15.4. The water cycle

Investigation 15d. To construct a model of the water cycle

Take a large beaker and add water to a depth of about 4 cm. Place it on a tripod stand and gauze over a bunsen burner. On top of the beaker, place a large clock-glass, and on this, pieces of ice. Light the bunsen burner, and adjust it to give a gentle flame (see Figure 15.4). Watch the beaker carefully to see what happens. Explain what is happening. Why do we only have a very gentle flame? Why is the ice placed on the clock-glass?

This is a simple model of the water cycle. As we discovered in

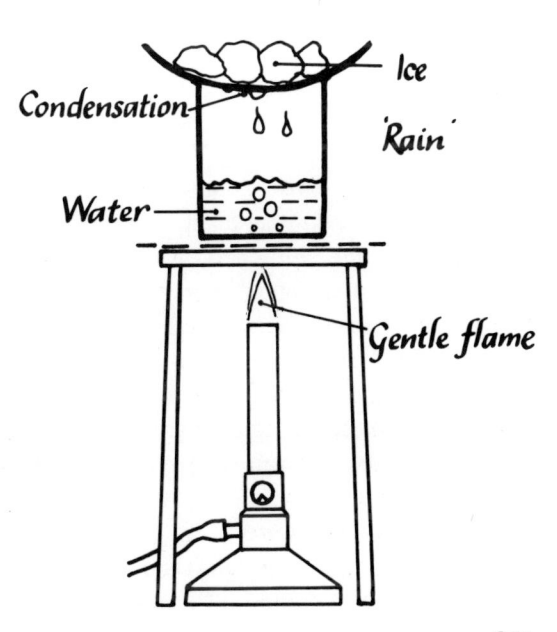

Figure 15.4 Model of the water cycle

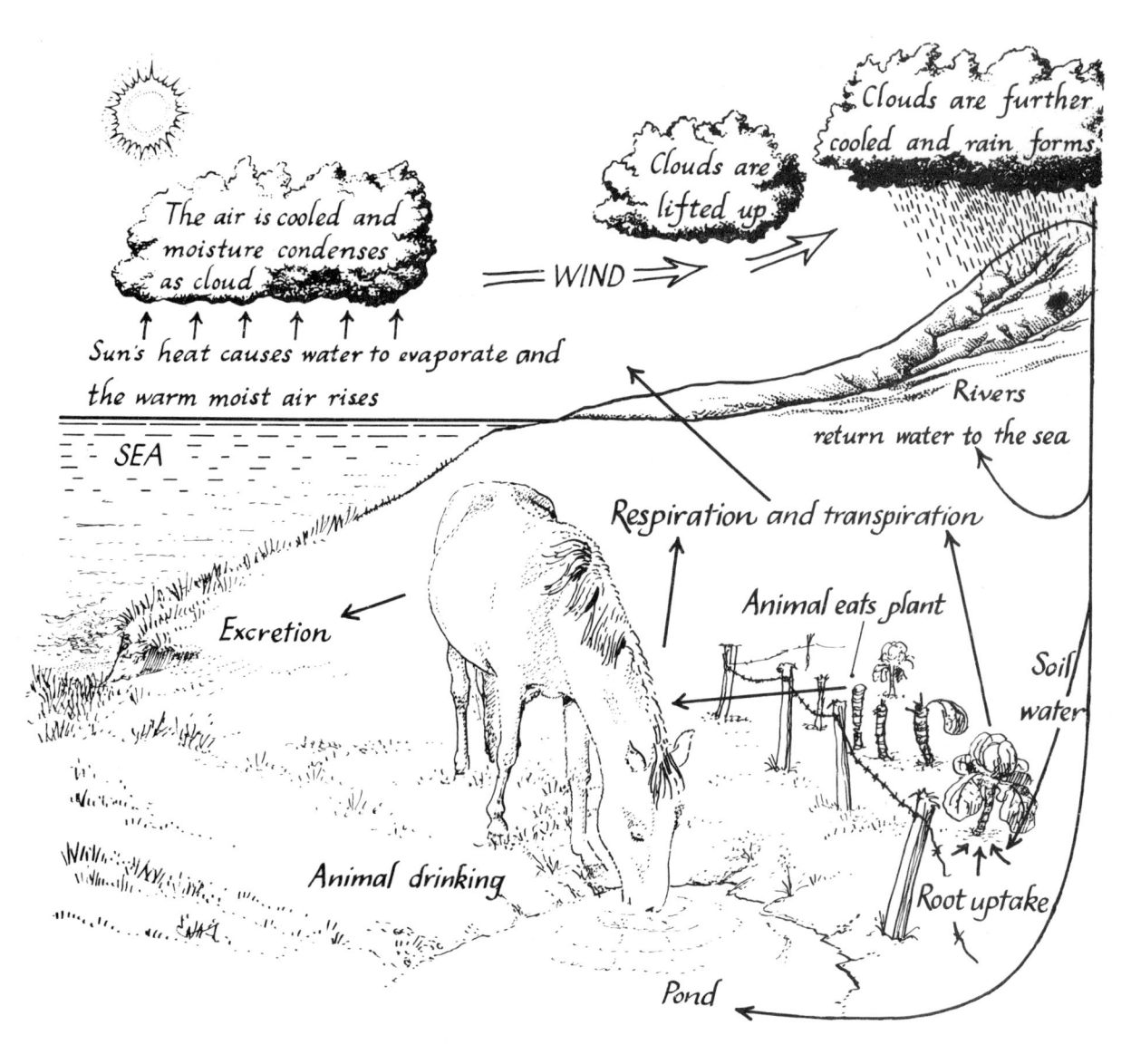

Figure 15.5 The water cycle

Chapter 11, life cannot exist without water, so it is vital that the water in the environment should circulate. In the beaker, the water vapour meets the cold surface of the clock-glass and condenses into droplets of water which fall back into the beaker. Usually water leaves the atmosphere and falls back to earth as rain or snow. It may fall directly into the seas, or it may fall on to the land, where it starts to trickle down the hills into streams and springs. These flow into rivers which eventually carry water to the sea. Some of it returns to the atmosphere from all these places by evaporation. There is a general circulation from the atmosphere to the land and seas, and back again, as in Figure 15.5.

Both plants and animals take in water, some of which becomes chemically incorporated into their living materials. This water is eventually returned to the environment through such processes as respiration, transpiration and excretion.

15.5. The source of energy

The most characteristic and vital property of living organisms is their ability to release and to use energy. Once the energy-transfer reactions cease in a cell, it is no longer living, and rapidly becomes disorganized and eventually disintegrates. A living cell can be compared with your bedroom. As long as you exert a little energy from time to time and put things away and clean up dirt, it remains reasonably neat and tidy, but if you completely neglect to put things away or clean, then it rapidly becomes a shambles.

Energy is the capacity to do work; in our bodies it is used for moving, talking, pumping blood, building new body materials, and so on. We have already learnt that we are consumers and obtain our food from other animals or from plants, the producers. We can link energy with carbon-containing compounds here because the carbohydrates, such as starch and sugar, are the energy-rich compounds which have a great deal of potential energy locked away in their chemical structure. When this chemical structure is broken down, as in respiration, much of the energy is released to do useful work.

If man, in common with other primary consumers, gets his energy from the green plants, the producers, where do they get it from? Green plants are unique, because they are able to harness the sun's energy and convert it to the chemical energy of carbohydrates during photosynthesis. Does *all* energy originate from the sun? What about the energy we get from, for example, a ham roll? The bread is made from flour of the wheat plant, which produces the starch as a result of photosynthesis. The butter comes from milk taken from a cow, which produced the milk from materials in the grass, which, in turn, obtained its energy from the sun. Work out how the energy in the ham got there.

When we sit by a coal fire, we get energy in the form of heat and light. Does this come from the sun also? Coal is the remains of prehistoric plants and consists largely of carbon. This resulted from the photosynthetic activities of the prehistoric ferns. Work out how you think the energy which cars get from petrol got there, and trace back the energy from the light bulb and gas cooker to the sun.

All energy appears to have come ultimately from the sun, giving us some idea of the importance of the sun to life on earth. One possible exception to this rule that all energy comes ultimately from the sun is atomic energy, which is obtained by disrupting the nuclei of atoms (nuclear reactions). However, increasing knowledge about the origin of the earth and its elements indicates that even this energy may have its origin in the sun or at least a 'sun'.

15.6. Food-chains: the interdependence of living organisms

Living organisms are linked together by their need for food and energy. We have already learnt that it is only the green plants which are able to harness the sun's energy and convert it into the chemical energy in carbohydrates. These are the producers. All other organisms, the animals and the fungi, are consumers and ultimately depend upon the producers for their food and energy requirements. Only first-order consumers feed directly on the producers, as is shown in the simple food-chain in Table 15.2 below.

TABLE 15.2. A SIMPLE FOOD-CHAIN

Hawks — Fourth-order consumer
↑
Tits — Third-order consumer
↑
Ladybirds — Second-order consumer
↑
Aphids — First-order consumer
↑
Lime tree — Producer

If you examine the undersurface of a leaf from a lime tree in summer, you will probably see a large number of greenish-white insects. These are aphids feeding on the sap in the leaves. You may also find ladybirds on the lime tree; they are probably feeding on the aphids. There are not nearly as many ladybirds as there are aphids, as each ladybird obviously eats many aphids every day. Each tit eats many ladybirds every day, so there will be more ladybirds than tits. Birds of prey, like the hawk, eat several small birds every day and the hunting territory of a single hawk may extend over several square kilometres in which a large number of lime trees may grow. Large numbers of small first-order consumers are necessary to support a single large fourth-order consumer.

In a pond or freshwater aquarium, the producers at the beginning of a food-chain are the bacteria and minute unicellular algae called **infusoria**, which are present in colossal numbers. Feeding on these bacteria and algae are filter-feeding crustaceans, the daphnia or 'water-flea', Daphnia is, of course, the first-order consumer which is present in considerable numbers, but not nearly in such large numbers as the bacteria and algae. Feeding on the crustaceans in the pond or tank are one or two sticklebacks, the second-order consumers.

Thus, there is a definite quantitative relationship between the stages of a food-chain, reflecting the food and energy requirements of the stages. This can be expressed as a **pyramid of numbers**, with the large numbers of producers at the base of the pyramid and the small numbers of large consumers at the apex of the pyramid (see Figure 15.6).

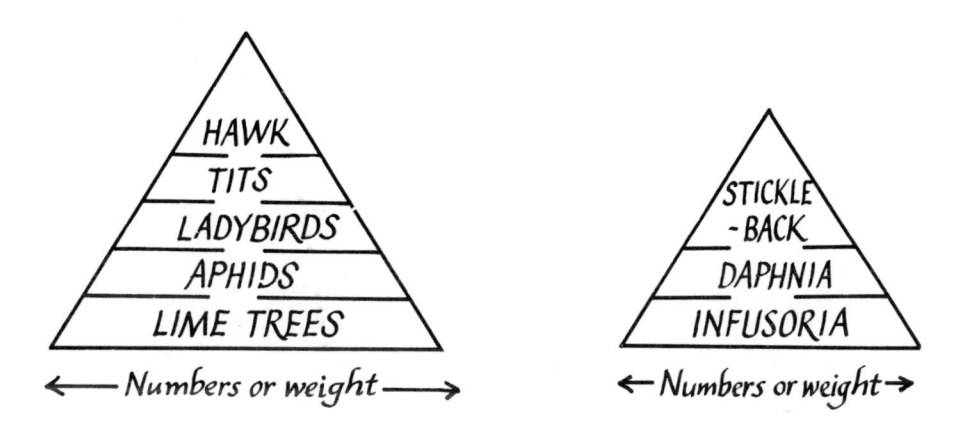

Figure 15.6 Two pyramids of numbers illustrating the food-chains mentioned in the text

15.7. Food-webs

What we have said is an over-simplification. Tits are not the only creatures that feed on ladybirds, nor do ladybirds comprise the sole diet of tits. Some birds may feed directly on the aphids, and the sparrowhawk will feed on any small bird or mammal that it can capture. Water-boatmen may feed on daphnia. The feeding and energy relationships of a community are better expressed as a **food-web** which may show some of these variations. The food-web shown below in Figure 15.7 is still very simplified.

Figure 15.7 A food-web

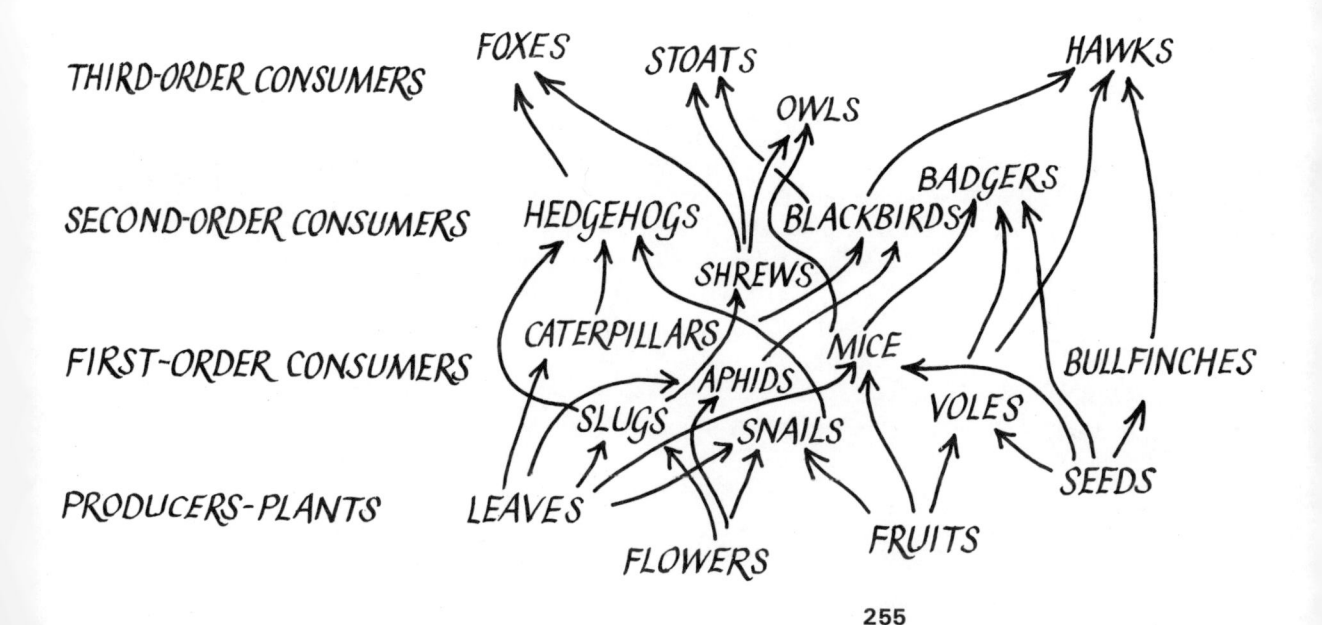

15.8. The balance of nature

Let us suppose that a population of deer is increasing. Eventually the plants on which the deer feed will become scarce. This means that some deer will emigrate from the area in search of food. Those which remain may be undernourished, and will more easily be caught by the second-order consumers that feed on them, or will fail to rear their young successfully. Thus, emigration (migration *out* of the area), increased death rate and reduced birth rate all tend to check the rise in the population. This eventually leads to a reduction in the population. As the population declines, fewer plants are eaten so the plants flourish, enabling the remaining deer to become well fed and able to evade their predators and to produce large numbers of healthy young. The second-order consumers by this time may have turned to other food. The abundant food supply attracts deer from other areas (immigration) and thus the population increases again.

Living organisms do not exist as isolated individuals but as breeding populations. The size or density of a population may increase or decrease from time to time. This size is determined by the following factors: birth rate, death rate, immigration and emigration. These will in turn depend upon environmental factors, the most important being food supply, shelter and conditions for breeding.

Test your understanding

1. Which six elements are most important to living organisms?
2. How would you show that both plants and animals contain carbon?
3. Mention four activities carried out by bacteria in the soil.
4. Explain why thunderstorms may make soil more fertile.
5. Explain what is meant by 'symbiosis'.
6. Mention three ways in which atmospheric nitrogen can be converted into nitrates.
7. Explain how the energy from your electric fire could be said to have come from the sun.
8. Write out a simple food-chain that might occur in your garden. Explain the role of each member.
9. Explain what is represented by a 'pyramid of numbers'.
10. Mention four factors which influence population density.

Chapter 16

Soil

In Chapter 8 we learnt that the simplest plants, the algae, live in water or in damp situations. More advanced plants such as the water-lily and duckweed also live in water. However, the vast majority of plant types inhabit the land and rely for their existence on the soil which covers it. Where there is little or no soil, as on rock faces, only the simplest plants such as lichens can live.

In this chapter we shall try to discover what soil is like, and why it is so important to plant life.

16.1. The meaning of soil

Investigation 16a. Examination of a soil profile

With a garden spade, dig a hole in the ground about one metre deep, preferably in a situation which has not recently been disturbed. Alternatively, if there is a nearby quarry or road cutting, you may visit this, and so avoid the necessity of digging.

Examine the sides of the hole or cutting. Do you notice that there are layers, or **strata**? In what respects do the strata differ from each other? How far down do plant roots extend? Measure the depth of each layer and draw a simple plan of the soil profile, indicating colour, texture and depth. Finally, remove a small sample of the material from each layer, to be studied in greater detail in the laboratory.

This investigation shows us that the plant roots are confined to the upper strata, this region being referred to as the **true soil**. True soil is usually darker than the coarse **subsoil** which lies below it, though the subsoil may be composed of layers varying in colour from pale grey, through brown, to almost black. If you have been fortunate enough to visit a quarry, you will have seen that lower down the subsoil gives way to rock, the upper layer of which is cracked (see Figure 16.1). What does this suggest about the way in which soil is formed?

16.2. The composition of soil

Our examination of the soil profile has shown us that as we pass deeper into the earth the components of the layers become larger

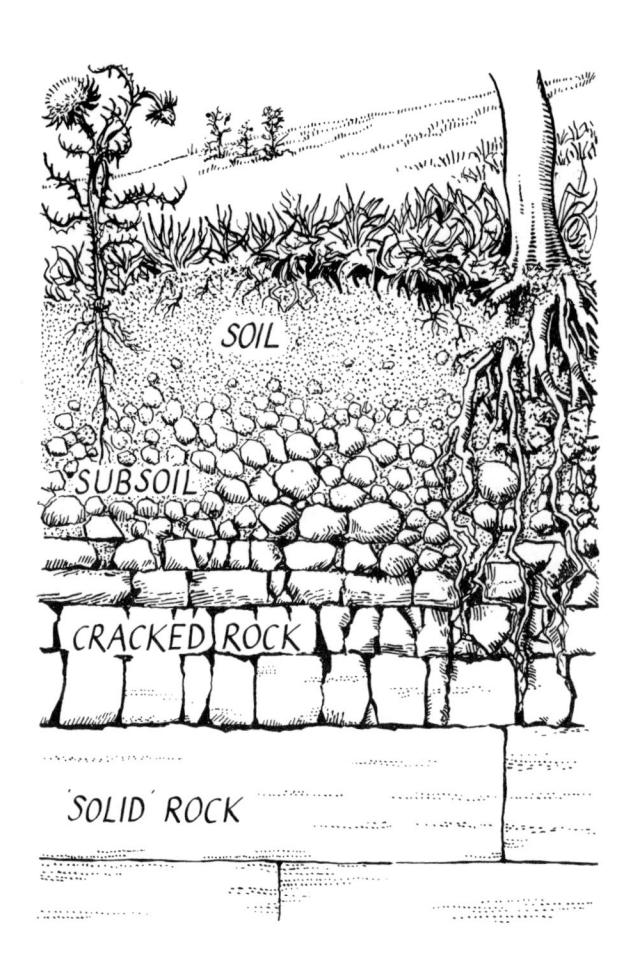

Figure 16.1 A soil profile

until, eventually, we reach solid rock. From this, we might expect that the particles forming the true soil would also vary in size, and would be smaller than those of the subsoil. We may now perform a simple investigation to see if this is so.

Investigation 16b. Separating true soil into its components

For this investigation it is best if each member of the class brings a small quantity of garden soil from his or her own garden (two or three tablespoonfuls will be sufficient).

Pour water into a measuring cylinder, gas jar, or other tall jar, until it is about two thirds full. Add some soil to the water. As it sinks, what do you observe escaping from it? Continue adding soil until you have 30–40 mm at the bottom of the jar. Now place a greased cover over the jar and invert it several times, in order to mix the soil and water thoroughly. Allow the soil to settle, observing closely what is happening in the jar (see Figure 16.2).

How do the particles at the bottom of the jar differ from those just above? What factor is causing the particles to separate into layers?

Have all of the particles settled, or are some still settling? Leave the jar for five minutes and see if the soil water becomes clear. What does this suggest about some of the particles? What is left at the surface of the water, amongst the froth of air bubbles?

Now measure the depths of the various layers in your jar and calculate what fraction of the soil is occupied by each. Compare your results with those of other members of the class who have used different soils. What conclusion can you draw regarding soils from different areas?

Investigation 16c. Soil under the microscope

The last investigation showed that soil particles vary in size, the smallest being invisible to the naked eye and being small enough to remain in suspension in the water. Moreover, the investigation showed that the relative proportions of the various particles vary from one soil to another. Thus one soil may have more fine and less coarse particles than another. Finally, the investigation showed the presence of air and rotting matter (humus) in soil.

That soil is composed of particles of varying size may also be

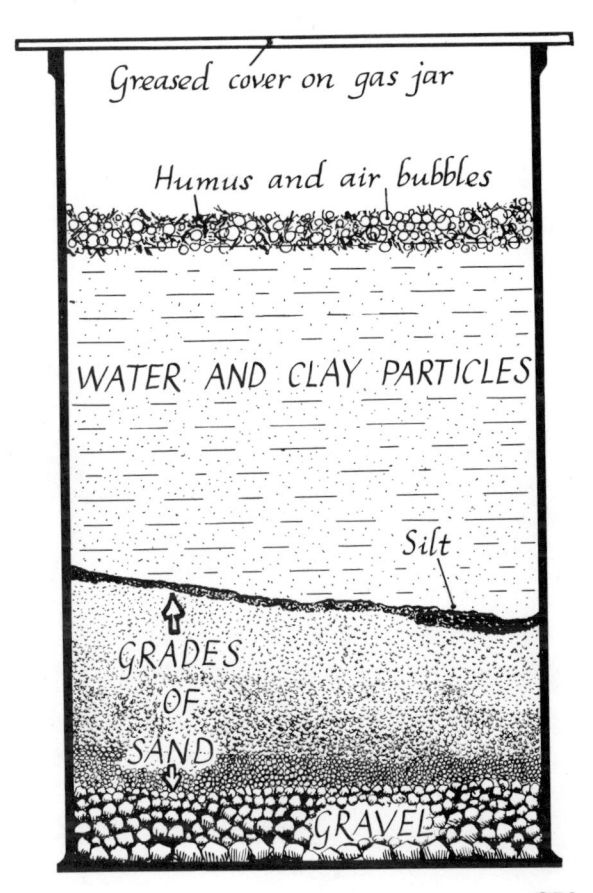

Figure 16.2 Shaking soil with water

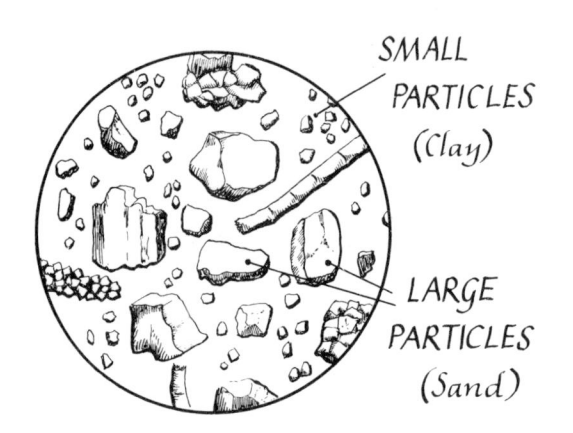

Figure 16.3 Soil under the microscope

shown with the aid of a microscope (see Figure 16.3). Sprinkle a pinch of dry soil on to a watchglass or microscope slide and examine under the low power of the microscope (*do not use the high-power lens, which may easily be scratched by the sharp soil particles*). It is best if the microscope lamp is shone down on to the soil so that the particles are seen by reflected light.

A rough estimation of the size of the soil particles may be made in the following way:

1. Select a particle of a particular size and estimate how many such particles would be needed to stretch across the field of view, if placed in a row. Record this number.
2. Replace the slide or watchglass with a transparent ruler and focus on the millimetre markings. The microscope mirror should be used so that the light is shone through the ruler (transmitted light). Adjust the ruler so that you are able to measure the width of the field as you look down the microscope. Record the width of the field.
3. Calculate the size of one particle thus:

$$\text{Size of one particle} = \frac{\text{Width of field in millimetres}}{\text{Number of particles across field}}$$

Note: It is more convenient to quote the size of the smaller particles in micrometres (microns), where

$$1 \text{ micrometre } (\mu m) = \frac{1}{1\,000} \text{ mm}$$

Of course, the soil particles vary continuously in size, but, for convenience, the following division may be made:

PARTICLE	DIAMETER
Gravel	above 2 mm
Coarse sand	2 mm–200μm
Fine sand	200 μm–20 μm
Silt	20 μm–2 μm
Clay	below 2 μm

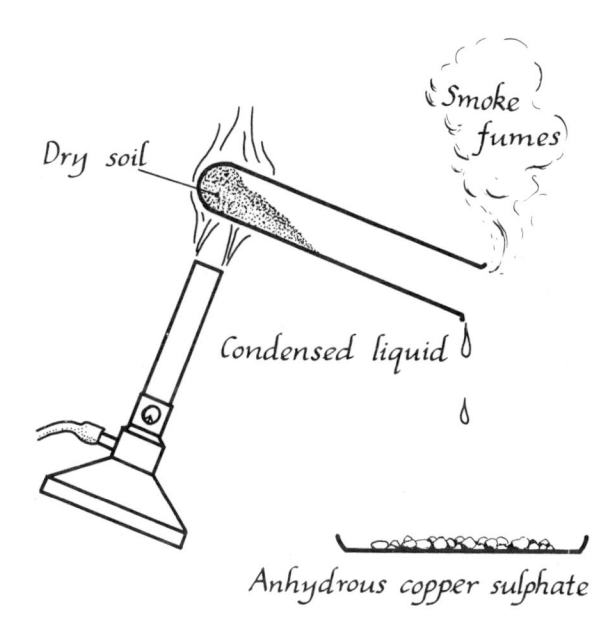

Figure 16.4 The effect of heat on soil

Apart from their difference in size, soil particles also differ in chemical composition. The most common constituent is silica, and various silicates.

Investigation 16d. The effect of heat on soil

Place in a hard glass tube some soil which has been dried by exposure to the air. Heat, very gently, with a bunsen burner (see Figure 16.4). What do you notice collecting at the cooler end of the tube? Allow a little of this liquid to fall on to some white, anhydrous copper sulphate. Does the powder change colour? What does this show? Continue heating the soil—more stongly now. What do the fumes smell of? Think what must be burning to give off these fumes. When fumes cease to be produced, examine the cooled residue from the tube. What part of the soil is left?

Investigation 16e. Testing soil for the presence of salts

Place a small quantity of garden soil in a beaker and just cover it with distilled water. Stir thoroughly, and then filter the dirty water (see Figure 16.5). The resulting filtrate should be clear. Pour 5 to 10 cm^3 of this filtrate into a clean evaporating basin and evaporate to dryness (to avoid 'spitting' remove the bunsen just before dryness is reached). Allow the basin to cool and then examine the inner surface carefully. What do you notice? Scrape the surface with a spatula. Has any residue been left by the soil water? Is there much of this residue? Can it be re-dissolved in water? Why did we use distilled water in this investigation?

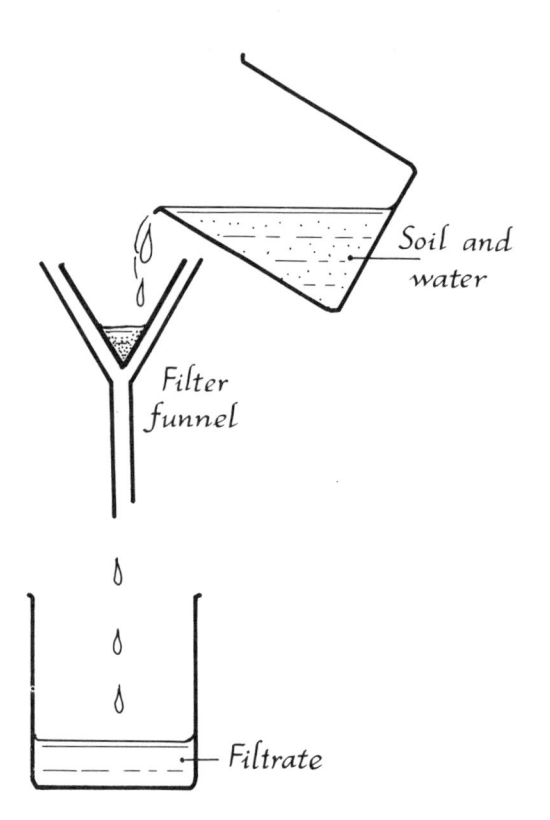

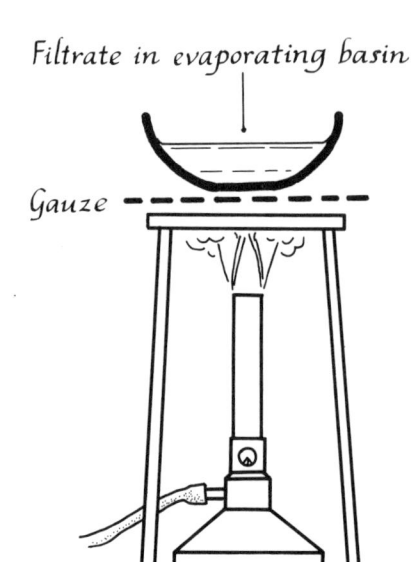

Figure 16.5 Testing soil water for mineral salts

Investigation 16f. Testing soil with limewater

Divide 50 cm³ of garden soil into two equal portions. Heat one portion strongly for a few minutes, in a hard glass tube or on a tin tray. Allow the soil to cool and then enclose it in a muslin bag. Place the unheated soil in a similar bag. Suspend each bag in a flask containing a little freshly made limewater (see Figure 16.6). Cork the flasks, allow to stand, and note any change in the limewater. How do you account for the difference between the two flasks? What was the purpose of the unheated soil?

Summary of results of Investigations 16d, 16e and 16f

Investigation 16d has shown us that:
a. Air-dried soil still contains some water.
b. Soil contains rotting animal and vegetable matter (humus).
c. When all the water and humus have been removed from the soil by heating, the mineral (rock) particles are left. The pale colour of the residue indicates that the dark colour of the original soil must have been due to the humus content.

Investigation 16e indicates that soil water contains small quantities of soluble mineral salts.

Figure 16.6 Testing soil with limewater

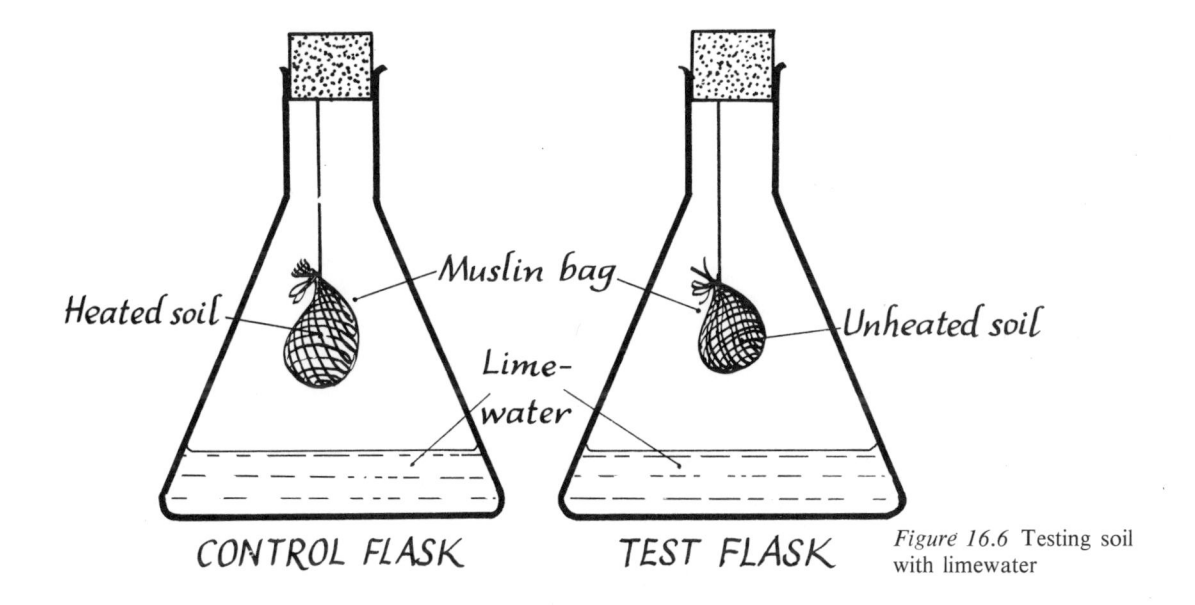

Investigation 16f shows the presence in soil of living organisms. These give out carbon dioxide which turns limewater cloudy.

We may now list the components of garden soil as shown by our investigations:
1. Mineral, or rock, particles of varying size.
2. Humus, or rotting animal and vegetable matter.
3. Air.
4. Water.
5. Mineral salts, dissolved in the soil water.
6. Living organisms.

16.3. Soil analysis

If one soil is to be compared with another, it is necessary to discover not only what components are present but in what quantity. The following investigations give simple methods of soil analysis.

Investigation 16g. Measuring water content

Weigh a clean, dry crucible and record the mass. Place a known mass (approximately 10 g) of soil into the crucible and then heat it gently with a bunsen burner, supporting the crucible on a pipeclay triangle and tripod. Stir the soil continually. The heat must be sufficient to evaporate the soil water, but not to burn the humus. Alternatively, the crucible may be heated in an oven at 105 °C. After warming, allow the soil to cool in a desiccator and then re-weigh the crucible and soil. Why is the soil cooled in a desiccator? Repeat the warming and cooling until two successive weighings are the same, when it may be taken that all the water has been driven off. Record the results in this manner:

$$\text{Mass of crucible} = a$$
$$\text{Initial mass of crucible and soil} = b$$
$$\text{Final mass of crucible and soil} = c$$
$$\text{Mass of water} = b - c$$
$$\text{Percentage of water content} = \frac{b-c}{b-a} \times \frac{100}{1}$$

Investigation 16h. Measuring the humus content

Return the crucible and dry soil, from Investigation 16g, to the pipeclay triangle and heat strongly so as to burn off all of the humus. Stir continuously. Cool and re-weigh at five-minute intervals, until two successive weighings are the same. Calculate the percentage of humus content in the same way as you calculated the water content.

Investigation 16i. Measuring the air content

For this investigation you will need a container, such as a copper calorimeter, of 100–150 cm^3 capacity. If the exact volume is not known, it should be found by using a measuring cylinder. Pour a quantity of water into the measuring cylinder and note the level. Then find how much of this water has to be poured into the calorimeter to fill it completely.

Pack soil into the dry calorimeter until it is quite full. Now tip the soil into 150 cm^3 of water in a measuring cylinder and shake well. Note the final volume of the combined soil and water (see Figure 16.7)

Calculate the air content of the soil as follows:

$$\text{Volume of soil} = x \text{ cm}^3$$
$$\text{Volume of water} = y \text{ cm}^3$$
$$\text{Total volume of soil} + \text{water} = x + y \text{ cm}^3$$
$$\text{Actual volume of soil} + \text{water} = z \text{ cm}^3$$
$$\text{Air content of soil} = (x+y) - z \text{ cm}^3$$
$$\text{Percentage of air content} = \frac{(x+y)-z}{x} \times \frac{100}{1}$$

In this investigation we have measured the air content of soil by discovering the volume of water required to fill the same spaces as were previously occupied by air.

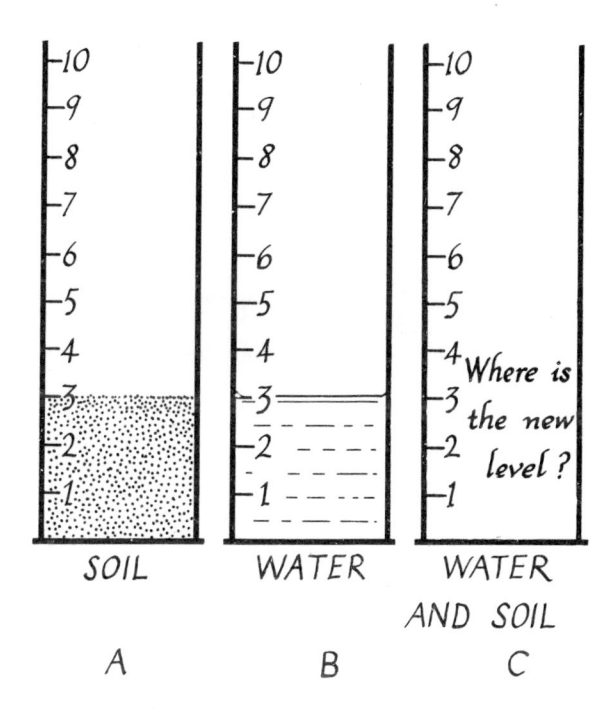

Figure 16.7 Finding the amount of air space in soil (the numbers have been simplified)

Investigation 16j. Mechanical analysis of soil

To discover the relative proportion of the various sizes of particle, a set of graded sieves must be used. Place 100 g of dry soil in the top (coarsest) sieve and shake for five to ten minutes. Collect the fractions from each sieve and weigh them separately, thus discovering the percentage content.

16.4. Types of soil and their properties

We have learnt earlier in this chapter that the larger particles in soil are called sand, whilst the smallest particles are clay. Moreover, soils vary in the proportion of each type of particle present. Soils with a greater proportion of sand particles are said to be **sandy soils,** whilst those in which clay particles predominate are said to be **clay soils.** Normal soils do not contain only one type of particle, but form a natural series from extreme sandy soils (as in deserts) to extreme clay soils (as in the clay used for pottery). A **loamy soil** is one which contains approximately equal proportions of sand and clay.

Which type of soil will be best for the gardener or farmer? The following investigations will help us to answer this question, by comparing some of the properties of sandy and clay soils.

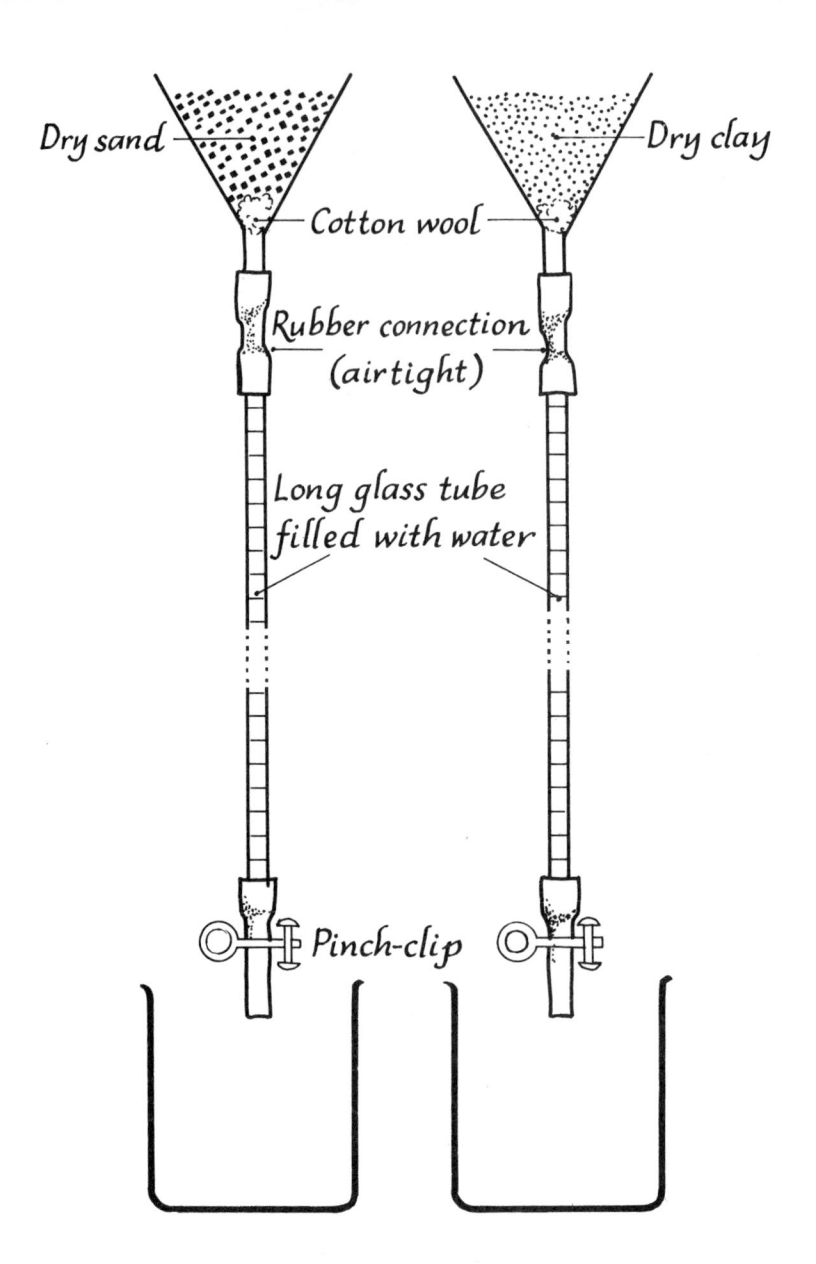

Figure 16.8 Comparing the porosity of sand and clay

Investigation 16k. Comparing porosity

The porosity of a soil is the degree to which it allows air and water to pass between its soil particles.

Fill a large funnel with dry sand and a similar funnel with an equal volume of dry clay. Retain the soils in the funnels with loose plugs of cotton wool. By means of rubber tubing, attach to each funnel a piece of glass tubing, 1–1½ metres long (see Figure 16.8). The tubes should be completely filled with water, retained by a pinch-clip.

Release the pinch-clips and record the time taken for the water to leave the tubes. Can you see why this is a measure of the porosity of the soils? Which type of soil is more porous to air? What result would you expect if loamy soil was used?

Investigation 16l. Comparing drainage

Lightly plug two similar funnels with cotton wool. Into one put some dry sand and into the other put an equal quantity of dry clay. Stand each funnel over a measuring cylinder (see Figure 16.9). Pour equal quantities of water on to each soil, and note (a) the time taken

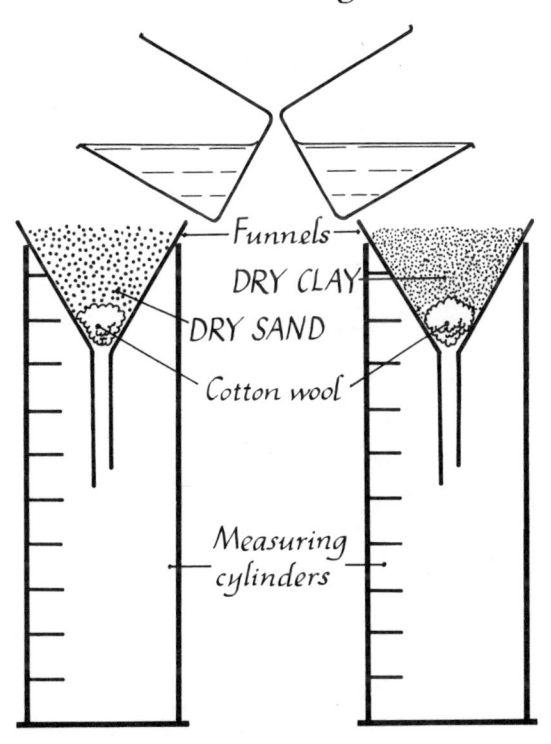

Figure 16.9 Comparing the drainage of sand and clay

for water to pass through, and (b) the volume of water draining through. Which type of soil allows the better drainage?

Investigation 16m. Comparing capillary rise

Select two equal lengths of glass tubing approximately 30 × 300 mm. Close one end of the tubes with muslin and then pack one tube with dry sand and the other with dry clay. Support the tubes with the closed end immersed in water to a depth of about 30 mm (see Figure 16.10). At intervals, mark the level to which water has risen in each tube. In which tube does water rise faster? In which tube does water reach the greater height?

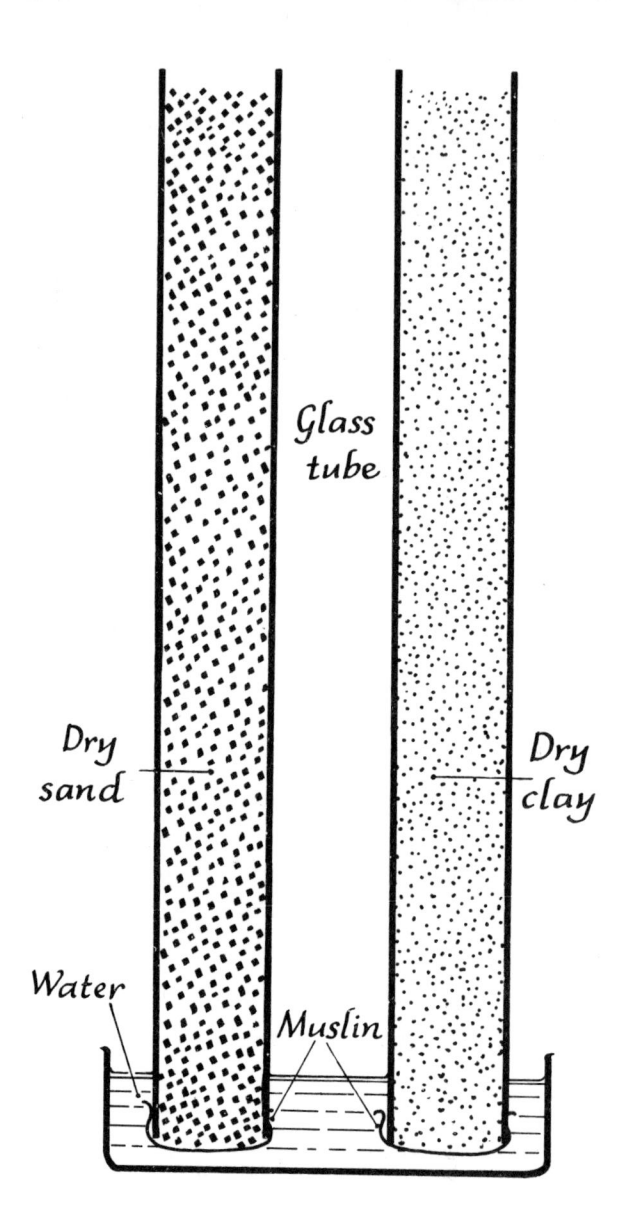

Figure 16.10 Comparing the rise of water, by capillarity, through sand and clay

Investigation 16n. Comparing masses

Weigh a dry container, such as a copper calorimeter, and re-weigh it when completely filled with oven-dry sandy soil. Empty out the sand, re-fill the container with oven-dry clay, and weigh again. Which type of soil has the greater mass? Why do you think that clay soils are said to be 'heavy'?

Investigation 16o. Comparing heat retention

Into a copper calorimeter pack some sandy soil and, into another calorimeter, an equal volume of clay. Insert a thermometer into each, so that the bulbs are central in the soil. (In order to prevent the thermometer bulbs from being damaged, it is best to bore pathways in the soils with a pencil or other implement.)

Place the calorimeters in a water-bath and raise the water temperature, taking readings of the soil thermometers at regular intervals. Which soil warms up most rapidly?

Finally, remove the calorimeters from the bath and notice the rate at which the soils cool. Which is the better retainer of heat?

Summary of results of Investigations 16k to 16o

Investigation 16k showed that sandy soil is more porous than clay. This is due to the fact that the smaller clay particles pack more tightly together and, therefore, have less air space. This also explains why, in *Investigation 16l*, it was found that water drained more readily through the sandy soil.

In *Investigation 16m* the rise of water was due to capillarity, the natural tendency for liquids to rise up tubes. The extent of the rise depends on the diameter of the tube, the rise increasing as the diameter decreases. Thus it was found that, although there was a rapid initial rise in the tube containing sand, the greater rise occurred in the clay, where the channels between the soil particles are narrower.

Investigation 16n showed that the density of clay is less than that of sand. Clay is said to be a heavy soil because it retains more that clay warms up more slowly, but retains heat longer than sand.

The rapid drainage of sandy soils is a disadvantage in that valuable mineral salts become washed out by the water percolating through. This is referred to as **leaching**, and accounts for the relative infertility of sandy soils. Sandy soils are, however, lighter and easier to work than clay soils.

TABLE 16.1. COMPARISON OF SANDY AND CLAY SOILS

Sandy Soils	Clay Soils
1. Composed mostly of large particles with large air spaces between.	1. Composed mostly of small particles with small air spaces between.
2. Drain well, but retain little water.	2. Drain badly, but hold water well.
3. Poor capillary rise.	3. Good capillary rise.
4. Warm rapidly, but cool quickly.	4. Warm slowly, but retain warmth.
5. Light soils, which are easy to work and crumble on drying.	5. Heavy, sticky soils, which are hard to work and tend to crack on drying.
6. Lose salts by leaching, hence lack fertility.	6. Hold valuable salts, hence grow good crops.

It is evident that neither a sandy nor a clay soil is satisfactory for the gardener. A loamy soil, that is a mixture of sand and clay, is preferable.

16.5. Soil and plant life

There are many factors which control the type of vegetation which grows in a particular area, but one of the most important is the nature of the soil. Thus, from our work in the last section, it follows that plants living in sandy soil must be able to tolerate dry conditions, with a shortage of mineral salts. An important controlling factor that has not been mentioned is the **soil acidity**, or pH. This depends on the amount of bases, such as calcium carbonate (limestone or chalk), present. Neutral soils have a pH of 7; those with a pH above 7 are alkaline those with a pH below 7 are acid. Plants which are confined to acid soils are called **calcifuges**, whilst those that require alkaline conditions are called **calcicoles**. The sandy soil of heathland is usually acid, because its bases are soon leached out. Thus heathland has a characteristic vegetation of such calcifuges as heather, gorse, bracken and rhododendron.

In gardening, therefore, it is important to realize that some crops will prefer alkaline and others acid conditions. Most crops, such as cabbages and root crops, prefer the soil to be slightly alkaline. Potatoes, on the other hand, grow better if the soil is slightly acid.

Investigation 16p. Testing soil acidity

★ WARNING. *Direct the open end of the tube away to avoid spray.*

A simple test to see if a sample of soil contains calcium carbonate is to add some dilute hydrochloric acid. If this is done in a test-tube, the amount of calcium carbonate present may be estimated by the degree of fizzing which occurs.

Alternatively, the pH of the soil may be determined by a soil test outfit. If this is not available shake a few cubic centimetres of the soil with 10 cm^3 of distilled water; allow it to settle and then add a few drops of Universal Indicator. By comparing the resulting colour with the colour standards, the approximate pH may be found.

16.6. Soil organisms

The number of different organisms in the soil is very large indeed, and it is beyond the scope of this chapter to deal with many of them. We will confine ourselves to mentioning three important groups, namely soil bacteria, soil fungi and earthworms.

A gramme of good soil may contain a billion **bacteria** of many different species. Some of these play a vital role in the decomposition of dead organic matter, and the subsequent release of substances essential for plant growth. Other, nitrogen-fixing, bacteria assist in the circulation of nitrogen (see Section 15.3). Acid conditions inhibit the growth of bacteria, which accounts for the accumulation of semi-rotted matter in peat bogs.

Soil **fungi** also play an important part in the process of decomposition, forming dense networks of threads (hyphae) among the soil particles. We are usually only conscious of their presence when some of their fruiting bodies, the mushrooms and toadstools, appear above the surface.

The burrowing activities and the feeding of **earthworms** is of great benefit to the soil, a fact that was first made clear by Charles Darwin in his famous book, *The Formation of Vegetable Mould Through the Action of Worms, with Observations on their Habits* (1881). Some detail of the way in which worms improve the soil was discussed in Section 5.3.

16.7. Soil improvement

There are many things that can be done to improve the fertility of a soil, the methods used depending on whether the soil is sandy or clay. Both types of soil are improved by the regular application of **lime** (calcium hydroxide). This neutralizes the acidity of sandy soils and improves the porosity of clay soils by causing the clay particles to **flocculate**, or aggregate in clumps.

The main problem with sandy soils is to increase the water-retaining capacity, and this is best done by the addition of abundant humus in the form of manure or compost. Before the winter, it is best to dig the clay soil and leave the frost of winter to break down the large clods of compacted soil.

Fertilizers

The best fertilizers are **natural**; in other words, they come from organic matter. Animal manure is becoming increasingly scarce and is being replaced by vegetable manures, such as hop manure and compost. Sewage sludge, dried and powered, is also widely used. The beneficial substances in natural manures have to be released by bacteria and fungi. As this takes time, these fertilizers are slow acting and should be applied in the autumn.

Artificial fertilizers are faster acting, but are more rapidly leached out of the soil. They should, therefore, be applied in the spring. Some of the more common chemical fertilizers are listed in Table 16.2.

TABLE 16.2. SOME FERTILIZERS AND THEIR USES

Essential Ion	Essential For	Good Sources
Nitrate	Healthy green growth	Sulphate of ammonia, nitrate of soda
Phosphate	Healthy root growth	'Superphosphate' (a mixture of calcium sulphate and calcium phosphate), bone meal
Potash	Fruit and vegetable formation	Wood ash, sulphate of potash, nitrate of potash (a dual fertilizer)

Test your understanding

1. What is meant by (a) a sandy soil, (b) a clay soil and (c) a loamy soil?
2. Give reasons why a loamy soil is preferable to either a sandy or clay soil.
3. What physical feature accounts for most of the differences between sand and clay?
4. Why are clay soils said to be 'heavy'?
5. Why do sandy soils tend to be infertile?
6. What causes some soils to be more acid than others?
7. What is meant by (a) a calcifuge and (b) a calcicole?
8. Name the three most important groups of soil organism.
9. Distinguish between natural and artificial fertilizers and suggest the advantages and disadvantages of each type.
10. Why is lime added to (a) sandy and (b) clay soils?

Chapter 17

Communal Life

17.1. The habitat

All living organisms, both animals and plants, live in places suited to their survival. The place where an organism lives is called its **habitat**. If an organism is to live successfully, its habitat must provide three basic requirements. These are an adequate supply of suitable food, somewhere to shelter and somewhere suitable to breed.

Investigation 17a. Setting up a habitat

Select an area of soil in a fairly sheltered place and dig it over to remove any plants. In the centre, place a lump of fresh meat or the carcass of a small bird or animal. Anchor it with a skewer to prevent cats or dogs from removing it. Take several pieces of sacking, about half a metre square, and cut a hole in the centre of each about the size of the bait. Place the sacking in layers on the soil with the bait exposed through the holes. Lightly water the sacking from time to time to keep it slightly damp. It is a good idea to cover the experiment with wire netting (see Figure 17.1). A piece of wire netting 70 cm × 70 cm is easily bent into a box 50 cm × 50 cm × 10 cm high. Peg it down with U-shaped pieces of wire. Do not forget to gently loosen the soil under everything you have placed on the ground. Inspect the piece of meat, the layers of sacking and the ground beneath every two days, and carefully record all the changes that occur.

If you use a lump rather than a slice of meat, it will not dry out so quickly. Why is this important? Note the changes that the meat undergoes. Its smell will become more noticeable and it will become darker and slimy.

Record the exact whereabouts of any animals that occur. Look under the meat as well as on its surface. Look carefully between and beneath the layers of sacking. Loosen and examine the upper layers of soil. If the meat disappears, look beneath the soil as it may have been buried. If so, look for any animals on or near it. Examine a little of the meat in the laboratory.

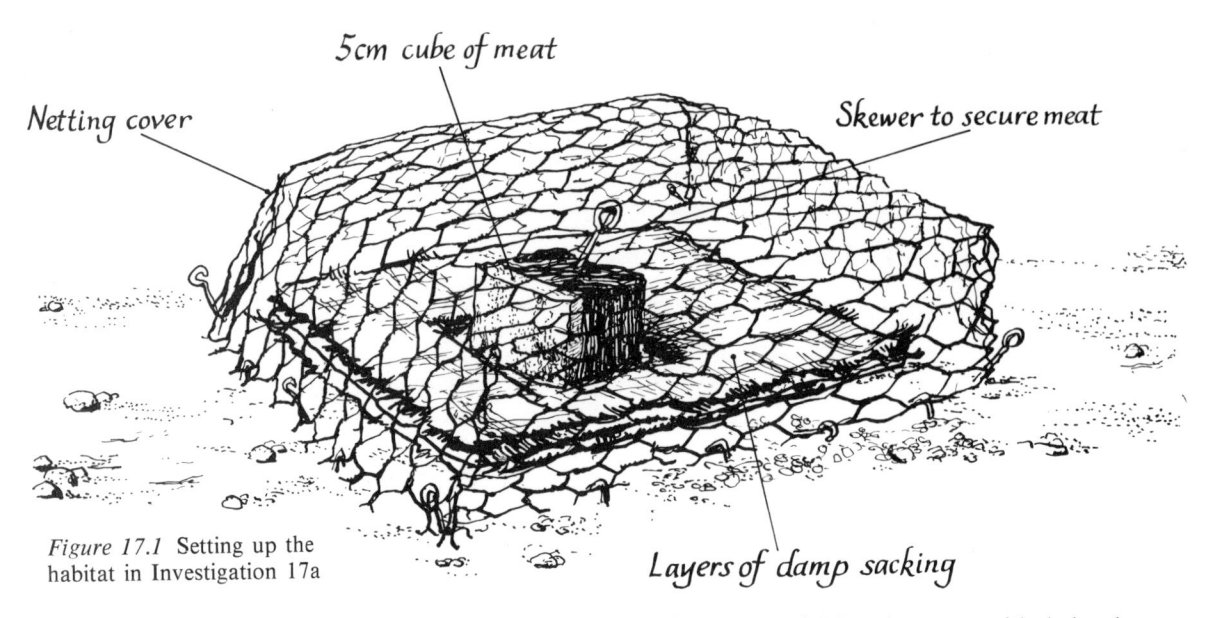

Figure 17.1 Setting up the habitat in Investigation 17a

Labels on figure: Netting cover; 5cm cube of meat; Skewer to secure meat; Layers of damp sacking

What has the investigation shown? You have provided the three basic requirements of a habitat: food, shelter and somewhere to breed. Try to sum up how each organism you found was attracted to your experiment, why it went there and what the meat and the sacking offered that particular organism.

17.2. Communities

Organisms do not live as isolated individuals, but in breeding populations. Populations of organisms usually occupy a characteristic type of habitat; for example, a population of wood-mice will live in the undergrowth of a wood, a population of cockles will live in a muddy beach, a population of winkles will be found on a rocky shore and a population of milk-souring bacteria will live in milk.

A habitat is normally occupied by several populations, which together often form a recognizable entity. Such a characteristic grouping of organisms, which almost always live together in a particular type of habitat, form a **community**. A wood is a good example of a community. A wood does not consist merely of a group of trees. A wood is made up of trees and shrubs; herbs and bryophytes (mosses and liverworts); together with the birds living in or on the trees and shrubs; the mice and voles amongst the herbs; the woodlice, snails and centipedes in the leaf litter; the insects in the bark and the worms in the soil. In most cases, the animals and plants will be typical woodland species which are suited to or adapted to the conditions in the woodland habitat. You would be unlikely to find a wood-mouse in your pantry, or a jay on a salt-marsh, or a banded snail on the sea-shore.

Can you think of any other communities? You have probably

often referred to them without thinking of them as communities. They include a pond or lake, a stream, a hedge, a meadow, a fen and a bog, a heath, a chalk pit, a muddy beach, a rocky shore, mountains and moorlands.

Sometimes one particular population of organisms gives the whole community its characteristic feature; for example, a wood which consists mainly of oak trees is called an oak wood and is very different from a beech wood. The organism that gives such a community its characteristic feature is said to be **dominant**. Obviously, the dominant organism in a birch wood is the birch tree, in the sedge fen it is the sedge, in the bilberry heath the bilberry, and so on.

17.3. Habitat factors

The distribution of animals and plants is determined by the conditions under which they live most successfully. By successfully, we mean they are able to breed efficiently enough to maintain and increase the size of the population, and to extend the geographical distribution of the population. The conditions are produced by the interaction of the climate, the geological features and the effect of other living organisms.

The **climatic** factors include rainfall, temperature, humidity, light intensity, wind speed and direction, and water availability. Some plants need a high light intensity, such as the large dominant trees in a wood, whilst others, such as dog's mercury growing within the wood, need a much lower light intensity. The marsh marigold grows in very damp situations whilst the prickly pear thrives in the dry desert.

The **geological** features include the slope of the ground, its aspect in relation to the sun, and the soil type. The soil type will depend on the nature of the parent rock. The pH of the soil, that is its acidity or alkalinity, is important, and linked with this is the presence or absence of calcium carbonate in the soil. Plants such as foxglove, tormentil and bracken are examples of plants which grow well on acid soils. Clematis, wild thyme and sainfoin thrive better on basic soils.

The effects of other living organisms, including man, on a habitat are known as the **biotic** factors. For example, sheep grazing on a pasture encourage the fine grasses and discourage the coarse ones. The seeds of any shrubs or trees which germinate in the pasture are soon cropped off by the sheep and their growth is suppressed, but if an area of the pasture is penned off so that the sheep cannot graze it, the coarser grasses soon develop, followed by the bushy shrubs and eventually the trees. Every known plant is the food for at least one animal, so the distribution of plants is affected by animals.

17.4. Field studies

In the following sections four studies are mentioned which will introduce you to the study of communities in the field. It is not possible within the scope of this single chapter to deal with more than a few examples of the methods and techniques which are suitable for a school study of communities. Other books should be referred to for more detailed information and help with identification. The communities chosen for consideration are the wood, the hedge, the meadow and the pond or stream. Exercises can be carried out on waste land, a lawn or the school field. In most schools it should be possible to study field biology without a long journey. Do not forget, if you do decide to carry out a survey or experiments on someone else's land, to get permission first.

17.5. Colonization of bare ground

If you have a piece of ground available for a period of several months, or better still, if earth moving or building operations nearby have left an area of bare soil, you can study the way in which it is colonized.

Investigation 17b. To study the colonization of bare ground

Dig an area of about a metre square thoroughly, removing all traces of seeds, plant and animal life. Fix pegs at each corner of the metre square and tie a piece of string between the pegs to mark out your square metre clearly. This is a permanent metre square or **quadrat**. Visit your quadrat at least once a fortnight and keep a diary of the changes that take place in it. Try to identify (without pulling up) the seedlings which appear. Sketch your quadrat in your notebook or on graph paper and draw in the numbers and position of plants that have become established. Every month draw the plan of your quadrat, and either show each plant by a symbol, or shade the area where the soil is completely covered by a particular plant. Do not forget to make the meaning of your symbols very clear. Also, tie a piece of string across the diagonal of your permanent quadrat and every month record the type and height of each plant touching the line at 10 cm intervals. This is called a **line transect**. Draw your transect with its fourteen points, or **stations**, on to graph paper. Show each type of plant with a different symbol, but draw the height of the symbol to scale (see Figures 17.2 to 17.5).

The first plants to appear in your quadrat will probably be short-lived, ephemeral plants, like groundsel and chickweed. They will probably be succeeded by the annuals, including knot grass, and true grasses, and then by dandelions, docks and nettles. Try to

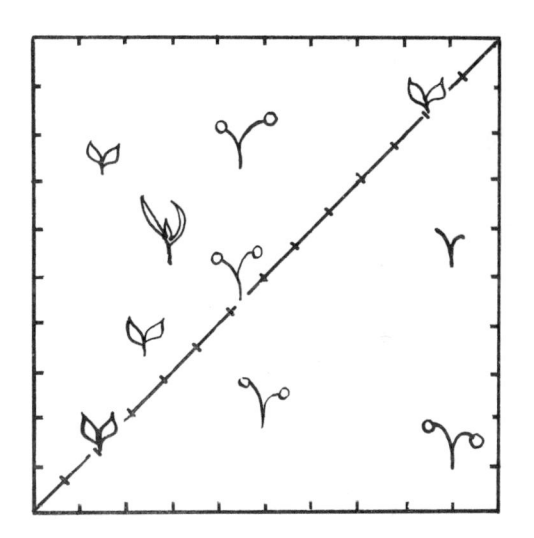

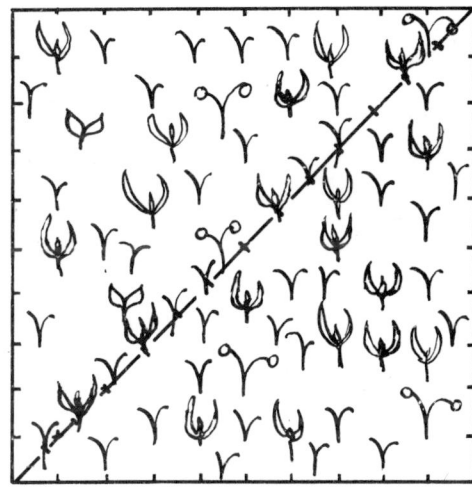

Figure 17.2 (above left) An early quadrat

Figure 17.3 (above right) The same quadrat later in the year

Figure 17.4 An early line transect (of Figure 17.2)

Figure 17.5 A line transect later in the year (of Figure 17.3)

suggest how each of the plants reached your quadrat. If you are able to study your plot for long enough, you may see brambles, or even hawthorn seedlings, beginning to appear.

The colonization of bare earth, mud, rock or water by plants, followed by the **progressive** development of increasingly complex communities, is called a **plant succession**. The final stable stage of a succession is usually woodland, and is known as the **climax community**. The reason for a succession is that each colonizer changes the nature of the habitat, making it suitable for the succeeding colonizer. A bare patch of ashes left by a bonfire or the loose earth on the bank of a new road make ideal virgin territories on which you can study the colonization of bare soil.

17.6. A woodland study

A wood is usually a stable community as it represents the final stage, or climax, of a plant succession. If possible it is best to repeat

TREE LAYER

SHRUB LAYER
FIELD LAYER
GROUND LAYER

Figure 17.6 Diagram showing the layers in a wood

a woodland study at different seasons of the year, as a wood shows an interesting **seasonal succession**. The plant distribution and the structure of the community change with the seasons. This is due partly to habitat factors which vary with the seasons. What factors do you think might vary according to the time of the year? Can you suggest reasons for such changes?

Investigation 17c. To study the structure of a woodland community

Select a wood to which you have easy access, and make a note of its map reference. Draw a sketch map of the wood from an Ordnance Survey map showing the main paths and its position in relation to the surrounding roads and fields. As you approach the wood, look at it carefully from a distance. Is it composed mainly of one type of tree? If so, what is the dominant tree? Is it an oak wood, a beech wood or a birch wood? Is no one species of tree particularly noticeable. In other words, is it a mixed wood?

Select the area of the wood you intend to study and spend some time examining the common plants and those animals you can see. Identify as many as possible.

When you feel you can recognize most of the common plants in your part of the wood, choose a line, preferably from the edge of the wood towards the centre, along which to make a transect. You should work in groups of three for this investigation. You can use a line marked at metre intervals or you can simply pace out the transect. The length of the transect and the distance between the stations at which you make observations will depend on the size and nature of your wood. In a large wood, a transect 50 metres long with a station every 5 metres should be suitable.

In a wood the plants are arranged into four horizontal layers (see Figure 17.6). The large trees with long trunks, whose leaves form the canopy of the wood, make up the highest layer, the **tree layer**, which controls the amount of light reaching the other plants in the wood. The next layer is formed by the shrubs like hazel and hawthorn, and is called the **shrub layer**. The flowers, ferns, grasses and other herbaceous plants form the **field layer**, whilst the mosses, liverworts and lichens (bryoids) form the **ground layer**, actually on the surface of the soil. The trees, shrubs, herbs and bryoids represent four life forms which you should show by different symbols on your transect (see Figure 17.7). The layering of plants in the wood is known as **stratification**.

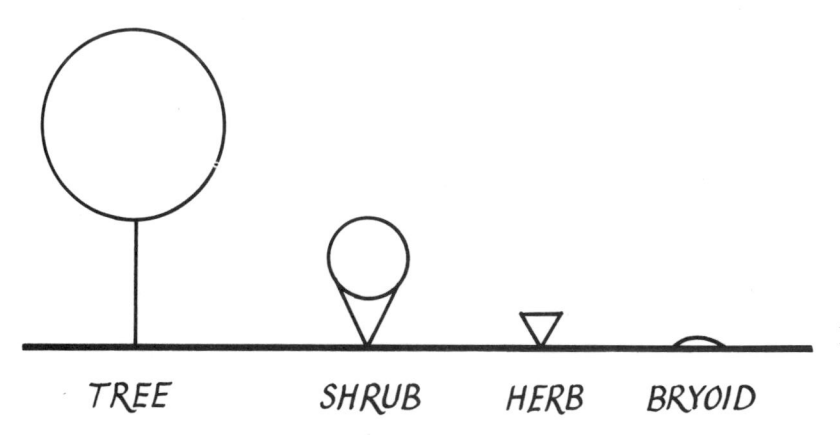

Figure 17.7 Symbols which can be used to represent the different life forms

Starting at the beginning of the transect, make a note of each plant at each station. Estimate or measure the height of the plants and also the area on either side of the trunk that is shaded by the branches of a tree. Either using diagrams or symbols, show these plants to scale on your transect. Repeat at the next station, and so on. You can estimate the height of a tree by standing someone of known height by the trunk of the tree and then standing at a distance and estimating how many times taller the tree is. (See Figure 17.8).

In the field, record your results on the chart in your notebook, which should be similar to that in Table 17.1. Then, back in the laboratory, make a careful record of the transect on graph paper,

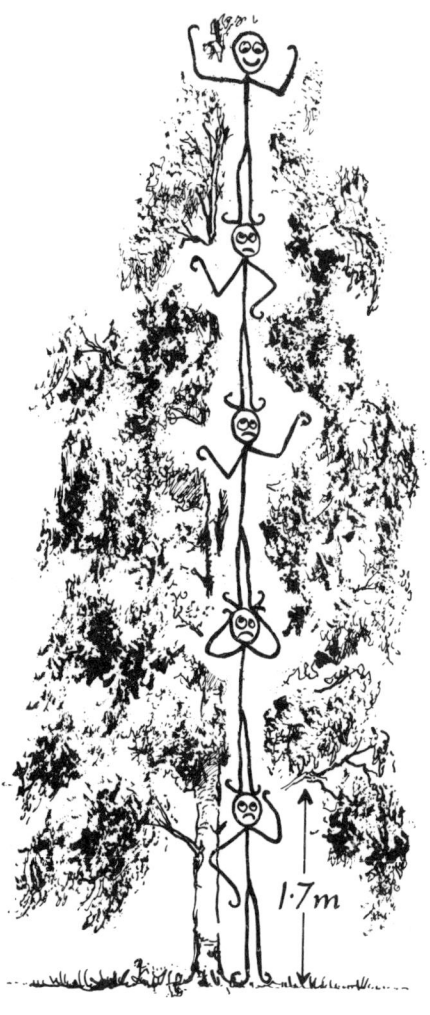

Figure 17.8 Estimating the height of a tree

$$5 \times 1.7\,m = 8.5\,m$$

using appropriate scales and symbols (see Figure 17.9). You will adapt both the recording grid and the final transect to your own particular case.

TABLE 17.1. RECORD OF THE TRANSECT DATA

Station	0	1	2	3	4	5	6	7	8
Species	Oak	Hazel	Dog's mercury	Ash	Moss				
Height	9 m	3 m	0·6 m	17 m	0·02 m				
Length of Shadow	6 m	2 m	0·2 m	8 m	—				

Figure 17.9 A line transect of the wood

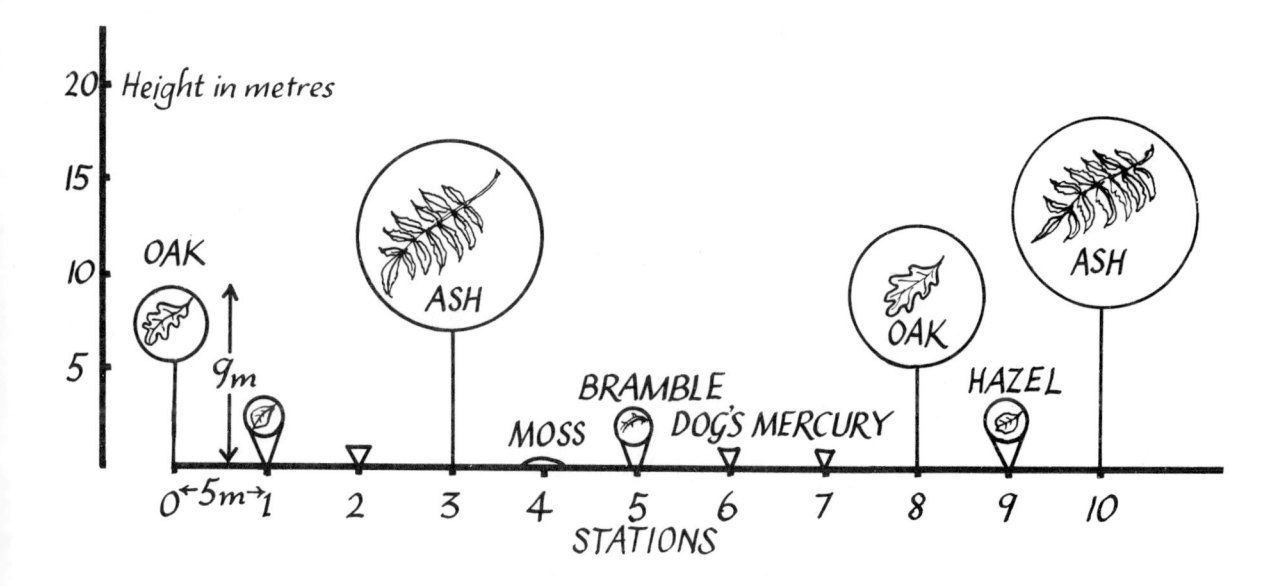

Are the same plants found on the edge of the wood as in the centre? Is the vegetation in the clearings the same as that under the trees? If possible, carry out your study in February or March, repeat it towards the end of April or May, again in late June or July and finally in October.

If possible, as part of each season's study, take a colour photograph of your particular part of the wood. At the end, compare the photographs. Do they look like the same place? What are the differences between the photographs?

As part of each study, record the temperature. If possible, leave out a maximum and minimum thermometer for a day to record the highest and lowest temperatures reached during a twenty-four hour period. Use a light meter to measure the light intensities on each occasion. These readings will almost certainly be relative ones. Simply record the figure on the meter scale at the same time of day on each occasion, both inside the wood and in the open. It would also be useful to measure these factors, together with humidity, outside the wood as well as inside. Also note the depth of leaf litter. Is it damp or dry?

Investigation 17d. To study a 5 metre square in a wood

Select an interesting part of the wood and, with stakes hammered in at the corners, mark out a square with each side 5 metres long. With a tape-measure or a piece of string marked at 0·1 metre intervals, plot the plants found in the square and indicate which plants are growing on each part, as in Figure 17.10. As with your transect, display your results on graph paper, using a suitable scale and symbols.

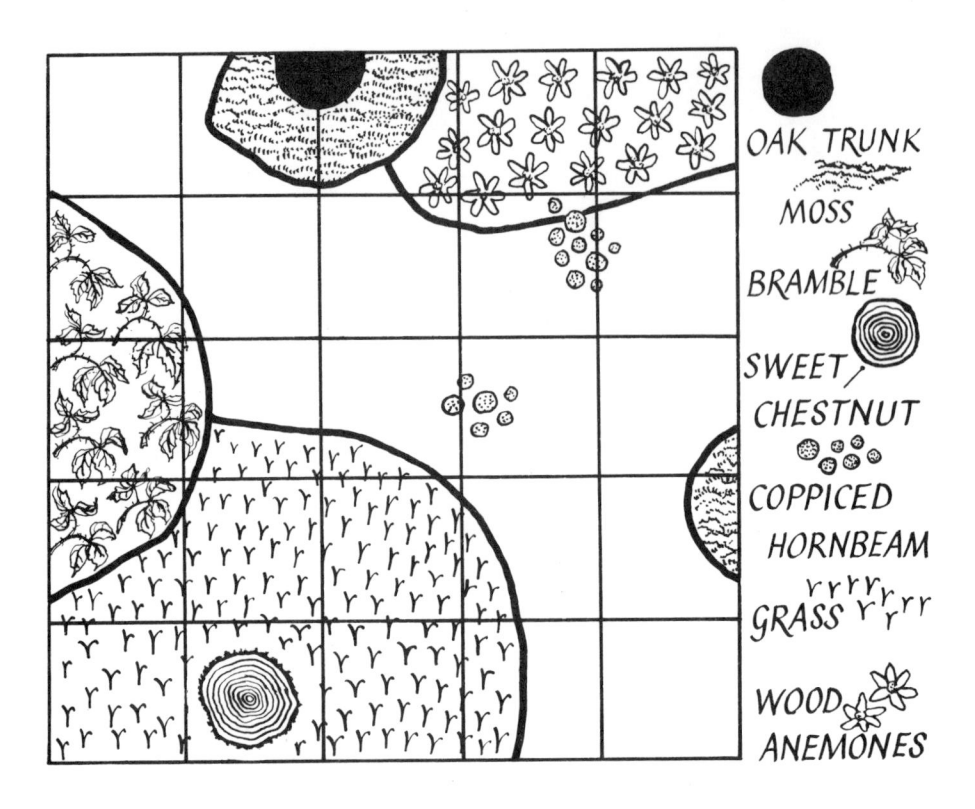

Figure 17.10 A 5 metre square recorded

In both woodland investigations, do not ignore the animal life or the evidence of it. Do not collect for collecting's sake. If you do need to take a creature back to school to identify it, try to keep it alive and *return it*, if possible, after you have finished with it. There is never need to collect more than just one or two individuals of a species. Try to decide how the habitat in which you found a creature satisfies its need for food, shelter and somewhere to breed. Look at fallen fruits to see if they have been gnawed. Look for leaves and bark that have been chewed. Watch for footprints in the soft soil, and also for the faecal pellets of animals. Examine the leaf litter around the base of trees for woodlice, centipedes, millipedes and spiders. Look out for snails, and for birds and their nests.

In both of the above investigations it is important to test the alkalinity or acidity of the soil, or in other words the pH (see Investigation 16p). It might be interesting to compare the pH in an oak wood with that in a beech wood, and if possible the pH of a bog with that of a fen.

Obviously, you can do a great deal more work on a wood, and some of the books listed at the end of the chapter will be of help to you in extending your studies or with identifying the organisms you find.

17.7. A hedgerow study

Investigation 17e. To study a hedgerow community

First of all, make sure that you can recognize most of the commoner plants and animals in the hedge you have chosen. If it is on a bank with a ditch in front of it, then it is all the more interesting.

Figure 17.11 Measuring the profile using (a) a tape-measure and (b) a 2 metre pole

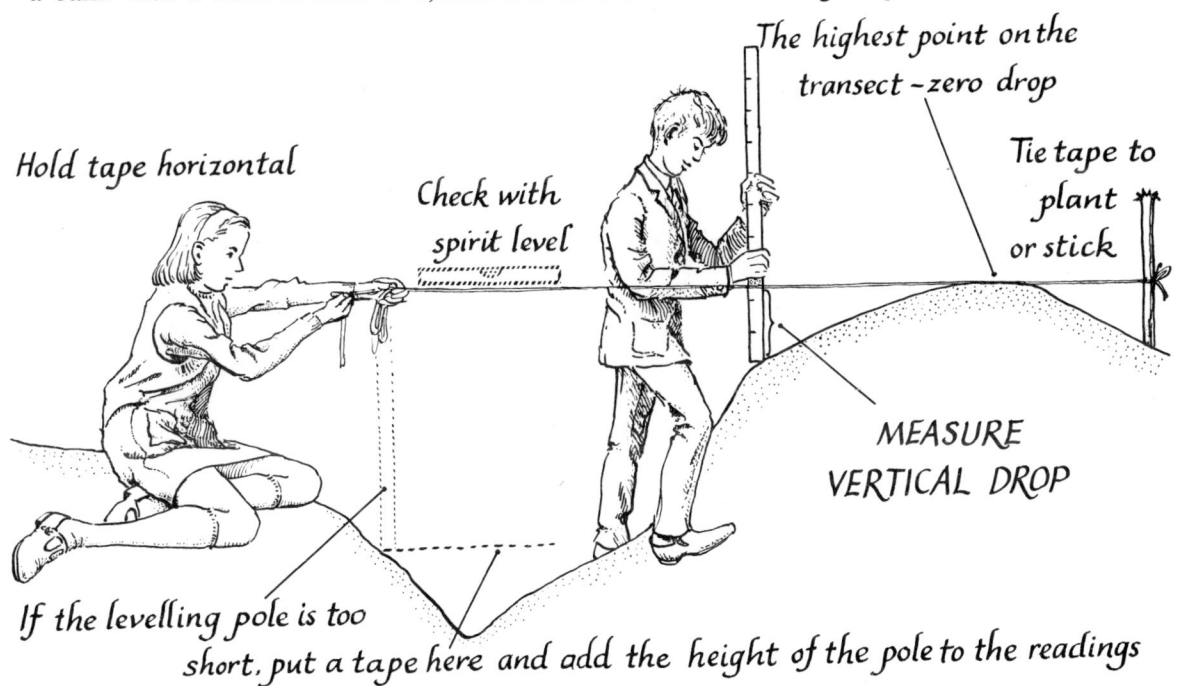

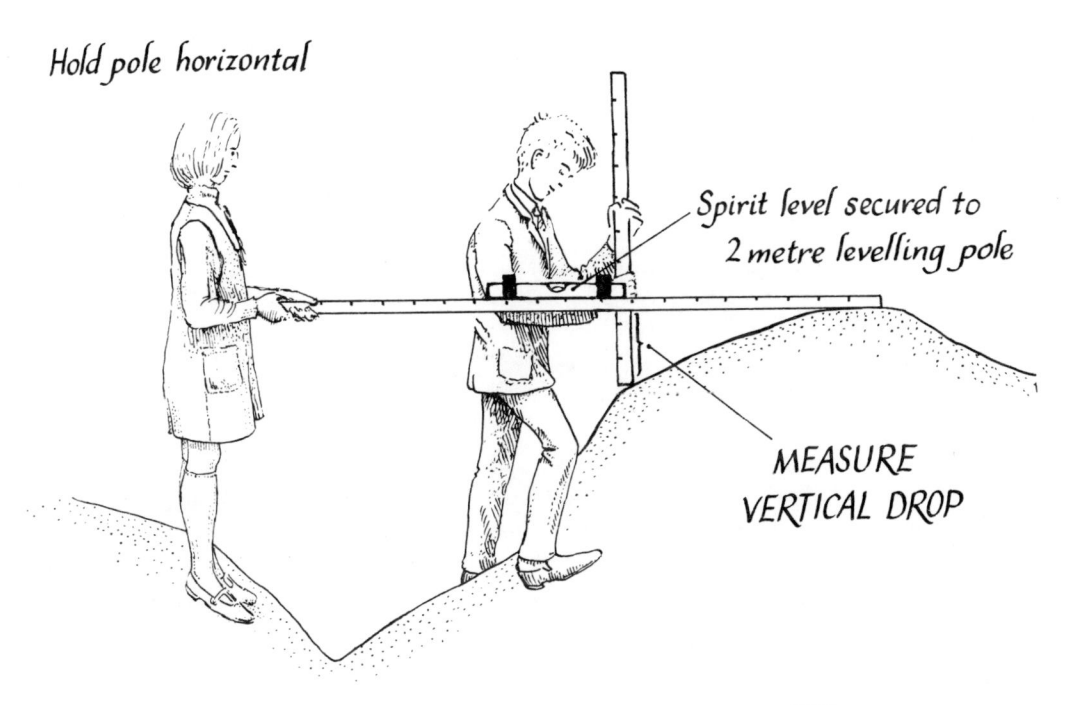

Hold tape horizontal

Check with spirit level

The highest point on the transect – zero drop

Tie tape to plant or stick

MEASURE VERTICAL DROP

If the levelling pole is too short, put a tape here and add the height of the pole to the readings

Hold pole horizontal

Spirit level secured to 2 metre levelling pole

MEASURE VERTICAL DROP

283

You will need a tape-measure *or* a line marked at 0·1 metre intervals, a levelling pole (a straight piece of wood, 1 or 2 metres long, marked at 0·1 metre intervals) and a spirit level.

Fix your line or tape firmly on the far side of the hedge, so that when the line is held horizontally it just touches the highest piece of ground in the section. Get one of the group to hold the other end of the line, making sure with a spirit level that it is horizontal (see Figure 17.11). You may find it easier to use a 2 metre levelling pole, held horizontally, instead of the line. In this case, the spirit level can be secured to the pole with elastic bands. Work on one side of the line only. Do not trample the plants on the other side. Rule up a chart similar to that in Table 17.2, and call the point at which the line is secured station 0. The vertical drop at the highest point in the section is 0, and if there is, for example, a 2 metre hazel bush at that point it should be recorded as such on the chart. Now take a levelling pole and hold it exactly vertical, with its base firmly on the ground immediately below the first 0·1 metre mark. Record the height from the bottom of the pole to the horizontal tape. Record also the height of any plant that touches the tape or is immediately below it at this point. Repeat this process every 0·1 metre, until you are out of the hedge and across the ditch. In this way you will be able to fill in the table shown in Table 17.2. Your results will enable you to draw a profile of the hedge and ditch on graph paper.

TABLE 17.2. RECORDING THE RESULTS OF THE HEDGE STUDY

Station	0	1	2	3	4	5	6	7	8
Vertical Drop									
Total Drop									
Species									
Height									

Using a suitable scale, make the horizontal axis of your profile represent the total distance reached horizontally along the line. Draw a faint horizontal line across your profile passing through the highest point. This represents your line or horizontal pole. Using the figures entered on Table 17.2, measure the vertical drop (in the appropriate scale) from the horizontal line and plot the level of the ground with a small cross at each station. When this is complete, join up the points you have plotted and you have the **profile** of the hedge and ditch. You can now rub out the faint line and plotting marks.

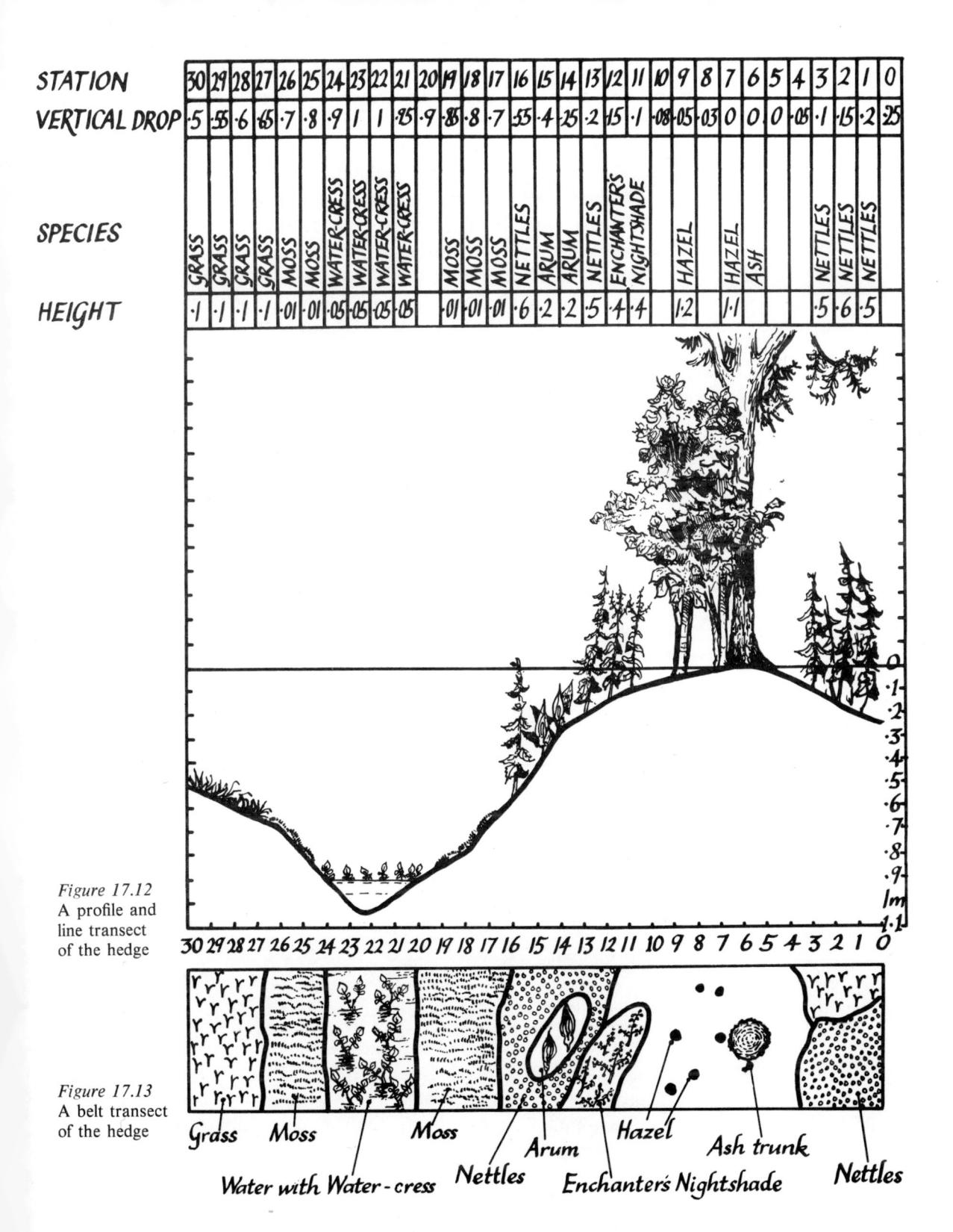

STATION	30	29	28	27	26	25	24	23	22	21	20	19	18	17	16	15	14	13	12	11	10	9	8	7	6	5	4	3	2	1	0
VERTICAL DROP	·5	·55	·6	·65	·7	·8	·9	1	1	·95	·9	·85	·8	·7	·55	·4	·25	·2	·15	·1	·08	·05	·03	0	0	0	·05	·1	·15	·2	·25
SPECIES	GRASS	GRASS	GRASS	GRASS	MOSS	MOSS	WATER-CRESS	WATER-CRESS	WATER-CRESS	WATER-CRESS	MOSS	MOSS	MOSS		NETTLES	ARUM	ARUM	NETTLES	ENCHANTER'S NIGHTSHADE		HAZEL		HAZEL ASH					NETTLES	NETTLES	NETTLES	
HEIGHT	·1	·1	·1	·1	·01	·01	·05	·05	·05	·05	·01	·01	·01		·6	·2	·2	·5	·4	·4		1·2		1·1					·5	·6	·5

Figure 17.12
A profile and line transect of the hedge

Figure 17.13
A belt transect of the hedge

Grass   Moss   Water with Water-cress   Moss   Nettles   Arum   Enchanter's Nightshade   Hazel   Ash trunk   Nettles

A **line transect** may now be added to your profile. First devise suitable clear symbols for the plants recorded on the profile. At each station, draw the symbol for the plant touching the line at that point. Draw the height of the symbol to scale. You have then made and recorded a line transect across the ditch (see Figure 17.12).

Do not think this is the end of the investigation, as the most interesting part is yet to come. This is interpreting and explaining your results. Why, for instance, is a particular plant found growing close to the shrubby parts of the hedge? Why is another plant found only some distance from the hedge? Why are some plants found on one side of the hedge and not on the other? Why, say, is one plant growing at station 5 much taller than a plant of the same species growing at station 2?

In addition to the line transect, you should carry out a **belt transect**. It is important that the vegetation should not be too trampled, so when observing, recording and measuring, always work on one side of the tape or line only so that the vegetation on the other side is fit to study. Take a strip of ground a metre wide over the length of the transect on the undisturbed side of the line. With the aid of a metre rule, plot the position of the plants. You should show large individual plants as such. For example, you might show a large tree by a circle indicating the relative size and position of its trunk, but where a large number of small plants such as moss cover the ground, outline the area of the patch and shade it in a distinctive way, as in Figure 17.13.

When it is complete, try to explain the distribution of plants. In addition to the plants, do not forget to record all the animal life you discover. Most important, make a note of exactly where the animal lives and try to suggest how its way of life (its food and method of feeding, how it moves, how it breathes and how it reproduces) is adapted to the position in which you found it.

You may find that some of the books mentioned at the end of the chapter are of help to you.

17.8. A grassland study

Investigation 17f. To study a grassland community

You will simply need a sampling square of a suitable size (say a wire square with sides 0·25 metre long). This can easily be made up from about 10-gauge galvanized wire (3·25 mm diameter).

First of all, have a look around to see if you can recognize most of the common plants. Grasses are rather difficult to identify, particularly if they are not in flower, but the Pelican book *Grasses* by Hubbard will help you. Even so, you might prefer to refer to the many different species of grass plants simply as 'grass'.

It is important that you throw your sampling square completely at random. If you attempt to 'hoop-la' interesting-looking plants, then your final results will not give a true picture of the composition of the field.

This investigation is best carried out in pairs, the class results being pooled. If there are twenty in the class, this gives ten groups of two. If each group throws ten samples, then the class will record one hundred sample squares, so the results can easily be expressed as a **percentage occurrence**. For example, if a daisy is found in a total of thirty-seven of the squares, then it has a percentage occurrence of 37%.

Before starting to throw your sample squares, draw out a grid similar to the one in Table 17.3, and write down the names of the plants you identified on your first look round. Throw your first square and carefully examine the plants it comes to enclose. As you identify a plant, put a tick by its name in the first column, and then, for your second throw, if it is present again put your tick in the second column. As you can see from the partly completed chart, grass and buttercups were found in the first sample square, and grass and daisies in the second.

TABLE 17.3. RECORDING WHAT IS FOUND IN THE SAMPLE SQUARES

Species	Samples Number									
	1	2	3	4	5	6	7	8	9	10
Grass	✓	✓	✓	✓	✓	✓	✓	✓	✓	✓
Buttercup	✓		✓				✓			
Daisy		✓			✓				✓	
Dock				✓						
Plantain										
Clover										
Hawkweed										
Lichen										
Moss										

When you have completed your samples, count the number of squares in which a particular species occurred. Then pass on your results to be included in the class result. These will give a much more accurate picture than your own individual result, because a much larger number of samples has been included.

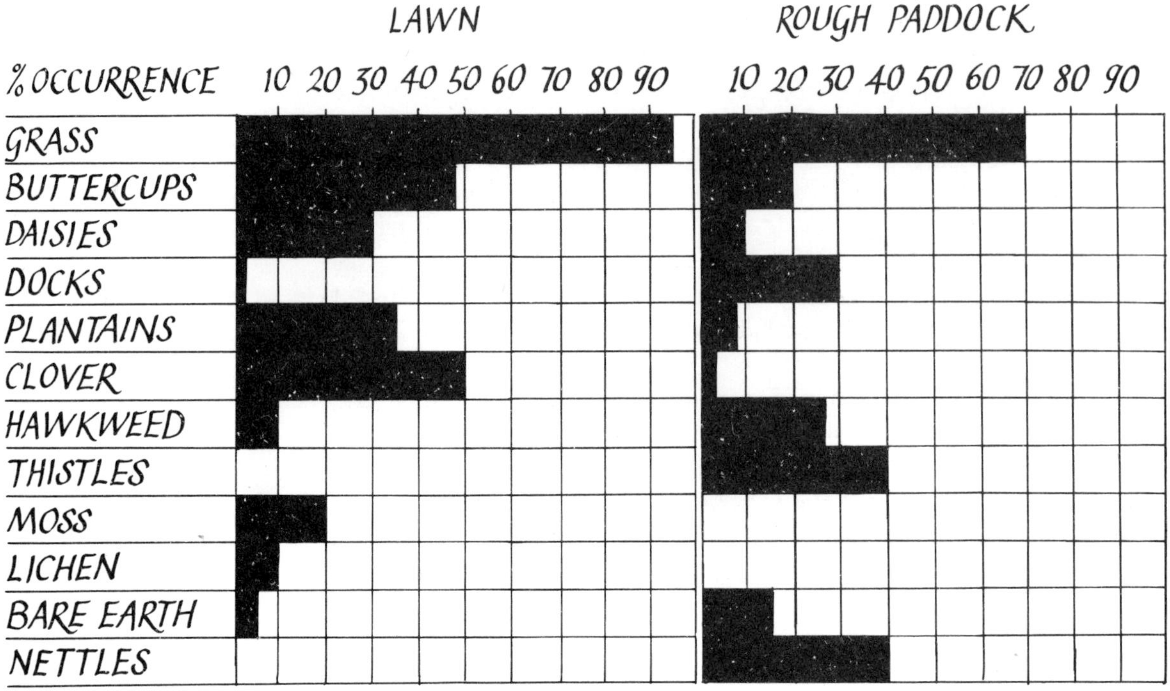

% OCCURRENCE	LAWN 10 20 30 40 50 60 70 80 90	ROUGH PADDOCK 10 20 30 40 50 60 70 80 90
GRASS	80	70
BUTTERCUPS	40	60
DAISIES	30	50
DOCKS	20	50
PLANTAINS	30	40
CLOVER	40	30
HAWKWEED	20	50
THISTLES	0	40
MOSS	10	0
LICHEN	10	0
BARE EARTH	10	30
NETTLES	0	60

Figure 17.14 A histogram comparing the percentage occurrence of plants in two types of grassland

The investigation might be more interesting if you compare two different areas of grass. You might compare a meadow (grass grown and cut for hay) with a pasture (grass which is grazed by livestock), the lawn with the orchard grass, long untended grass with a fine, regularly cut lawn, a cricket square with the outfield, or grass on acidic soils with grass on basic soils. If you are fortunate to have access to grass which is cut at different intervals, you can carry out an interesting comparative study. The results of such comparisons can be expressed on a histogram, as in Figure 17.14.

When you have your results in an easily compared form, try to account for any differences between them. Does cutting or cropping grassland tend to decrease or increase the number of species found?

17.9. A pond or stream study

Investigation 17g. To study a pond or stream community

To study freshwater life, work if possible in groups of three. Each group needs a net. A suitable net can easily be made from a broom handle, a metre of very stout galvanized wire, two jubilee clips and half a square metre of hessian, as shown in Figure 17.15. In addition, each group needs four Kilner-type jars or screw-top honey jars, a white pie dish or enamel tray, a small plastic spoon, a number of corked tubes and a teat-pipette with a wide nozzle.

Make a note of the geographical position of your pond or stream and make a sketch map of it. Again, the first task is to become familiar with the commoner plants and animals in this habitat. On your first visit to the locality, be content with noting the plants on the bank and in the water, and with taking several sweeps with your net to collect the animals from various parts of the pond. Put your net into the water and sweep it from right to left and back again, two or three times, before taking it from the water. Keep the net moving just fast enough to prevent organisms from swimming out of the net, and turn the net at the end of each sweep for the same reason. Hold the net over the pie dish or white enamel tray and turn it inside out, emptying its contents into the dish. Look out for creatures clinging to the side of the net. The organisms should be quite obvious against the light-coloured dish. Use the plastic spoon, or a teat-pipette, to pick out individual organisms. Identify those you can, and put just a few individuals that you cannot identify into the jars to study back in the laboratory. Some books which might be helpful are listed at the end of the chapter.

Be careful not to put carnivorous creatures such as a great diving beetle larva or dragonfly nymph with other creatures in a jar, or you will end up with just one large beetle larva or dragonfly nymph! When carrying aquatic specimens in screw-top or similar jars, take

Figure 17.15 Making a net for a pond or stream study

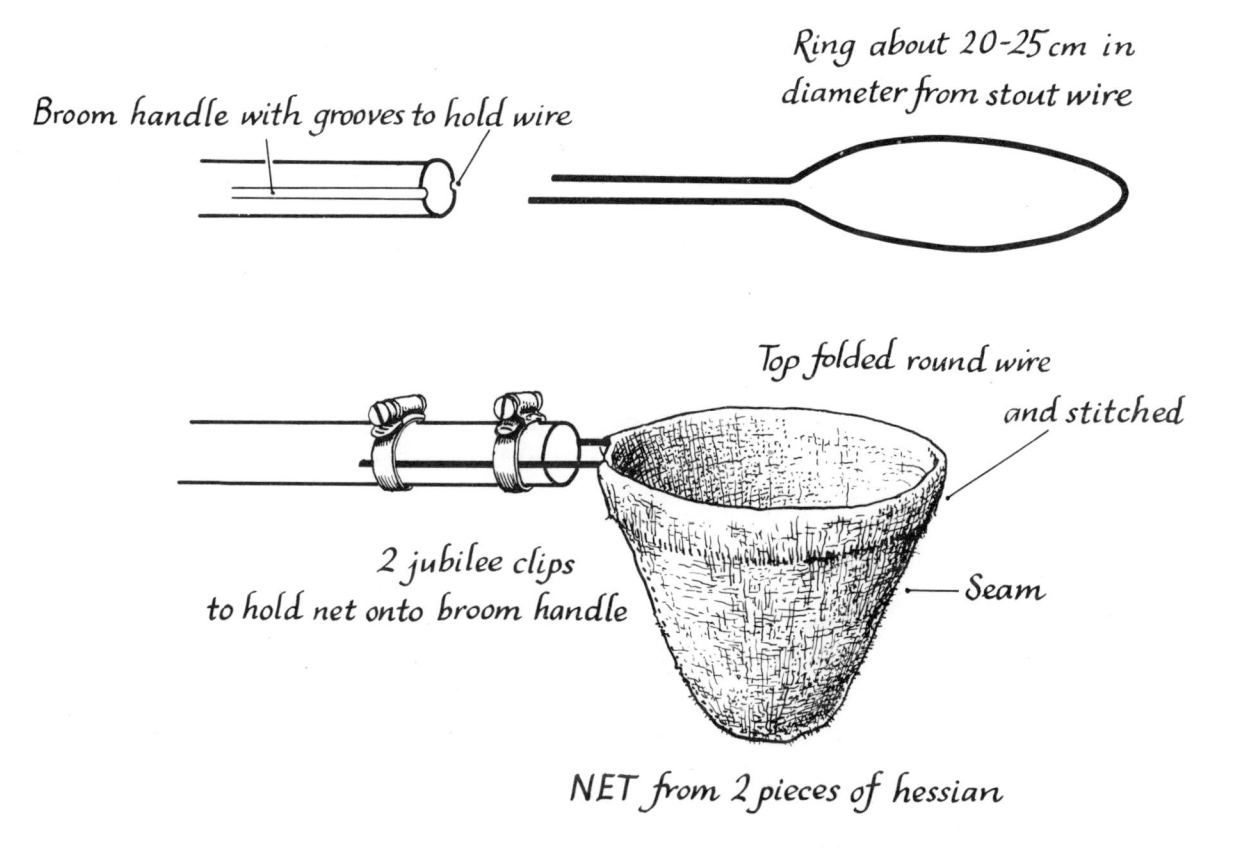

Broom handle with grooves to hold wire

Ring about 20-25 cm in diameter from stout wire

2 jubilee clips to hold net onto broom handle

Top folded round wire and stitched

Seam

NET from 2 pieces of hessian

care only to fill the jar two-thirds full of water; when the jar is jogged about, the air in the remaining third of the jar can then be mixed with the water. What good will this do?

Back in the laboratory, identify as many of the organisms as you can. Use a dissecting or binocular microscope to examine the smaller specimens (keeping the specimen in water, of course, in a watchglass or petri dish). Make a note of the phylum or major group to which each creature belongs. Make sure you know which characteristics it shares with other members of its phylum.

On your next visit to the pond or stream, try to discover in what particular freshwater habitat each organism lives, how it is adapted to that particular set of conditions, how it moves, how and on what it feeds, how it gets its oxygen requirements and how it breeds. The pond or stream can be divided into four main habitats:

1. The surface of the water.
2. The shallow water around the edge of the pond or stream.
3. The deep water.
4. The muddy or stony bottom.

Collect systematically from these regions, examining the same number of netfuls from each habitat. Record your catch from each locality and keep those you wish to study further from a particular habitat together in the same jar. It is difficult to label wet tubes and jars to indicate where the creatures were caught. These details are best written in *pencil* on a piece of paper placed directly in the jar or tube.

In addition to the major habitats, there are many microhabitats such as logs dragged from the mud. Such habitats can be very rewarding if examined carefully, in this case by slowly peeling away the rotting bark and examining all the crevices. If the bases of aquatic plants such as rushes are examined and broken open under water in the pie dish, these may reveal an interesting array of animal life. Other microhabitats may include submerged bottles, cans or boots and, of course, the undersides of floating leaves.

If you wish, you might like to set up a freshwater aquarium with the animals you have collected. The procedure for this is fairly straightforward, provided that you exclude voracious carnivores such as the great diving beetle larvae and the dragonfly nymphs. Further details are given in the Universities Federation for Animal Welfare pamphlet, *Fresh Water Life: Cold-water Aquaria*.

You can show the results of this work as a chart. A comparison between a pond and a stream is interesting and the results can be compared on a histogram (see Figure 17.16).

Another method of presentation is to draw a profile of a section across the pond or stream on a large piece of card, or perhaps sugar paper, so that the four habitats mentioned can be clearly shown. Then draw the various creatures boldly on coloured card or paper,

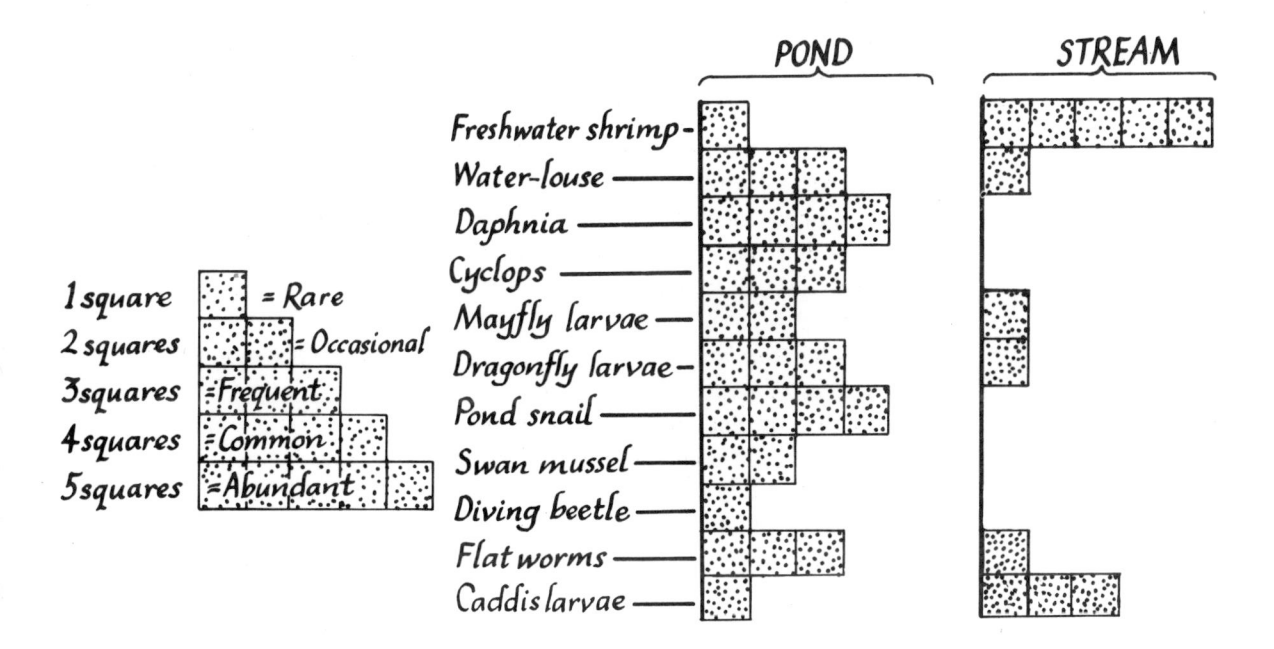

Figure 17.16 Histograms comparing animal life found in a pond with that found in a stream

exaggerating their size in relation to the pond but keeping the sizes of the various creatures roughly proportional to one another. Cut round the drawings and stick them on the pond profile in the appropriate habitat. If you cut animals belonging to a particular group, for example the molluscs, from card of the same colour your display will have more meaning.

17.10. The habitat of the earthworm

Investigation 17h. To compare earthworm populations in soils of different types and under different types of vegetation.

If you are fortunate enough to have access to both acidic and basic soils, then you can use the following method to compare the earthworm populations. Similarly, if very sandy soil, very clayey soil and loamy soil are available, compare the earthworm populations in the three types of soil. However, most of you will have access to soils which have differing vegetation, such as the soils of a grassland, an orchard or a wood and open soil which is frequently disturbed by digging. Whichever you tackle, you will need a large sample square with either metre or half metre sides, a watering can with a rose, a solution of formaldehyde (25 cm^3 of 40% formalin to 5 litres of water) and a pie dish with a little water in it.

Place the sampling square on the ground to be studied. If you are using a square metre sampling square, pour 5 litres of the formaldehyde solution evenly within it. Wait a minute or so for the worms to come up and, when they are about two-thirds out of the soil, seize them with blunt forceps. If the worms are seized too soon, they will retreat and will not re-emerge. Place them in the dish of water, counting as you do so. Wash the formaldehyde solution from the worms and they will live. It is possible to carry out this experiment with a saturated solution of potassium permanganate, but the worms may die. After about twenty minutes, a second 5 litres of solution should be applied and, shortly after, extraction should be more or less complete. Release the worms as soon as you have counted them. The total will give you an estimate of the population in the area of ground studied.

Take soil samples from the areas to be compared and try to explain your results. Do earthworms prefer acidic or basic soils? Do they prefer cultivated land to grassland? Do they prefer sand, loam or clay soils? Are there more worms under trees than in the open? Are there more worms on pasture than on meadow grassland? If so, why?

If you wish to discover the earthworm population per hectare then sample an area of a square metre and multiply the population by 10 000.

It should be possible for you to tackle at least some of the field study investigations, even if you only have the school field or a piece of waste ground available. Do not forget that even water butts and gutters house quite interesting life. Many of the investigations in this chapter will have to be adapted to your own locality.

Test your understanding

1. What three basic demands are made by an organism on its habitat?
2. What are the main habitat factors?
3. What is the difference between a community and a habitat?
4. What is meant by the dominant species in a habitat?
5. What is meant by stratification in a wood?
6. Explain what a plant succession is.
7. What is the main factor influencing plant life in a wood?
8. What might influence the distribution of animals and plants on the sea-shore?
9. How would you study life on the sea-shore?

Reference books

The following books will help you to identify the animals and plants discovered whilst doing field work. (The publisher is given in brackets.)

Woodland

How to begin your field work—Woodland by V. E. Ford (John Murray)
Woodland Ecology by Miles and Miles (Hulton)
Woodland Ecology by E. Neale (Methuen)
The Young Specialist looks at Trees by A. Kosch (Burke)

Concise British Flora by Rev. Keble Martin (Ebury Press/Michael Joseph)
Life of Wayside and Woodland by E. Step (Warne)
Trees and Shrubs by Prime and Deacock (Heffer)
Woodland Life by G. Marshall Barth (Blandford)

Grasses

Grasses by Hubbard (Pelican)

Freshwater life

The Young Specialist looks at Pond Life by W. Engelhardt (Burke)
The Observer's Book of Pond Life (Warne)
Animal Life in Freshwater by Helen Melanby (Methuen)
Water Animal Identification Sheets by Eric Marson (School Natural Science Study Leaflet No. 8)
Pond and Stream Life by G. Marshall Barth (Blandford)
Puffin Picture Book—*Pond Life*

Analytical Contents List

1 Features of Living Organisms

1.1 Living and non-living things
1.2 Movement 1.3 Respiration 1.4 Growth 1.5 Nutrition
1.6 Excretion 1.7 Irritability 1.8 Reproduction
1.9 Summary of the characteristics of living organisms
1.10 Comparing plants and animals
1.11 The balance of nature

2 Cells: The Units of Life

2.1 Looking at cells: cell structure
2.2 Plant and animal cells
2.3 The parts of the cell and their uses 2.4 Types of cell
2.5 How cells arise: cell division 2.6 The fate of dead cells
2.7 Cells, tissues, organs and organisms

3 Naming and Grouping

3.1 The meaning of classification
3.2 Early methods of classification
3.3 The work of Linnaeus 3.4 What is a species?
3.5 Grouping species together 3.6 The use of keys
3.7 The value of classification

4 Simple Animals

4.1 The simplest animals: protozoans
4.2 Amoeba: a common protozoan 4.3 How an amoeba moves
4.4 How an amoeba feeds
4.5 Respiration, excretion and the control of water content
4.6 Reproduction 4.7 Encystment 4.8 Other protozoans
4.9 Multicellular animals: metazoans
4.10 Hydra: a simple multicellular animal
4.11 The structure of the body 4.12 Locomotion
4.13 Feeding and digestion
4.14 Respiration and excretion
4.15 Reproduction and life-history
4.16 Animals related to the hydra
4.17 Three layers of cells
4.18 Planaria: a simple three-layered animal
4.19 Other flatworms

5 More Animals without Backbones

5.1 The segmented worms: annelids
5.2 Various annelids 5.3 Earthworms
5.4 Animals with jointed legs: arthropods
5.5 Crustaceans: aquatic arthropods
5.6 Insects: highly successful land arthropods
5.7 Arachnids 5.8 Myriapods: the many-legged arthropods
5.9 The soft-bodied animals: molluscs
5.10 The spiny-skinned animals: echinoderms

6 More about Insects

6.1 The insect body 6.2 The butterfly
6.3 The life-history of the large white butterfly
6.4 The meaning of metamorphosis
6.5 A social insect: the honey bee 6.6 Castes of bees
6.7 The life-history of the honey bee
6.8 The duties of the worker
6.9 Development of the queen and drone
6.10 A harmful insect: the housefly
6.11 The life-history of the housefly 6.12 Flies and disease
6.13 The mosquito 6.14 The life-history of the mosquito
6.15 Mosquitoes and malaria

7 Animals with Backbones

7.1 The general features of chordate animals
7.2 Fishes 7.3 Locomotion in fishes
7.4 Other adaptations shown by fishes
7.5 Conquest of the land: amphibians 7.6 Reptiles
7.7 Birds 7.8 Mammals 7.9 Diversity among mammals

8 The Plant World: Plants without Flowers

8.1 From the past 8.2 The algae
8.3 Chlamydomonas: a free-swimming, unicellular, freshwater alga
8.4 Spirogyra: a filament of similar cells
8.5 Marine algae: seaweeds
8.6 The fungi: simple plants without pigments
8.7 Pin mould: a saprophytic fungus
8.8 Mushrooms and toadstools: gill fungi
8.9 The plant division Thallophyta: algae and fungi
8.10 The division Bryophyta: liverworts and mosses
8.11 The mosses 8.12 The division Pteridophyta
8.13 The ferns 8.14 Reproduction in the ferns
8.15 Ancient ferns and coal formation
8.16 The division Spermatophyta: the seed-bearing plants
8.17 The pine with its naked seed and tree form

9 The Flowering Plant

9.1 Flowering plants 9.2 The shoot system
9.3 The stem 9.4 Secondary growth in stems
9.5 Spring and autumn wood: annual rings
9.6 The functions of the stem 9.7 Buds 9.8 The leaves
9.9 The root system 9.10 The functions of the root

9.11 Comparison between stems and roots
9.12 Monocotyledons and dicotyledons
9.13 Deciduous and evergreen plants

10 Food-making by Plants: Photosynthesis

10.1 The need for food 10.2 Van Helmont's experiment
10.3 Gaseous exchange in plants
10.4 Is carbon dioxide necessary for the plant to manufacture starch?
10.5 Is oxygen given off by a plant during starch production?
10.6 The importance of light
10.7 Photosynthesis—the synthesis of food with the aid of light
10.8 Is chlorophyll essential for photosynthesis?
10.9 The overall process of photosynthesis
10.10 The chemistry of photosynthesis
10.11 The site of photosynthesis

11 Plants and Water

11.1 The need for water
11.2 Where do plants get their water from?
11.3 How is the root adapted to absorb water from the soil?
11.4 How does water enter the root hair cells?
11.5 A simplied explanation of osmosis
11.6 Plant and animal cells as osmotic systems
11.7 Is live tissue necessary for osmosis?
11.8 The entry of water into the plant
11.9 The loss of water from the plant: transpiration
11.10 The effect of external conditions on the rate of transpiration
11.11 The transpiration stream
11.12 Plants and water availability

12 Reproduction in the Flowering Plant

12.1 Sexual reproduction
12.2 The problem of fertilization
12.3 The structure of a flower
12.4 The gametes of the flowering plant
12.5 Pollination
12.6 Why not self-pollination? 12.7 Insect pollination
12.8 Pollination of the buttercup flower
12.9 Pollination by the wind
12.10 The wind-pollinated flower of the oat plant
12.11 A comparison of wind pollination and insect pollination
12.12 Fertilization
12.13 The formation of the seed
12.14 The formation of the fruit
12.15 The dispersal of fruits and seeds
12.16 The dispersal of fruits and seeds by wind
12.17 The dispersal of fruits and seeds by water
12.18 The dispersal of fruits and seeds by animals
12.19 The dispersal of fruits and seeds by contact
12.20 The dispersal of fruits and seeds by explosion
12.21 False fruits: pseudocarps 12.22 Classifying fruits
12.23 Seed structure 12.24 Germination
12.25 The conditions needed for germination to take place

13 Surviving the Winter

13.1 The problems facing a plant in winter
13.2 The annual plant 13.3 The ephemerals
13.4 The biennial plant 13.5 The perennial plant
13.6 Herbaceous perennials
13.7 The crocus corm 13.8 Rhizomes
13.9 The potato tuber 13.10 Bulbs 13.11 Root tubers
13.12 The materials in storage organs
13.13 Vegetative reproduction
13.14 Natural methods of vegetative reproduction
13.15 Artificial methods of vegetative reproduction
13.16 The advantages of vegetative reproduction

14 Plants and their Senses

14.1 Plant responses 14.2 The nature of a plant response
14.3 Perception of the stimulus 14.4 Response to water
14.5 The adaptive nature of the responses
14.6 The mechanism of tropic responses 14.7 Plant hormones
14.8 Types of response in plants
14.9 Differences between plant and animal responses

15 The Economy of Nature

15.1 The materials of life 15.2 The carbon cycle
15.3 The nitrogen cycle 15.4 The water cycle
15.5 The source of energy
15.6 Food-chains: the interdependence of living organisms
15.7 Food-webs 15.8 The balance of nature

16 Soil

16.1 The meaning of soil
16.2 The composition of soil
16.3 Soil analysis
16.4 Types of soil and their properties
16.5 Soil and plant life 16.6 Soil organisms
16.7 Soil improvement

17 Communal Life

17.1 The habitat 17.2 Communities 17.3 Habitat factors
17.4 Field studies
17.5 Colonization of bare ground
17.6 A woodland study 17.7 A hedgerow study
17.8 A grassland study 17.9 A pond or stream study
17.10 The habitat of the earthworm

Analytical Contents List for Book II

For the convenience of the users of this book, we are setting out below the contents of the companion volume, *Human Biology and Hygiene*, Biology Book II.

1 Food and Digestion
Why food is necessary   Types of foodstuff   Testing foods for chemical content   What should we eat?   The energy requirement: carbohydrates and fats   The growth requirement: proteins   The health requirement: vitamins and minerals   The value of milk   Water   The purpose of digestion   The agents of digestion: enzymes   How food is moved through the alimentary canal   Digestion in the mouth   Swallowing   Digestion in the stomach   Digestion in the small intestine   Absorption of the digestive products   Fate of the undigested matter

2 The Release of Energy: Respiration
Meaning and purpose of respiration   Combustion of glucose   Respiration and combustion   Detecting respiration   Internal and external respiration   External respiration   Ventilation of the lungs   Lung capacity   Failure of breathing   Artificial respiration   Gaseous exchange in lungs and tissues   Internal or tissue respiration   Energy release without oxygen   Control of respiration   The lungs and health

3 The Transport System: Blood
The nature of blood   Functions of the blood system   How blood is circulated   Blood vessels   Types of blood circulation   The heart   Blood pressure   Lymph and the lymphatic system   Blood clotting   Blood groups and transfusion   The Rhesus factor

4 Getting Rid of Waste: Excretion
Why is excretion necessary?   Origin and nature of excretory products   The organs of excretion   The fine structure of the kidneys   Functioning of the kidneys   Composition of urine

5 The Skin and Temperature Control
Functions of the skin   Structure of the skin   Skin colour   Cold-blooded and warm-blooded animals   Regulation of body temperature in man   Illness and body temperature

6 The Senses of the Body
The collection of information   A simple sense organ: taste buds on the

tongue Sense of smell Sense organs of the skin Sense of sight The muscles of the eye Structure of the eye The formation of an image The accommodation or focusing of the eye The retina Defects of vision and their correction Sense of hearing Structure of the ear Working of the ear Causes of deafness

7 Co-ordination: The Nervous System
The need for co-ordination Receptors and effectors Reflex actions The reflex arc Conditioned reflexes The central nervous system Nerves The synapse The autonomic nervous system

8 Chemical Control: Endocrine Organs and Hormones
Chemical co-ordination Endocrine organs The pituitary gland The thyroid gland The thymus The pancreas The adrenal glands The gonads

9 Having Young: Reproduction
The purpose of reproduction Asexual reproduction Sexual reproduction Fishes Amphibians Reptiles and birds Sex organs in mammals Mating and fertilization Development of the embryo Birth Early growth of the baby How twins arise Growing up: puberty Menstruation

10 The Skeletal System
Movement Why is a skeleton necessary? Regions of the skeleton The skull The vertebral column: backbone Summary of functions and adaptations of the vertebral column Structure of long and flat bones The appendicular skeleton The thoracic skeleton

11 Movement: Muscles and Joints
Types of joint Joint structure Types of muscle Muscles and movement Posture

12 Teeth and Dentition
Tooth structure Types of teeth Milk and permanent teeth Care of teeth Prevention of tooth decay Fluoridation of water Dentition and diet

13 How Life Began
In the beginning Origin of the Universe Origin of the solar system Age of the earth The ancient atmosphere Some old ideas of the origin of life Current theories of the origin of life

14 The Changing World: Evolution
Life in the past: the fossil record How fossils are dated Great periods of the earth's history Fossil horses Geographical distribution of plants and animals Homologues and vestiges Meaning of evolution Mechanism of evolution: Darwin and natural selection Example of natural selection at work Artificial selection Importance of isolation Causes of extinction Evolution of man

15 How Life Is Handed On
Sexual reproduction Structure of the nucleus Function of the chromosomes Chromosomes at fertilization Some breeding investigations *Drosophila* culture Handling *Drosophila* Breeding experiments with mice Gregor

Mendel   How are the 'instructions' inherited?   Why is each chromosome duplicated?   An explanation of Mendel's results and your own   The back cross or test cross   The dihybrid cross: two-character inheritance   Inheritance of sex   Incomplete dominance   Mutations   Chromosome mutations   Gene mutations   Effect of radiation on mutations

16 Micro-organisms and Disease
Bacteria   Types of bacteria   How bacteria may be killed   Bacteria and disease   Viruses   How bacteria and viruses enter the body   The body's reaction   Prevention of disease: immunity   Vaccination   Antibiotics: discovery of penicillin   Other causes of disease   Malaria

17 Maintaining a Healthy Environment
Clean air   Ventilation   Heating and lighting   Clean water   Purification of water   Sewage disposal   Refuse disposal   Clean food   Clean milk   Clean living   Safety in the home   Industrial safety and hygiene   Doomwatch

Index

Where the subject is illustrated the page number is shown in bold type

Adaptation 93–5
Adventitious root 146
Algae 106, **107**
Amoeba 36–41
  cyst **40**
  excretion **39**
  feeding 37, **38**
  movement 37, **38**
  occurrence 36
  reproduction 39, **40**
  respiration **39**
  structure **37**
Amphibians 95, **96**
Anabolism 18
Androecium 185
Angiosperms 129
Animals and plants compared 8
Annelids 54, **55**
Annual plant 211, **212**
Annual rings 134, **135**, **136**
Anther **186**
Arachnids **61**
Aristotle 25
Arthropods 58
  key to 31
Asexual reproduction 7
Auxin 237, 239, 240
Axillary bud 137

Bacteria, denitrifying 250
  nitrifying 250
Balance of nature 9, 256
Barnacle **59**
Bee (Honey bee) 70–7
  castes of 71
  life-history 72–5
Biennial plants 211, **212**
Bilateral symmetry 51
Binary fission **40**
Binomial nomenclature 25

Biotic factors 275
Birds 100, **101**
  history 102
Bony fishes (*see* Osteichthyes)
Boysen-Jensen, Peter 235
Bracken 122, 123, 124
Broad bean seed **205**, 206, 207, **208**
Brown, Robert 15
Bryophyllum **224**
Bryophytes 118
Budding, of hydra 47, **48**
  of plants **225**
Buds 137–9
  Brussels sprout **137**
  horse-chestnut 138, **139**
Bulbil **224**
Bulbs 219, **221**
Buttercup flower 185–**8**, **191**, **192**
Butterfly 66, **67**
  life-history 68–70

Calyx 185
Cambium 134
Carbon cycle 245, **246**, 247
Carbon dioxide, and plants 156–7
Carnivores 8
Carpel 186, **187**, **195**, **196**
Cell division **20**
Cell doctrine 17
Cell sap 16
Cell wall 16, 18
Cells, examples of 18, **19**
  in cheek lining **15**
  in cork 12
  in hydra 43, 44, **45**
  in moss leaf **16**

Cells, contd.
   in onion epidermis 13, **15, 172**
   plant and animal compared 16, **17**
Cellulose 16
Centipedes **62**
Chitin 40
Chlamydomonas 107, **108**
   reproduction **108**
Chlorophyll 18, 160, 161
Chloroplasts 16, 18
Choice chamber 6, **7**
Chondrichthyes **90**, 91
Chordates 87, **88, 89**
   key to 31–2
Chromosomes 18
Cilia 51
Class 28
Classification 24–35
Cleavage 41
Clinostat **231**, 232
Club mosses 121, **122**
Cnidoblast cells 43, **45**
Coal 125
Coelenterates 49, **50**
Coelom 54
Coenocyte 114, **115**
Coleoptile 232
Comb 72, 73, **74**
Community (plant) 274, 275
   climax 277
Composition, of plants 244 (table)
Compound eyes 65
Cones 126, **127**
Conifers 126
Conjugation 109
Consumers 8, 159, 245
Contractile vacuole 39
Corals 49, **50**
Corm 215, **216**
Corolla 185
Cotyledons 196
Crustaceans 58, **59**
Cuticle **58**
Cuttings 224
Cysts 40
Cytoplasm 14, 18

Darwin, Charles 56
Deciduous plants **148**
Decomposition 247, 250
Denitrification 250
Dicotyledons 147

Differentiation 41
Dinosaurs **98**, 99
Disease, and flies 80–1
Division, of labour 19, 41, 70
   of plants 226
Drone **71**, 76
Dysentery 41

Earthworm 55–8
Echinoderms 63, **64**
Ectoderm 43
Ectoplasm 37
Embryo 7
Embryo sac 188, **190**
Endoderm 43
Endoplasm 37
Energy, source of 253
Entamoeba 41
Enteron 43
Ephemeral plants 211
Evergreen plants **148**
Excretion 5
Exoskeleton 58

Family 28, **29**
Ferns 121, 122, **123**, 124–6
   and coal formation 125
   reproduction 124
Fertilization 7
   in flowering plants 184, 195
   in hydra 48
Fertilizers 251, 271, 272 (table)
Fibrous root 146
Field studies 276
Fishes 90–5
   adaptations in 93
   movement in 91, **92**
Flagellate cells **45**
Flowering plant 129, **130**
Flowers **184–94**
Flukes 52
Food chain 9, 254–**5**
Food web 9, **10**, 255
Fruits 197–205
   classification of 203, 204 (table) 205
   dispersal of (*see* Seeds)
   false **203**
   formation of 197
Fungi 112–18

Gametes 7
Gaseous exchange, in plants 153, 154
Genes 18

Genus 26, 28
Geotropism 232
Germination, of seeds 207
   conditions for **209**, 210
   epigeal 208
   hypogeal 207
Gibberellins 239, 240
Gill slits 87
Gills 94
Glandular cells 44
Glume 193
Grafting 225, **226**
Gristly fishes (*see* Chondrichthyes)
Growth 4, **5**
Gymnosperms 126
Gynoecium 186

Habitat 273
Halophytes 183
Halteres 79
Hedgerow study **283**, **284**, **285**, 286
Herbivores 8
Hermaphrodite 48, 191
Heteroauxin 239, 240
Hooke, Robert 13
Hormones, in plants 239–42
Horsetails 121, **122**
Housefly 77–81
   and disease 80, 81
   life-history 77–9
   structure 78, **79**, **80**
Hybrids 28
Hydra 41, 43–9
   culture 41
   locomotion **46**
   nutrition 46, **47**
   reproduction 47, **48**, **49**
   respiration and excretion 47
   structure 43, **44**
Hydrophytes **182**
Hydrotropism 234
Hyphae 113, 114

Ichthyosaurs **98**, 99
Indolylacetic acid (IAA) 239
Infusoria 254
Insects **60**–1, 65–86
   features of 61, **65**, 66
Integuments 196
Internode 130
Interstitial cells 44, **45**
Irrigation technique 14
Irritability 6, 7
Isotopes 162

Jellyfish 49, **50**
Joints 58

Katabolism 18
Keys (classification) 30–2
Kingdom 28
Kinins 239

Larva, of butterfly **68**, 69
   of honey bee 74, **75**
   of housefly **77**, 78
   of mosquito **83**
Lateral-line organs 94
Layering **225**
Leaf, structure **140–3**
Leech **55**
Lemma 193
Lenticels 138
Light, importance to plants 159
Linnaeus, Karl 25, 26, 28
Liverworts 118, **119**
Lodicules 193
Lugworm 55
Lungfish **95**

Malaria 82, 85
Mammals 103, **104**, 105
Marsupials 103
Medusa 49
Mesoderm 50
Mesogloea 43
Mesophyll 142
Metamorphosis 70
Metazoans 41
Micropyle 195
Millipedes **62**
Mitochondria 18
Mitosis (*see* Cell division)
Molluscs **62**, 63
Monocotyledons 147–8
Monotremes 103
Mosquito 82–5
Mosses 119, 120, **121**
Mouth-parts 66
Movement 3
   of fishes 91, **92**, 93
   of newt 96, **97**
Musculo-epithelial cells 43, **45**
Mushrooms (and toadstools) **116**, **117**, 118
Mycelium 113
Mycorrhiza 117
Myriapods **62**

Naphthalene acetic acid (NAA) 240
Nasty 241
Nectar, nectary 185
Nerve cell 44, **45**
Nerve chord 87
Nerve net 44
Nitrates 249
Nitrification 250
Nitrogen cycle 247, **248**, 249–51
Nitrogen fixation 247
Node 129
Notochord 87
Nucleus 14, 18
Nuptial flight 76
Nutrition 5

Oat flower 193, **194**
Order (classification) 28
Organ 21
Organism 21
Osmosis 167–71, 173–4
Osteichthyes **90**, 91, **92**
Ovary 186, **187**
Ovules 186
Oxygen (production in plants) 157, 158

Palea 193
Panicle 193
Parasite 41, 52, 113
Pedicel 186, 193
Perennation 137, 214
Perennials 213, **214**, 215
  herbaceous 214
  woody 214
Perianth 185
Pericarp 197
Petal 185
Photosynthesis 8, 18, 140, 159–63
Phototropism 231
Phloem 133, **135**, 181
Phylum 28
Pine (Scots) **127**
Pin mould 113, **114**, 115, 116
Pistil 186
Planaria **51**
Plants and animals compared 8
Plasma membrane 17
Plasmagel 37
Plasmasol 37
Plasmodium 85
Platyhelminthes 50–2

Plumule 196
Pollen 186, 188, **189**
Pollination 189–94
  cross 190
  in buttercup 191, **192**
  in oat 193
  insect and wind compared 190–92, 194 (table)
  self 190
Pond study 288–91
Portuguese Man-of-war 49, **50**
Potato blight 113
  tuber **218**, 219
Potometer 178, **179**, 180
Proboscis 67, **68**
Producers 8, 159, 245
Prothallus **125**
Protoplasm 14
Protozoans 36, 41, **42**
Pseudocarp (*see* Fruit, false)
Pseudopodia 37
Pseudopodial cells **45**
Pteridophytes 121
Pterodactyl **98**, 99
Pupa, of butterfly **69**
  of honey bee **75**
  of housefly **78**
  of mosquito 83, **84**
Pyramid of numbers 254–5

Quadrat 276
Queen bee **71**, 76

Radial symmetry 64
Radicle 196
Ragworm 54, **55**
Ray, John 25
Receptacle 186
Regeneration **51**
Reproduction 7
Reptiles 97, **98**, **99**, 100
Respiration 3
  in fishes 94
Responses, plant and animal compared 241–2
Rhizome 122, **123**, **217**, 218
Root 129, 143–6
  and stem compared 146 (table)
  functions of 146
  hairs 145, **166**, **167**
  nodules 247, **249**
  pressure 174
  tip **144**, 145, **166**
Royal jelly 74
Runner 222, **223**

Sampling technique 287
Saprophytes 113
Scales, of butterfly **67**
Schleiden and Schwann 15
Sea anemones 49, **50**
Seaweeds **111**, 112
Secretory cells **45**
Seed, endospermous 196
   food store in 206, 207
   formation 196
   non-endospermous 196, 206
   structure **205**, 206
Seed dispersal 197–203
   by animals **200**, 201
   by contact **201**
   by explosion 201, **202**, 203
   by water **199**, 200
   by wind 197, **198**, 199
Segments 54
Self-pollination 190
Semi-permeable membrane 169
Sensory cells 44, **45**
Sepal 185
Sexual reproduction 7, 184
Sleeping sickness 41
Snakes 100
Soil 257–72
   analysis 263–5
   and plant life 270
   components of 257–63
   improvement 271
   organisms 270, 271
   particles 259, **260**, 261
   profile 257, **258**
   sandy and clay compared 265–9 (table)
   types of 265–70
Sorus 123, **125**
Species 25–8
Spikelet 193
Spiracles 65
Spirogyra 109, **110**
Stamen 185, **186**
Starch production in plants 155–6
   conditions for 156–61
Stem 129–37
   and root compared 146 (table)
   functions 136, 137
   secondary growth of 134, **135**, 136
   structure 131, **133**
Stigma 186

Stolon **223**
Stratification 279
Style 186
Succession 277, 278
Sucker 223, **224**
Swarm (honey bee) 72, 73
Swim-bladder 93
Symbiosis 46, 117, 249

Tapeworms 52
Tap-root **213**
Taxis 241
Tentacles 43
Terminal bud 138
Testa 196
Tissue 21
Tracheae 65
Transect, belt **285**, 286
   line 276, **285**, 286
Transpiration 175–82
   stream 180, **181**
Tropism 230, 241
Tuber, root 220, **222**
   stem **218**, 219
Turgidity 164, **172**, **173**
Twig, horse-chestnut **138**, 139

Vacuole (cell) 16
Van Helmont's experiment 152, **153**
Variegated leaves 160, **161**
Vascular bundles 133
Vegetative reproduction 137, 222–6
Vertebrae 89
Vertebrates 89
Virchow, Rudolf 20
Viruses **2**

Water, and plants 164–83
Water cycle 251, **252**, 253
Wax 73
Went, Friedrich 237
Woodland, study 277–82
   layers in **278**, 279
Woodlice **60**
Worker bee **71**–3, 75–6

Xerophytes **182**
Xylem 133, 181

Zoochlorellae 46
Zygote 7